The Art of Evolution

INTERFACES: STUDIES IN VISUAL CULTURE

Editors Mark J. Williams and Adrian W. B. Randolph, Dartmouth College

This series, sponsored by Dartmouth College Press, develops and promotes the study of visual culture from a variety of critical and methodological perspectives. Its impetus derives from the increasing importance of visual signs in everyday life, and from the rapid expansion of what are termed "new media." The broad cultural and social dynamics attendant to these developments present new challenges and opportunities across and within the disciplines. These have resulted in a trans-disciplinary fascination with all things visual, from "high" to "low," and from esoteric to popular. This series brings together approaches to visual culture—broadly conceived—that assess these dynamics critically and that break new ground in understanding their effects and implications.

For a complete list of books that are available in the series, visit www.upne.com

Barbara Larson and Fae Brauer, eds., *The Art of Evolution: Darwin, Darwinisms, and Visual Culture*

Jeffrey Middents, *Writing National Cinema: Film Journals and Film Culture in Peru*

Michael Golec, *The Brillo Box Archive: Aesthetics, Design, and Art*

Rob Kroes, *Photographic Memories: Private Pictures, Public Images, and American History*

Jonathan Beller, *The Cinematic Mode of Production: Attention Economy and the Society of the Spectacle*

Ann B. Shteir and Bernard Lightman, eds., *Figuring It Out: Science, Gender, and Visual Culture*

Anna Munster, *Materializing New Media: Body, Image, and Interface in Information Aesthetics*

Luc Pauwels, ed., *Visual Cultures of Science: Rethinking Representational Practices in Knowledge Building and Science Communication*

Lisa Saltzman and Eric Rosenberg, eds., *Trauma and Visuality in Modernity*

The Art of Evolution

Darwin, Darwinisms, and Visual Culture

Edited by Barbara Larson and Fae Brauer

DARTMOUTH COLLEGE PRESS
Hanover, New Hampshire

Published by University Press of New England
Hanover and London

Dartmouth College Press
Published by University Press of New England
One Court Street, Lebanon, NH 03766
www.upne.com

Printed in the United States of America

First paperback edition 2016
Paperback ISBN: 978-1-61168-977-8

The Library of Congress cataloged the previous edition as:
The art of evolution: Darwin, Darwinisms, and visual culture / edited by Barbara Larson and Fae Brauer. — 1st ed.
p. cm. — (Interfaces: studies in visual culture)
Includes bibliographical references and index.
ISBN 978-1-58465-775-0 (cloth: alk. paper)
1. Science and the arts. 2. Arts and society. 3. Natural history—Social aspects. I. Larson, Barbara (Barbara Jean) II. Brauer, Fae.
NX180.S3A772 2009
700.1'05 — dc22 2009012354

5 4 3 2 1

The editors dedicate this volume to their children, who have been much affected by cultural and social dimensions of post-Darwinian thought: to Vivian Johnson for her childhood years in America's creationist deep south and for her punishment for asking a classmate if she knew her ancestors had been monkeys; to Marcus Brauer and Lara Brauer for the joy of survival and for "adapting" in ways that would make any "hairy, tailed arboreal creature" justly proud.

Contents

Preface

This book is the result of years of Darwin research on the part of both editors and most recently a jointly chaired conference stream on Darwin and visual culture for the Society for Literature, Science, and the Arts in 2006 (sponsored by the Dactyl Foundation and New York University). The research behind several of the essays in this volume was first presented there. Other contributors were involved in ongoing Darwin projects that spanned a variety of issues, periods, and cultures, which enhanced the possibilities for a volume that moved beyond the relatively narrow time frame of the late nineteenth century and the somewhat circumscribed arenas of England and France common to Darwin studies. The enthusiasm of the authors and the excellence of their work have made the editing of the volume a pleasure and an education. We thank them wholeheartedly for their efforts to maintain deadlines on a very tight schedule and provide fruitful feedback. Their outstanding collegiality and the richness of their contributions have generated additional momentum, resulting in a second conference on Darwin and visual culture in London sponsored by the Courtauld Institute of Art, University of London, in July 2009 at the time of The Darwin Festival. The editors also wish to extend special thanks to the University Press of New England's excellent editor Richard Pult. His professionalism, generosity of spirit, and extraordinary efforts to produce this volume in record time for the Darwin bicentennial year have spurred the project on from inception to publication. Thanks also to Rachael Cohen for her impeccable copyediting and to Sebastian Seifert, who patiently worked on organizing the reproductions found in the book from their various international sources.

The Art of Evolution

Introduction

BARBARA LARSON

Darwin's effect on culture is perhaps greater than that of any other scientist in modern times. Beginning in the late nineteenth century, his evolutionary theories were called upon to support ideas on human romance and mating, uphold the progress of capitalism, and add a scientific underpinning to anti-clerical politics. The subject of evolution was by no means new in 1859 when Darwin published his revolutionary *On the Origin of Species by Means of Natural Selection*, but his bold assertions concerning open-ended transformation of species guided by a process that was amoral struck at the heart of prevailing currents of creationism with its divine dimensions.

Darwin's views on evolution are distinguished by two main mechanisms: natural selection and sexual selection. Darwin defined natural selection as follows:

> As many more individuals of each species are born than can possibly survive, and as, consequently, there is a frequently recurring struggle for existence, it follows that any being, if it varies however slightly in any manner profitable to itself, under the complex and sometimes varying conditions of life, will have a better chance of surviving and thus be naturally selected.[1]

The Darwinian idea of competitive advantage allowing for the greater propagation of organisms better suited for particular environmental conditions and the necessity of making full use of favorable characteristics to compete for food to the eventual detriment of the less lucky, was condensed into the popular phrase "survival of the fittest." As advantageous traits accumulated, new species then came into being. Sexual selection refers to the preference for mates based on characteristics deemed desirable, even within subjective categories of "beauty." It explained the sometimes extraordinary and even dangerously exaggerated attributes of a given species, such as the peacock's tail (which in this case could also attract predators).

Despite outright hostility to Darwin by believers, Darwinism rapidly infiltrated the Western world on a variety of levels, significantly influencing its visual culture. Yet Darwinism's intersection with the arts and popular culture has been little studied. It is a surprising lacuna, for example, that no major volume has been published on Darwin and *monkeyana* despite the fact that the most sensationalistic aspect of Darwin's theories from the public perspective was the idea that humans were tied intimately to the animal world with relatively recent ancestry among the apes. Anthropomorphized apes or simianized humans are found from advertising to the decorative arts to cartoons and caricatures and the fine arts. However, Darwinism in visual culture is also far more extensive than the obvious ape references. Philosophies about human behavior, society and its institutions, and politics in light of Darwinism are embedded in much of art and graphic production of the modern period. This volume, which moves through nations and across visual cultures, is an effort to illuminate the richness of this topic.

Darwinian Visual Culture and Literary Studies

The field of literature, which has a lengthy history of examining Darwin's influence on poets and novelists, made early headway on visualizing Darwin's ideas, even if through descriptive means. Ever since Gillian Beer published *Darwin's Plots* in 1983, the analysis of Darwinian narratives has been a steadily growing subfield in literary studies, constituting a significant part of what has been called the "Darwin Industry."[2] In the same year, Evelleen Richards initiated a new and continuing trajectory of feminist studies with her "Darwin and the Descent of Women" in *The Wider Domain of Evolutionary Thought*. Darwin and visual culture studies per se can claim no such iconic text. Its authors are dispersed across a variety of fields: art history, literary history, history, culture studies, the history of photography, and the history of science. As such, they bring a variety of methodologies or borrow from other fields. In 1986, Bram Dijkstra offered *Idols of Perversity: Fantasies of Feminine Evil in the Fin de Siècle*, a richly illustrated text on images of the *femme fatale* in the fine arts as she emerged in part from Darwin's ideas of the procreative female with a limited brain. This read as an art-historical book based in cultural history, but was written by a scholar of comparative literature. Like many art historians of that period, Dijkstra was influenced by feminist work within visual culture studies, where the uncomplicated "gaze" upon the female depicted is always masculine and generally misogynistic. Also like many feminist art historians of the 1980s, he interpreted the domineering presence of the *femme fatale* as critical of the New Woman or the rootless and poisonous prostitute, with references to inappropriate female power as culturally and socially unacceptable.

Coming at "visuals" from a completely different angle, literary historian James Krasner's *The Entangled Eye: Visual Perception and the Representation of Nature in Post-Darwinian Narrative* (1992) demonstrated how nature writers, naturalists, and novelists came to portray nature as the locus of optical illusion and visual failure following Darwin's descriptions of the natural. Although remaining within the realm of the written text, in his interpretation of evolutionary biology and perceptual theory, Krasner comes tantalizingly close to modernist sensibilities as realized in Impressionist or Symbolist painting. Another area within literary history that can be bound to visual culture is reception theory, as in James Secord's *Victorian Sensation* (2000) on the evolutionary work of Robert Chambers in *Vestiges of the Natural History of Creation* (1844). Secord argues that this enormously popular work, whose cultural importance has since been eclipsed by *Origin of Species*, established a template for a grand tale of evolution linked to a taste for spectacle and showmanship. The epic style that Chambers employed was derived from conventions of historical fiction that domesticated the dangerous idea of evolution. While the visual was implicit rather than explicit, *Vestiges* then cleared the way in the public imagination for Darwin's work.

Art History and Darwinian Visual Culture

Visual culture as a conceptual field of study within art history was marginalized until the growth of the social history of art in the 1970s and 1980s. The history of institutions, training, and media, along with gender issues, all informed new concerns. A recognition of the explosion of image making in the modern period with the improvement of printing technologies and ways in which it is tied to the modern visual experience was also important. Darwin intersects with pictorial practices in the larger context of cultural studies.

In 1988, art historians Douglas Druick and Peter Zegers initiated studies on Darwin and individual artists with an important essay on Degas. They used a range of visual culture references, convincingly arguing that periodical reviews of Darwin's work with reproductions of imagery from *Expression of Emotions*, ethnological displays of nonwhite races that exhibited "simian" physiognomy, popular notions of the criminal as atavistic with its ties to Darwinian science, and friendships with amateur naturalists interested in Darwin were all behind Degas' satirical pastels of working-class café singers, profile drawings of murderers, and depiction of a less-than-idealized lower-class ballet dancer in his unique sculpture of a fourteen-year-old dancer. Other individual artists subsequently examined through a Darwinian lens include Van Gogh, Redon, Fernand Cormon, Klinger, Klimt, and Carl Rungius. These projects have explored individual artists' responses to Darwin across a range of styles and have considered the reception of Darwinism, political engagement of evolutionary ideas, and the importance of related circulating images in the popular press and elsewhere. Broader studies have speculated on Darwin and art movements. This writer explored Symbolist tropes informed by Darwinism in a 1993 publication.[3] In 1996, Kathleen Pyne examined the influence of Herbert Spencer on American artists in light of popular interpretations of the way that Darwin could be applied to progress and politics (social Darwinism), but with a preference for Spencer's ideas on an environment that shapes organisms. In arguing for the importance of an aesthetic environment, Pyne made use of the then-popular sociological theories of Bourdieu on ways in which dominant classes stake out boundaries and meanings through shared cultural signals. Scholarship in gender studies within art history also has found Darwinian science to be a crucial resource. In 2002, feminist art historian Linda Nochlin convened a conference on Darwin and visual culture in conjunction with her student Martha Lucy, who was then writing a dissertation on Darwin and the evolutionary body. Lucy made use of contemporary theories of the body as fluid and "leaky," including the writings of Deleuze and Guattari on the body as a nontotalizable series of processes of becomings. More central to her thesis is the work of Julia Kristeva on abjection and the body of dissolution. Lucy argues that such postmodern conceptions of the body are applicable to the destabilized Darwinian body ever in flux and that "Darwin's bodies" as referenced in art produced one of the most significant challenges to the classical ideal after the middle of the nineteenth century.[4] The 2009 Darwin bicentennial year undoubtedly will offer a further range of ideas on Darwin and the fine arts through the exhibitions *Endless Forms: Charles Darwin, Natural Science and the Visual Arts* at the Fitzwilliam Museum in Cambridge and the Yale Center for British Art in New Haven, and *Darwin: Art and the Search for Origins* at the Schirn Kunsthalle in Frankfurt.

Science and Darwinian Visual Culture

In history and the history of science, Darwin and visual culture studies have taken three directions: 1) the popularization of Darwinism through cartoons, science illustrations, fictional book illustrations, theatrical productions, traveling fairs, museum installations, and scientific exhibitions at international expositions; 2) the examination of scientific illustrations used by Darwin himself; and 3) ways in which art and aesthetics shaped Darwin's own worldview.

The first category is complex and does not benefit from a consideration of a totalizing historical trajectory, except to observe that, by the 1970s and 1980s, a sociological approach became central within the history of science and this propelled Darwin and visual culture studies. Bernard Lightman traces the sociological turn in the introduction to his *Victorian Science in Context* (1997), citing groundbreaking works like Walter Cannon's *Science and Culture: The Early Victorian Period* (1978), John Greene's *Science, Ideology and World View* (1981), and Robert Young's *Darwin's Metaphor: Nature's Place in Victorian Culture* (1985).

Mary Cowling's *The Artist as Anthropologist: The Representation of Type and Character in Victorian Art* (1989) traces the history of physiognomy and its linkages to animal heads and skull measurement and the implications of this to a public understanding of Darwinian science. While Darwin refuted the earlier popular sciences of physiognomy and phrenology (himself famously nearly rejected from the Beagle voyage by the displeasure of Captain Fitzroy over the shape of the young scientist's nose), he supported craniometry (skull measurement) as an index of evolutionary hierarchy from apes to humans and among all the living races. The dissolution of bound categories between animals and humans in Darwin's work seemed to confirm to the public the tradition of atavistic constructions of lower classes and primitives in physiognomy. Cowling looks at animalized illustrations of physiognomic types by anthropologists, cartoonists working for popular journals, and painters who claimed scientific validity under Darwinian science. Caricatures of Irish patriots, whose already animalistic features become increasingly ape-like in the 1860s, exemplify the growing awareness of Darwinian ideas.[5]

In craniometry, visual comparisons of profile views of ape skulls, those of nonwhites, and whites became an iconic visual reference for racial hierarchy before and during the Darwinian period, beginning with Pieter Camper's "The Evolution of Man" from *The Works . . . on the Connexion between the Science of Anatomy and the Art of Drawing, Painting, and Statuary* (1794), an example of a scientific illustration by an anatomist that crossed over into the arts as authoritative. Camper's importance in terms of visuals where Darwin would be concerned lies in his interest in primatology and dissection of apes. Despite the appearance of illustrating "evolution" from ape to human, Camper's ideas were based in the Great Chain of Being, with species fixed on rungs of a ladder with humans at the top. Never-the-less, Camper's work, based on comparative skull measurements resulting in his famous "facial angle," provided a foundation for the pseudoscience of craniometry used by anatomists and anthropologists. Although Camper's manual for artists only implied the direct relationship of ape to human, later treatises with scientific illustrations made references to evolution. The physiologist Mathias-Marie Duval, for example, who held joint positions as Professor of Zoological Anatomy at the École d'anthropologie in Paris and Professor of Anatomy at the École des Beaux-Arts, updated Camper's work with frequent references to Darwin in his *Précis d'Anatomie à l'usage des Artistes* (1881). Skull measurements were now part of the mobile vision of evolution. Duval applied the contemporary work of the anthropologist Paul Broca on craniometry as well as Cesare Lombroso's influential interpretations of comparative criminal physiognomy and simian atavism. Comparative imagery of simian and racial skulls in art texts and science illustration before the age of Darwin no doubt allowed the public to quickly grasp the implications of evolution in class and race politics.

While illustrative line drawing such as that used by Camper and Duval has a lengthy history in science, in the mid-nineteenth century photography was a relatively recent means of using comparative images to demonstrate "truth." Darwin was one of the first to use this convincing medium to illustrate a science book (see below), but early on, those who connected evolution to crime made use of comparative and composite photographs to show the connections among deviancy, atavism, and skull formation. Allan Sekula gives a succinct history of the use of photographs in the work of Lombroso, by Darwin's cousin the eugenist Frances Galton, and in police archives in his "The Body and the Archive" (1989). His analysis makes use of Foucault's theories of social control and the identification of deviancy among the poor and disenfranchised. Peter Hamilton fleshes out further the implications of photography of the marginalized in regard to Darwinian science in *The Beautiful and the Damned: The Creation of Identity in Nineteenth-Century Photography* (2001). The connection of deviancy to atavism with animal features inscripted on the body moved beyond eccentric applications by a few individuals and was applied widely to culture based on post-Darwinian fears of cultural and social degeneration in Europe and America, issues explored by Robert Nye, Daniel Pick, and Sander Gilman.

Photography and linear illustration were also used in measurements, cranial and corporeal, of living tribal populations. These measurements helped to refine the hierarchical relationships within the schema of animal to Caucasian. Camper's facial angle and perceived deformations of the body were used to signal animal origins as well. *Images of Savages: Ancient Roots of Modern Prejudice in Western Culture* (1999) by Gustav Jahoda, and Jan Nederveen Pieterse's *White on Black: Images of Africans and Blacks in Western Popular Cul-*

ture (1992) are two texts that explore a variety of visuals where nonwhite races are shown in animal-like depictions in both scientific and popular illustrations, lending authority to racial discrimination and imperialist expansion.

Although Darwin did not take on the discussion of the simian ancestry of humans directly until his *Descent of Man*, and evolution with its connections to apes and other animals has a much longer history than Darwin, he was identified with "the monkey thesis" immediately after the publication of *Origin of Species* in 1859 by scholars and the public alike. When English biologist and Darwin popularizer Thomas Huxley debated the issue of evolution with Anglican Bishop Samuel Wilberforce in 1860, the believer inquired as to whether it was through his grandfather or grandmother that Huxley claimed descent from an ape. Huxley famously quipped, "If, then . . . the question is put to me, would I rather have a miserable ape for a grandfather, or a man highly endowed by nature and possessing great means and influence, and yet who employs those faculties and that influence for the mere purpose of introducing ridicule into a grave scientific discussion—I unhesitatingly affirm my preference for the ape."[6] While animalistic nonwhites were more acceptable in visual culture than simianized Caucasians, cartoons in popular publications, mainly aimed at the educated, used the anthropomorphized ape as a subversive trope to resist that aspect of evolution that many found to be the most frightening and threatening to the increasingly powerful middle class: the evisceration of divine creation from human history.

For those prepared to consider Darwin's "hairy, arboreal" ancestor as a possibility, there were multiple sites where science and popular entertainment converged. Scientists arranged for exhibitions of tribal peoples in human zoos, where they generally were perceived as barely evolved beyond animals, a practice that was used to support imperialism and missionary activity. Darwin's own response to Fuegians in South America is typical of the response of thousands to tribal exhibitions seen in Europe: "The astonishment which I felt on first seeing a party of Fuegians on a wild and broken shore will never be forgotten by me, for the reflection at once rushed into my mind—such were our ancestors."[7] After Darwin, indigenous populations were not only thought of as animalistic but as Stone Age survivors, offering windows on past lifestyles and barely evolved bodies. The developmentalist approach in anthropology, wherein civilization was thought to follow a uniform series of stages beginning in the deep past, both was influenced by Darwinian evolution and in turn influenced the scientist's later work.[8] Archaeologist Stephanie Moser has examined visual representations of the hairy "cave man" in light of Darwinian science, referring to comics, popular science books, paintings, museum murals, and installations.[9]

A growing fascination with the idea of "the missing link" coupled with the recent discovery in 1847 of gorillas by Westerners led many to speculate that a transitional ape-man was still living. Locally, people with genetic conditions that rendered them hairy, such as Lionel the "Lion-Faced Boy" and Julia Pastrana, were included in traveling exhibitions and labelled "missing links." Chimps and orangutans as well as people from indigenous cultures were displayed as missing links, discussed in a number of "What Is It?" essays.[10] While missing-link exhibitions were popular following a widespread interest in Darwin and even considered scientific, museum installations of stuffed animals, wax replicas of indigenous peoples, and prehistoric groups brought the growing authority of Darwinian science to the populace in a somewhat more professional light. In America, where social Darwinism and the idea of survival of the fittest were popular, installations and painted scenery emphasized competition among and between species. Charles Henry Knight created paintings for the American Museum of Natural History in New York that featured menacing predators. Dioramas often emphasized threatening aspects of nature. Donna Haraway in "Teddy Bear Patriarchy" (1989) and Sally Kohlstedt in "Nature by Design: Masculinity and Animal Display in Nineteenth-Century America" (2006) have written about the presentation of gender in museum primate displays. Stephanie Moser has noted that wax figure dioramas in natural history museums of indigenous peoples and prehistoric groups stressed their closeness to nature, showing them to be "little different from the animals in adjoining habitat dioramas."[11] Men often were depicted as hunters, with women involved in domestic activities. These installations catered to contemporary notions of gendered activities, supported by Darwin himself.

Darwinism was further deployed through popular science writers, who often infused his work with agendas of their own and with illustrations to support their ideas. For example, in his work on evolutionary popularizers, Bernard Lightman notes how Arabella Buckley's writings on evolution had a spiritual subtext misread by Darwin as a means to escape persecution.[12] Geoffrey Cantor and Sally Shuttleworth have demonstrated ways in which science, including Darwinian evolution, was intricately interwoven with cultural spheres in popular journals in *Science Serialized: Representations of the Sciences in Nineteenth Century Periodicals* (2004).

In a broader cultural context, the spread of Darwin's ideas and their application to society were influenced by geographical sites as well as political agendas.[13] David Kohn's volume *The Darwinian Heritage* (1985) remains a landmark in the spread and cultural considerations of Darwin's ideas. Ronald Numbers and John Stenhouse's *Disseminating Darwinism: The Role of Place,*

Race, Religion and Gender (1999) focuses largely on North America and Australia. Anne-Julia Zweirlein's anthology, *Unmapped Countries: Biological Visions in Nineteenth-Century Literature and Culture* (2005), with its essays on Darwin, considers cultural issues concerning politics, popularization, feminism, and anthropology.

Charles Darwin's Use of Visuals

In his 1976 article "The Emergence of a Visual Language for Geological Science, 1760–1840," the touchstone text for science and visual culture studies, Martin Rudwick discusses traditions in geological representation; these can be easily tied to Darwin's schematic "Tree of Life" diagram from *Origin of Species* with its horizontal "strata," an example of applying existing visual conventions to new ideas. While *Origin* contained but a single image, other volumes are richly illustrated, often by well-known artists and photographers and, in many cases, with illustrations created with other scientific work in mind. Jonathan Smith has looked at the way that Darwin has exploited and resisted existing illustration styles and conventions to convey his messages of natural and sexual selection. In his *Charles Darwin and Victorian Visual Culture* (2006), he examined Darwin's imagery over a thirty-year period, making use of W. J. T. Mitchell's concept of imagetext in which the image and surrounding text are fluid in communicating Darwin's ideas. While images most often come from existing practices (illustrations intended for other sources, for example), they are selected for their perceived sympathy regarding his outlook. Though some of these illustrations may have originated with other arguments in mind, Darwin reinterprets their meaning in his texts. Darwin reenvisions conventional imagery or makes use of the unconventional as in the use of photography in a scientific text to emphasize the truth of his ideas. Julia Voss structured her book *Darwins Bilder: Ansichten der Evolutionstheorie 1837–1874* around four Darwinian images (the evolutionary tree, finches, pheasants, and smiling apes) and three theoretical paradigms (the wheel, net, and collage) to examine Darwin's pictures comparatively within a local, global, and historical context of scientific activity. She documented the centrality of pictures to his work through his collection of visual material, his involvement with the illustrations for his publications, and his activities as a draughtsman, which, as demonstrated by his sketchbooks, were instrumental in his ability to conceptualize evolution. Her studies have revealed that, in contrast to his collaborators, followers, and opponents, Darwin's drawings and illustrations visualized random chance, disorder, variation, and imperfection and were notable for what they omitted. For example, nowhere did Darwin depict debased primitive races, apes figured as monsters, or visualizations of the survival of the fittest.

Janet Browne has examined Darwin's collection of photographs of the insane intended for *Expression of the Emotions in Man and Animals*, one of the earliest scientific texts to make use of this medium and Darwin's only volume to use photography as illustration (1985). Phillip Prodger has studied the manipulation of photographic imagery in *Expression of the Emotions*. The case of the very first image is itself of interest, given the fact that the photograph of a crying baby caught in action seemed to be a near impossibility in terms of available technology. As it turns out, it was, in fact, too good to be true, although Darwin never let on about the circumstances surrounding its production.[14] It was a photographed drawing. The seemingly remarkable instantaneous look of the image made it immediately popular and the well-known photographer sold tens of thousands of copies separately with no explanation regarding its scientific origins. Instead, in its popular life, it was likened to the central character of a novel of the period and dubbed "Ginx's Baby."[15] In other photos, theatrical positions were held to illustrate a particular kind of emotion, which though socially recognizable—as in hands raised in the air and an open mouth to register astonishment—were more theatrical convention than science. Prodger has further discussed Darwin's reasoning behind the dual use of wood engraving (a traditional medium in science illustration in the nineteenth century) and photography in *Expression of Emotions*.

Darwin as Shaped by Art and Aesthetics

Bernard Smith has demonstrated that Darwin's vision of separate geographical regions in the context of evolution can be traced indirectly to artists aboard Captain Cook's ships who resolved problems of unfamiliar landscapes by conjoining training in landscape painting with naval traditions of topography. In particular, William Hodges emphasized distinct regions with their own climate and ecology, directly influencing Alexander von Humboldt's ideas about conditions where distinct zones support particular wildlife. Humboldt in turn influenced Darwin.[16] If somewhat academic yet ecologically exotic paintings of the eighteenth century influenced Darwin's vision, Jane Camerini argues from the pragmatic side that maps used to document distribution of species, water level, and climate were central to Darwin's developing ideas.[17] Traditions of Romanticism and the sublime in literature and landscape art have informed James Paradis and David Kohn's work on Darwin.[18]

The Chapters

The authors of this volume are scholars of literature, the history of science, photography, and the history of art. They consider visual culture broadly, from comics to salon sculptures and computer programs, although several focus on a limited area within visual culture based on the questions posed. Collectively, they examine the relationships among media, representation, and message and have considered the following: What is the identity of the artists/artisans as they intersect with audiences? How do audiences of satirical cartoons differ from those of propaganda posters or avant-garde paintings? What is the locus of the image maker within Darwinian ideas? How is Darwin appropriated or undercut as an authoritative voice? What kinds of Darwinian messages are being communicated and by what method? Some of the essays contribute to cultural theory or reception and viewer response theory without engaging in a discussion based exclusively on those perspectives.[19] The essays take into consideration historical and personal moments in terms of artists/artisans and broader cultural agendas. They are arranged roughly in chronological order from Darwin's lifetime to the present. In regions considered, they range from England to France, Germany, and Russia, all important centers for the dissemination of Darwin's ideas.

Janet Browne examines the origins of the cartoon as a visual form that accompanied the introduction of Darwinism in England and its subsequent use to conflate the invisible (and for many, unacceptable) process of evolution from ape to human to the very scientist popularly identified with this aspect of his theories. After the publication of *The Descent of Man* in 1871, Darwin himself entered monkeyana, humorously deflating the seriousness of his proposals. At the same time, Browne argues that the popular identification of Darwin with evolution reduced the role of Huxley, Lyell, Spencer, and Wallace, other important evolutionists. While science relies on the visual in many ways, in presenting theoretical propositions in pictorial or diagrammatic form, for example, even seemingly "dry" inscriptions can be used to popular ends. In the case of Darwin as monkey, his famous tree of descent reproduced in *Origin* becomes the monkey's own habitat, providing the branches from which he swings. Browne points out that cartoons both rely on familiar stereotypes and create them, generally reinforcing middle-class values.

Natural selection has long been thought of as the most central of Darwinian evolutionary mechanisms, but recent scholarship has turned to sexual selection, which gained increasing attention in Darwin's own work. Phillip Prodger discusses a little-known conversation between Darwin and his famously adversarial aesthetic opponent Ruskin. Prodger argues that Darwin carefully prepared his illustrations for *Descent of Man* and *Expression of Emotions* as well as enlarging his argument over beauty in the 1869 edition of *Origin* based on the negative press he was receiving because of Ruskin and the importance of proving his biological view of beauty. As sexual selection based on the experience of "beauty" as an attractant throughout the animal kingdom moved to center stage in Darwin's work along with the animalization of emotions, he was sensitive to the power of Ruskin, who believed beauty to be a divine gift.

The image of ape-man in German "high art" in the *Darwinismus* of the end of the century is explored by Marsha Morton. The biologist Ernst Haeckel is well known as Darwin's greatest popularizer in Germany, although his theory of monistic pantheism diverges significantly from Darwinism. Himself a gifted artist, Haeckel's brand of visual culture is most often identified with his intricate illustrations of sea life, a major influence on Art Nouveau around 1900. However, Morton explores an earlier phase of Haeckel's work, in which a more programmatic Darwinism in his writings influenced references to a violent and amoral nature found in the work of Arnold Böcklin, Max Klinger, Alfred Kubin, Gabriel von Max, Franz von Stuck and Richard Müller. Their ape-man imagery is often dark spirited and filled with irony; like Browne's cartoons, they respond to cultural anxieties.

Haeckel's substantial influence on visual culture beyond Art Nouveau outside of German-speaking countries has not been generally recognized despite the international translations of his many publications, both those aimed at a scientific audience and those meant for popular reading. Of great influence was his theory about the earliest and most rudimentary of life forms that gave rise to all others—*monera*—comprised of nonnucleated blobs of active protoplasm. Protoplasm then became the substance of life found in all cells, a gelatinous, vital fluid. Robert Brain examines the popularization of Haeckel's challenge to Darwin's theory of heredity—wherein particles of the body's cells are transmitted to reproductive organs or *pangenesis*—through Haeckel's proposal that the protoplasm itself stores organic memory in waveform motions that are then transferred to the next generation. The widespread audience that embraced this concept included none other than Darwinian proselytizer Huxley. Brain demonstrates that the theory of vibratory protoplasm intersected with wave force theory in physics and engineering. Beginning with graphs that dominated physics as well as physiology, Brain argues that waveform phenomena extended into various cultural domains; in art it influenced Munch and Picabia and eventually contributed to abstraction.

Darwin's cousin Galton, originator of the popular science of eugenics, applied sexual selection and information gleaned from animal breeding to humans, arguing for eugenic marriage. Fae Brauer focuses on the visual features of the first eugenic exhibition of 1912 (one year after Galton's death), in which Darwin was represented as a key figure. Among the materials she examines are Galton-Darwin pedigree charts establishing their lineage in terms of heredity and the production of great men of science. The identification of Darwin's authority prompted eugenics legislation in England, a history that previously has been obliterated from Darwin studies.

James Krasner offers a Darwinian twist to the readers' assumed male gaze concerning the original illustrations for Darwinist Thomas Hardy's *Tess of the d'Urbervilles*. The illustrations render the viewer complicit with the protagonist Angel Clare in sexual selection. Krasner argues that the near uniformity and linear distribution of women across the imagery is related to Darwin's own descriptions of sexual selection in human populations, which in turn owes to contemporary aspects of social control, standardization of women's bodies, and spectacle.

While Hardy's audience is much like that of Darwin's own dominant social class, which shaped the scientist's vision of sexual selection, not all Caucasian Western men had equal access to the most desirable of women. This writer undercuts the notion of a uniform male gaze in paintings by modern male artists around the turn of the twentieth century who were disenfranchised from the mainstream of the middle class through social and self perceptions of degeneracy. The many fatal women in modern art of the period have been interpreted as misogynistic representations, but they may often represent the elusive beloved woman who rejects the weak male artist. These representations of women are compared with the familiar circulating imagery of "wife capture" in literature and art, where aggression and strength are the basis of patriarchy.

Broad cultural implications for those who embraced Darwin, but opposed his ideas on a random, undirected, and open-ended universe as Haeckel ultimately did, affected political agendas and their visual culture. In a chapter on the early twentieth-century French painter Henri Rousseau, Brauer examines the artist in light of anarchist politics. She interprets his animal paintings in terms of the mutualist politics of Kropotkin and Rèclus and considers ways in which they applied Darwin to society. She anchors Rousseau's images of "tame primates" and rapacious beasts to politics abroad and longed-for harmony. While the anarchist vision of society had a limited audience in France, Darwinism was absorbed into the agenda of Marx and Engels and their followers in Russia. They too opposed the notion of social struggle. Patricia Simpson examines ways in which Darwin was combined with Lamarckian evolution in Russia to support the evolution of the ideal, laboring body after the Russian Revolution. Simpson examines the development of "biomechanics" through photographs and avant-garde theater and art.

In the post-war period, Darwin's influence on visual culture is often not straightforward. Gavin Parkinson explores Surrealism's complicated relationship with Darwin, focusing on the drawings by André Masson for his book *Anatomy of My Universe* (1943). Masson quotes Goethe, Darwin, and Spencer, among others who together suggest the connectedness of forms in nature, but Parkinson explores the equal importance of Nietzsche, who refuted Spencer and Darwin. Patrizio and Barnes explore a range of contemporary artists working with a variety of media from drawings and photographs to computer programs who explore the human experience of deep time and the nature of the universe. This occurs in a number of ways: how fossils intersect with local politics, exhibition, and economy; the sublime experience of geological processes; and an interest in the state of animality. The latter dimension is one that has been taken up in recent postmodern theoretical writings such as that of Derrida ("The Animal that Therefore I Am"), Cary Wolfe, and Deleuze and Guattari.

Future Directions

Future directions on Darwin and visual culture will no doubt become increasingly nuanced, tracking perhaps the scientist's reception and meaning among specific groups of individuals within cultures. Hopefully, the studies will move past the immediate post-Darwinian period, undeterred by the complexities of Darwinian resistances after 1900 as is the case with five of the essays in this volume. "Neural Darwinism," examining the brain and selection of neurological connections in terms of adaptation along with neuroaesthetics, is an avenue being pursued by art historians and artists. Current artistic ideas concerning animal intersubjectivity and embodiment are benefiting from an exploration of Darwin's heirs in ethology like Nikolass Tinbergen (founder of ethology), Donald Griffin (founder of cognitive ethology), and the later work of Marc Bekoff, Frans de Waal, or Marc Hauser.

Where Darwin himself is concerned, questions need to be raised about just which Darwin one is talking about. Is it the Darwin who eradicates a spiritual dimension from the natural world or is it the Darwin who slipped the words "by the Creator" into the final sentence of *The Origin* beginning with the second edition, which then read: "There is grandeur in this view of life, with its several powers, having been originally breathed by the Creator into a few forms or into one"? Is it the Darwin supporter of abolition and hypothesizer of racial variation as based on cultural standards of beauty or is it the Darwin who positively cited Karl Vogt on the proof of craniometry and facial angles and therefore of intellectual variation among the races? Is it the Darwin who famously established the law of natural selection as unbending and of central importance or the Darwin who admitted in the *Descent of Man* that he had given far too much weight to natural selection and found sexual selection to be at least of equal importance, often eclipsing natural selection? And what of Darwin's interest in the older science of embryological recapitulation that held so much value for Haeckel? Will we eventually divide Darwin into "periods" rather than refer to pre- and post-Darwinian eras?

In terms of interdisciplinary approaches to Darwin, do visual features need to be treated differently following the methodologies within fields or can we set aside our staked territories concerning representational practice? It is, of course, important to carefully examine the materials used in the reproduction of images and the intended audience—a scientific illustration is not received in the same way as a fine arts painting even if both aim to replicate geological strata, of course. However, while media and visualization practice are mutually dependent, images circulate not only through their material manifestation, but through ideas as well. Boundaries between art and science often blur, for both are rooted in culture. The authors of this volume have spent many years reading in fields not initially their own, perhaps with even greater passion, have met and exchanged information at interdisciplinary conferences, and in some cases have ventured far from where they initially thought they might go in light of perspectives offered from various disciplines. Perhaps Gillian Beer's speculations about intersections in interdisciplinary approaches that need not arrive at the conclusions of a familiar agenda might prove fruitful. We might consider the following thoughts from her *Open Fields* (1996) with its essays on Darwin and culture:

> Encounter . . . between disciplines . . . brings into active play unexamined assumptions and so may allow interpreters . . . to tap into unexpressed incentives. Exchange, dialogue, misprision, fugitive understanding, are all crucial within disciplinary encounters as well as between peoples. Understanding askance, with your attention fixed elsewhere, or your expectations focused on a different outcome, is also a common enough event in such encounters and can produce effects as powerful, if stranger, than fixed attention.[20]

NOTES

I would like to thank Marsha Morton and Janet Browne for their helpful commentary on this essay.

1. Charles Darwin, *On the Origin of Species by Means of Natural Selection* (1859), republished with a new foreword by Patricia Horan (New York: Avenel Books, 1976).

2. Beer was not the first to write about Darwin and literature. Early works include Leo Henkin, *Darwinism and the English Novel, 1890–1910: The Impact of Evolution on Victorian Fiction* (New York: Corporate Press, 1940); Lionel Stevenson's *Darwin among the Poets* (Chicago: University of Chicago Press, 1932); and Tom Gibbons, *Rooms in the Darwin Hotel: Studies in English Literary Criticism and Ideas 1880–1920* (Nedlam: University of West Australia Press, 1973). However, Beer's explorations of Darwin's use of language with a basis in Romantic literature and the formulation of his "stories" within that context, along with arguments of their deployment in novels of the period, sparked renewed interest in this area. Other recent landmark studies include George Levine, *Darwin and the Novelists: Patterns of Science in Victorian Fiction* (Chicago: University of Chicago Press, 1988) and Bert Bender, *The Descent of Love: Darwin and the Theory of Sexual Selection in American Fiction, 1871–1926* (Philadelphia: University of Pennsylvania Press, 1989).

3. Barbara Larson, "La génération symboliste et la révolution darwinienne," in *L'âme au corps: arts et sciences, 1793–1993*, ed. Jean Clair and Pierre Changeaux, 322–42. (Paris: Réunion des musées nationaux, 1993).

4. Kelly Hurley makes a similar argument within literature in *The Gothic Body: Sexuality, Materialism and Degeneration at the Fin de Siècle* (Cambridge: Cambridge University Press, 1996), where she also cites Kristeva's work along with Mary Douglas's model of abomination as she employs the term "abhuman" in her discussion of how Darwinism as a disruptive force opened up morphic structures, leading to a renewed interest in the Gothic horror novel with its monstrous bodies.

5. See L. P. Curtis, *Apes and Angels: The Irishman in Victorian Caricature*, rev. ed. (Washington: Smithsonian Institution Press, 1997).

6. Quoted in Adrian Desmond, *Huxley: From Devil's Disciple to Evolution's High Priest* (Reading, Mass.: Helix Books, 1999), 278–79.

7. *The Descent of Man and Selection in Relation to Sex* (1871), reprinted with an Introduction by John Tyler Bonner and Robert M. May (Princeton: Princeton University Press, 1981), 919–20.

8. On the developmentalist approach to physical and cultural evolution, see George Stocking, *Victorian Anthropology* (New York: The Free Press, 1987), especially "The Darwinian Revolution and the Evolution of Culture," 144–85. On ways in which developmentalist anthropology influenced Darwin, see Rosemary Jann, "Darwin and the Anthropologists: Sexual Selection and its Discontents," in *Sexualities in Victorian Britain*, ed. Andrew Miller and James Adams, 79–95. (Bloomington: Indiana University Press, 1996).

9. For an introduction, see her *Ancestral Images: The Iconography of Human Origins* (Ithaca: Cornell University Press, 1998).

10. See, for example, *Freakery: Cultural Spectacles of the Extraordinary Body*, ed. Rosemarie Garland Thomson (New York: New York University Press, 1996); Robert Bogdan, *Freak Show: Representing Cultural Oddities for Amusement and Profit* (Chicago: University of Chicago Press, 1988); Diana Snigurowicz, "Sex, Simians and Spectacle in Nineteenth-Century France; or, How to Tell a 'Man' from a Monkey," *Canadian Journal of History* 34 (April 1999): 51–81; Jean-Louis Fischer, *Monstres: histories du corps et de ses défauts* (Paris: Syros-Alternatives, 1991); and Neil Harris, *Humbug: The Art of P. T. Barnum* (Chicago: University of Chicago Press, 1973).

11. Stephanie Moser, "The Dilemma of Didactic Displays, Habitat Dioramas, Life Groups,

and Reconstructions of the Past," *Making Early Histories in Museums*, ed. N. Merriman (London: Leicester University Press, 1999), 102.

12. Bernard Lightman, *Victorian Popularizers of Science: Designing Nature for New Audiences* (Chicago: University of Chicago Press, 2007), 253.

13. On the reception of Darwin, see Thomas Glick, ed., *The Comparative Reception of Darwinism*, reprinted with a new preface (Chicago: University of Chicago Press, 1988); and Ronald L. Numbers and John Stenhouse, eds., *Disseminating Darwinism: The Role of Place, Race, Religion, and Gender* (Cambridge: Cambridge University Press, 1999).

14. For a history of the relationship between developing printing technologies and scientific illustration, see Estelle Jussim, *Visual Communication and the Graphic Arts: Photographic Technologies in the Nineteenth Century* (New York: R. R. Bowker Co., 1974, reprinted in 1983).

15. See Phillip Prodger, "Illustration as Strategy in Charles Darwin's 'The Expression of Emotions in Man and Animal,'" in *Inscribing Science: Scientific Texts and the Materiality of Communication*, ed. Timothy Lenoir (Stanford, Calif.: Stanford University Press, 1998), 139–181.

16. Bernard Smith, *European Vision and the South Pacific: 1768–1850* (New Haven: Yale University Press, 1959, reprinted in 1985).

17. Noted in Soojung-Kim Pang, "Visual Representation and Post-Constructivist History of Science," *Historical Studies in the Physical and Biological Sciences* 28 (2005): 153–54.

18. James Paradis, "Darwin and Landscape," in *Victorian Science and Victorian Values: Literary Perspectives*, ed. James Paradis and Thomas Postlewait, 85–110. (New Brunswick: Rutgers University Press, 1985); and David Kohn, "The Aesthetic Construction of Darwin's Theory: in *The Elusive Synthesis: Aesthetics and Science*, ed. Alfred Tauber, 13–48 (Dordrecht: Kluwer, 1996).

19. Landmark studies include Roger Cooter and Stephen Pumfrey, "Separate Spheres and Public Places: Reflections on the History of Science Popularization and Science in Popular Culture," *History of Science* 32 (1994): 237–67; David Freedberg, *The Power of Images: Studies in the History and Theory of Response* (Chicago: University of Chicago Press, 1989); and James Hay, Lawrence Grossberg, and Ellen Wartella, eds. *The Audience and Its Landscapes* (Boulder, Colo.: Westview, 1996).

20. Gillian Beer, *Open Fields: Science in Cultural Encounter* (Oxford: Oxford University Press, 1996), 2.

CHAPTER 1

Darwin in Caricature

A Study in the Popularization and Dissemination of Evolutionary Theory

JANET BROWNE

In the years that followed publication of *On the Origin of Species*, Charles Darwin became one of the most famous naturalists in the world, "first among the scientific men of England," as Edward Aveling put it, his name inextricably linked with the idea of evolution and with the larger shifts in public opinion gathering pace as the century drew toward a close.[1]

Few other scientific theories have spread as widely as Darwin's theory of evolution by natural selection. Within ten years of publication in London of *Origin of Species* in 1859, sixteen different editions had appeared in England and America, and translations had been made into German, French, Dutch, Italian, Russian, and Swedish, accompanied by important commentaries, criticisms, and supporting texts.[2] There would be many more to come. Through these means, people all over the developed world were able to read Darwin's work in a language accessible to them and, if they wished, participate in what was one of the first truly international scientific debates.

This extraordinary phenomenon has attracted much scholarly attention. Much of Darwin's prominence was expressed in characteristically nineteenth-century form through a proliferation of texts, commentaries, reviews, and translations. Analyses by Thomas Glick, whose admirable volume pioneered comparative reception studies of Darwinism, and by Alvar Ellegärd, on the reception of Darwin's ideas in the British periodical press, are standard works.[3] Since then, an expansion of the historiographical approach, especially in considering scientific and religious issues in broader cultural context, has brought remarkable scholarly achievements in understanding the spread and transformation of concepts on a global basis, as seen, for example, in Ronald Numbers's and John Stenhouse's recent book, *Disseminating Darwinism*.[4] Many other works will be published for the Darwin commemorations of 2009. If this were not sufficient, the collected *Correspondence of Charles Dar-*

win, edited by the late Frederick Burkhardt and Sydney Smith, and now by James Secord, reveals in copious detail the impact of Darwin's book on a wide variety of readers.[5] "It is curious how nationality influences opinion," said Darwin, noting the differing responses to his work in France and Germany.[6]

One of the most striking aspects of recent research into the history of evolution, however, is an increasing interest in probing nonscientific realms, both textual and nontextual, in order to ask how Darwin's work became part of the richly varied world of nineteenth-century popular culture that flourished beyond the domains of scientific devotees. Studying the popular response to Darwin's theories has a great deal to tell us about the ways that science and society met at various times in history. Most ordinary people in nineteenth-century Europe and America, after all, usually encountered science through newspapers and magazines, sometimes at a public lecture, museum or art gallery, or through fiction, biographies, and memoirs. There were plenty of sites of production and consumption in Victorian Britain in which scientific ideas could be found. These included exhibitions, menageries, agricultural contests, horticultural displays, music halls, and consumer goods, as well as fashionable crazes that caught the imagination, such as mesmerist displays.[7]

Darwin's theory was no exception. If they wished, individuals could acquire a pottery statuette, crafted by Hugo Rheinhold, of a monkey contemplating a human skull. The Soviet leader Vladimir Lenin displayed one of these on his Kremlin desk in the 1920s.[8] Or they might pay to gape at Julia Pastrana, the "Missing Link," whose mummified body toured Eastern Europe in 1862.[9] British connoisseurs were able to commission an elegant piece of Wedgwood chinaware decorated by Emile Lessore with cherubs clustering around the tree of life.[10] They could sing a duet at the piano on the "Darwinian Theory," read edifying popular romances such as *Survival of the Fittest*, or give their children nursery primers called *Daddy Darwin's Dovecot*. Spanish gourmets might drink a glass of anis from a bottle depicting a Darwinian imp: "science says it is the best—and that's the truth," declared the label.[11] And farmers in upstate New York could medicate their livestock with Darwin's unknowing blessing. The agricultural firm of G. W. Merchant, of Lockport, near Rochester, New York, advertised its veterinary Gargling Oil (a medicated drench for animals) with an ape that sang:

> If I am Darwin's Grandpa,
> It follows, don't you see,
> That what is good for man & beast
> Is doubly good for me.[12]

These consumer products made Darwin's ideas—or what were commonly understood to be Darwin's ideas—fully tangible to his own generation and the one that followed him.

Darwin was also one of the few scientists to have been portrayed in an extraordinary variety of printed cartoons, caricatures, humorous songs, and written satire. Indeed, it is a little surprising that apart from a number of classic studies focusing on medical lampoons and geological caricature, as well as Jim Paradis's study of Victorian scientific satire, and Patricia Fara's work on the iconography of Isaac Newton and Joseph Banks, caricatures have not featured very much in the history of science.[13] This may relate to a relative paucity of resources. Satirical images of scientists do not turn up nearly as often as researchers wish. Nevertheless a recent turn toward the material culture of science is opening the field, and the visual aspects of science are widely appreciated.[14] As this volume attests, science relies on the visual in a multitude of ways, on the one hand in presenting theoretical propositions in pictorial or diagrammatic form, and on the other hand in constructing the data itself, such as in the visual materials produced by a seismograph or CAT scanner. In interesting epistemological ways, images *are* the data. Science, at its very heart, is about making visible the invisible.

And in equal measure, science as an activity appears in images created for viewing by nonscientists. Caricatures, for example, vividly present the perceptions of the people. A humorous cartoon is a unique form of communication between human beings that makes obvious the content of new ideas or points up the difficulties inherent in new ideas. We have only to think of modern cartoons, with their fertile juxtaposition of themes, and of the way that humor does not travel very well from country to country or from group to group, to understand how each item is specific to a particular cultural moment. With their free use of stereotypes and topical allusion, cartoons can provide insight into the way at least some of the people of a specific national grouping might regard science.

It is not possible here to dwell on the rich and well-documented history of satirical tradition except for a word or two of definition. Caricatures, as the term's origin indicates, tend to emphasize prominent features of a person's character, often with cruel intent, as in the biting political satires of Rowlandson or Gillray in Britain at the end of the eighteenth century.[15] Cartoons, as commonly understood, on the other hand, are simple line drawings, often accompanied by text, and became popular in Britain from about 1843 via the humorous magazine *Punch*, although the term previously was applied to working sketches or outlines for a fresco or tapestry. *Punch* at first used the title "Punch's Pencillings" to describe the big picture of the week that dealt variously with political or social topics. Then, in response to publicity surrounding proposed decorations for the rebuilding of the Houses of Parliament in London, the magazine adopted the word "cartoon."[16] These new forms of drawing, usually accompanied by a printed caption, were altogether milder, offering gentle topical comment. They were—and remain—for the most part mass-produced items that depend on publication or circulation for their intended effect. The rise of such images clearly relates to the rapid development and diversification of printing technologies in nineteenth-century Europe and America and to the expansion of audiences for all forms of periodical literature, audiences eager to engage with an unprecedented wave of material.[17] *Harper's Weekly, Punch, Fun,* and illustrated journals like *Household Words* were widely distributed from 1850 onwards. They became the mainstays of a sector of the English-speaking market that aimed for well-to-do readers. In the 1860s, at W. H. Smith's, a newsagent in the Strand, in London, a prospective purchaser could find some 150 different periodicals for sale. Similarly, at Mudie's Circulating Library, also based in London, a reader could have found mass-circulation editions of Dickens's novels illustrated by Hablot Brown (Phiz). The impact of the visual here can hardly be overstated. These were domesticated line drawings, relying on familiar stereotypes and middle-class values. In the hands of great illustrators like John Doyle ("HB"), and his son Richard Doyle, along with the social artists John Leech, Charles Keene, and John Tenniel, followed by Edward Linley Sambourne and Ernest Griset, popular books and magazines came to shape public opinion by codifying the ideals of the emerging middle classes in Britain.[18]

Victorian humorists grabbed their chance when the *Origin of Species* was published in 1859. "Am I a Man and a Brother?" asked a gorilla in the May 1861 number of *Punch,* echoing the popular perception of Darwin's work (figure 1.1). Although Darwin did not mention human evolution or the possible ancestry of mankind in the *Origin of Species,* this was the controversial subject that dominated debate after publication. A host of published reviews and commentaries, and the personal confrontation between Bishop Samuel Wilberforce, Thomas Henry Huxley, and Richard Owen at the British Association for the Advancement of Science meeting in Oxford, in July 1860, made the point clear. Apes and angels quickly became the issue on which Darwin's and Alfred Russel Wallace's theories were discussed, an example of the public vigorously exploring themes that were not present in the original books or articles. Concepts of progressivism and transmutation were already circulating in Europe and North America through the writings of Robert Chambers, Jean-Baptiste Lamarck, Étienne Geoffroy Saint-Hilaire, Herbert Spencer, and others, and ape ancestry was not a new topic for discussion. Yet Darwin's

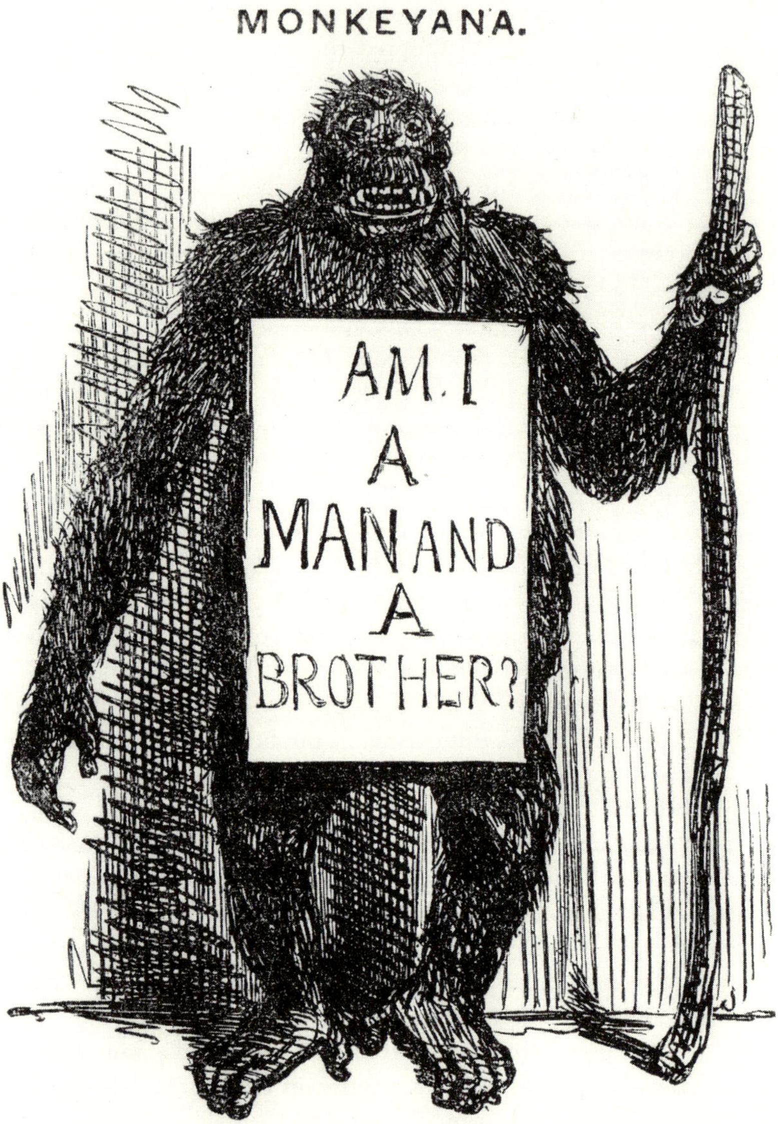

Figure 1.1 Monkeyana. The first and most famous of *Punch*'s images to display the implications of evolutionary theory. The cartoon also plays on contemporary anti-slavery movements in Britain. *From* Punch, *18 May 1861. Courtesy Wellcome Library London.*

book sharpened the problem dramatically. The 1861 *Punch* cartoon played specifically on the British anti-slavery campaign of the 1830s, taking up the motto of the crusade while also drawing on highly topical references to Paul Du Chaillu's accounts of gorillas in West Africa and the recent Oxford confrontation.[19] The artwork and accompanying poem are unattributed.

> Am I satyr or man?
> Pray tell me who can,
> And settle my place in the scale. A man in ape's shape,
> An anthropoid ape,
> Or monkey deprived of his tail?

Over the following decade, *Punch* cartoonists had a great deal of fun with the evolution controversy. Irresistibly, they indicated in pictorial form that apes were an integral part of the human world, often portraying them as more intelligent or well-behaved than ourselves, as in Mr. Gorilla, beautifully dressed in evening clothes, pictured arriving as a guest at a high-society party.[20] In the printed columns of the magazine, word play linked the Irish political question with Mr. O'Rilla, contributing to *Punch*'s long-running attack on the Irish nation, which even before Darwin's writings often included the simianization of Irish facial features.[21] Appreciative of the public taste for apes, *Punch* dedicated its 1861 Christmas Annual to the gorilla, and showed Mr. Punch playing leapfrog with his alter-ego for the year. Yet these *Punch* cartoons were always mild in tone, scarcely more than allusions to the follies of the world. Although *Punch* had certainly begun life with a campaigning air, under the editorship of Mark Lemon and the social activist Henry Meyhew, it became much less inclined to attack the establishment when falling under increasing financial difficulties. By the 1860s, *Punch* cartoons confirmed cosy middle-class Victorian values. One significant consequence in the United Kingdom was that Darwin's ideas were thereby rendered safe for the readership. Indeed, a few cartoons represented just such a family atmosphere, and could truly be described as "domesticating" Darwin (figure 1.2)

A set of cartoons not published in *Punch* showed an equally distinctive hand at work. In 1863, Charles Bennett depicted spiraling transformations of humans into inert objects such as a cooked leg of mutton (figure 1.3). The satire, again, was muted. Bennett published six of these images in a series under the title "The Origin of Species." Circularity as a motif also came over very strongly in Henry Woolf's full-page cartoon in *Harper's Weekly* of "The Darwinian Student's After-Dinner Dream," in which knives and forks metamorphosed into the girl the student wishes to marry.[22] These circular images of evolutionary change are worthy of note when compared with Darwin's

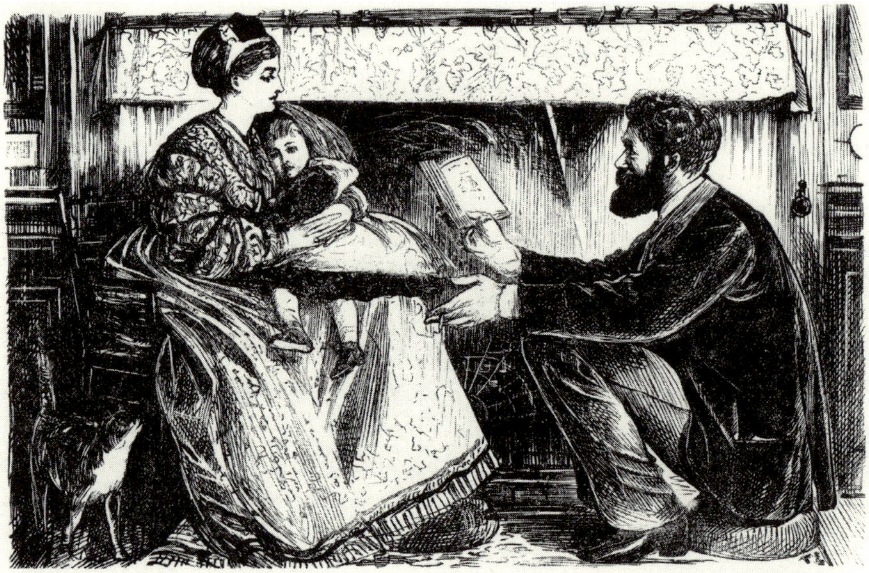

A LOGICAL REFUTATION OF MR. DARWIN'S THEORY.

Jack (who has been reading passages from the "Descent of Man" to the Wife whom he adores, but loves to tease). "SO YOU SEE, MARY, BABY IS DESCENDED FROM A HAIRY QUADRUPED, WITH POINTED EARS AND A TAIL. WE *ALL* ARE!"

Mary. "SPEAK FOR *YOURSELF*, JACK! *I'M* NOT DESCENDED FROM ANYTHING OF THE KIND, I BEG TO SAY; AND BABY TAKES AFTER ME. SO, THERE!"

Figure 1.2 A Logical Refutation of Mr. Darwin's Theory. In Britain, comfortable middle-class values were simultaneously critiqued and confirmed by evolutionary caricatures. The caption reads: "Jack (who has been reading passages from the 'Descent of Man' to the Wife whom he adores, but loves to tease): 'So you see, Mary, Baby is Descended from a Hairy Quadruped, with Pointed Ears, and a Tail. We *all* are!' Mary: 'Speak for *yourself*, Jack! *I'm* not descended from Anything of the Kind, I beg to say; and Baby takes after me. So there!" *From* Punch, *1 April 1871. Courtesy Wellcome Library London.*

strictly linear motif of a branching tree. In the *Origin*, Darwin took pains to emphasize that evolution was neither progressive nor circular. Such ad hoc representations of progressive change indicate the range of available interpretations of Darwinian evolution.

The British magazine *Fun* also ran cartoons of Darwin. When Princess Louise, the oldest daughter of Queen Victoria, married the Marquis of Lorne in 1874, *Fun* parodied the wedding procession by including the figures of "Dr. Darwin and our distinguished ancestor" among the trumpeters and royal guests. This was a drawing of Darwin escorting an ape down the aisle.[23] A representation of Darwin similarly appeared in the pages of the London edition of *Figaro* politely inviting an ape to contemplate itself in a hand-mirror, supported by quotations from Shakespeare (figure 1.4).[24] These cartoons not only posed the question whether humans were descended from apes. As

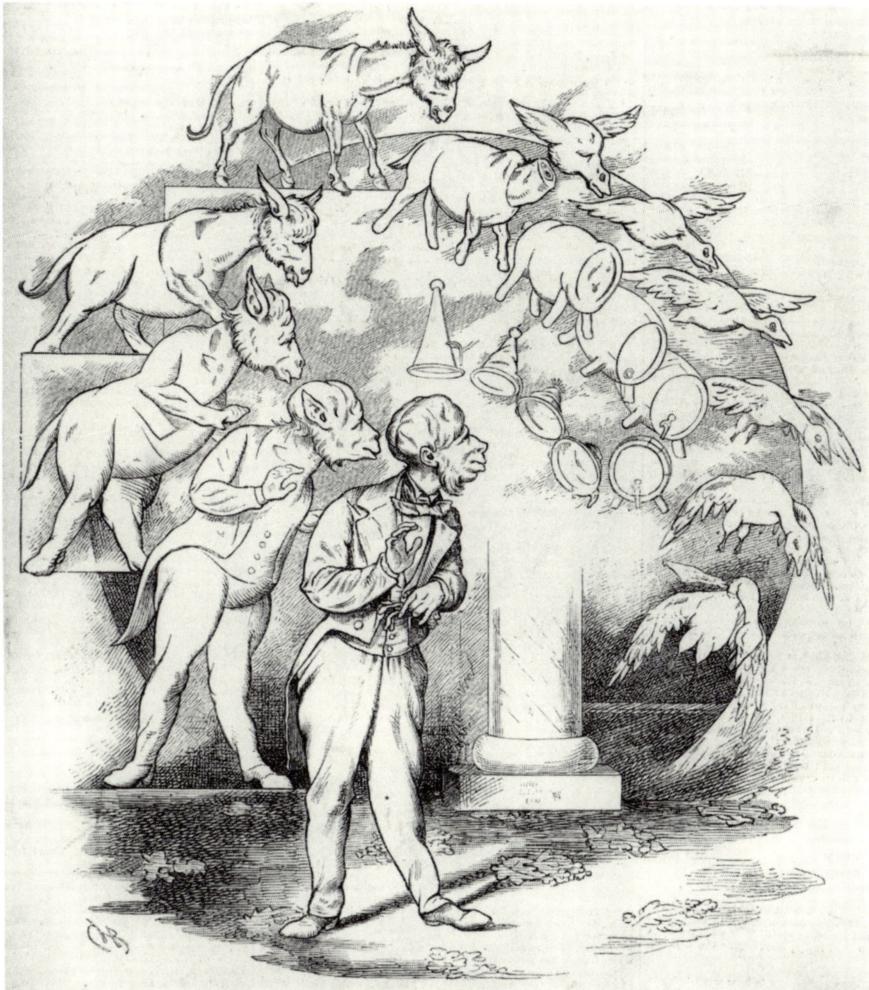

Figure 1.3 What Makes Your Ears So Long? The evolution of a high-society gentleman into a dunce's hat and goose indicating human folly and stupidity. *Woodcut after Charles H. Bennett,* Illustrated Times, *6 June 1863, 396, from a series called* "The Origin of Species, Dedicated by Natural Selection to Dr. Charles Darwin." *Courtesy Wellcome Library London.*

many viewers have noted, they also drew on age-old themes of metamorphosis and the animal traits that seemingly reside in mankind, using long-lasting themes of apes and monkeys as the mirror of humanity.[25] Some played into the old cultural tradition of "vanitas," images that reflected on human foolishness. As such, they provided a nontextual way of commenting on the implications of Darwin's theory.

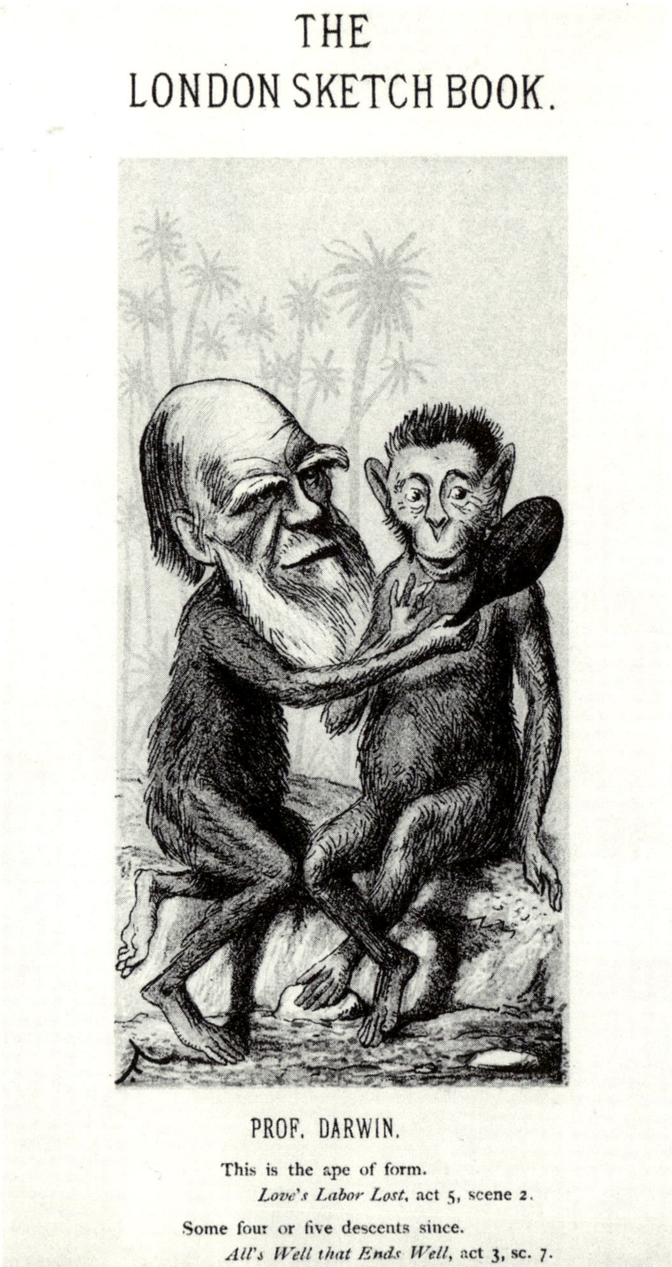

Figure 1.4 Prof Darwin. After the *Descent of Man* was published in 1871, Darwin was frequently caricatured as an ape. *From* Figaro's London Sketch Book of Celebrities, *18 February 1874. Courtesy Wellcome Library London.*

Such visual commentaries were not confined to Britain. Talented caricaturists such as André Gill in *La Charivari* (founded 1832), Wilhelm Busch in *Fliegende Blätter* (founded 1844), and Thomas Nast in *Harper's Weekly* (founded 1851), who memorably documented the Civil War and etched elephant and donkey political symbols into the American mind, purveyed Darwinism along with the ironies of their own culture. In 1871, when Darwin's *Descent of Man* was reviewed widely in American journals, Nast produced a cartoon for *Harper's Weekly* in which a gorilla accused Darwin of wanting to claim his pedigree (figure 1.5). Nast linked this to Henry Bergh, the founder of the American Society for the Prevention of Cruelty to Animals. Such idiomatic transformations of high science are ripe for a great deal more study by historians of popular culture.

With publication of the *Descent of Man* in 1871, followed by *Expression of the Emotions* in 1872, Darwin himself entered the cartoons, usually as the ape itself. His personal facial attributes, such as his beard, prominent eyebrows, and the great dome of his skull were becoming relatively familiar to the public from a *Vanity Fair* chromolithograph of 1871 and photographic images reproduced in the *Illustrated London News* and elsewhere.[26] Such recognition was unusual at a time when mass publicity was only in its infancy, even more so for a scientist. Nevertheless, Darwin's facial features were heavily emphasized in every caricature around the time of the publication of *Descent of Man* and the *Expression of the Emotions*.

At one level, the cartoonists probably were utilizing acknowledged bodily conventions that signify intellectuality.[27] Any caricaturist of the day would have been able to refer confidently to one or another of the accepted attributes of knowledge, such as spectacles, a balding head, books, and so on. One picture in *Fun* (27 July 1871), titled "A little lecture by Professor D———n on the development of the horse," showed Darwin as an absent-minded professor in front of a blackboard, with a handkerchief tumbling out of his trouser pocket to mimic a monkey's tail (figure 1.6). The joke lay in his earnest explanation of the transmutation of a horseradish plant into a racehorse through ten nonsensical horsy stages, including a clothes-horse, Louis Quart-horse, and a Hors-de-combat.

But there was also an element of creative construction going on. Darwin's general hairiness could easily be turned into the animal fur of anthropoid apes. Add a tail, and there was an image immediately conveying the idea of human evolution from primates. *The Hornet* displayed Darwin as a "Venerable Orang-Outang: A Contribution to Unnatural History" in March 1871, a direct reference to Darwin's *Descent of Man*. The following year, the Dalziel brothers (Edward and Thomas), the most eminent team of British wood-

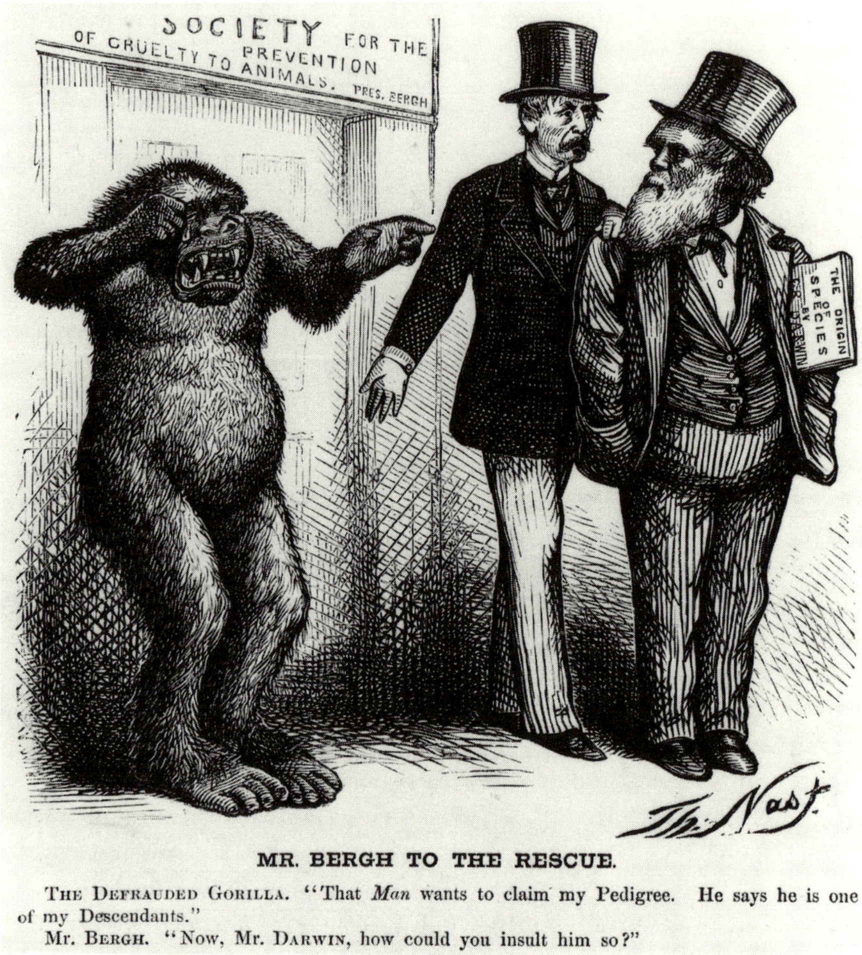

Figure 1.5 Mr. Bergh to the Rescue. Thomas Nast, the crusading American cartoonist, contributed several politicized gorilla sketches to *Harper's Weekly* during the 1870s. *From* Harper's Weekly, *19 August 1871. Courtesy British Library.*

engravers of the period, produced much the same set of symbolic devices in an image referring to *The Expression of the Emotions in Man and Animals* (1872), titled "That troubles our monkey again." This now widely distributed image shows a well-bred young woman whose pulse is being held by a monkeyish Darwin.[28] Today we can discern considerable sexual innuendo. However, these readings surely were unintended in a family journal like *Fun*. The aim was to surprise readers with the implication of a shared social world as well as common ancestry. These pictures of Darwin-as-ape or Darwin-as-

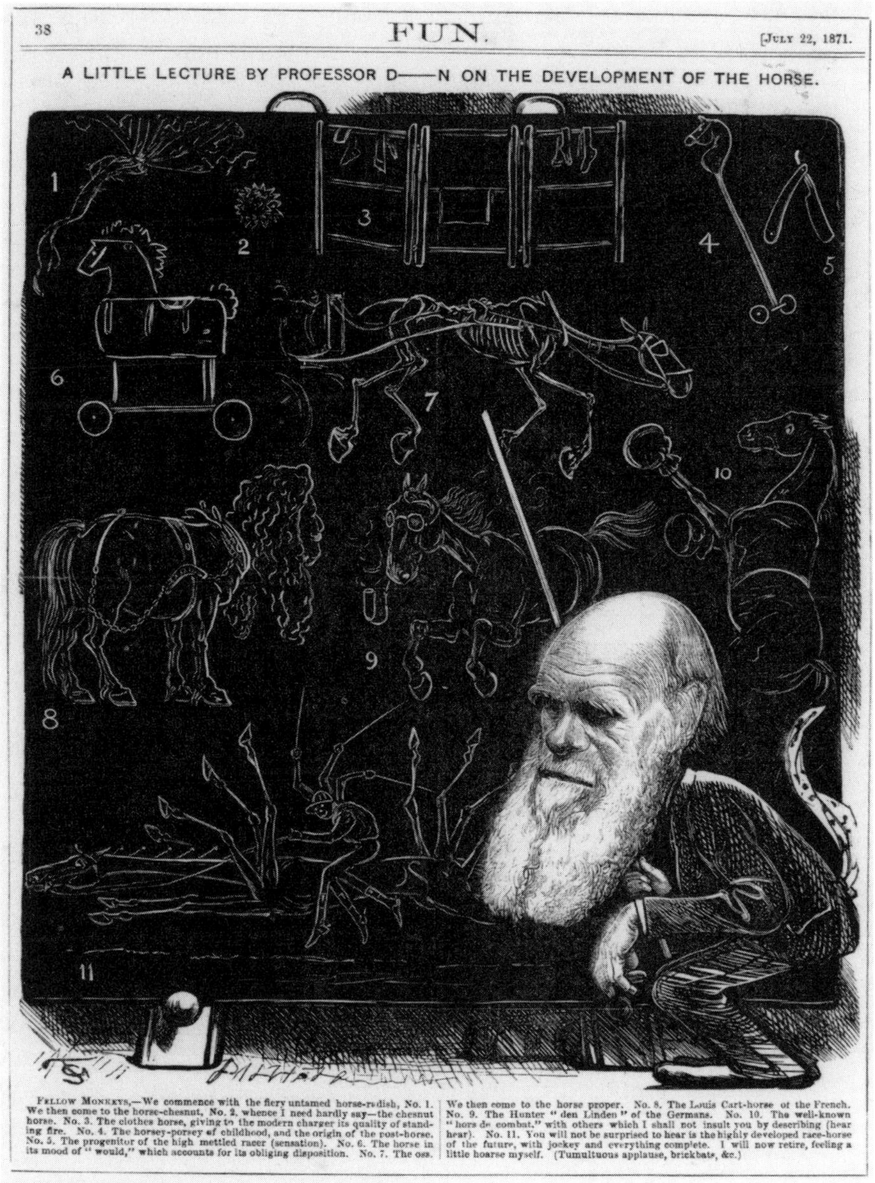

Figure 1.6 A Little Lecture by Professor D———n on the Development of the Horse. By the famous team of woodcut artists, the Dalziel brothers. The image is of Darwin as a professor in front of a blackboard. Note how his handkerchief mimics a monkey's tail. *From* Fun, *22 July 1871. Courtesy Wellcome Library London.*

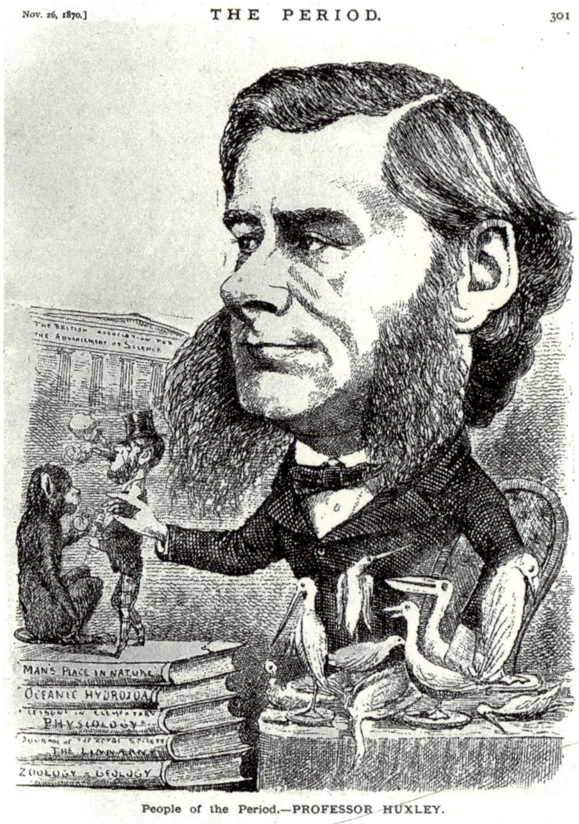

Figure 1.7 Of the other evolutionists who appeared in cartoons, Thomas Henry Huxley was the most frequent. Unlike Darwin, however, he is not portrayed as an ape. His contributions to the debate are characterized by books and natural history specimens. The ape in this image is matched to a stereotypical Victorian "swell" or dandy. *Wood engraving from* The Period, *26 November 1870. Courtesy Wellcome Library London.*

monkey readily identified him as the author of the theory, in much the same way as a tricorne hat signaled Napoleon. Inventing and popularizing such visual markers was the tool of the caricaturist's trade. "Ah, has *Punch* taken me up?" Darwin asked a friend in 1872. "I keep all those things. Have you seen me in the *Hornet?*"[29]

It is significant that hardly any of the other Victorian evolutionists appear in cartoons, and of those who do appear, Huxley is by far the most regular (figure 1.7).[30] None appear as an ape. This simplification of complex moments of discovery and exposition is perhaps to be expected. Yet it goes to show how quickly—and how easily—evolution by natural selection became associated almost exclusively with Darwin's face, reducing the important roles of Huxley, Charles Lyell, Herbert Spencer, Asa Gray, and especially Alfred Russel Wallace. The high visibility of one compelling figure in the imagery of the day probably played a significant role in this rising association between Darwin,

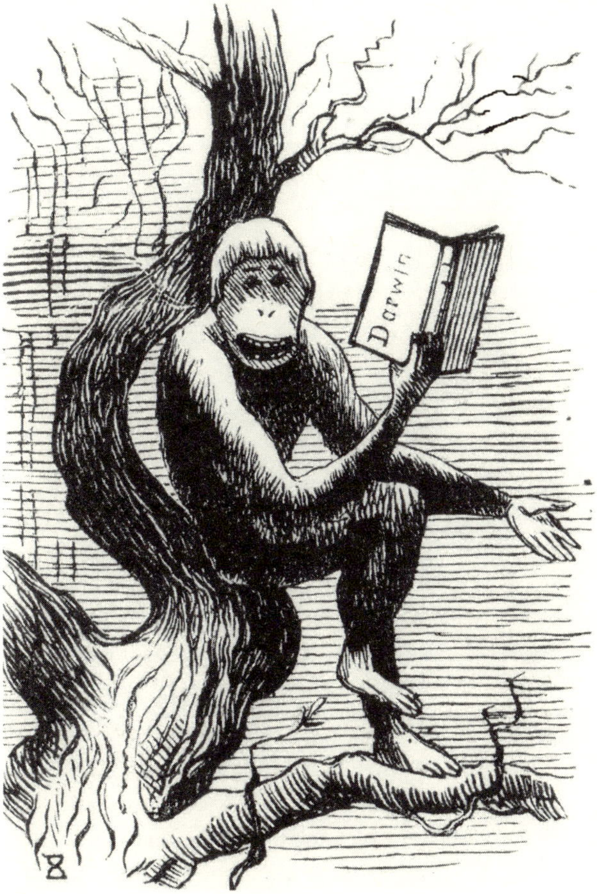

Figure 1.8 Piety and Parallel. During the 1870s, caricaturists increasingly included the motif of a tree, making allusion to the apish origins of human beings as well as the evolutionary tree itself. This ape is reading a book marked "Darwin." The accompanying text likened Darwin to a monkey in the London Zoological Gardens. *From* Punch, *30 November 1872, 222. Courtesy Wellcome Library London.*

the man, and the body of evolutionary work that was rapidly (frequently inaccurately) becoming known as Darwinism.[31]

At the same time, the evolutionary tree made a literal appearance. Darwin sometimes was depicted as a monkey sitting in or swinging from a tree, which was in turn sometimes labeled the "tree of life." *Punch* caricaturists put an ape in a tree diligently reading a copy of Darwin's works (figure 1.8). *Figaro* showed a hairy Darwin among the branches of "A Darwinian hypothesis." André Gill in the Parisian satirical journal, *La Petite Lune,* dangled him from the "arbre de la science" with his tail elegantly draped over an arm.[32]

The twin images of an ape and a tree established that the theory of human descent was the message. Few other scientific theories would have been so quickly identified in the public prints of the day. A hairy, apish Darwin and a tree became easily recognizable images of the evolutionary debate—as recog-

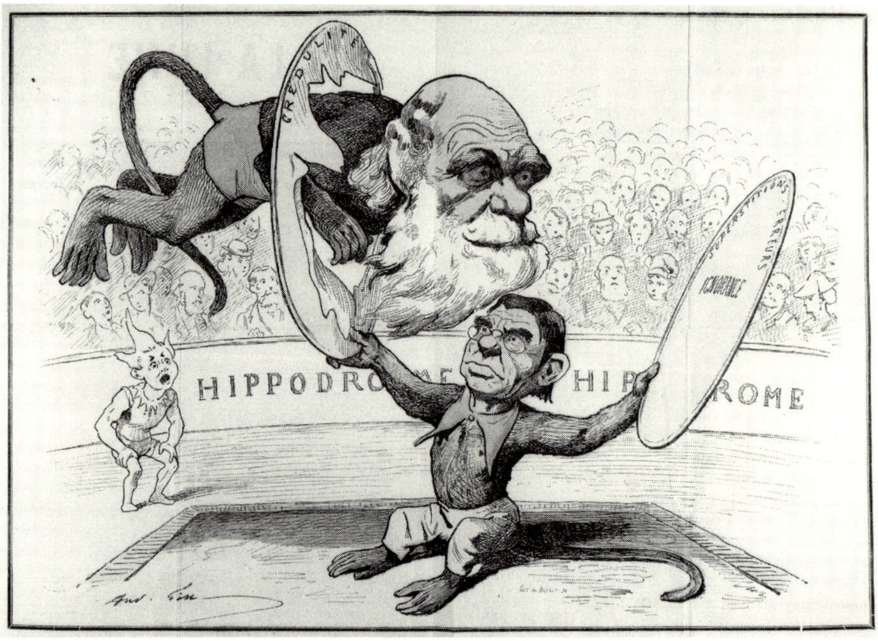

Figure 1.9 L'homme Descend du Singe. André Gill, the Parisian caricaturist, here used Darwin's image to make a trenchant political and philosophical point. The figure of Emile Littré, the materialist philosopher, is represented as a circus ring-master, and encourages a monkey-Darwin to jump through circus hoops labelled "Credulité," "Superstitions," "Erreurs," and "Ignorance." *From* La Lune, *18 August 1878. Author's collection.*

nizable an image to Victorians as the double helix of DNA is today.[33] In general, there seems to have been little allusion to any other aspects of Darwin's evolution by natural selection. Darwin's and Wallace's theory, after all, is in the history books for offering a mechanism for evolutionary change. At this point in time, and in this context, however, there were few, if any, visual references to big ideas like competition, inheritance, variation, or selection, or even to the fossil record. Rather, emphasis was focused on the likely relationship between humans and apes. In this, pictures reflect the emphasis of written commentaries. British cartoonists chose to highlight certain aspects of the theory in order to suit their visual needs. They chose to connect with popular topics of conversation.

As an antidote to this genteel portrayal of Darwin in the British press, at least one French cartoon carried more of a menacing air. A print made by André Gill brought the radical nature of natural selection to the fore. It was published in the Parisian magazine *La Lune* in August 1878 (figure 1.9). Under the caption "L'homme descend du singe," Darwin appeared as a monkey at the

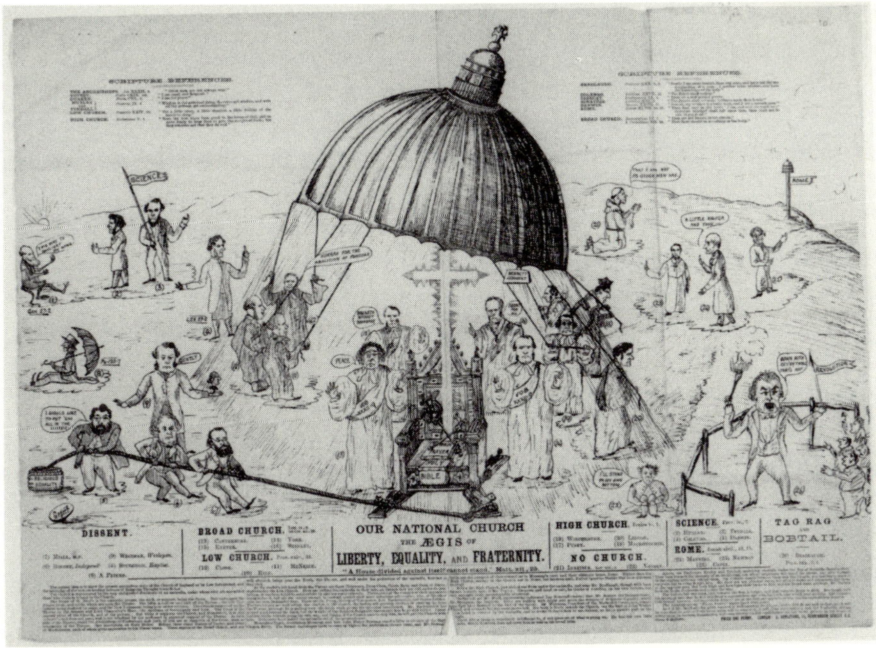

Figure 1.10 Our National Church 1873, attributed to George Holyoake. A multitude of dissenting religious groups disrupt the foundations of the Anglican faith, which is represented by the dome of St. Paul's Cathedral in London. Darwin is shown at top left, indicating the way to rationality to scientific followers Thomas Henry Huxley and John Tyndall, both prominent critics of the established church. Cambridge University Library, Darwin Collection DAR 141.10. *Courtesy of the Syndics of Cambridge University Library.*

circus, bursting through a paper hoop marked "Credulité" and aiming for another marked "Ignorance," "Erreurs," and "Superstition." The hoops are held by Emile Littré, the medical writer and popularizer of Comte, who was denounced repeatedly in France as a prominent supporter of scientific positivism. The message was that rational thought would smash through Catholic ignorance, a powerful force for change.

In Britain, Darwin was included in a large and comprehensive satirical attack on the Anglican religion, labeled "Our National Church," known in two versions, one published in 1873 (figure 1.10), followed by a modified and more sophisticated version in 1883.[34] The central feature is the dome of St. Paul's Cathedral serving as an umbrella in a storm, indicating the position of the Church of England in the state. But the umbrella cannot shelter all the dissenting groups, shown here as Broad Church, Low Church, High Church, No Church, Catholicism, and Science. Darwin is shown indicating the way to rational thought, "This way to daylight my sons." T. H. Huxley and John Tyndall, prominent supporters of evolutionary theory and pugnacious critics of establishment religion, carry flags on the path toward him.

These two theological caricatures—the French and the English—bring a sense of immediacy to the debate surrounding Darwin's work. In both of them, the idea of evolution is presented as a liberating force that reaches far beyond the boundaries of science.

In conclusion, it seems very probable that these visual statements were active participants in propelling the idea of evolution (however it might be understood) out of the arcane realms of learned societies into the ordinary world of humor, newspapers, and demotic literature. Without Mr. *Punch*'s gorillas, or *Figaro's* monkeys, the full implications of Darwin's densely packed *Origin of Species* would have taken much longer to sink in.

Furthermore, the cartoons fused the notion of evolution with the personal identity of Darwin, a matching of theory with author that surely contributed to the highly personalized response to the *Origin of Species* and perhaps also to the increasing use of the term Darwinism to represent a highly diverse body of evolutionary thought rather than (say) Spencerism or Wallaceism.[35] Generally speaking, it is not easy for an artist to draw a picture of scientist that also conveys his or her theory. Newton has his mythical apple, Einstein his blackboard or bicycle.[36] But these are totemic devices, not intrinsic to the knowledge produced, merely pictorial conventions for representing abstract achievements in much the same way as a scientist often is depicted in a laboratory or book-lined study.[37] The cartoons of Darwin, by contrast, show him *as* his theory.

Without wanting to claim too much for published caricatures and cartoons as a means of understanding what has come to be known as the Darwinian revolution, it does seem possible to view these mass-produced drawings in socially positive terms, as contributing to a greater group identity in specific national context, perpetuating a shared ideology, and drawing to public attention the implications and consequences of troubling new proposals. These images, few as they were, were not just a transparent medium of communication, not just illustrations, but also participated in the shaping of British nineteenth-century popular thought.

NOTES

First published in *Proceedings of the American Philosophical Society* 145, no. 4 (December 2001): 496–509. Reprinted by permission. I am so grateful to the American Philosophical Society for permission to republish. A few corrections and amendments have been made. I wish to thank Ellen Guarente of Harvard University, Mary McDonald of the American Philosopical Society, and Fae Brauer for their generous assistance.

1. Edward Aveling, *Students' Magazine of Science and Art*, 2 September 1878; and Thomas Henry Huxley, "Charles Darwin, Obituary," *Nature* 25 (27 April 1882): 597.

2. The standard bibliography for Darwin's works is Richard Freeman, *The Works of Charles Darwin: An Annotated Bibliographical Handlist*, 2nd ed. (Folkestone: Dawson, 1977). See also the online resource, "The Complete Work of Charles Darwin Online," http://darwin-online.org.uk/, which makes available an updated electronic version of Freeman, as well as digital versions of many of the books and editions cited.

3. Thomas F. Glick, ed., *The Comparative Reception of Darwinism*, reprinted with a new preface (Chicago: University of Chicago Press, 1988); Alvar Ellegård, *Darwin and the General Reader: The Reception of Darwin's Theory of Evolution in the British Periodical Press, 1859–1872*, with a new foreword by D. L. Hull (Chicago: University of Chicago Press, 1990).

4. Ronald L. Numbers and John Stenhouse, eds., *Disseminating Darwinism: The Role of Place, Race, Religion, and Gender* (Cambridge: Cambridge University Press, 1999). A wide range of authoritative thought about Darwinism is still to be found in David Kohn, ed., *The Darwinian Heritage* (Princeton, N.J.: Princeton University Press in association with Nova Pacifica, 1985). Peter Bowler provides an updated survey in *Evolution: The History of an Idea*, 3rd ed. (Berkeley: University of California Press, 2007). See also Gregory Radick and Jonathan Hodge, eds., *The Cambridge Companion to Darwin* (Cambridge: Cambridge University Press, 2003); Janet Browne, *Darwin's* Origin of Species: *A Biography* (New York: Grove Press, 2006); Browne, *Charles Darwin: The Power of Place* (Princeton, N.J.: Princeton University Press, 2005); and Abigail Lustig, Robert J. Richards, and Michael Ruse, eds., *Darwinian Heresies* (Cambridge: Cambridge University Press, 2004). For a recent account of evolutionary thought in domains other than science, see Anne Julia Zweirlein, ed., *Unmapped Countries: Biological Visions in Nineteenth-Century Literature and Culture* (London: Anthem Press, 2005).

5. Frederick H. Burkhardt and Sydney Smith, eds., *The Correspondence of Charles Darwin*, vols. 1–15 (1821–1867) (Cambridge: Cambridge University Press, 1983–2008). Extant letters to and from Darwin (some 14,000 items) are summarized in Frederick H. Burkhardt and Sydney Smith, eds., *Calendar of the Correspondence of Charles Darwin*, rev. ed. (Cambridge: Cambridge University Press, 1994).

6. Francis Darwin, ed., *The Life and Letters of Charles Darwin*, 3 vols. (London: John Murray, 1887), vol. 3, 118.

7. Richard D. Altick, *The Shows of London* (Cambridge, Mass.: Harvard University Press, 1978); and Nicholas Jardine, James A. Secord, and Emma Spary, eds., *Cultures of Natural History* (Cambridge: Cambridge University Press, 1996). For popular scientific culture, see

especially Aileen Fyfe and Bernard Lightman, eds., *Science in the Marketplace: Nineteenth-Century Sites and Experiences* (Chicago: University of Chicago Press, 2007).

8. Axel Smetz provides information about this statue on his website http://library.uwsp.edu/aschmetz/Rheinhold's_Monkey. It is illustrated in Robert Service, *Lenin: A Biography* (London: Macmillan, 2000). There were probably several such statuettes, for example a "monkey with Darwin's head" was exhibited in the Darwin Centenary Exhibition, Cambridge 1909; see Richard Freeman, who gives a list of artworks and portraits in *Charles Darwin: A Companion* (Folkestone: Dawson, 1978), 98. A revised list of imagery is available in the *Oxford Dictionary of National Biography* entry on Darwin, authored by Adrian Desmond, Janet Browne, and James R. Moore. A comprehensive iconography is under way in "The Complete Work of Charles Darwin Online" (see note 2).

9. Jan Bondeson, *A Cabinet of Medical Curiosities* (New York: Tauris, 1997); Martin Howard, *Victorian Grotesque: An Illustrated Excursion into Medical Curiosities, Freaks and Abnormalities Principally of the Victorian Age* (London: Jupiter Books, 1977); Janet Browne and Sharon Messenger, "Victorian Spectacle: Julia Pastrana, the Bearded and Hairy Female," *Endeavour* 27 (2003): 155–59.

10. Illustrated in Robin Reilly, *Wedgwood*, 2 vols. (London: Macmillan, Stockton Press, 1989), vol. 2, 130, under the title, "The Darwinian Theory." It was designed by Emile Lessore in 1862. I doubt whether it was ever available in mass-produced form.

11. I am very grateful to Jaume Josa-Llorca, the great collector of Darwiniana in Spain. See Alberto Gomis-Blanco and Jaume Josa-Llorca, *Bibliografia critica ilustrada de las obras de Darwin en España 1857–2005* (Madrid: CSIC, 2007).

12. I am grateful to A. Walker Bingham for providing me with information about this firm and its advertisements. See also Henry W. Holcombe, *Patent Medicine Tax Stamps: A History of the Firms Using United States Private Die Proprietary Medicine Tax Stamps* (Lawrence, Mass.: Quarterman Publications Inc., 1979), 367–77.

13. Standard sources are Mortimer Frank, "Caricature in Medicine," *Bulletin of the Society of Medical History of Chicago* 1 (1911–1916): 47–57, and Andreas Weber, *Tableau de la caricature medicale* (Paris: Hippocrate, 1936). More recently, see Fiona Haslam, *From Hogarth to Richardson: Medicine in Art in Eighteenth-Century Britain* (Liverpool: Liverpool University Press, 1996); and Roy Porter, *Bodies Politic: Disease, Death and the Doctors in Britain, 1650–1914* (London: Reaktion Books, 2001). For geology, see especially Martin S. Rudwick, "Caricature as a Source for the History of Science: De la Beche's Anti-Lyellian Sketches of 1831," *Isis* 66 (1975): 534–60; Rudwick, "The Emergence of a Visual Language for Geological Science, 1760–1840," *History of Science* 14 (1976): 149–95; and James A. Secord, "Scrapbook Science: Composite Caricatures in Late Georgian England," in *Figuring It Out: Science, Gender, and Visual Culture*, ed. Ann B. Shteir and Bernard Lightman, 164–91 (Hanover, N.H.: Dartmouth College Press, 2006). James G. Paradis, "Science and Satire in Victorian Culture," in *Victorian Science in Context*, ed. Bernard Lightman, 143–75 (Chicago: University of Chicago Press, 1997); Patricia Fara, "Faces of Genius: Images of Newton in Eighteenth-Century England," in *Heroic Reputations and Exemplary Lives*, ed. Geoffrey Cubitt and Allen Warren, 57–81 (Manchester: Manchester University Press, 2000); and Fara, "The Royal Society's Portrait of Joseph Banks," *Notes and Records of the Royal Society* 51 (1997): 199–210. For verbal humor, see Janet Browne, "Squibs and

Snobs: Science in Humorous British Undergraduate Magazines around 1830," *History of Science* 30 (1992): 165–97.

14. The scope of new studies is indicated by Norton Wise, "Making Visible," *Isis* 97 (2006): 75–82. See especially, Soraya de Chadarevian and Nick Hopwood, eds., *Models: The Third Dimension of Science* (Stanford: Stanford University Press, 2004). General themes of science and the visual are discussed in Peter L. Galison and Caroline A. Jones, eds., *Picturing Science, Producing Art* (New York: Routledge, 1998); and Lorraine Daston and Peter L. Galison, *Objectivity* (Boston: Zone Books, 2007). Darwin's visual thinking is receiving close attention; see Julia Voss, *Darwin's Bilder. Ansichten der Evolutionstheorie 1837–1874* (Frankfurt am Main: Fischer, 2007); Horst Bredekamp, *Darwin's Korallen: die fruhen Evolutionsdiagramme und die Tradition der Naturgeschichte* (Berlin: Wagenbacht, 2005); and Jonathan Smith, "Picturing Sexual Selection: Gender and the Evolution of Ornithological Illustration in Charles Darwin's *Descent of Man*," *Figuring It Out*, 85–109; and Smith, *Charles Darwin and Victorian Visual Culture* (Cambridge: Cambridge University Press, 2006). For material culture associated with Darwin and Darwinism, see Janet Browne, "Presidential Address: Commemorating Darwin," *British Journal for the History of Science* 38 (2005): 251–74.

15. Mark Hallett, *The Spectacle of Difference: Graphic Satire in the Age of Hogarth* (New Haven: Yale University Press, 1999); Mary Lee Townsend, *Forbidden Laughter: Popular Humor and the Limits of Repression in Nineteenth Century Prussia* (Ann Arbor: University of Michigan Press, 1992); Tamara L. Hunt, *Defining John Bull: Political Caricature and National Identity in Late Georgian England* (Aldershot: Ashgate, 2003), and Judith Weschler, *A Human Comedy: Physiognomy and Caricature in Nineteenth-Century Paris* (London: Thames and Hudson, 1982). See also M. Dorothy George, *English Political Caricature: A Study of Opinion and Propaganda* (Oxford: Clarendon Press, 1959). An interesting sidelight is cast on the caricatures of intellectuals by David Kunzle, "Goethe and Caricature: From Hogarth to Topffer," *Journal of the Warburg and Courtauld Institute* 48 (1985): 164–88. Roots of celebrity caricature are explored in Wendy Wick Reeves, *Celebrity Caricature in America* (New Haven: Smithsonian Institution in association with Yale University Press, 1998).

16. John Leech's drawing in *Punch* 105 (5 July 1843), usually is stated to be the first drawing to be called a cartoon in this modern sense. It was entitled "Substance and *Shadow*: the Poor ask for *Bread*, and the Philanthropy of the State accords—an Exhibition."

17. Richard D. Altick, *The English Common Reader: A Social History of the Mass Reading Public, 1800–1900* (Chicago: University of Chicago Press, 1957); and John Feather, *A History of British Publishing* (London: Croom Helm, 1988). For reader response theory, see James A. Secord, *Victorian Sensation: The Extraordinary Publication, Reception, and Secret Authorship of Vestiges of the Natural History of Creation* (Chicago: University of Chicago Press, 2000); and Umberto Eco, *The Role of the Reader: Explorations in the Semiotics of Texts* (Bloomington: Indiana University Press, 1979). A useful account of the rise of illustrated texts is by John R. Harvey, *Victorian Novelists and Their Illustrators* (London: Sidgwick and Jackson, 1970). Special attention to science in Victorian periodicals can be found in Geoffrey N. Cantor et al., *Science in the Nineteenth-Century Periodical: Reading the Magazine of Nature* (Cambridge: Cambridge University Press, 2004); and Geoffrey N. Cantor and Sally Shuttleworth, eds., *Science Serialized: Representations of the Sciences in Nineteenth-Century Periodicals* (Cambridge, Mass.:

MIT Press, 2004). See also Peter W. Sinnema, *Dynamics of the Pictured Page: Representing the Nation in the Illustrated London News* (Aldershot: Ashgate, 1998).

18. Richard Price, *A History of* Punch (London: Collins, 1957). The magazine *Punch* was particularly noted for its exhaustive chronicling of Benjamin Disraeli's ascendancy. Representations of science form only a very small proportion of the visual imagery in the magazine. See http://punch.co.uk/cartoonhistory02.html.

19. "Monkeyana," *Punch* 40 (18 May 1861): 206. For Du Chaillu, see Stuart McCook, "'It May be Truth, but It Is Not Evidence': Paul Du Chaillu and the Legitimation of Evidence in the Field Sciences," *Osiris* 11 (1996): 177–97. See also Janet Browne, *The Power of Place* (Princeton, N.J.: Princeton University Press, 2002), 114–25.

20. Discussed in Paradis, "Science and Satire," 158.

21. L. Perry Curtis, Jr., *Apes and Angels: The Irishman in Victorian Caricature*, rev. ed. (Washington, D.C.: Smithsonian Institution Press, 1997). More recently, see Michael de Nie, *The Eternal Paddy: Irish Identity and the British Press, 1798–1882* (Madison: *University of Wisconsin Press*, 2004).

22. Bennett is most well known for his illustrations to children's books. See Charles H. Bennett and Robert B. Brough, *Character Sketches, Development Drawings and Original Pictures of Wit and Humour* (London: Ward, Lack, and Tyler, 1872). The evolutionary cartoons ran for several weeks in *The Illustrated Times*, a weekly journal published in London 1862–1872 under the title "The Origin of Species Dedicated by Natural Selection to Charles Darwin." For Woolf, see "The Darwinian Student's After-Dinner Dream," *Harper's Weekly*, 23 December 1871, 1209.

23. "The Wedding Procession," *Fun*, 25 March 1871, 126.

24. "Prof. Darwin," *Figaro (Figaro's London Sketch Book of Celebrities)*, 475 (18 February 1874): 1.

25. Horst W. Janson, *Apes and Ape Lore in the Middle Ages and the Renaissance* (London: Warburg Institute, University of London, 1952). The ape and the owl were early emblems of animality and the devil. By the time David Teniers painted "Guardroom with Monkeys" around 1633, monkeys appeared in images as diverse as playing cards, Dürer prints, and paintings, usually associated with human sinfulness and folly.

26. "Men of the Day, No. 33. Natural Selection," *Vanity Fair*, September 1871, by Carlo Pellegrini under his customary byline of "Ape" (although the Darwin print was in fact unsigned). Steel-engraved portraits of Darwin (based on photographs) were reproduced in *Illustrated London News* 58 (1871): 244, and *Harper's Weekly* 1871:308. Some of these issues of recognition are touched on in Janet Browne, "I Could Have Retched All Night: Charles Darwin and His Body," in *Science Incarnate: Historical Embodiments of Natural Knowledge*, ed. Christopher Lawrence and Steven Shapin, 240–87 (Chicago: University of Chicago Press, 1998); and "Charles Darwin as a Celebrity," *Science in Context* 16 (2003): 175–94. See also Walter Benjamin, "*The Work of Art in the Age of Mechanical Reproduction*," *in* many different anthologies, here taken from *Illuminations* (London: Fontana, 1973), 219–53.

27. Christopher Lawrence and Steven Shapin, eds., *Science Incarnate: Historical embodiments of Natural Knowledge* (Chicago: University of Chicago Press, 1998).

28. "A venerable Orang-Outang. A contribution to unnatural history," *Hornet*, 22 March 1871, and "That troubles our monkey again," *Fun* (16 November 1872). On sexuality and the

Victorian response to Darwinism, see Gowan Dawson, *Darwin, Literature and Victorian Respectability* (Cambridge: Cambridge University Press, 2007).

29. James Hague, "A Reminiscence of Mr. Darwin," *Harper's New Monthly Magazine* 69 (1884): 759–63, on p. 760.

30. Warren R. Dawson, *The Huxley Papers: A Descriptive Catalogue of the Correspondence, Manuscripts and Miscellaneous Papers of Thomas Henry Huxley* (London: Published for the Imperial College of Science and Technology by Macmillan, 1946).

31. James R. Moore, "Deconstructing Darwinism: The Politics of Evolution in the 1860s," *Journal of the History of Biology* 24 (1991): 353–408.

32. "A Darwinian Hypothesis," *Figaro*, 18 October 1871, 9, and front cover of *La Petite Lune* 10, no date given.

33. Although Michael Baxandall argues that we can never truly recover the "period eye." *Baxandall*, Patterns of Intention: On the Historical Explanation of Pictures (New Haven, Conn.: Yale University Press, 1985). See Dorothy Nelkin and M. Susan Lindee, *The DNA Mystique: The Gene as a Cultural Icon*, rev. ed. (Ann Arbor: University of Michigan Press, 2004).

34. The later version is discussed and illustrated in Warren Sylvester Smith, *The London Heretics, 1870–1914* (London: Constable, 1967), xiii–xvi. Smith attributes the text of the print to George Holyoake. This complex picture primarily draws on James Martineau's attempt during the 1870s to unite all clergymen under the single umbrella of a "national" church, and the looming menace of evolutionary theory was merely one of several perceived threats to the establishment. Darwin had copies of both images in his personal collection, Cambridge University Library, Darwin Collection, DAR 141:10 and 11. I am grateful to Jim Moore for his help on this issue.

35. Moore, "Deconstructing Darwinism."

36. Richard Yeo, "Genius, Method and Morality: Images of Newton in Britain, 1760–1860," *Science in Context* 2 (1988): 257–84; and Alan J. Friedman and Carol C. Donley, *Einstein as Myth and Muse* (Cambridge: Cambridge University Press, 1985).

37. There is a large body of relevant literature on the history of portraiture. Scientific portraiture is authoritatively explored by Ludmilla Jordanova, *Defining Features, Scientific and Medical Portraits 1660–2000* (London: Reaktion Books, 2000). See also Patricia Fara, "Framing the Evidence: Scientific Biography and Portraiture," in *The History and Poetics of Scientific Biography*, ed. Thomas Söderqvist, 71–91 (Aldershot, Hampshire: Ashgate, 2007); Though not directly about portraiture, modes of representing science, and scientists, are discussed in Christopher Frayling, *Mad, Bad, and Dangerous? The Scientist and the Cinema* (London: Reaktion, 2005); and Pnina Abir Am and Clark A. Elliott, eds., "Commemorative Practices in Science: Historical Perspectives on the Politics of Collective Memory," *Osiris* 14 (1999).

CHAPTER 2

Ugly Disagreements

Darwin and Ruskin Discuss Sex and Beauty

PHILLIP PRODGER

John Ruskin, a long-time acquaintance and former school friend of Charles Darwin, made no attempt to hide his contempt for Darwin's evolutionary theories. "Had Darwinism been true," he wrote in *The Eagle's Nest* (1872), "we should long ago have split our heads in two with foolish thinking, or thrust out, from above our covetous hearts, a hundred desirous arms and clutching hands; and changed ourselves into Briarean Cephalopoda."[1] Such bluster was typical of Ruskin, who frequently seasoned his criticism with flamboyant rhetoric. Yet it contained a serious point that Darwin was forced to address. Along with several other prominent scholars, Ruskin challenged Darwin's explanation of the rise of higher-order animals from lower ones on aesthetic grounds. If natural selection were the only force guiding evolution, he argued, life would have stagnated with functional, simple animals like ancient squid. He refused to accept that complex, beautiful creatures could be explained through worldly mechanisms alone; divine will must be at work. Railing against the idea that random variation propels change, he condemned Darwinian evolution as "arbitrary" and "apparently causeless."[2]

Questions of aesthetics swirled around Darwin as he finalized the manuscript for *The Expression of the Emotions in Man and Animals* in 1872. Published within a year of each other, *Expression* and *Descent of Man and Selection in Relation to Sex* (1871) are closely related texts; although Darwin was accustomed to assaults on his theories, these two books pushed evolution into sensitive new territory. Evolution by natural selection, described in *Origin of Species,* had polarized opinion, but it focused largely on animals other than humans, and organisms were considered for their physical attributes—the way bodies are adapted to survive in harsh environments. This kept arguments relatively impersonal and abstract. But with *Expression* and *Descent,* Darwin raised the question of cognition. How, he ventured, might feelings be explained by evolution? What attracts and repels people, and why do they react to stimuli as they do?

Ruskin seized on the question of natural beauty as the centerpiece of his attack on Darwinian theory. This line of attack enjoyed considerable vogue in the late 1860s and early 1870s, just as Darwin was assembling *Descent* and *Expression*. Understanding the debate that ensued is important for two reasons. First, it reveals the atmosphere in which Darwin prepared his illustrations for *Descent* and *Expression*. The arguments of Ruskin and his allies concerning beauty were inherently visual, and Darwin's use of illustration was informed by these arguments. Second, Darwin's approach to the problem casts light on the strategies that he used to gain converts and dissuade his critics, in these two books and throughout his career.

In Ruskin's view, Darwinian theory amounted to little more than disguised atheism. "Very positively can I say to you that I have never heard yet one logical argument in its favour," he declared," and I have heard, and read, many that were beneath contempt."[3] Yet in spite of such caustic comments, he held Darwin in high esteem personally and professed respect for the thoroughness of his research. Although he became known as an artist and art critic, Ruskin had studied natural history at Oxford at nearly the same time that Darwin enrolled at the University of Cambridge. He retained an interest in biology and geology throughout his career, frequently citing biological concerns in his essays. Whereas Darwin seldom hazarded opinions about visual art in his writings, Ruskin embraced opportunities to address questions of natural history in both his writings and his art. To him, the elements of painting were inseparable from the natural environment, and he rejected Darwin's conclusions on the subject almost completely.

Beauty and Design

Ruskin's views were characteristic of a generation of anti-Darwinian critics who took the view that evolution by natural and sexual selection, even if it could be shown to exist, was just one element of a complex system that Darwin failed to comprehend fully. Darwin himself took a strictly biological view of beauty, arguing that the forms and colors of organisms that humans consider beautiful represent little more than a complex series of signals and attractants. The beauty of flowers, for example, can be explained by the need of plants to lure insects to pollinate them; they are shaped and colored to facilitate reproduction of the parent plant. Such pleasure as humans derive from them, he maintained, is either the vestigial result of evolution from animal progenitors, or merely coincidental.

Animal beauty, he believed, was also linked to reproductive success. Birds, baboons, insects, and even humans, he argued, have evolved to appeal to potential mates, with structures of only one function: to advertise reproductive availability to the opposite sex. Animals that are most effective in displaying themselves to others are consequently most likely to attract mates. According to this view, sexual partners are resources for which organisms compete, much as Darwin envisaged competition for food and shelter in his theory of evolution by natural selection. This additional means of competition Darwin termed his theory of sexual selection. This was the focus of *Descent.*

While Ruskin agreed that flowers probably are structured to attract insects, unlike Darwin, he believed this to be evidence of divine intent rather than competitive advantage. Whereas Darwin attributed the evolution of such mechanisms to felicitous mutation, Ruskin considered them evidence of God's handiwork. Only God, he argued, was capable of creating structures simultaneously delightful to humans and useful to plants. In *The Queen of the Air* (1869) for example, he offered a theistic interpretation of floral beauty, centered on the feelings elicited in a human beholder:

> The main fact, then, about a flower is that it is part of the plant's form developed at the moment of intensest life: and this inner rapture is usually marked externally for us by the flush of one or more of the primary colours. What the character of the flower shall be, depends entirely upon the portion of the plant into which this rapture of the spirit has been put. Sometimes the life is put into its outer sheath, and then the outer sheath becomes white and pure, and full of strength and grace; sometimes the life is put in the common leaves, just under the blossom, and they become scarlet or purple; sometimes the life is put into the stalks of the flower, and they flush blue, [. . .] but in all cases, the presence of the strongest life is asserted by characters in which the human sight takes pleasure, and which seem prepared with distinct reference to us, or rather, bear, in being delightful, evidence of having been produced by the power of the same spirit as our own.[4]

Unlike Darwin, Ruskin emphasized the inexplicable in the appeal of flowers. While acknowledging the utility of certain structures, he stressed the importance of human pleasure in their presence.

Ruskin reserved his fiercest criticisms for Darwin's explanation of animal sexuality. The theory of sexual selection, he argued, required not just an evolution of display by one organism, but a simultaneous evolution of taste by another. Even if one could explain the development of a male bird's elaborate tail feathers, for example, by selective forces, one could not, according to Ruskin, account for the concomitant evolution of preference among female birds for elaborately adorned mates. Darwinian sexual selection, he believed, requires a co-evolution between display and reception that cannot be explained by simple biological forces. On this point he wrote:

> Nay, we might even sufficiently represent the general manner of conclusion in the Darwinian system by the statement that if you fasten a hair-brush to a mill-wheel, with the handle forward, so as to develop itself into a neck by moving always in the same direction, and within continual hearing of a steam-whistle, after a certain number of revolutions the hair-brush will fall in love with the whistle; they will marry, lay an egg, and the produce will be a nightingale.[5]

He rejected Darwin's argument that animals might be born with a predisposition for certain characteristics that are not already abundant in their population. To him, this was a simple matter of cause and effect. Animals could not develop appetites for enticements that they had never seen before. For Darwin's theory of sexual selection to be true, he argued, one must prove that taste can evolve in a population to enable animals with a certain appearance to be preferred over others. The argument echoed that of Louis Agassiz on the inviability of mixed-race Brazilian peoples.

Lessons from the Peacock

Ruskin's strongest objection to Darwinian theory was his belief that many forms in nature are too complex to have arisen randomly. This was especially evident, for example, in the elaborate forms of peacock and pheasant feathers, which he maintained are immune to scientific analysis because the intricate patterns and sumptuous coloration of such feathers could not be explained by natural and sexual selection alone. He was so convinced of this argument that he repeated it in two separate publications, *The Eagle's Nest* and *Proserpina* (1882–1886). In the former, he described reading Darwin's explanation of the phenomenon in *Descent:* "I went to it myself, hoping to learn some more of the existing laws of life which regulate the local disposition of colour. But none of these appear to be known; and I am informed only that peacocks have grown to be peacocks out of brown pheasants, because the young feminine brown pheasants like brown feathers."[6] He concluded: "When you have drawn some of the actual patterns of plume and scale with attention, I believe you will see reason to think that spectra of organic species may be at least as distinct as those of metals or gases; but learn at all events what they are now, never mind what they have been."[7] Ruskin himself repeatedly drew and painted peacock feathers in the early 1870s. At least one, the watercolor *Pea-*

cock and Falcon Feathers, now in the Ruskin Library at Lancaster University, is over one meter tall—suggesting that he used them to illustrate formal lectures (figure 2.1). In *Proserpina,* Ruskin explained:

> All these materialisms [various unspecified theories on the evolution of colouration in plants and animals], in their unclean simplicity, are essentially the work of human bats; men of semi-faculty or semi-education, who are more or less incapable of so much as seeing, much less thinking about, colour; among whom, for one-sided intensity, even Mr. Darwin must be often ranked, as in his vespertilian treatise on the ocelli of the Argus pheasant, which he imagines to be artistically gradated, and perfectly imitative of a ball and socket. If I had him here in Oxford for a week, and could force him to try to copy a feather by [Thomas] Bewick, or to draw for himself a boy's thumbed marble, his notions of feathers, and balls, would be changed for all the rest of his life. But his ignorance of good art is no excuse for the accurately illogical simplicity of the rest of his talk of colour in the *Descent of Man.*[8]

Ironically, Darwin did almost precisely as Ruskin suggested. The illustrations of three sections of pheasant ocelli, Figs. 56, 58, and 59 of *Descent,* are all based on sketches from his hand, although they are uncredited in the text (figure 2.2). However, he did not draw the one illustration of a peacock tail, which appears as Fig. 53. This was prepared by G. H. Ford, an artist who supplied a number of other illustrations for the work.[9]

The Darwin Archive at the University of Cambridge Library contains the original sketches for Darwin's pheasant feather illustrations, which may have been drawn with the assistance of a camera lucida.[10] Darwin was familiar with the device, which he first mentioned in correspondence to his son William in 1862.[11] At that time, William was helping his father to prepare preliminary illustrations for *Different Forms of Flowers on Plants of the Same Species* (1877). Shaky and irregular, Darwin's later drawings of pheasant feathers have the characteristic look of pictures made with the unwieldy instrument (figure 2.3). They resemble well-made tracings: The placement of the lines is highly precise, but the lines themselves are uneven. The specimens from which they were made included two feathers, one of a Java peacock and one of an argus pheasant, still held in the Archive.[12] Lacking confidence in his ability to draw, and fearful that his "eyesight is not so good" as he would write near this time to John Murray, the sketches were passed to someone else, possibly another artist, one of Darwin's sons or the engraver himself, to be refined before engraving.[13] Darwin proofed and labeled these revised drawings (figure 2.4). Ultimately they were given to the artist G. Pearson, who prepared most of the wood engravings in *Descent.*

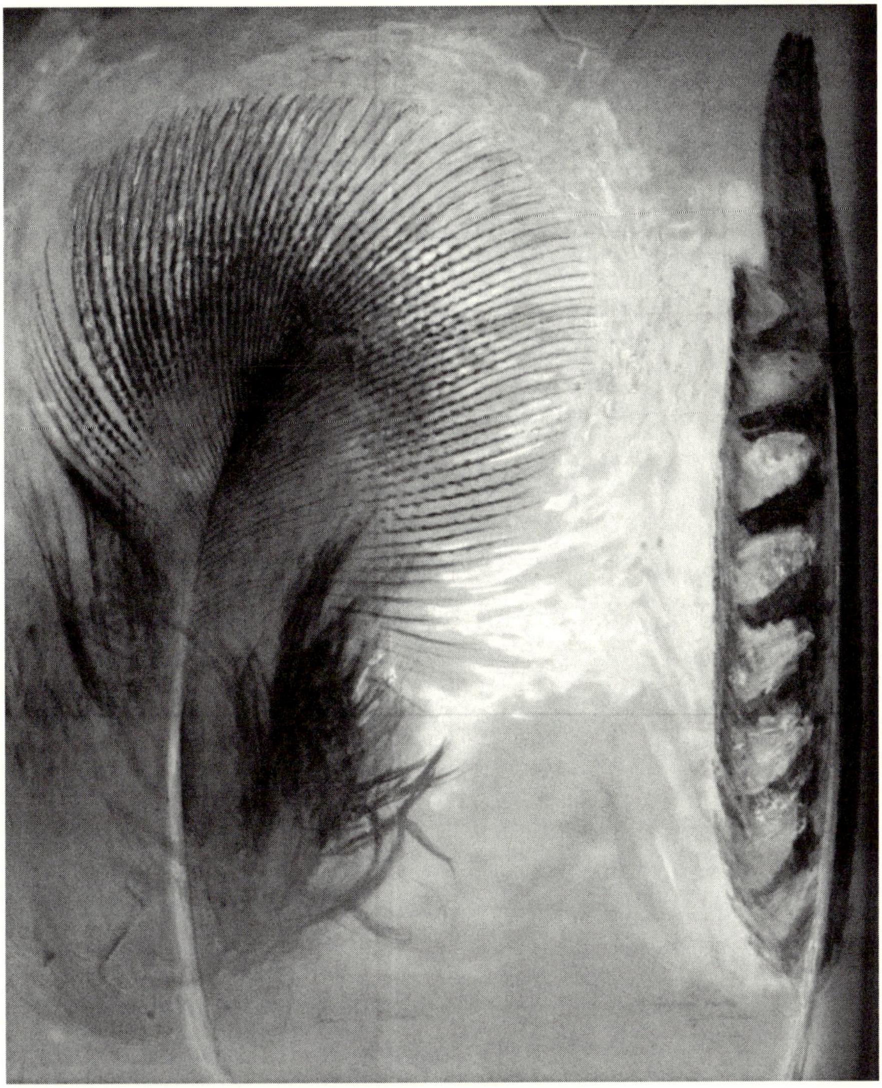

Figure 2.1 John Ruskin, *Peacock and Falcon Feathers*, 1872, watercolor and gouache. *Ruskin Foundation (Ruskin Library, Lancaster University).*

Ruskin supposed that by drawing structures like the tails of peacocks or pheasants, Darwin could not help but be moved by their complexity. The act of close inspection and replication, he believed, would force him to rethink his views on sexual selection: Confronted with the task of rendering the minutiae of pattern and color in such feathers would convince him that they are far more complex than could be accounted for by random mutation. It might

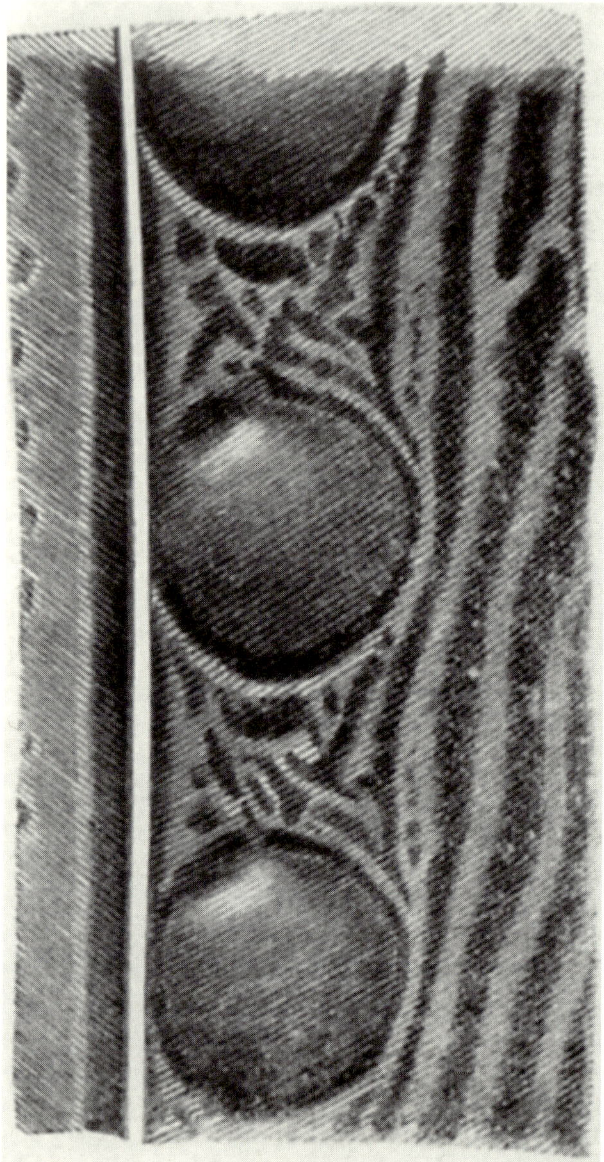

Figure 2.2 G. Pearson after Charles Darwin, *Part of Secondary Wing-Feather of Argus Pheasant,* wood engraving, c. 1870. *Figure 56 of* Descent of Man *(Darwin's original proof). Darwin Papers, reproduced by kind permission of the Syndics of Cambridge University Library.*

have surprised him to know that Darwin had performed the exercise, but it had not affected him as Ruskin anticipated. To the contrary, he used these renderings to illustrate his theory.

In his biography of Ruskin, the painter Arthur Severn (1842–1931) recorded Darwin's visit to Ruskin's home at Coniston in 1879. Severn described

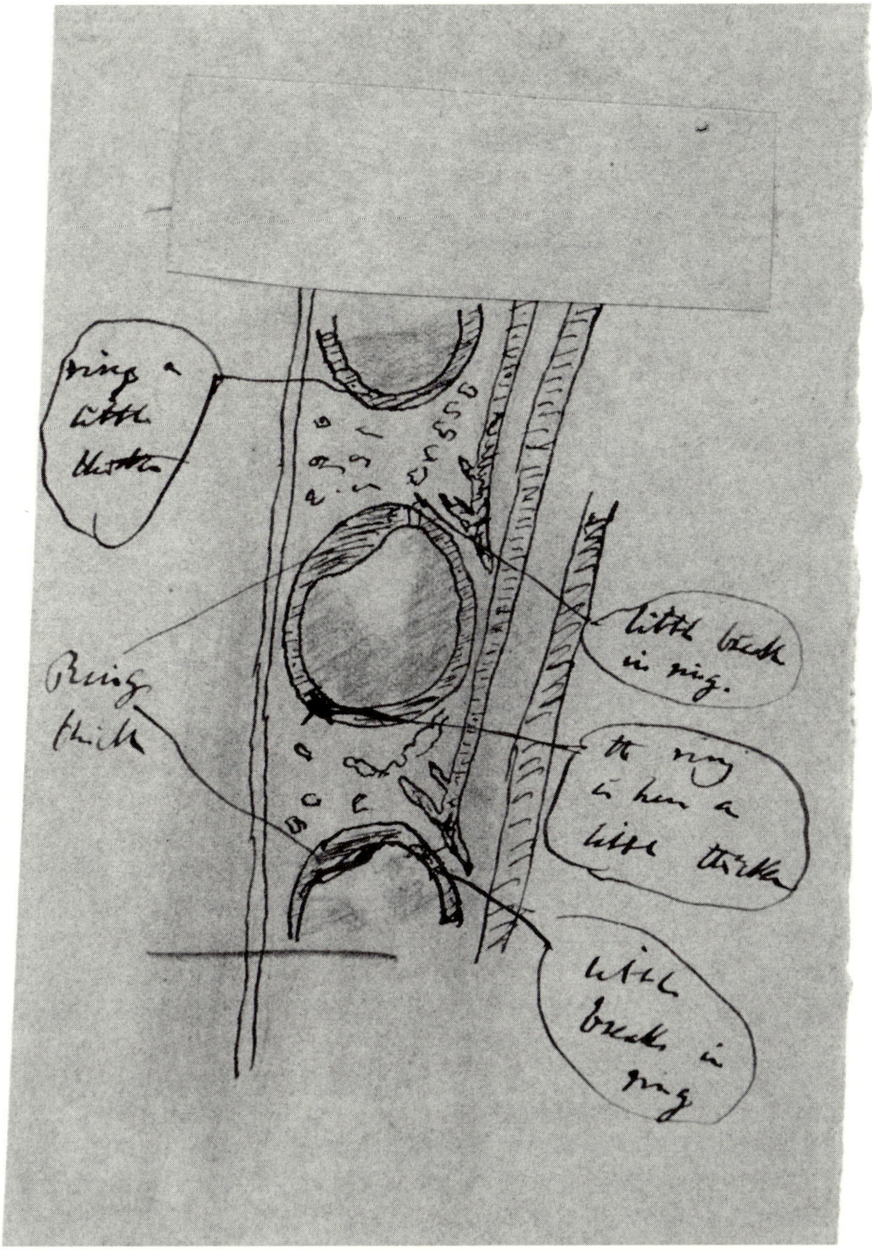

Figure 2.3 Charles Darwin, *Part of Secondary Wing-Feather of Argus Pheasant,* pencil and ink drawing, c. 1870. *Darwin Papers, reproduced by kind permission of the Syndics of Cambridge University Library.*

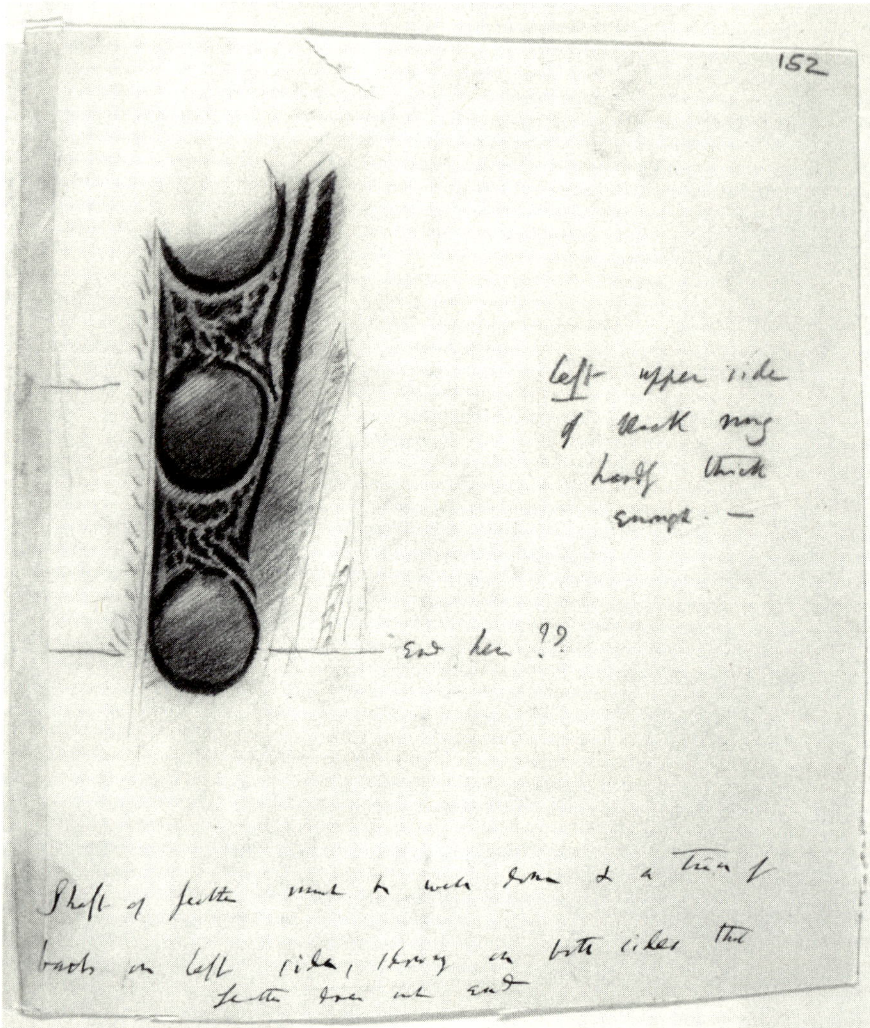

Figure 2.4 Unknown artist after Charles Darwin, *Part of Secondary Wing-Feather of Argus Pheasant*, pencil and ink drawing, with Darwin's pencil annotations, c. 1870. *Darwin Papers, reproduced by kind permission of the Syndics of Cambridge University Library.*

Darwin as "one of the most charming visitors we ever had," noting that "although Ruskin hated his theory, they seemed to get on very well." He remembered one especially amicable exchange, when "going into a room one day to see how they were getting on, I found them discussing the eyes on a peacock's tail—Darwin full of interest in the subject."[14] Nearly ten years after *Descent* was published, the two men still found the peacock a lively subject of conversation. Darwin, however, did not look on such discussions as fondly as Severn supposed. Privately, he confided, "The sight of a peacock's tail, whenever I gaze at it, makes me sick!"[15]

As the scholar Helena Cronin has written, the peacock's tail was, for Darwin, a tail "with a sting in it."[16] During the late 1860s and early 1870s, as Darwin wrote *Descent* and *Expression*, it was the subject around which criticisms of his theories coalesced. The problem was not just one of complexity, as Ruskin had it, but of excessive complexity—an ornament so extravagant in its effect as to sap the resources of the animal host. Cronin puts the point eloquently. As she describes it, a peahen could have been designed by a hard-headed, cost-cutting engineer; her mate could have stepped off the set of a Hollywood musical.[17] The conspicuous inefficiency of a male peacock is what Darwin found most complicated to explain. In it, his theories of natural and sexual selection seemed to contradict one another: While the tail might indeed draw the attention of females, it also cost precious resources that could help its owner survive in a harsh environment. Skeptics reasoned that both could not be true. If the evolution of the peacock had occurred according to rules of natural selection, then it should not have developed such costly and largely useless adornment. If it instead had evolved according to sexual selection, then natural selection would seem to be a much less potent force than he suggested.

In *Color and Culture*, the art historian John Gage has written of the historical association between the peacock and the alchemical tradition. As a conspicuous natural form containing an immense variety of colors, like a rainbow the peacock came to be associated with the spectrum.[18] Alchemists sometimes referred to the shimmering iridescence visible in some metallurgical reactions as "peacock-colored." In addition, the circular fan of the tail in full display and the numerous round ocelli present on individual feathers suited schemes of color organization visualized as a circle. This use of the peacock's tail as a color rubric was the opposite of the role it assumed in the evolutionary debate. Both alchemists and natural historians saw it as a source of wonder. However, while medieval scholars saw harmony in the peacock's tail, nineteenth-century scholars saw discord.

Evolution and the Art of Gradualism

Darwin was confident that evolutionary forces could explain even complex adaptations such as peacock feathers. The key to understanding the problem, he stressed, was the gradual nature of change amplified over time. Even "highly complex ornaments may have been acquired by small successive steps," he wrote, noting especially the "splendid decoration" of a peacock's tail.[19] This argument was particularly effective in responding to Ruskin's criticisms, as Ruskin famously considered gradation essential to successful painting. In *The Elements of Drawing* (1857), Ruskin advised his students, "No colour exists in nature without gradation. If you do not see this, it is the fault of your inexperience; you will see it in due course if you practice enough. But in general you may see it at once."[20] It was not the peacock's tail but its neck to which he directed his attention in *Elements:* "I have actually heard people say that blue and green were discordant; the two colours which Nature seems to intend never to be separated, and never to be felt, either of them, in its full beauty without the other!—a peacock's neck, or a blue sky through green leaves, or a blue wave with green lights through it, being precisely the loveliest things, next to clouds and sunrise, in this coloured world of ours."[21]

Speaking to the question of complexity in the tail of the peacock's close cousin, the argus pheasant, Darwin wrote:

> The ocelli on the wing feathers of the Argus pheasant [. . .] are shaded in so wonderful a manner as to resemble balls lying within sockets, and which consequently differ from ordinary ocelli. No one, I presume, will attribute the shading, which has excited the admiration of many experienced artists, to chance—to the fortuitous concourse of atoms of colouring matter. That these ornaments should have been formed through the selection of many successive variations, not one of which was originally intended to produce the ball-and-socket effect, seems as incredible, as that one of Raphael's Madonnas should have been formed by the selection of chance daubs of paint made by a long succession of young artists, not one of whom intended at first to draw the human figure.[22]

Natural history, Darwin argued, is like the history of art. Elements are resolved as they pass from one generation to the next; some are picked up and amplified in subsequent iterations while others are diminished. According to this conception, Perugino prefigures Raphael in the same way a small wing spot on an ancient pheasant prefigures the fully developed ocellus on a modern one.

The analogy is somewhat strained, and the reason Darwin chose to invoke it in his discussion of the pheasant's tail is unclear. It may have been conceived as a private message to Ruskin. By comparing a pheasant's tail to a figure painting, Darwin spoke to those who sought to dispel the theory of sexual selection through aesthetic claims. Likening the evolutionary development of an ornate feather to the process of painting served to remind his readers that even the most complex works of art could be created from the hand of a single man. Paintings, as Ruskin asserted in the *Elements of Drawing*, are developed gradually. In biology, complex structures can be developed through simple but repeated variations in approach, much as a painter can develop a compelling canvas with a limited palette and a few types of brush stroke. By naming Raphael, Darwin cited not just one of the most revered historical painters of his time, but also one distinguished by the logic and clarity of his vision. He may have had in mind Ruskin's own characterization of Raphaelesque beauty in *Modern Painters* (1843):

> John Bellini, Leonardo, Angelico, Dürer, Perugino, Raphael—all of them hated fog, and repudiated indignantly all manner of concealment. Clear, calm, placid, perpetual vision, far and near; endless perspicuity of space; unfatigued veracity of eternal light; perfectly accurate delineation of every leaf on the trees, every flower in the fields, every golden thread in the dresses of the figures, up to the highest point of calm brilliance which was penetrable to the eye, or possible to the pencil,—these were their glory.[23]

Raphael, according to Ruskin, was a painter who embraced complexity. Evolution, Darwin believed, was at least as eloquent as an Old Master artist.

By the end of the 1860s, those who disputed Darwin's account of evolution began to rally around the beauty problem as the Achilles' heel that would finally disprove evolution by natural and sexual selection. As with all thoughtful criticisms, Darwin took such arguments seriously. He was sufficiently alarmed by challenges of the beauty question that in preparing the fifth edition of *Origin* in 1869, he inserted several new pages explaining his view of the role of beauty in natural selection. This insertion is one of the most significant differences between the final editions of the work and its predecessors. In it, Darwin defended himself against allegations that he failed to account for the delight humans feel in the presence of natural forms:

> With respect to the belief that organic beings have been created for the delight of man,—a belief which it has been pronounced is subversive to my whole theory,—I may first remark that the sense of beauty obviously depends on the nature of the mind, irrespective of any real quality in the admired object; and that the idea of what is beautiful, not innate or unalterable. We see this, for instance, in the men of different races admiring an entirely different standard of beauty in their women. If beautiful objects had been created solely for man's gratification, it ought to be shown that before man appeared, there was less beauty on the face of the earth than since he came on the stage. Were the beautiful volute and cone shells of the Eocene epoch, and the gracefully sculptured ammonites of the Secondary period, created

> that man might afterwards admire them in his cabinet? Few objects are more beautiful than the minute siliceous cases of the diatomaceae: were these created that they might be examined and admired under the microscope? The beauty in this latter case, and in many others, is apparently due wholly to [the] symmetry of growth. Flowers rank among the most beautiful productions of nature; but they have been rendered conspicuous in contrast with the green leaves, and in consequence at the same time beautiful, so that they might easily be observed by insects. Hence we may conclude that, if insects had not been developed on the face of the earth, our plants would not be decked with beautiful flowers; one kind open and coloured so as to attract insects; the other closed, not coloured, destitute of nectar, and never visited by insects.[24]

Ironically, although these ideas would not find voice in his work until late in his career, they nevertheless are present in notes from the formative period of *Origin*. Remarks in his Notebook "N," written between 1838 and 1839, demonstrate that Darwin was weighing such considerations long before the manuscript was written. He wrote: "Negress beautiful,—[male glow worm doubtless admires female, showing no connection with male figure]—as forms change, so must idea of beauty.—[Old Graecians living amongst naked figures, & observing powers common to savages???]—The existence of taste in human mind is to me clear evidence, of the general ideas of our ancestors being impressed on us. Surely we have taste naturally all has not been acquired by education."[25] Indeed, it would seem that Darwin was troubled by the notion of beauty even when a young man, just beginning to develop his theory of evolution by natural selection.

The discussion of symmetry as a primary force in the determination of beauty is curious, given contrary accounts in literature that Darwin studied. William Hogarth, for example, offered a conflicting view in his *Analysis of Beauty* (1753), arguing that the prevailing notion that beauty results from symmetry has "little or no foundation."[26] Equating symmetry with regularity of form, he used the analogy of painting a building:

> It is a constant rule in composition in painting to avoid regularity. When we view a building, or any other object in life, we have it in our power, by shifting the ground, to take that view of it which pleases us best; and in consequence of this, the painter, if he is left to his choice, takes it on the angle, rather than in the front, as most agreeable to the eye; because the regularity of lines is taken away by their running into perspective, without losing the idea of fitness: and when he is of necessity obliged to give the front of a building, with all its equalities and parallelisms, he generally breaks (as it is termed) such

> disagreeable appearances by throwing a tree before it, or the shadow of an imaginary cloud, or some other object that may answer the same purpose of adding variety, which is the same with taking away uniformity.[27]

Hogarth held that for a picture to be beautiful, symmetrical forms must be broken up with contrasting elements. In contrast to Darwin, he argued that deformity could be beautiful. In a series of undated notes on *Analysis of Beauty,* Darwin acknowledged this stance. Of Hogarth's description of the Laocoön, he wrote, "Deformity is required—The existence of a number of discordant parts, which the eye must never be able to comprehend at a single glance in order to awaken in the opposite tendencies to those which beauty excites!!—I do not see the force of this argument: but deformity is a curious subject."[28]

Mivart's Challenge

Arguably the central figure in the anti-Darwinian movement of the early 1870s was St. George Jackson Mivart (1827–1900), who published his influential refutation of Darwinian evolutionary theory, *Genesis of Species,* in 1871. Mivart's handsomely illustrated book became the standard textbook of evolutionary unbelievers. Theologians wasted little time before embracing it, and it is perhaps some measure of its success that in 1876, Pope Pius IX conferred on Mivart an honorary degree of doctor of philosophy for his efforts. Like Ruskin, he conceded that evolution exists, but concentrated his attacks on the mechanisms of change proposed by Darwin. Writing before *Descent* was published, Mivart argued that the theories of natural and sexual selection (as they would later be known) are scientifically unacceptable. As he noted, each of these theories posits random variation as an engine of change. To him, they were theories of "vague, aimless, and indefinite variations in all conceivable directions."[29]

Mivart connected his discussion of the peacock's tail to an analysis of women's breasts. Mivart believed that breasts represent particular difficulties for evolutionary theory. He held that it was "inconceivable" that the young of any animal, let alone humans, could ever have been saved from destruction by suckling from a mother with enlarged breasts, or what he termed "accidentally hypertrophied cutaneous glands."[30] Even if enlarged mammary glands could be shown to be advantageous in rearing young in times of scarce resources, argued Mivart, their marginal utility would be outweighed (figuratively at least) by the potentially considerable disadvantage to the mother of having to obtain surplus nutrition to sustain them.

To Mivart, human breasts were clear examples of organs that could not be explained by natural selection alone. He considered them the human equivalent of a peacock's tail, which he addressed directly later in the book:

> Mr. Darwin explains the brilliant plumage of the peacock or the humming-bird by the action of sexual selection: the more and more brilliant the males being selected by the females (which are thus attracted) to become the fathers of the next generation, to which generation they tend to communicate their own bright nuptial vesture. But there are peculiarities of colour and of form which it is exceedingly difficult to account for by such action. Thus, amongst apes, the female is notoriously weaker, and is armed with much less powerful canine tusks than the male. When we consider what is known of the emotional nature of these animals, and the periodicity of its intensification, it is hardly credible that a female would risk life and limb through the admiration of a trifling shade of colour, or an infinitesimally greater though irresistibly fascinating degree of wartiness.[31]

John Ruskin shared the sentiment. The charm of a peacock's tail, he argued, was indisputable. But the appeal of the vulgar, fleshy rumps of baboons was beyond comprehension, an issue Ruskin evidently discussed with Darwin during his stay at Coniston. After Darwin left, Ruskin's friend V. Marshall wrote to him, confiding Ruskin's impressions of the visit. Ruskin had been telling friends that he believed Darwin had an unhealthy interest in the coloration of baboons' hind quarters.[32]

In 1876, Darwin clarified his views on the subject in the journal *Nature*. In formulating his theory of sexual selection, he wrote, "no case interested and perplexed me so much as the brightly-coloured hinde ends and adjoining parts of certain monkeys." He explained, "as these parts are more brightly coloured in one sex than the other, and as they become more brilliant during the season of love, I concluded that the colours had been gained as a sexual attraction."[33] One can only imagine Ruskin's reaction to Darwin's remarkably detached report that monkeys' bottoms are indeed secondary sexual organs: "von Fischer remarks that his monkeys like to have their naked hinde ends patted or stroked, and that they then grunt with pleasure."[34]

The existence of sexual attractants in the animal kingdom that humans find distasteful was actually one of Darwin's best weapons against the arguments of Mivart and Ruskin. Examples such as the baboon's hind quarters served as an antidote to the peacock's tail, as they enabled Darwin to counter the argument that God made animals for the enjoyment of humans. Darwin treasured accounts of elaborately ugly creatures, and collected articles describing particularly unusual findings. One such clipping, taken from the journal *Land and Water* in 1868, described a never-before-seen chimaera fish, which the author described as "not unlike an elongated carrot with wings." "It is among the fish that we find some of the most beautiful as well as the most hideous of created things," he wrote. "The chimaera can certainly not be classed among the 'court beauties' but should rather sit for a model to artists who desire to represent nightmares and other demons of darkness in their most hideous form."[35]

Consequences of the Beauty Problem

In the book *Mr. Darwin Misread Miss Peacock's Mind* (1999), the zoologist Merle Jacobs has argued that Darwin's theory of sexual selection languished for decades because Darwin mistakenly anthropomorphized the behaviors he sought to explain. Regarding the peacock, for example, Jacobs holds that Darwin erroneously attributed human thoughts such as choice, desire, and even an appreciation of beauty to the female peacock:

> Physical prowess is part of the dossier of the males. After a victorious male has intimidated his rivals, openly proving his physical condition by means of brute force, he entertains the females with various types of prancing displays of his grandeur. This is where the subjective judgement of the female, along with a high degree of intellectual visualisation, enters the picture. Beauty, to be sure, is a subtle thing, dependent on the eyes of the beholder. After prolonged and intensive observation, like a human artist squinting at a subject from various angles, the female finally makes her choice. This is Darwin's reading of the mind of the female.[36]

By Jacobs's reasoning, Darwin's theory of sexual selection is flawed because it assumes that animals have the mental capacity and will to make decisions in a similar way to humans.

In fact, the converse is true. Jacobs identified but misread one of the fundamental points concerning Darwin's writings on beauty and expression. Far from ascribing human values to animals, Darwin did the reverse: He explored the animal origins of the most complex human mental functions. Darwin's investigations in *Descent* and *Expression* represent the height of his heterodoxy. The place of humans in the continuum of life is a theme that beset many of his critics. It is also a theme that Darwin acknowledged numerous times in his work, but avoided commenting on explicitly until late in his career. Nevertheless, even in his early writings, the implications for understanding the nature of the human species were largely self-evident. *Origin of Species* prompted debate over the place of *Homo sapiens* in nature by focusing primarily on the physical adaptations that enable animals to thrive in their environments. The theory of natural selection was based largely on observations of the morphological similarities between species—the homologies between structures of modern animals and their ancestral relatives.

Descent and *Expression* took this one step further, describing the spectrum of behaviors, and consequently of mental functions, seen in the animal kingdom. At this point, Darwinism had breached the confines of physical appearance, and moved into the realm of the mind. *Descent* and *Expression* were particularly threatening to those who held the mental qualities of humans sacrosanct. In these books, humans begin to be regarded as machines, biological structures acting according to a set of scientific principles. There is no place in this theory for spirit, sentience, or personal experience. At stake was no less than the origin of thoughts and feelings, the essence of what would appear to make people unique.

It was for later scholars, such as Sigmund Freud (protégé of Jean-Martin Charcot, 1825–1893, and he, in turn, of Guillaume-Benjamin Duchenne de Boulogne), to probe the psychological elements of the animal origins of the human mind. Darwin himself made no direct claims on the subject. His works, however, identify numerous parallels between the actions of humans and their animal progenitors. Even to those who sympathized with his views, the logic was potentially shocking. It was one thing to claim that evolution was a self-contained system, responsible for the immense variety of life around the globe, and independent of divine forces. It was another to argue that experiences of love, hate, admiration, fear, and even pleasure itself were no more than manifestations of survival needs, originating in the adaptations of animal progenitors.

Ruskin, who had a penchant for touching raw nerves, had put his finger on one of the most sensitive elements of late Darwinian science. The beauty problem, and the question of the peacock's tail in particular, typified a new phase of research that confronted the traditional view of humans as being unique in their ability to experience emotions. If, as Darwin claimed, beauty is nothing more than evidence of reproductive pressures, and the enjoyment of such beauty is merely coincidental, then the full spectrum of human emotions can be reduced to the level of biological forces. Taken to its extremes, the expression of the emotions, no longer an embodiment of the soul as Descartes had it, could be stripped of its spiritual underpinnings. This was dangerous ground, even for a scientist well-versed in controversy. Darwin was wary of the reaction his new theories would provoke. While preparing the manuscripts for *Descent* and *Expression,* he was mindful of the resistance he was likely to encounter.

NOTES

1. John Ruskin, *The Eagle's Nest*, in *The Works of Ruskin*, vol. 22, ed. E. T. Cook and Alexander Wedderburn, (London: George Allen, 1903–1905].

2. Ibid.

3. Ibid., 247.

4. Ruskin, *The Queen of thc Air*, in *Works of Ruskin*, vol. 19, 358.

5. Ruskin, *Love's Meinie*, in *Works of Ruskin*, vol. 25, 36.

6. Ruskin, *The Eagle's Nest*, 247.

7. Ibid., 248.

8. Ruskin, *Proserpina*, in *Works of Ruskin*, vol. 25, 268–69.

9. The artist's name does not appear in standard reference works, but is credited in the Murray ledgers.

10. The Darwin Archive contains at least seven miscellaneous sketches of peacock and pheasant feathers. These are: Darwin Papers, volume 84.1, folios 152, 158–161, 168, and 169.

11. Charles Darwin to William E. Darwin, 2–3 August 1862, in Frederick Burkhardt and Sidney Smith, eds., *The Correspondence of Charles Darwin*, vol. 10, 1862 (Cambridge: Cambridge University Press, 1989), 349.

12. Darwin Papers, vol. 142.

13. "Main Ledger for Descent," 1871, p. 398, Murray Archive. The ledger credits Pearson with the "cut feather" engravings. According to the ledger, the other engraver was Butterworth & Co., but their role in preparing the engravings seems to have been relatively small. G. Pearson may have been George Pearson, a figure who appears in the Union List of Artist Names. His full name is not given.

14. Arthur Severn, *The Professor: Arthur Severn's Memoir of John Ruskin*, ed. James Dearden (London: George Allen & Unwin Ltd., 1967), 127.

15. Charles Darwin, as cited in Helena Cronin, *The Ant and the Peacock: Altruism and Sexual Selection from Darwin to Today* (Cambridge: Cambridge University Press, 1991), 113. It is one of the curiosities of history that the man who first wrote to Professor John Henslow in 1831, asking him to nominate a naturalist to accompany the now legendary voyage of the *Beagle* to South America, was the former dean of Ely and professor of Astronomy at Cambridge, one George Peacock.

16. Ibid.

17. Ibid.

18. John Gage, *Color and Culture: Practice and Meaning from Antiquity to Abstraction* (New York: Bulfinch Press, Little Brown & Co., 1993), 140. Chapter 8, "The Peacock's Tail," provides an excellent historical discussion of the subject.

19. Charles Darwin, *Descent of Man and Selection in Relation to Sex* (London: John Murray, 1871), 135.

20. John Ruskin, *The Elements of Drawing* (1857; reprint, New York: Dover Publications, 1971), 147.

21. Ibid., 156.

22. Darwin, *Descent*, 142.

23. John Ruskin, *Modern Painters: Their Superiority in the Art of Landscape Painting to the Ancient Masters, Proved by Examples of the True, the Beautiful, and the Intellectual, from the Works of Modern Artists, Especially from those of JMW Turner, Esq., RA, by a Graduate of Oxford* (1843), reprinted in Joan Evans, ed., *The Lamp of Beauty: Writings on Art* (London: Phaidon, 1995), 86.

24. Charles Darwin, *On the Origin of Species*, Thinker's Library edition, (London: Watts & Co., 1929), 152–53.

25. Charles Darwin, "Notebook N," in *Charles Darwin's Notebooks: 1836–1844*, ed. Paul Barrett et al., 570–71 (Ithaca: Cornell University Press, 1987).

26. William Hogarth, *The Analysis of Beauty; Written with a View of Fixing the Fluctuating Ideas of Taste* (London: Samuel Bagster, 1753), 55.

27. Ibid., 57–58.

28. Undated notes, "Hogarth—Analysis of Beauty," Darwin Papers, vol. 189, folio 113.

29. St. George Jackson Mivart, *On the Genesis of Species* (London: MacMillan, 1871), 54.

30. Ibid., 47.

31. Ibid., 48.

32. Unpublished correspondence, V. A. E. G. Marshall to Charles Darwin, 7 September 1879, Darwin Papers, vol. 171.

33. Charles Darwin, "Sexual Selection in Relation to Monkeys," *Nature*, 2 November 1876, 18.

34. Ibid., 19.

35. Frank Buckland, "The Arctic Chimaera," *Land and Water*, 4 July 1868, 377. Darwin Papers, vol. 82, folio 69.

36. Merle E. Jacobs, *Mr. Darwin Misread Miss Peacock's Mind: A New Look at Mate Selection in Light of Lessons from Nature* (Ashland, Ohio: Naturebooks, 1999), 9.

CHAPTER 3

From Monera *to Man*

Ernst Haeckel, *Darwinismus,* and Nineteenth-Century German Art

MARSHA MORTON

Darwinism was embraced by scientists, the media, and the general public in Germany more readily than in other countries, prompting Darwin to remark in 1861 that "the support which I receive in Germany is my chief ground for hoping that our views will ultimately prevail."[1] *Origin of Species* was translated into German in 1860 by the paleontologist Heinrich Georg Bronn and in 1866 by Victor Carus, who also provided a collected edition of Darwin's works in 1875.[2] The German public was exposed continually to information about natural history through extensive scientific coverage in newspapers like the Leipzig *Illustrirte Zeitung,* numerous periodicals serving the general reader such as *Die Gartenlaube, Die Gegenwart,* and *Westermanns Monatshefte,* and illustrated popular science books that included Alfred Brehm's highly successful multivolume *Tierleben [Brehm's Life of Animals]* (1864–1869) . Further contact was afforded by lectures and visits to zoos, museums, and aquariums with microscopes such as the one that opened in Berlin in 1875.[3] By that decade, evolutionary theory was commonplace enough to be satirized throughout the pages of the Munich weekly *Die Fliegende Blätter* and parodied in a three-act comedy at a Berlin theater.[4]

Almost uniformly, the science that was popularized in Germany was tied to Darwinism and the man behind this phenomenon was the University of Jena zoology professor Ernst Haeckel. His influence cannot be overestimated, whether one gauges it by his own prodigious output or by his students and followers, such as Brehm; the biologists Oscar and Richard Hertwig; Anton Dohrn, the founder of the marine biology station in Naples; and Carus Sterne (writing under the pen name of Ernst Krause) and Wilhelm Bölsche, both popular science writers. Haeckel published more than twenty technical books as well as texts for the general reader that included *Natürliche Schöpfungsgeschichte* [*The History of Creation*], a pioneering model for subsequent cosmological histories that went through twelve German editions between 1868 and 1919 and two English translations; *Anthropogenie* [*The Evolution of Man*], 1874; and his later *Die Welträtsel* [*The Riddle of the Universe*], 1899, which was translated into twenty-four languages by 1912.[5]

Haeckel initially read Darwin in the summer of 1860, first cited him in a footnote for his 1862 monograph on radiolarians, and launched what is considered to be the German public debut of Darwinism in a combative paper delivered in September 1863 at the annual conference of the Association of German Scientists and Physicians in Stettin. He corresponded with Darwin, sent him books, and visited him in Kent in 1866 and 1876.[6] Nonetheless, *Darwinismus,* as formulated by Haeckel, reveals on closer inspection not only disorienting differences from many Darwinian precepts but also shifting emphases during his lifetime. The materialist foundations of his 1860s and 1870s publications, which acknowledged the savagery of nature, yielded in the 1890s to a more benign sacred pantheism, although aspects of both views were present to varying degrees in all of his writings. The monistic message of world unity, based on the indestructible presence of force and matter, was further reiterated and untethered from Darwin in the writings of his popularizer Bölsche. Despite this, Haeckel never wavered in his opposition to notions of divine creation and free will, and remained a tireless foe of Catholicism.

Previous studies of Haeckel's artistic legacy have focused on individuals who responded to his writings espousing a unified evolutionary life force. These have included Jugendstil/Art Nouveau designers such as Hermann Obrist and René Binet, painters associated with the *Lebensreform* (life reform) movement, and individuals like Edvard Munch.[7] This scholarly orientation is not surprising, considering that Haeckel turned increasingly to issues related to aesthetics in his later publications, celebrating natural beauty as a central component of his monist religion (in *The Riddle of the Universe*) and providing sumptuous color illustrations, primarily of microscopic and marine creatures, that visually embodied proofs of evolution in *Art Forms in Nature* (1899–1904). Most of them were drawn by Haeckel, who was an amateur landscape painter, and were intended for adaptation by artists and architects. Their beauty was seductive, possessing a bold clarity that displayed the certainty of the author's convictions and the order he found in nature.

To limit Haeckel's influence to this context, however, presents a view of the zoologist when he was furthest removed from his Darwinian roots during a time when scientific popularization was at its most sentimentalized, anthropomorphic, and affirmative. Aptly characterized as the "re-enchantment of nature," this was a period when many writers endeavored to redress the analytical and alienating effects of professional scientific specialization and to counterbalance the philosophical pessimism of Schopenhauer and Nietzsche. This direction reached its apogee in the writings of Haeckel's friend and biographer Bölsche, whose *Das Liebesleben in der Natur* [*Love Life in Nature*], 1898, was an immediate bestseller.[8]

This essay will seek to recontextualize Haeckel by charting the impact of his more programmatic Darwinian views on a broad spectrum of earlier painters and printmakers prior to the turn of the century. Their work, which eschewed a progressive optimism, helped to shape the public face of Darwinism in Germany and established a direction against which later art movements, both Jugendstil and *Lebensreform*, reacted in efforts to rehabilitate the human soul. These artists, who included Arnold Böcklin, Max Klinger, Ernst Moritz Geyger, Franz von Stuck, Gabriel von Max, Richard Müller, and Alfred Kubin, were receptive to a bleaker evolutionary narrative of competition, struggle, and death. For them, the presence of man "in," rather than "above," nature, evoked anxious, and frequently ironic, visions of human and animal parity in a world of violence, suffering, and carnality.[9]

The Darwinian strands of their work, absorbed from scientific publications and popular culture, will be considered in conjunction with other influences that reinforced evolutionary truths but also led to frequent reformulations and divergences from Haeckel's viewpoints. Foremost among these were aspects of German Romanticism associated with the "dark side of nature" and explorations of the unconscious, including paranormal states, which were receiving renewed attention in the late nineteenth century.[10] Just as German Romantic *Naturphilosophie*, together with Goethe, has been credited with anticipating theories of descent, so too were the attendant fears of estrangement, destabilization, and nihilism also present earlier.[11] These can be traced from the literature of Jean Paul, E. T. A. Hoffmann, and Heinrich Heine, with their descriptions of nightmarish hallucinations, frequently cosmological and oceanic, to the biologically oriented philosophy of Schopenhauer and the young Nietzsche.

All German artists, however, whether they regarded a Darwinian inflected nature with wonder or misgiving, found common ground in themes specific to Haeckel. They pursued similar explorations about man's unity with nature, his origins (monera or apes), primal states (radiolarians or the unconscious), and transitional forms of life. All of them depicted aquatic and/or simian animals, those areas that, according to Bölsche, comprised Haeckel's signal refinements to Darwin's system, both "at the bottom of the tree, where life begins" and at "the crown of all terrestrial evolution: the manner in which man is connected with the tree."[12]

Haeckel's Hylozoic Universe and the Orderly Descent of Life

Haeckel's *Darwinismus* was the product of German specializations in history, cell biology, embryology, and comparative morphology; his own research on marine organisms; his penchant for philosophical interpretation that led him to package evolutionary theory as a grand worldview; and his personality, which was averse to hesitation or ambiguity. Despite Haeckel's lifelong role as Darwin's self-appointed champion, he promoted a theory from which the random, undirected, and open-ended were ironed out in favor of a generally optimistic view of a harmonious universe governed by regular laws that evolved progressively towards greater order, beauty, and self-perfection.[13] Co-operation among species came to play a role as prominent as competition. Indebted to the beliefs of Goethe, Alexander von Humboldt, and the Romantic *Naturphilosophie* of Friedrich Schelling and Lorenz Oken, Haeckel perceived telic structures within nature and insisted on the monistic unity of matter and spirit (energy/consciousness) as well as the inorganic and organic.

Haeckel's vision of a hylozoic universe posited an active force, also characterized as growth, which operated according to immutable laws and was manifested in affinities that could be found in the "vibration of atoms," the bonding of elements, magnetism, the sensitivity of plants to touch, and sexual attraction.[14] For Haeckel, the world comprised a chain of connections unified not only by mechanistic forces but also by the shared building material of sentient cells with "souls" (a notion based on Gustav Fechner's "soul life" in plants), which in the lowest forms of life (the Protista kingdom) amounted to properties of irritability, sensation, and motion that presaged the development of the nervous system and brain in animals.

Haeckel was drawn to evolutionary theory because it provided an ordered system of universal kinship. This is revealed in his first public statement about Darwin, in which Haeckel praised *Origin of Species* "as the first serious scientific attempt to explain all the manifestations of organic nature from the marvelous, unified point of view and to replace the incomprehensible wonders with comprehensible natural laws."[15] He immediately set about to close the gaps in Darwin's work and to account for the origin of life, prompting Darwin to "tremble" at his "boldness."[16] The goal of Haeckel's first ambitious work, *Generelle Morphologie* (1866) was to prove "the unity of all organic and inorganic nature" through their related "substance, form and energy" and to "apply the theory of evolution to the entire classification of organisms."[17] Darwin supplied Haeckel with interpretative tools through which similarities and differences of form were now expressions of shared ancestry.[18]

Within Haeckel's cosmology, specific organisms assumed prominent roles due to their significance as key transitional forms proving evolutionary kinship. Life began through spontaneous generation via the bonding propensities of carbon with oxygen, nitrogen, and hydrogen to form albumineous bodies, or non-nucleated blobs of protoplasm that he termed monera. These "arose from the primeval ocean through the operation of purely physical and chemical conditions" and were the origin of all living forms.[19] The illustration of monera (circular in shape with thread-like attachments) in *The History of Creation* (plate I) represents developmental processes of nutrition (eating) and propagation through self-division. Described by Haeckel as "primeval parents," monera provide an artistic model of organic abstraction whose representation conveys a meaning similar to the tale of Genesis. For Haeckel, they are additionally significant as the missing link between organic and inorganic form, whose distinction "loses all importance" because of their discovery.[20] Cells are formed by the condensation of a central mass within the monera that through separation becomes a nucleus.

While most Darwinian authors featured fossil forms of prehistoric flying reptiles (many are illustrated in books by Sterne and Bölsche), Haeckel highlighted the marine organisms that represented his most significant zoological contributions: the radiolarians and medusa (jellyfish) of which he had identified hundreds of new species. These comprised the majority of images in *Art Forms in Nature* with illustrations taken from earlier, more specialized publications.[21] Radiolarians are microscopic, single-celled, free-swimming protozoa that date to the Precambrian geological era. Their bodies are contained in helmet-like siliceous skeletons whose diversity and complexity fascinated Haeckel and inspired comparisons with crystals. The medusa, whose "delicate" flowing tentacles reminded him of the blond hair of his beloved first wife Anna Sethe, were valued from an evolutionary perspective as embodying one of "the strongest proofs of the truth of the theory of descent" through their method of procreation involving generational alternation (figure 3.1).[22]

Haeckel also promoted embryonic evidence as the most reliable method for proving man's descent from lower organisms and popularized the biogenetic theory according to which the developmental stages of the human embryo (ontogeny) are a condensed recapitulation of the evolution of the species (phylogeny). Thus, the egg of a mammal resembles an amoeba, while the human embryo is initially similar to that of the fish, tortoise, salamander, hen, pig, deer, and dog (*The Evolution of Man*, plates IV and V). These comparative illustrations of embryos were among his most controversial, eliciting accusations of falsifying data that his admission of re-using the same plate for the earliest embryonic stages in different animals did little to resolve.[23] Bold images such as *The Evolution of the Face* drove home the message that

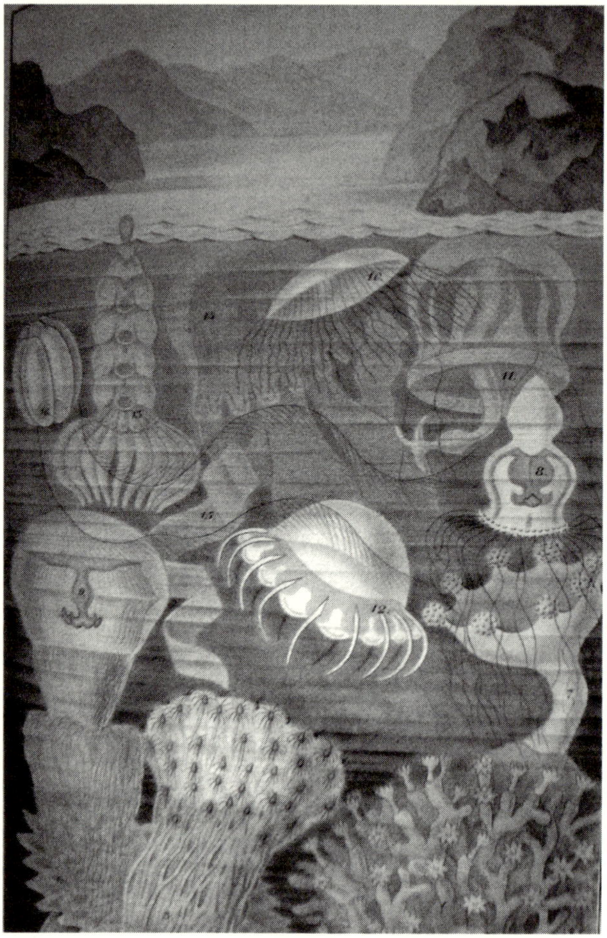

Figure 3.1 Ernst Haeckel, *Group of Animal-Trees (Zoophytes, or Coelenterate) in the Mediterranean.* This illustration depicts medusae, ctenophore, corals, and hydroid polyps. *From* Natürliche Schopfungsgeschichte (*The History of Creation*) *3rd ed. (Berlin: Georg Reimer, 1872), Plate VII.*

man contained within himself primordial states (figure 3.2). Haeckel's choice of the Hellenistic Zeus of Otricoli sculpture conveys multiple readings: evolutionary theory as subverting the existence of divine beings, undercutting the pinnacle of humanist achievement (and human behavior) through linkages with the bat, and opposing the classical ideal of art with the "peculiar beauty" of nature.[24] Haeckel was among the first to proclaim man's descent from the catarhine apes, an accomplishment noted by Darwin, and stressed similarities between tribal man and higher primates.[25] Predictably, this theory was illustrated in unequivocal fashion with an African man perched in a tree surrounded by his arboreal progenitors the chimp, gorilla, and orangutan (figure 3.3).

By the 1890s, Haeckel's activity in empirical research was largely over and

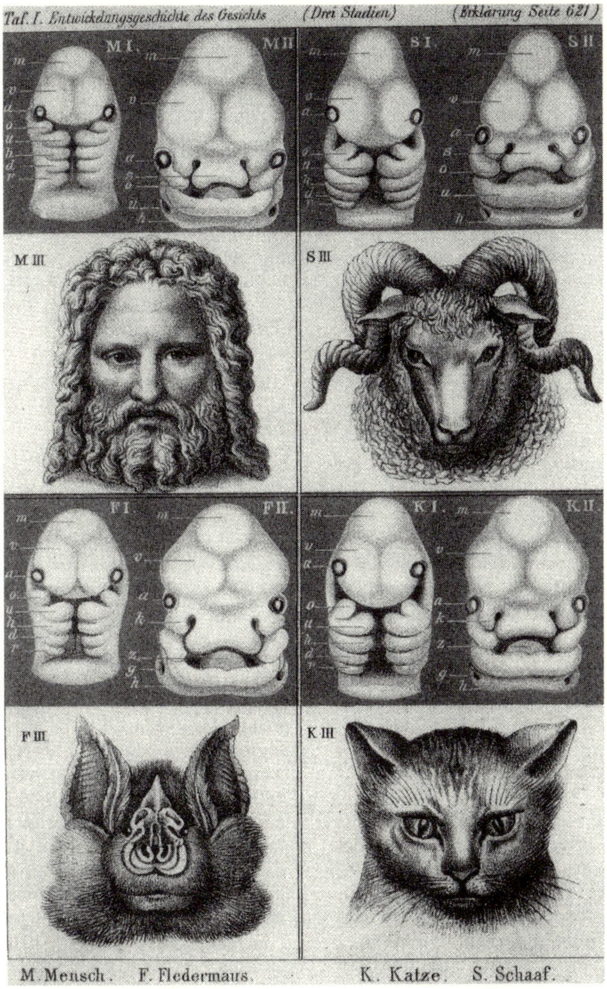

Figure 3.2 Ernst Haeckel, Development of the Face. From *Anthropogenie* (*The Evolution of Man*), 2nd ed. (Leipzig: Wilhelm Engelmann, 1874), Plate I.

the pan-psychism latent in his earlier work fully emerged as a monist, almost mystical, religion that would lead to the foundation of the Monist Society in 1906.[26] Accompanying the increasingly sacred tenor of his writings was the attempt to foster a more accessible, less-alienating image of science. Nature was seen as a wonderland of new "aesthetic enjoyment," provided by the telescope and microscope, in which poetry was immanent.[27] In his essay "Cell Souls and Soul Cells," Haeckel argued that although the "nymphs and Naiads, Dryads and Oreads" and semi-human gods of the ancient Greeks were gone, they had been replaced by the countless "elementary spirits of cells"—a reference, no doubt, to the legendary folk creatures of Heinrich Heine's *Ele-*

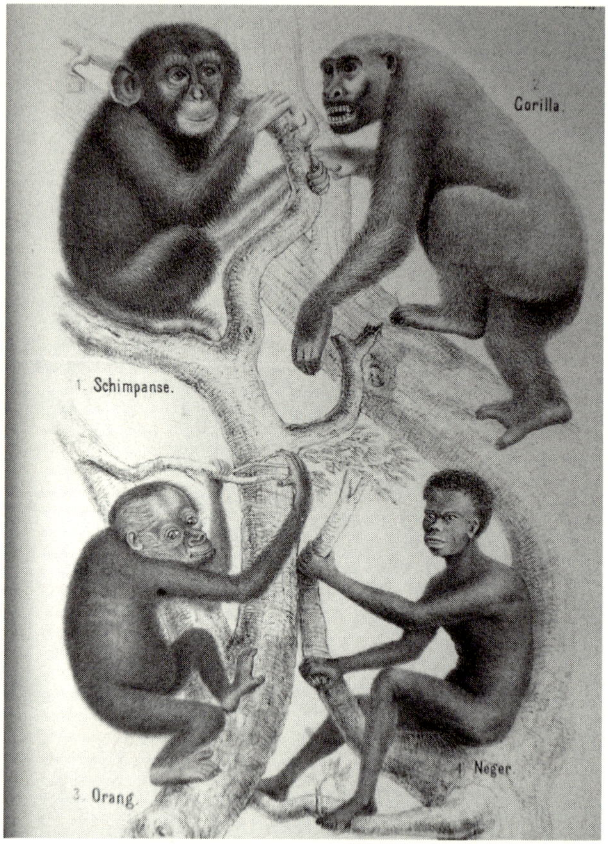

Figure 3.3 Ernst Haeckel, *Anthropogenie*, 2nd ed. (Leipzig: Wilhelm Engelman, 1874), Plate XI, *Four Catarhines (Chimpanzee, Gorilla, Orang, Negro).*

mentargeister [*Elemental Spirits*].[28] Modern artists, however, would find inspiration in both myths and cells, and, like Heine, discover that an enchanted nature could be not only nurturing but dangerous, a source of beauty or horror.

Haeckel's populist approach was taken much further through the widely read writings of his friend Wilhelm Bölsche, who injected a decidedly more erotic dimension that was relentlessly optimistic. Bölsche's background was in literature, not science, and he adopted a folksy, chatty tone (the essay form known as the *Plauderei*) that featured verbally painted landscapes, artistic metaphors, and references to fairy tales and legends. He regarded nature as a vast art work developing toward aesthetic perfection (the "rhythmic-ornamental principle") and powered, like evolution, by love. Basing his convictions on Darwin's theory of sexual selection, in which partners are chosen in part for beauty, Bölsche regarded the erotic drive as the central unifying principle of the universe, equivalent to Haeckel's "force."[29] This was, in essence, Schopenhauer's *Will* stripped of suffering. In Bölsche's sensational three-volume book *Love-Life in Nature*, the reader is taken on a comprehensive tour of the sexual practices of organisms (radiolarian to snails to flies to primates), recounted with enthusiastic brio, and invited to re-experience the evolutionary process or, as David Kelley has observed, to "tap the primeval memory of your body that will link you to the primitive wild love orgies of bygone eons."[30]

Imaging Genealogical Kinship: Klinger, Böcklin, Geyger, von Max, and Schopenhauer's "Wild Beast"

The upbeat promotion of nature's recuperative powers celebrated at the end of the century by Haeckel and Bölsche, as well as Büchner and Sterne, evidenced a response to growing industrialization and urbanization, as well as an attempt to "spin" Darwinism in a positive light.[31] Earlier artistic portrayals of evolutionary theory, by contrast, had delved into more disturbing aspects. These painters and printmakers, despite differences of style and tone, directed their attention to the implications of the new science with regard to human behavior as they probed the now-porous borders between man and animal and explored the origins and primitive states of human ancestry. Many artists absorbed a fusion of Darwin, Haeckel, and other scientific popularizers in their readings, observed animals firsthand in zoos and aquariums, were collectors themselves, and, in the case of Gabriel von Max and Arnold Böcklin, were personal friends with scientists. The artistic translations of biological research, however, frequently produced results that shifted attention to the darker features of Darwinian theory vis-à-vis man—aggression, death, suffering, self-interest—that belied the assertions of progressive human perfection trumpeted by most natural science authors. Artists generally regarded man's perch at the top of Haeckel's evolutionary tree with skepticism.

This viewpoint was in part shaped by a conjunction of scientific information with the philosophy of Schopenhauer and romantic literary traditions, the latter evidenced pictorially through figures derived from myths and legends, demonic monsters, and attitudes of irony and melancholy. Schopenhauer, whose writings greatly influenced the art of Klinger, Böcklin, von Max, and Kubin, theorized the presence of an instinctual *Will* present in all of nature. Unlike Haeckel's pantheistic conception of a sentient intelligent universe, Schopenhauer's *Will* was a blind irrational force, centered in the genitals, that was opposed to intellect and reason and secretly determined human behavior. Perennially insatiable, the *Will* represented bondage to inescapable physical drives. Modern man was, according to Schopenhauer, a "wild beast,"

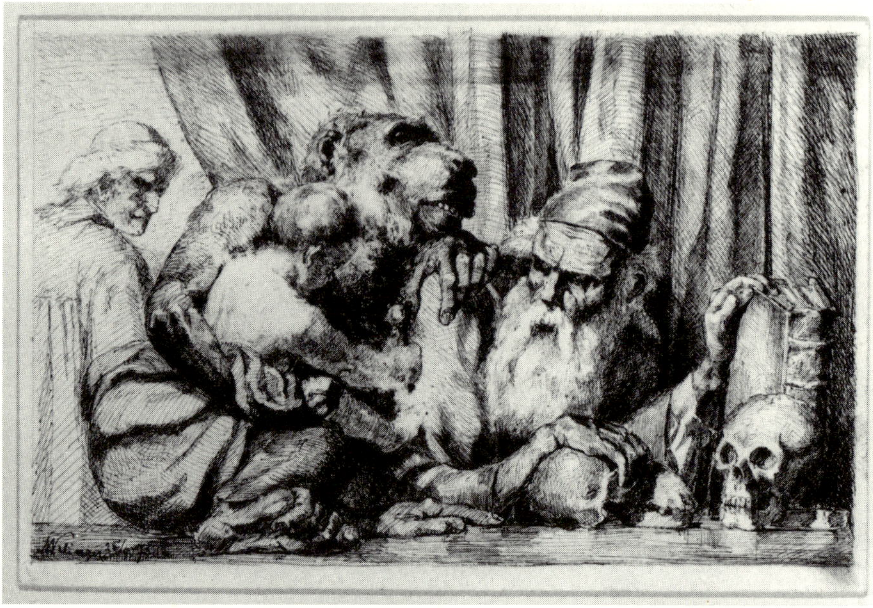

Figure 3.4 Max Klinger, *Darwinian Theory*, 1875, pen and ink, 9.8 × 14.6 cm. *Kupferstichkabinett, Staatliche Museen zu Berlin, Bildarchiv Preussischer Kulturbesitzt / Art Resource, New York.*

only superficially "bridled and tamed" by the civilizing process.[32] While differing profoundly in their messages, both men nonetheless posited a force or spirit (developed partly from research on the nervous system) that linked man to other organisms, denied free will, denounced Christianity, and adhered, primarily, to a materialist world view. Schopenhauer, who was influenced by Cuvier and Lamarck, employed biological imagery throughout his writings, and was quoted by both Darwin and Haeckel to bolster their arguments on the significance of sexual selection.

Several German artists created pictures that directly addressed the pithecoid theory, beginning with Klinger's *Darwinian Theory* from 1875 (figure 3.4). Inspired by his reading of Darwin, Klinger depicted the scientist with a book and two skulls, simian and human, which offer paleontological proof of man's ancestry through comparative anatomy.[33] The intimacy between the child and ape reveals man's origins and attests to the intense maternal affection observed in monkeys by Haeckel and Darwin. Haeckel maintained that human behavior derived from "the instinct which is found in its extreme form in the exaggerated tenderness of the mother-ape."[34] He also considered the less-developed intelligence of children, in comparison to the adult, as proof that mental capacities grow, like physical ones, and are therefore present in

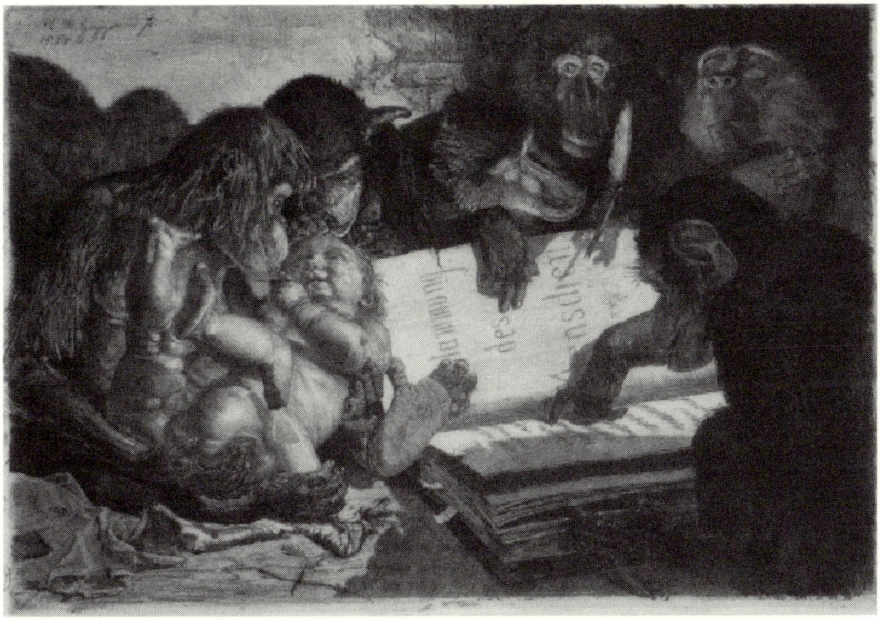

Figure 3.5 Ernst Moritz Geyger, *Darwinian Disputation*, 1888, etching, 45.4 × 56 cm. *Städel Museum, Frankfurt am Main.*

rudimentary form in animals.[35] The retreating figure of an angry priest references the threat posed by evolutionary theory to traditional theological beliefs, as well as the anticlericalism of most German Darwinists. Haeckel first sounded the alarm in his controversial speech in Stettin in 1863, declaring that "neither the weapons of tyrants nor the curses of priests" could suppress evolutionary biology.[36] During the 1870s in Germany, hundreds of Catholic clergy were imprisoned or exiled as a result of a Prussian ban on monastic orders orchestrated by Bismarck and the liberal political parties.

Klinger's references to propagation, genealogical descent, and the mother-child relationship were expanded into a narrative by Ernst Moritz Geyger in his etching *Darwinian Disputation*, exhibited in the 1888 Munich International Art Exhibition (figure 3.5). Geyger, a printmaker and sculptor, specialized in animal themes, a skill he developed as a student at the Berlin Academy under the instruction of Paul Meyerheim, who was known for his scenes of the Berlin Zoo. Meyerheim was one of several artists, including Heinrich Leutemann and the Brehm illustrators R. Kretschmer and Gustav Mützel, whose zoological pictures appeared frequently in newspapers and journals, and whose careers benefited from the surging public enthusiasm for natural history. In comparison to Klinger's drawing, *Darwinian Disputation* reveals its origins in traditional anthropomorphic representations, now adapted to incorporate evolutionary kinship. Behavior is gender specific, as the female ape grips the baby's milk bottle and the males (silver baboon, chimp, gorilla, and orangutan) pursue scholarly research.[37] Looking perplexed, they attempt to identify the human infant through extensive consultation with a volume inscribed "Descent of Man." The dramatic lighting illuminates the book and baby, inspiring one contemporary critic to compare it, perhaps ironically, to Renaissance paintings of the birth of Christ. It also casts an eerie glow on the faces of the apes, establishing an ambiance of primal mystery.[38]

Geyger's print reflects transformations in post-Darwinian animal depictions away from the tradition of moral parables or comic human satires in the manner of Alexander Decamps and, occasionally, Meyerheim.[39] The awareness of shared kinship inspired many artists to render simian physiognomies with heightened degrees of intelligence, thereby burnishing the quality of man's ancestral pedigree.[40] This direction was further encouraged in Germany by several studies in animal psychology initiated by Wilhelm Wundt's pioneering book, *Lectures on Human and Animal Souls* (1863).[41] Assertions about animal "ascent" to human capabilities led to a variety of pictorial responses, including satirical spoofs. An 1873 issue of *Fliegende Blätter*, for example, featured the autobiographical musings of an ape, "From the Diary of a Miocene Anthropoid: A Contribution to the Teachings of the Origin of Man," with a picture of the author seated on a tree stump penning his thoughts.[42] Alfred Kubin offered less-reassuring reactions to the pithecoid theory. In his drawing *Science* (c.1902) (Leopold Museum, Vienna) a victorious ape, deep in thought with a book tucked under his arm, is shown striding over a prone male corpse in a vacant landscape.

The sober, contemplative expressions in *Darwinian Disputation* are echoed in depictions of caged animals, such as the mournful *Orangutan* (1896 etching, now in the Museum der bildenden Künste Leipzig) by Richard Müller, a student of Geyger and follower of Klinger.[43] These reflect the public's increased contact with and empathy for primates through the expanding zoo collections in Germany and the arrival in 1876 of M'pungu, the first gorilla to be brought to Europe, at the Berlin Aquarium. M'pungu received major press coverage, together with full-page illustrated portraits, before his death a year later following a trip to London and Hamburg. The aquarium, whose founder and initial director was Haeckel's follower Alfred Brehm, brought the most pertinent areas of Haeckel's evolutionary study to life with a collection that featured aquatic creatures, anthropoid apes, chimpanzees, and orangutans.[44]

The most sympathetic portrayals of apes were done by Haeckel's friend Gabriel von Max, who owned several as pets. His identification with them is evident in his late painting *Self Portrait with Ape* (1910), now in the Reiss-Museum, Mannheim, where the artist tenderly cradles a young ape, and in his representations of anthropoids engaged in scientific activities that he pursued. These include *Apes as Geologists* (after 1900), where they sit surrounded by bones and fossils, and *Anthropological Lessons* (nd), which depicts an ape gazing thoughtfully at a small human skeleton while taking notes. Shunning narrative kitsch and humor, these paintings evoke a profound sensitivity that recalibrates the degrees of wisdom possessed by man and the highest primates. Von Max actually dissected his own deceased apes, conducted studies in comparative anatomy, maintained photographic documentation, and preserved their remains as taxidermic specimens in his extensive collection of paleontological, anthropological, and zoological objects. This private museum, installed in his homes in Munich and Ammerland, eventually contained between sixty and eighty thousand objects, and was visited by Haeckel in 1892.[45]

According to von Max, his acquisitions were motivated by an interest in human origins and ancestry. He wrote: "The question as to where people come from, that is the source of my collection."[46] The same goal drove his art and, like Haeckel, he sought to uncover a spiritual awareness, or consciousness, in matter that developed through evolutionary genealogy. A contemporary writer, Agathon Klemt, observed in 1886 that "Max . . . takes a deep and earnest interest in science. His most favored subject is the history of the existence of the soul; he pursues this in the first externalization of the psychic relations of animal existence to the early history of man."[47] It was towards this end that von Max tackled one of his most ambitious subjects in 1894, a portrait of transitional ape-man, *Pithecanthropus Alalus* that he gave to Haeckel as a sixtieth birthday present (figure 3.6). This "first family" was inspired by Dr. Eugène Dubois' 1894 discovery of fossil fragments of a Pliocene-age primate *Pithecanthropus erectus* (Java Man) amidst marine sediment. He was following a lead by Haeckel, who had earlier theorized that the original home of primitive man may have been a lost continent under the Indian Ocean.[48] Haeckel proclaimed Dubois' findings to be "the long-searched for 'missing link,' for which, in 1866 [*General Morphology*], I myself had proposed the hypothetical genus Pithecanthropus, species Alalus."[49] Haeckel was impressed with the painting and later reciprocated in 1900 with an honorary diploma bestowed on Max for his seventieth birthday.[50] This reconstruction, however, is of a blond-haired "middle-European" family in an ancient northern forest, thereby fostering a sense of kinship with the viewer when it was exhibited in Munich in 1894.[51] Linkages with modern man were additionally underscored by photographic illustrations of atavistic hair-covered bodies in scientific texts by Sterne and Bölsche.[52]

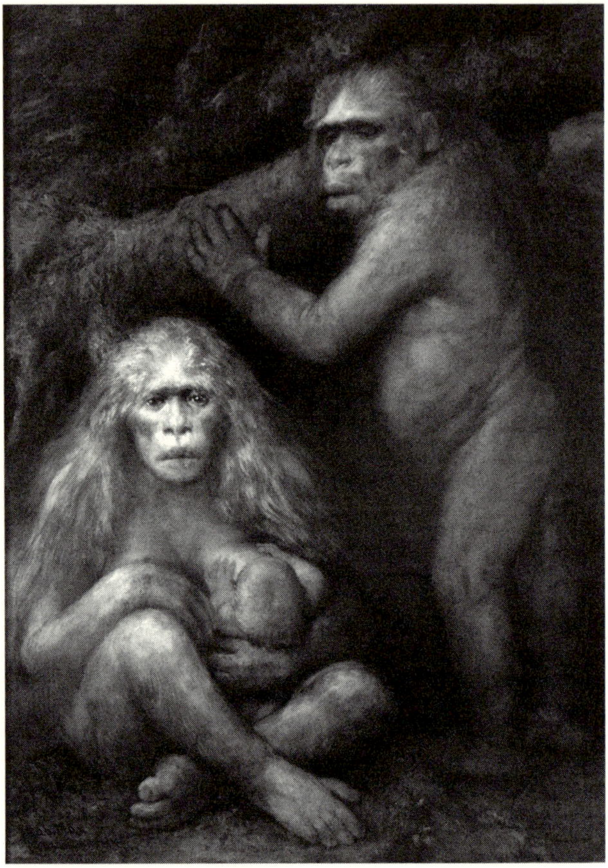

Figure 3.6 Gabriel von Max, *Pithecanthropus Alalus*, 1894, oil/canvas. *Reproduced with permission by Ernst-Haeckel-Haus, Friedrich-Schiller-Universität Jena.*

Although von Max's figures were compared by critics with other prehistoric denizens, in particular Böcklin's centaurs and fauns, nonetheless *Pithecanthropus Alalus* is an unusual vision of primitive man that rejects stereotypes of the "noble savage" and associations with brute force or sinister aggression typical of many such depictions, evident in Klinger's etching *Future III* (from the series *Eve and the Future*, 1880; Leipzig) or Franz von Stuck's painting *Battle over a Woman* (1899; The Hermitage, St. Petersburg).[53] Instead, an atmosphere of melancholy pervades this silent twilight scene and, as reviewers noted, human sensibility is established by the capacity to feel sorrow, manifested by a tear on the mother's face. Dubbed the "pithecoid Madonna," a reference to the evolutionary displacement of biblical texts as well as von Max's own fame as a painter of Marian themes, her expression was interpreted by Bruno Stern as a "presentiment of the whole misery which her human descendants will have to suffer."[54] This bleak pessimism, a mood also pronounced in von Max's paintings of apes, can be attributed to his deep admiration for Schopenhauer. His misanthropic views about contemporary society, attested to by his son, differed from the opinions of Haeckel and most other scientists who believed, at least in theory, that natural selection guaranteed improvement.[55] Von Max, by contrast, found greater decency among the ancestors of man.

Von Max also parted company with Haeckel in his fascination with mysticism and spiritualism. He was active in Munich circles investigating paranormal phenomenon led by the physician and psychologist Carl du Prey and Albert von Schrenck-Notzing, the former an admirer of Darwin and Schopenhauer who hoped to establish empirical proof of the human soul. Von Max participated frequently in séances, collected occult memorabilia, and was renowned for his portraits of female visionaries and mediums.[56] His dual interest in the supernatural and the scientific typified the period, and many artists most involved with evolutionary theory were intrigued with the paranormal.[57] Support for these concerns also came from Schopenhauer and from romantic writers like Heinrich von Kleist and E. T. A. Hoffmann (read by von Max, Klinger, Müller, and Kubin), whose plays and stories are filled with clinical descriptions of mesmeric states. In Schopenhauer's lengthy "Essay on Spirit Seeing" in *Parerga und Paralipomena*, which was an essential source for Klinger and Kubin, he declared that phenomenon like animal magnetism, magic, dreaming, and second sight corroborated the existence of the *Will* and were an important source for "every scholar and man of science to become thoroughly acquainted with."[58]

In the opinion of most artists, behavior experienced during irrational states revealed the unconscious and manifested a regressive level of human identity consistent with their exploration of evolutionary origins. An early book on von Max by his dealer and friend Nicolaus Lehmann discussed his paintings of somnambulist and hypnotic subjects in this context, interpreting them as an attempt to uncover the "primal state of mankind." Lehmann continued: "because his [Max's] thoughts are also directed to the investigation of the origin of all things, as well as the future and past of life forms, so he must be also naturally interested in the theories of Darwin."[59] The two areas merged in his painting *Hypnotic Studies* (nd) in which the scientific observer and trance-induced subject are apes.[60] The primeval nature of the dream experience was symbolized by artists like Klinger, Müller, and Kubin through the inclusion of paleontological and biological objects.[61]

Many artists shared von Max's dim assessment of modern man, but chose to convey this through an ancestry of behavior patterns determined by instinct rather than intellect and motivated by violence and carnality. Kubin, for example, crudely rendered inherited biological drives in his drawings *One for*

All (1900–1901) (Oberösterreichisches Landesmuseum, Linz) and *Lust* (c.1900) (Dichand Collection, Vienna), which featured apes with dripping penises and women in bondage. According to this viewpoint, a return to nature meant confrontation with a darker self. Surprisingly, Haeckel reinforced an unidealized evaluation of nature, in part as a way to discredit Christianity:

> If we contemplate the common life and the mutual relations between plants and animals (man included), we shall find everywhere, and at all times, the very opposite of that kindly and peaceful social life which the goodness of the Creator ought to have prepared for his creatures—we shall rather find everywhere a pitiless, most embittered *Struggle of All against All.* Nowhere in nature, no matter where we turn our eyes, does that idyllic peace, celebrated by the poets, exist; we find everywhere a struggle and a striving to annihilate neighbours and competitors. Passion and selfishness—conscious or unconscious—is everywhere the motive force of life. Man in this respect certainly forms no exception to the rest of the animal world.[62]

This passage, contained in *The History of Creation,* was kept in circulation through the publication of numerous revised editions, while the sentiments expressed did not ever completely disappear from his later writings. In his 1892 book, *Monism as a Bond Connecting Religion and Science,* pantheistic unity and natural beauty do not eliminate brutal Darwinian truths of survival and self-preservation: "Thousands of animals and plants must daily perish in every part of the earth, in order that a few chosen individuals may continue to subsist and to enjoy life . . . The raging war of interests in human society is only a feeble picture of the unceasing and terrible war of existence which reigns throughout the whole of the living world."[63] Scenes of conflict in nature can be found throughout German art, beginning in the 1860s with the animal battles conceived by the cartoonist Wilhelm Busch, who was a devoted reader of Darwin and Schopenhauer and a regular contributor to the pages of *Fliegende Blätter.*[64] Predatory zoological images also abound in the drawings of Klinger, Geyger, and Kubin.

Böcklin satirized Darwinian disbelievers with their faith in a divine benevolent universe in *St. Anthony Preaching to the Fish,* 1892 (figure 3.7). Conceived in the format of an "evolutionary" altarpiece, the retable depicts the monk preaching to a besotted shark whose hypnotic gaze is echoed on the faces of a school of fish in the distant water. Böcklin has selected a fish who is not only among the most rapacious in the aquatic world, but also, together with the seaweed on the rock, the most ancient of primitive species, as Haeckel noted in *The Evolution of Man.*[65] The shark's true nature is illustrated in the predella panel where he devours his prey. Böcklin's anticlerical message ac-

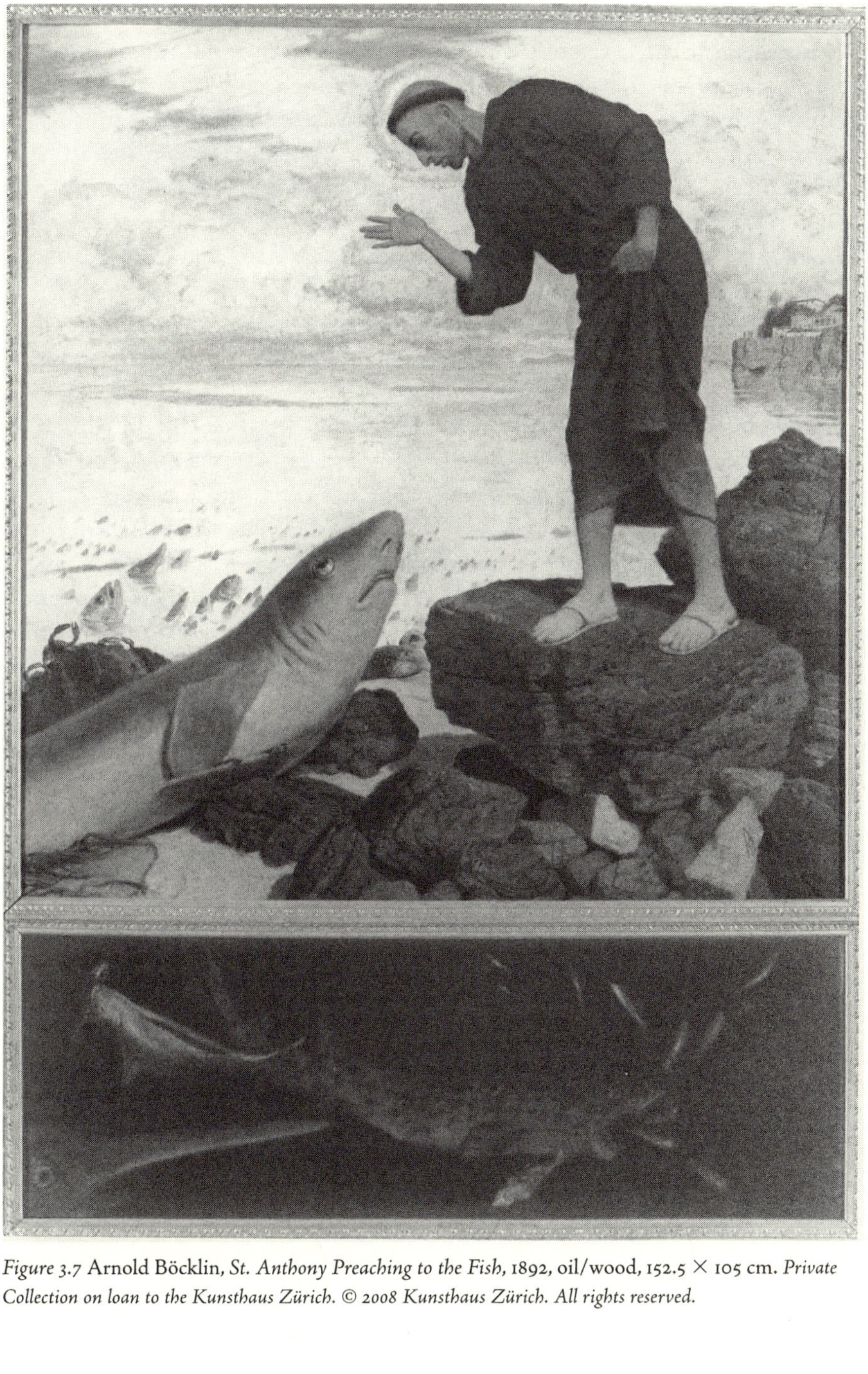

Figure 3.7 Arnold Böcklin, *St. Anthony Preaching to the Fish*, 1892, oil/wood, 152.5 × 105 cm. *Private Collection on loan to the Kunsthaus Zürich.*

cords with Haeckel's beliefs and, in combination with the ironic tone, are in the spirit of Heinrich Heine's writings and Busch's own parody of the saint published in 1870.[66] The predella, as Andrea Linnebach has observed, recalls the shape and lighting of an aquarium, and was probably based on the sea aquarium in the famous Zoological Station in Naples, which opened in 1874. The founder Dohrn was a student of Haeckel's and a friend of Böcklin's, who visited the research center. The aquarium, which contained numerous species, was designed for the general public to observe the daily behavior of aquatic animals. Bölsche recommended it as a place to watch the bizarre mating habits of medusa and cuttlefish and compared the experience to reading Karl Immermann's *The Adventures of Baron Münchhausen* or traveling in Jules Verne's submarine boat.[67]

Many artists envisioned the primeval past as a chthonic land inhabited by semi-animalized humans. Klinger's drawing *Fox Hunt* (1874–1877; Leipzig), reproduced in an 1896 edition of *Pan*, depicted the brutal savagery of pack animals with man's links to nature determined by mutual barbarism. More frequently these connections were established through mythic hybrid forms (centaurs, satyrs, fauns) as artists seized upon earlier products of literary imagination that seemed to have uncannily anticipated evolutionary themes of transformation. Scenes of fighting centaurs proliferated, beginning with Böcklin's *Battle of the Centaurs* (1873; Kunstmuseum Basel), and continuing with Klinger's narrative of pursuit and combat over a dead rabbit in the etching cycle *Intermezzi* (1881) and von Stuck's numerous prints and paintings of fighting fauns during the 1880s and 1890s. Set in environments reminiscent of the glacial Pleistocene era as illustrated in natural history books, the images by Klinger and Böcklin were interpreted as visualizations of cosmological "elemental forces" when "Creation emerg[ed] from . . . chaos."[68] The relevance of hybrid creatures as subject matter was confirmed by the scientists themselves, as Thomas Huxley acknowledged the prescience of Ovid and Sterne published a photograph of an Indian boy born with a tail. In Nietzsche's revisionist view of a Dionysian Greece in *The Birth of Tragedy* (1872), the centaur was posited as the embodiment of primal drives that still operated in modern man.[69]

"Our primordial birthplace": The Sea as Terror, Desire, and Evolutionary Origin

The artistic interest in the origins of human behavior, Darwin's emphasis on sexual selection, and Haeckel's specialized research on marine life came together in depictions of carnal drives that invariably were staged in aquatic environments. For Darwin, Haeckel, and their nineteenth-century scientific predecessors, the sea had replaced Eden as "our primordial birthplace, a shore washed by the tides."[70] Much of Haeckel's discussion of aquatic organisms, as with the medusa and radiolarians, centered on propagation and generation, while his illustrations of them in *Art Forms in Nature,* and in earlier books, frequently featured reproductive organs and processes that are explained in the descriptive texts. Haeckel presented sexuality in reductively materialist ways that stressed its profound significance to species survival and embedded human desire in the context of other natural affinities. Bölsche's book, as mentioned, went further in inviting readers to participate in nature through their amorous activities. Haeckel was more blunt, stating that "if we consider what an extraordinarily important part is everywhere played by the relation of the two sexes in organic nature, in the vegetable kingdom, as in animal and human life . . . we cannot over-estimate this retracing of 'love' to its primitive source, to the power of attraction between two differing cells," by which he meant "the sperm-cell and the egg-cell."[71]

Visualizations of erotic encounters by artists like Böcklin and Klinger portray couples, whether contemporary or mythic hybrids (tritons, sirens, and mermaids), in passionate embrace on the shore, in the surf, or submerged under oceanic depths. Böcklin's *Triton and Nereid,* 1873–1874, established the standard, and was the first painting by this artist to be seen by Klinger when it was purchased for the Berlin Nationalgalerie in 1875 (figure 3.8). In conjunction with his painting *Battle of the Centaurs,* set on a mountaintop, Böcklin vividly captured the imagined instinctual life of prehistoric creatures in locations of geographical and geological cosmological significance. Not surprisingly, Haeckel once confided to Darwin that "the Alps and the sea have always been the two things which have had the greatest influence on me."[72] Art critics and scientists responded to Böcklin's images within a culture shaped by evolutionary theory. Otto Julius Bierbaum noted that the sea in *Triton and Nereid* represented "life, love and the forces of nature," while Bölsche imagined the painter's mermaids with corsage "bouquets of gay medusae."[73] Other viewers were more mindful of the darker mood occasionally present in Böcklin's works and the reality of the ocean's destructive forces. Carus Sterne praised the verism of his sea serpents and the behavior of the creatures: "How wonderfully this cold, dripping female . . . conveys the nature of the sea; how merciless is the gaze of those cold, black, soulless eyes, just as merciless as the man-annihilating sea."[74]

This painting, and many prints by Klinger, reflects the extent to which modern scientific research merged in art with former associations of the sea as a site of mystery, danger, and female embodiment. In some ways, evolution-

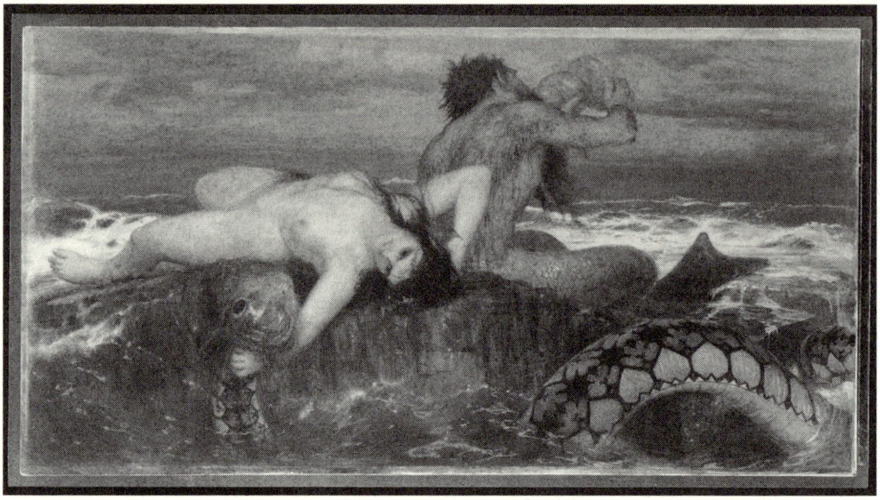

Figure 3.8 Arnold Böcklin, *Triton and Nereid*, 1873–1874, oil/canvas, 105 × 194 cm. *Bayerische Staatsgemäldesammlungen, Schackgalerie, München.*

ary theory had only served to strengthen those tropes. In *Arabian Corals*, Haeckel commented on the "mysterious ocean floor" and qualified his praise for the coral gardens, which surpassed the "legendary splendor of the magical Gardens of the Hesperides" with a cautionary note on the continuing "struggle for existence" (he mentioned poisonous plants) in the deep sea where "horror and danger" abound.[75] In Germany, these ideas derived from a romantic heritage. Klinger's (and Böcklin's) frequent pairing of women and marine creatures like crocodiles and crustaceans (or women and men/animals near bodies of water) evoke anxiety and reflect Darwin as filtered through the lens of Heine, both in his North Sea poetry and his book *Elemental Spirits*. In his discussion of the bewitching properties of nixies (water spirits), Heine noted that "Germans harbored a special love for all manner of water beings," and that submarine depths possessed "voluptuous hidden marvels and occult horrors."[76] The legacy of Klinger's visions of aquatic temptresses, such as the *Title Page* of his series *Etched Sketches* (1879; Leipzig) and the fish-eyed *Nymph* (c. 1879–1880 (lost), reproduced in *Jugend*, 1897 (Nr. 2, p. 29) can be traced to Kubin's drawings of primeval tropical forests populated by beauties and beasts and his grotesque group couplings of women, octopi, and sea serpents (as in *The Sucker*, c. 1903–1904; Oberösterreichisches Landesmuseum, Linz). Jugendstil designers produced more aestheticized and sanitized renderings of mermaids and amphibious creatures that, nonetheless, reflected a similar merger of natural history and myth.[77]

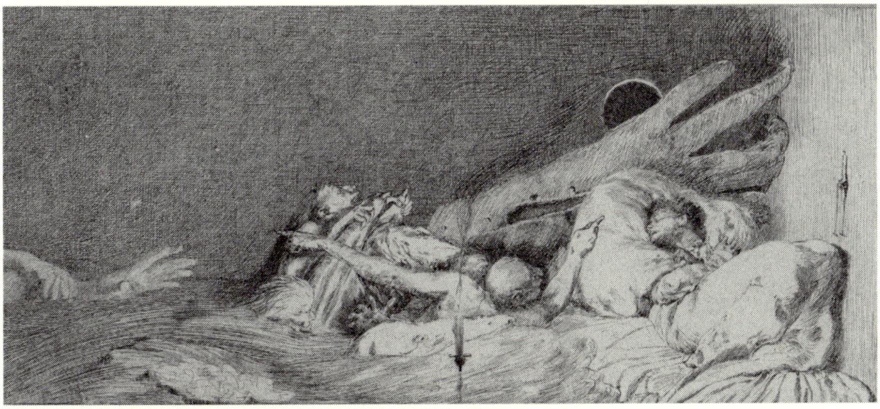

Figure 3.9 Max Klinger, *Fears* (from *The Glove*), 1878 (etching, 1881), ink drawing, 11.7 × 24 cm. *Stiftung Preussischer Kulturbesitz, Berlin, Bildarchiv Preussischer Kulturbesitz / Art Resource, NY.*

Klinger and Kubin most demonstrably incorporated Haeckel and Darwin within the philosophy of Schopenhauer and the literature of Jean Paul, Hoffmann, and Heine to produce works in which water and the sea were the site of terror, desire, the evolutionary past, and the unconscious.[78] Klinger's *Glove* series (ten etchings), which chronicles a tale of amorous longing, visualizes carnal desire through the extinct Pterosaur (a flying reptile) whose fossils recently had been excavated in Bavarian quarries in 1859. The creature first appears amidst ocean waves in *Triumph* and returns, together with other monsters, in *Fears* in an erotic water-flooded nightmare (figure 3.9). These scenes play upon Schopenhauer's equation of underwater depths with the *Will*, his description of sexuality as a "malevolent demon"—a notion reinforced by Haeckel, who stated that love was "a devouring flame . . . which has caused more misery, vice, and crime, than all the other evils of the human race"—and romantic literature in which instinctual drives and cosmic horrors were conveyed by visions of beasts emerging from the sea.[79] In Jean Paul's novel *Flegeljahre* [*Fledging Years*], for example, the hero Walt suffers through a nightmare of cosmological origins with a "shining sea . . . full of giant animals who slept, but in their sleep spoke, and told one another of an ancient hot hunger and thirst for blood."[80] Similar experiences in the writings of Hoffmann and Heine frequently were activated by sexual anxieties. Aquatic dream scenes of macabre metamorphic forms occur in Hoffmann's stories "Ritter Gluck" and "The Mines of Falun," and Heine's tale "The Hartz Journey" and his novella *Florentine Nights*, where "out of the red waves of blood" appeared "monsters of incredible hideousness, crocodiles with bats' wings, serpents with stags' horns, [and] monkeys capped with conch shells."[81]

Kubin's Primer of *Darwinismus*

Kubin, more than any other artist, realized Heine's dark, submarine depths and created a body of work that is virtually a compendium of Haeckel's *Darwinismus,* albeit a disturbingly grotesque one. Kubin's imagery spans primates, primitive man, primeval forests, microscopic and marine organisms, crystals, corals, and embryos. Under the influence of Schopenhauer and Klinger, whose *Glove* series triggered hallucinations in the young artist, Kubin visualized the aquatic origins of life in *The Hour of Birth,* 1901 (Leopold Museum, Vienna) as a baby's leap into a nihilistic void facilitated by a hybrid crustacean midwife with menacing sharp claws.[82] In other drawings, such as *Fertility* (1901–1902; Leopold Museum, Vienna), a scene of underwater birthing, and *The Egg* (1900–1901; Albertina, Vienna), evolutionary growth and progress are mocked repeatedly: pregnancy and fetal forms are monstrous and life is the gateway to death.

In 1906, Kubin completed a remarkable series of paintings that begin with underwater tableaus and develop into scenes of metamorphic forms set against darkened, indeterminate spaces. The submarine pictures, such as *From the Deep Sea,* 1906, portray murky depths populated by corals, fish, jellyfish, bristle worms, crustaceans, and other creatures, feathered or with tentacles, less easy to identify (figure 3.10). In some of the settings, organic shapes merge with witches and mythic beasts. Described by Kubin as "underwater landscapes reminiscent of large aquariums," the hazy environments and semiformed plants and animals are riffs on natural history illustrations such as Haeckel's (see figure 3.1) that visualize evolution at its mysterious source.[83] These paintings reflect Kubin's familiarity with Redon's series of underwater lithographs for Flaubert's *Temptation of St. Anthony* (1896) and Jugendstil imagery by designers in Munich, where he lived from 1898 to 1906. The composite hybrids appear to be culled from individual details in scientific illustrations found in publications such as Haeckel's *Art Forms in Nature,* Bölsche's *Evolution of Nature,* Brehm's *The Life of Animals,* and the magazine *Die Gartenlaube,* but assembled as organisms that belie the rational order of systemization and symmetry that are at the heart of Haeckel's work.[84]

Kubin's deep-sea pictures soon gave way to more abstracted images that were inspired by the artist's study of microscopic forms and his dissatisfaction with observed nature. He wrote that the "fairylike structures of delicate plant and animal substances" seen under a microscope had an "explosive" effect on his imagination, producing work that rejected "organized nature" in favor of "compositions formed out of bundles of veils and beams, of crystals or shell-like fragments, of bits of flesh or skin, leaf patterns and a

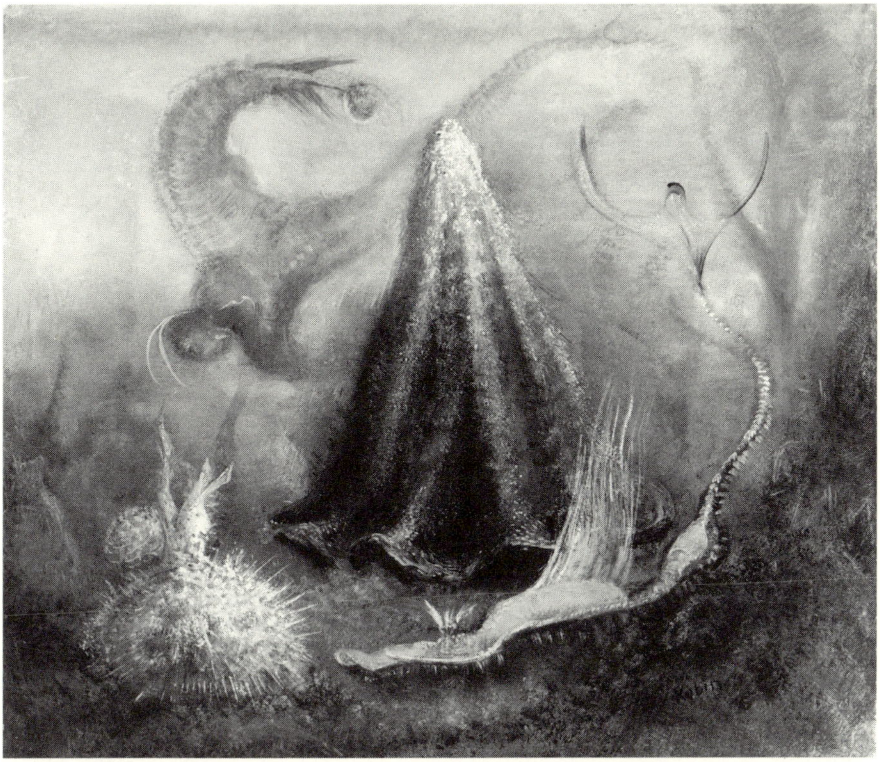

Figure 3.10 Alfred Kubin, *From the Deep Sea*, c. 1906, tempera, 32.3 × 36.2 cm. *Albertina Museum, Vienna. © 2008 Eberhard Spangenberg / Artists Rights Society (ARS), New York / VG Bild-Kunst, Bonn.*

thousand other things."[85] Liberated from the descriptive functions of art, he created creatures that are, in some cases, horrific fusions (with titles like *Chrysalis* and *Metamorphosis*) that evoke the helmet shapes of radiolarian, medusa, insects, and giant fish. The black backgrounds convey primordial states and recall those used in *Art Forms in Nature* and in Redon's lithographs. In other paintings, such as *Thunderstorm*, 1906, shell-rock materials explode in a cosmological moment of genesis, compared in a contemporary review to popular science illustrations and evolutionary theory (figure 3.11).[86] Visible to the far right are haloed circular shapes resembling Haeckel's illustrations of monera and radiolarians. *Thunderstorm* demonstrates the impact of Haeckel's microscopic imagery on emerging abstraction, evidenced also in another scene of cosmological origins, the *Balls of Bacilli* (c. 1900) by Obrist's student Hans Schmithals, to which the artist appended Haeckel's description of the nebular, or "gas theory," hypothesis regarding the origin of the universe.[87]

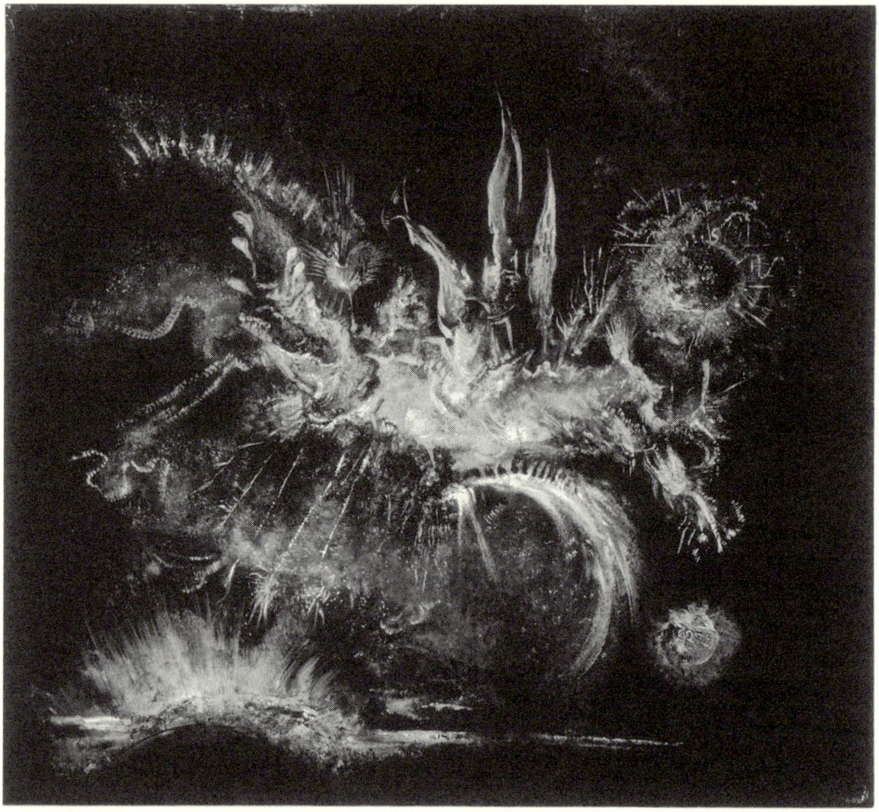

Figure 3.11 Alfred Kubin, *Thunderstorm*, 1906, gouache, 33.8 × 36.4 cm. *Städtische Galerie im Lenbachhaus, Munich.* *© 2008 Eberhard Spangenberg / Artists Rights Society (ARS), New York / Bild-Kunst, Bonn.*

In his early work, Kubin, together with the other artists discussed, found in *Darwinismus* a message that inspired an art of alienation, ambiguity, and debased instinctual behavior. Rejecting the progressive optimism of popular science writers and the reassuring monism of many professional scientists, these artists produced images of doubt and disenchantment that twisted the "new aesthetic sense" envisioned by Haeckel and the poeticization of nature espoused by Bölsche into cautionary warnings about the limits of evolutionary ascent.[88] Selectively inspired by aspects of Darwinian theory, their art looks forward to Surrealism and bears witness to German Romantic explorations of the "night side of nature."

NOTES

I would like to thank Barbara Larson for inviting me to contribute to this anthology, and Olaf Breidbach, who graciously spent time discussing Haeckel with me in Jena.

1. Charles Darwin, in Francis Darwin, ed., *The Life and Letters of Charles Darwin*, 3 vols. (New York: D. Appleton & Co., 1896), vol. 2, 270.

2. This included *Origin of Species, The Descent of Man, The Expression of Emotions in Man and Animals*, his travel accounts, and his work on insect-eating plants, together with over two hundred illustrations and a photograph of the author. Darwin was amazed at the productivity of German scientists, remarking that "in Germany a catalogue or bibliography on 'Darwinismus' has appeared every year or two." Cited in Paul Julian Weindling, *Darwinism and Social Darwinism in Imperial Germany: The Contribution of the Cell Biologist Oscar Hertwig (1849–1922)* (Stuttgart: Gustav Fischer Verlag, 1991), 26.

3. For an illustrated article on the Berlin aquarium, which featured fifty microscopes with prepared slides, see "Das Mikroscopische Aquarium in Berlin," in the Leipzig *Illustrirte Zeitung*, 10 February 1877, 111 and 113. The illustrations from this article are reproduced in Lynn Gamwell, *Exploring the Invisible: Art, Science, and the Spiritual* (Princeton, N.J.: Princeton University Press, 2002), 50. For the best analysis of scientific popularization and Darwinism in Germany, see Andreas W. Daum, *Wissenschaftspopularierung im 19. Jahrhundert: Bürgerliche Kultur, naturwissenschaftliche Bildung und die deutsche Öffenlichkeit, 1848–1914* (Munich: R. Oldenbourg, 1998); Alfred Kelly, *The Descent of Darwin: The Popularization of Darwinism in Germany, 1860–1914* (Chapel Hill: University of North Carolina Press, 1981); and Eve-Marie Engels, "Charles Darwin in der deutschen Zeitschriftenliteratur des 19. Jahrhunderts—Ein Forschungsbericht," in *Evolutionsbiologie von Darwin bis Heute*, ed. Rainer Brömer, Uwe Hossfeld, and Nicholaas A. Rupke, 19–57 (Berlin: Verlag für Wissenschaft und Bildung, 2000). Engels' essay provides a comprehensive bibiobiographical list of articles on Darwin in the German press. Efforts by publishers of journals were motivated partly by a pedagogical (and democratic) mission to fill the gap left by a public education system that did not include scientific instruction in the curriculum.

4. The play was titled *The Darwinians*. See Henry Vizetelly, *Berlin under the New Empire*, 2 vols. (1879; reprint, New York: Greenwood Press, 1968), vol. 2, 255.

5. Robert J. Richards, "The Foundation of Ernst Haeckel's Evolutionary Project in Morphology, Aesthetics, and Tragedy," in *The Many Faces of Evolution in Europe, c. 1860–1914*, ed. Patrick Dassen and Mary Kemperiuk, 2 (Leuven: Peeters, 2005). "Die Rätsel" actually means "riddles," but translators have always followed the original English title, which is in keeping with the book's thesis that only one "riddle"—the law of substance—remains. Robert Richards' book, *The Tragic Sense of Life: Ernst Haeckel and the Struggle over Evolutionary Thought* (Chicago: University of Chicago Press, 2008), appeared after this essay was written, but it is now the most comprehensive and authoritative source in English for all information pertaining to Haeckel.

6. Olaf Breidbach, *Visions of Nature: The Art and Science of Ernst Haeckel* (Munich: Prestel, 2006), 95, mentions a trip in 1864 rather than 1866. Mario Di Gregorio lists three trips to England in 1866, 1875, and 1876 in *From Here to Eternity: Ernst Haeckel and Scientific Faith*

(Göttingen: Vandenhoeck & Ruprecht, 2005), 98. Richards describes the 1866 trip in *The Tragic Sense of Life*, 174.

7. These studies include Siegfried Wichmann, *Hermann Obrist: Wegbereiter der Moderne*, exh. cat. (Munich: Villa Stuck, 1968,); Wichmann, *Jugendstil Art Nouveau: Floral and Functional Forms* (Boston: Little, Brown and Co., 1984); Christopher Kockerbeck, *Ernst Haeckel's "Kunstformen der Nature" und ihr Einfluss auf die deutsche bildende Kunst der Jahrhundertwende* (Munich: Peter Lang, 1986); Rosemarie Mann, "Ernst Haeckel, Zoologie und Jugendstil," *Berichte zur Wissenschafts-Geschichte* 13 (1990): 1–11; Erika Krausse, "Haeckel: Promorphologie und 'evolutionistische' aesthetische Theorie, Konzept und Wirkung," in *Die Rezeption von Evolutionstheorien im 19, Jahrhundert*, ed. Eve-Marie Engels, 347–94 (Frankfurt a. M.: Suhrkampf, 1995); Krausse, "L'influence de Ernst Haeckel sur L'Art Nouveau," in *L'âme au Corps: arts et sciences 1793–1993*, exh. cat. (Paris: Galeries Nationales du Grand Palais, 1993), 342–50; Kurt Bayertz, "Biology and Beauty: Science and Aesthetics in *Fin-de-siècle* Germany," in *Fin de siècle and its Legacy*, ed. Mikuláš Teich and Roy Porter, 276–95 (Cambridge: Cambridge University Press, 1990); Reto Niggl, "Hermann Obrist: Spitzenwirbelspirale," in *Wege in die Moderne: Jugendstil in München 1896–1914*, exh. cat., ed. Hans Ottomeyer, 23–37 (Munich and Berlin: Staatliche Museen Kassel, 1977); and Kai Buchholz et al., *Die Lebensreform: Entwürfe zur Neugestaltung von Leben und Kunst um 1900*, exh. cat., 2 vols. (Darmstadt: Institut Mathildenhöhe, 2001). This last catalogue includes articles on Haeckel and monism. Daniel Gasmann has discussed the influence of Haeckel on the Expressionists (Marc, Klee, and Kandinsky), Gauguin, Matisse, and Berlin Dada. See *Haeckel's Monism and the Birth of Fascist Ideology* (Frankfurt A. M.: Peter Lang., 1998), 76–100. Gasmann's comments on monism and Edvard Munch largely reiterate information found in Reinhold Heller, *Munch: His Life and Work* (London: John Murray, 1984), 63. For a recent discussion of Munch's monist beliefs, see Patricia Berman, "Edvard Munch's 'Modern Life of the Soul,'" in *Edvard Munch: The Modern Life of the Soul*, exh. cat. (New York: Museum of Modern Art, 2006), 34–51.

8. The project to "re-enchant" nature (the reference is from Max Weber) or "reconcile" science with a more harmonious worldview is discussed in Daum, *Wissenschafts popularierung*, 464–67, and Daum, "Das versöhnende Element in der neuen Weltanschauung: Entwicklungsoptimismus, Naturästhetik und Harmoniedenken im populäwissenschaftlichen Diskurs der Naturkunde um 1900," in *Von Weltbildwandel zur Weltanschauungsanalyse: Krisenwahrnehmung und Krisenbewältigung um 1900*, ed. Volker Drehsen und Walter Sparn, 203–15 (Berlin Akademie, 1996). Kurt Bayertz considers this phenomenon, embodied especially in monism, as an "attempt to ward off the threat" of a de-spiritualized science. See Bayertz, "Biology and Beauty," 276, 285–90. Bölsche's book was translated by Cyril Brown as *Love-Life in Nature: The Story of the Evolution of Love* (New York: Albert & Charles Boni, 1926).

9. Haeckel wrote that "Man is not above nature, but in nature." *The Evolution of Man*, 2 vols. (London: C. Kegan Paul & Co., 1879), vol. 2, 456.

10. The phrase "dark side of nature" derives from Gotthilf Heinrich Schubert's book, *Ansichten von der Nachtseite der Naturwissenschaften [Views from the Night (or Dark) Side of Nature]*, published in Dresden in 1808. Haeckel used the phrase in connection with the negative side of the "struggle for life" in *Monism as Connecting Religion and Science: The Confession of Faith of a Man of Science*, trans. J. Gilchrist (London: Adam and Charles Black,

1894), 74. For Nietzsche's engagement with Darwin, see John Richardson, *Nietzsche's New Darwinism* (Oxford: Oxford University Press, 2004).

11. For a study of evolutionary currents in Romanticism, see Robert J. Richards, *The Romantic Conception of Life: Science and Philosophy in the Age of Goethe* (Chicago: University of Chicago Press, 2002).

12. Wilhelm Bölsche, *Haeckel: His Life and Work*, trans. Joseph McCabe (Philadelphia: Georg W. Jacobs & Co., 1909), 178. The first German edition was published in 1900.

13. This has led Peter Bowler to label Haeckel, along with Thomas Huxley, a "pseudo-Darwinist" and a prime example of nineteenth-century biological historicism. See *The Non-Darwinian Revolution: Reinterpreting a Historical Myth* (Baltimore: The Johns Hopkins University Press, 1988), 96. Di Gregorio prefers the term "semi-Darwinist." See "The Importance of Being Ernst: Thomas Henry Huxley zwischen Karl Ernst von Baer und Ernst Haeckel," in *Die Rezeption von Evolutionstheorien im 19. Jahrhundert*, 197. Kurt Bayertz considers Haeckel's views to be conservative and essentially "pre-Darwinian." See "Die Deszendenz des Schönen: Darwinisierende Ästhetik im Ausgang des 19. Jahrhunderts," in *Fin de Siècle: Zu Naturwissenschaft und Literatur der Jahrhundertwende im deutsch-skandinavischen Kontext*, ed. Klaus Bohnen, 96 (Munich and Copenhagen: Wilhelm Verlag, 1984). Breidbach has also observed that Haeckel's ideology was not revolutionary, and that he turned Darwinism on its head Breidbach, *Visions of Nature*, 247. According to Weindling, *Darwinismus* "did not entail a pessimistic philosophy of purposeless conflict." "Ernst Haeckel, Darwinismus and the Secularization of Nature," in *History, Humanity and Evolution: Essays for John C. Greene*, ed. James R. Moore, 311 (Cambridge: Cambridge University Press, 1989).

14. Haeckel, *The Evolution of Man*, vol. 2, 457; and *The Riddle of the Universe*, trans. Joseph McCabe (1899; reprint, Buffalo: Prometheus Books, 1992), 216 and 224.

15. Haeckel, *Die Radiolarien* (Berlin: Georg Reimer, 1862), 232, translated and quoted in Olaf Breidbach, "The Most Charming Creatures: Haeckel's 1862 Monograph on Radiolarians," in *Art Forms from the Ocean* (Munich: Prestel, 2005), 11.

16. Darwin to Haeckel, 19 November 1868, in Darwin, *The Life and Letters*, 286.

17. Haeckel, *Generelle Morphologie der Organismen*, vol. 1 (Berlin: Georg Reimer, 1866), 2; and vol. 2, 446–47; and Haeckel, *The Evolution of Man*, vol. 1, 102.

18. As Olaf Breidbach has observed, this allowed Haeckel to continue to use classic taxonomic systems of comparative anatomy, modernized by virtue of their new phylogenetic meaning. Breidbach, *Visions of Nature*, 95–96.

19. Haeckel, *Generelle Morphologie*, vol. 1, 183. The same narrative is included in *The History of Creation*, vol. 1, 404–406. As Haeckel notes, his theories were based on earlier research by Oken regarding *Urschleim* (primordial slime), Max Schultze's work on protoplasm, or cell substance, and the cell theory of Schleiden and Schwann. Haeckel, *The History of Creation*, vol. 1, 98-100.

20. Haeckel, *The History of Creation*, vol. 1, 407. He wrote that "the whole body of these most simple of all organisms . . . consists, in fact, of only a single chemical combination, and is as perfectly simple in its structure as any crystal, which consists of a single inorganic combination."

21. These included the two-volume *Das System der Medusen* (1879–1980) and four volumes of research on radiolarian, medusa, siphonophoria, and keratosa published as part of the British deep-sea H.M.S. *Challenger* expedition report (1882–1889).

22. Haeckel, *The History of Creation*, vol. 2, 179. Haeckel named two medusa species after Anna as a memorial tribute following her tragic early death in 1864. His study in his house in Jena, called the Villa Medusa, was later filled with gifts from friends who created pillows, tables, and cabinets decorated with jellyfish. Medusa eggs produce polyps of the preceding class that form buds that detach themselves from the stationary polyp and become free-swimming medusa. For Haeckel, this amounted to a reenactment of the original phylogenetic process.

23. Darwin discusses this embryonic correspondence in *The Descent of Man* (New York: Modern Library, nd), 411. Images of embryos (tortoise, hen, dog, and man) first appeared in *The History of Creation*. The larger illustration (fish to man) from *The Evolution of Man* was reproduced in Otto Zacharias, "Ernst Haeckel's *Anthropogenie*," 4-part review, *Illustrirte Zeitung*, part 4 (20 February 1875, 140). The most complete account of the embryo controversy, which was revived after the turn of the century, can be found in Reinhard Gursch, *Die Illustrationen Ernst Haeckels zur Abstammungs- und Entwicklungsgeschichte* (Marburg: P. D. Lang, 1981) and in Richards, *The Tragic Sense of Life*, 277–312. Haeckel continued to reference embryos in *Art Forms in Nature*; plate 95 juxtaposes the larval forms of living echinoderms with fossilized versions from the Paleozoic era. See Olaf Breidbach, ed., *Art Forms in Nature: The Prints of Ernst Haeckel* (Munich: Prestel, 1998), 13.

24. Haeckel used this phrase in *The Riddles of the Universe* (341). This print was the frontispiece for *The Evolution of Man* (1874). Karl Clausberg regards the choice of Zeus, rather than Christ, as a deliberate rejection by Haeckel of Christian authority. He compares the illustration to the tradition of physiognomical metamorphosis in works by Pieter Camper and Johann Caspar Lavater. See "Psychogenes und Historismus: Verworfene Leitbilder und übergangene Kontroversen," in *Natur der Ästhetik—Ästhetik der Natur*, ed. Olaf Breidbach, 139–95 (Vienna: Springer, 1997). Haeckel's print is discussed within the context of other illustrations that demonstrate serial development in Julia Voss, *Darwins Bilder: Ansichten der Evolutionstheorie 1837–1874* (Frankfurt a. M.: Fischer Taschenbuch Verlag, 2007), chapter 3.

25. Darwin cited the *History of Creation* in *The Descent of Man*, 520, although Haeckel discussed human kinship with apes earlier in *Generelle Morphologie*, 435–37.

26. Haeckel, *Monism as Connecting Religion and Science*, 16. The final chapter of *Generelle Morphologie*, surprisingly, is titled "God in Nature." For a detailed discussion of his changing views of monism, see Niles R. Holt, "Ernst Haeckel's Monistic Religion," *Journal of the History of Ideas* 32 (1971): 265–80. The monist orientations of Haeckel, August Forel, and Wilhelm Ostwald are discussed by Olaf Breidbach in "Monismus um 1900—Wissenschaftspraxis oder Weltanschauung?" in *Welträtsel und Lebenswunde*, exh. cat. (Linz: Oberöstereiches Landesmuseum, 1998), 289–313. For a more comprehensive discussion, see Eric Paul Jacobsen, *From Cosmology to Ecology: The Monist World-View in Germany from 1770–1930* (Bern, Frankfurt a. M.: Peter Lang, 2005).

27. Haeckel, *Monism as Connecting Religion and Science*, 85.

28. Haeckel, "Zellseelen und Seelenzellen," *Deutsche Rundschau* 16 (1878): 59.

29. These ideas were first published in Bölsche, "Charles Darwin und die moderne Ästhetik," *Kunstwart* 1 (1888): 125.

30. Kelly, *The Discent of Darwin*, 55. See also his dissertation, "Between Poetry and Science: Wilhelm Bölsche as Scientific Popularizer" (Ph.D. diss, University of Wisconsin-Madison, 1975).

31. Daum, "Das versöhnende Element," 203 and 207.

32. Arthur Schopenhauer, *Parerga and Paralipomena,* vol. 2, trans. E. F. J. Payne (1851; reprint, Oxford: Clarendon Press, 1974), 210–11.

33. In a letter to his father dated 5 October 1875, Klinger mentioned an exchange of their Darwin books. The letter is published in Hans W. Singer, *Briefe von Max Klinger aus den Jahren 1874–1919* (Leipzig: E.A. Seemann, 1924), 13–14. For a more detailed discussion of Klinger and Darwinism, see Marsha Morton, "'Impulses and Desires': Klinger's Darwinism in Nature and Society," *Nineteenth-Century Art Worldwide: A Journal of Nineteenth-Century Visual Culture,* 2 (Spring 2003); online at www.19thc-artworldwide.org/spring_03/articles/mort.shtml.

34. Haeckel, *The Evolution of Man,* vol. 2, 738.

35. Haeckel, *The History of Creation,* vol. 2, 360.

36. Kelly, *The Decent of Darwin,* 22. Carus Sterne observed that scientists were the new priests of Europe in his book *Werden und Vergehen: Eine Entwicklungsgeschichte des Naturganzen,* 2 vols. (1876; reprint, Berlin: Gebrüder Borntraeger, 1901), vol. 1, 2.

37. Several types of anthropoids were identified in an article by M. Rapsilber, "Ernst Moritz Geyger," *Deutsche Kunst und Dekoration* 14 (1904): 364. A detail of an enlarged second version of *Darwinian Disputation,* dated 1890–1894, is reproduced on page 369.

38. Hans W. Singer, "Radierer unserer Zeit," *Die Kunst unserer Zeit* 7 (1896): 3. The etching, which is very rare, was reproduced in this article, opposite page 8. I would like to thank Mitchell Frank for calling my attention to this source.

39. For a nuanced examination of ape representation in the work of Meyerheim and Gabriel von Max, see Kai Artinger, "Der Beobachtete Mensch," *Münchner Jahrbuch der bildenden Kunst* 46 (1995): 163–74.

40. This itself was a new kind of anthropomorphism. Haeckel had maintained that "between the most highly developed animal souls, and the lowest developed human souls, there exists only a small quantitative, but no qualitative difference," in *The History of Creation,* vol. 2, 362. Darwin, of course, had made the same point, asserting that "the higher animals possess memory, attention, association, and even some imagination and reason" *Descent of Man,* 460.

41. Wundt, the Leipzig psychologist, continued through the 1890s to conduct experiments on animals' responses to stimuli in his laboratory. His earlier book was cited in Haeckel, *The History of Creation,* 365. Other explorations of animal sensibilities included Carus Sterne's *The Intellectual Life of Animals,* 1876, and Ludwig Büchner's *Love and Love-Life in the Animal World,* from 1879.

42. "Aus dem Tagebuch eines miocenen Anthropoiden," *Fliegende Blätter* 59 (1873): 137–39. The celebrated maternal instinct of apes was also caricatured by the end of the century in *Jugend* in an illustration, "The Untrustworthy Servant," where the nanny-ape has grabbed a screaming baby, climbed a tree, and is guzzling its bottle of milk. *Jugend* 1 (1896): 835.

43. Corinna Wodarz, *Symbol und Eros: Die Bildwelten Richard Müllers (1874–1954) mit dem Katalog des Gesamtwerks* (Göttingen: Duehrkohp & Radicke, 2002), fig. 13, p. 34. This publication contains numerous illustrations of Müller's prints related to natural history themes. Subsequent references to the Museum der bildenden Künste Leipzig will be designated as Leipzig.

44. Information and illustrations of the Berlin Aquarium can be found in Heinz-Georg Klös, *Tierwelt hinter Glas: Das Zoo-Aquarium Berlin* (Berlin: arani/Hauder & Spener, 1988), 9–50; and Ursula Harter, "Künstliche Ozeane oder die Erfindung des Aquariums," in *Das Meer im Zimmer: Von Tintenschnecken und Muscheltieren*, exh. cat. ed. Elisabeth Schlebrügge, 93–97 (Graz, Austria: Landesmuseum Joanneum Zoologie, 2005). The Aquarium was also famous as the inspirational source for a Jules Laforgue's poem incorporated in his short story *Salome*. Information about M'pungu can be found in Dr. Falkenstein, "M-pungu," *Die Gartenlaube* 24 (1876): 557–58, with a page of illustrations of the gorilla that include images of him playing and eating.

45. Margaret Mary Richter, "Gabriel Max: The Artist, the Darwinist, and the Spiritualist" (Ph.D. diss., New York University, 1998), 311. After von Max's death, the collection was purchased by the city of Mannheim and is today in the Reiss Museum. For a discussion, see Axel von Gagern, "Vor Fünfzig Jahren: Die Erwerbung der Sammlung Gabriel von Max," *Mannheimer Hett* 2 (1967): 20–28. An installation photograph (c.1885) while the objects were still in Max's home is reproduced in Harald Siebenmorgen, "Gabriel von Max und die Moderne," in *Festschrift für Johannes Langner*, ed. Klaus Gereon Beuckers and Annemarie Jaeggi, 215–39, ill. 6 (Münster: Lit Verlag, 1997). This excellent article also reproduces the paintings *Self-Portrait with Ape* and *Apes as Geologists*, which are in a private collection (ills. 10 and 11). For an image of *Anthropological Lessons*, see Richter, "Gabriel Max," 702. Contemporary accounts of his collection list hundreds of skulls, human and animal skeletons, preserved organs, crustaceans, shells, and tribal objects from South America, Africa, and Austrailia. These are mentioned in an unsigned article, "Ausstellungen und Sammlungen," *Die Kunst für Alle* 7, no. 14 (1892): 219; and Richard Müller, "Ein Besuch bei Gabriel Max," *Beilage zur Bohemia*, 19 November 19, 1879, 1–3. Von Max's scientific collecting interests had begun as a child in Bohemia, when he acquired discarded objects from the natural history museum in Prague. See Siebenmorgen, "Gabriel von Max," 220–21; and Richter, "Gabriel Max," 52. Selections from von Max's collection were exhibited in *Darwin: Kunst und die Suche nach den Ursprüngen*, curated by Pamela Kort, Frankfurt a. M: Schirn Kunsthalle, 2009.

46. Artinger, "Der Brobachtete Mensch," 163.

47. Agathon Klemt, "Gabriel Max und seine Werke," *Die Graphische Künste* 9 (1886–1887): 1–12 and 25–36; translated in Richter, "Gabriel Max," 305.

48. Haeckel, *The Evolution of Man*, 183. For a detailed account of Dubois' discovery, the painting, and the artist's relationship with Haeckel, see Erika Krausse, "Pithecanthropus erectus Dubois (1891) in Evolutionsbiologie und Kunst," in *Evolutionsbiologie von Darwin bis Heute*, 69–87.

49. Haeckel, *The Last Link: Our Present Knowledge of the Descent of Man* (London: Adam and Charles Black, 1898), 26. This book was the publication of a speech Haeckel had delivered in Cambridge, England, at the Fourth International Congress of Zoology.

50. The two men frequently corresponded and later collaborated in 1903 on a final plate for *Art Forms of Nature* (titled "Apotheosis of Evolutionary Thought") depicting various apes with a female nude in a forest grotto. According to Haeckel, it was rejected by the printer because of technical difficulties, but it seems to have been very inconsistent with the character of the other illustrations. For an account of this project, see Richter, "Gabriel Max," 314–16. The drawing is reproduced in Buchholz et al., *Die Lebensreform*, 572 and Krausse, 83.

51. Bruno Stern, "Pithecanthropus Alalus. Gemälde von Professor Gabriel Max," *Die Kunst unserer Zeit* 5 (1894): 56; and Franz Hermann Meissner, "Gabriel Max," *Die Kunst unserer Zeit* 20 (1899): 19. Max originally titled the painting *Pithecanthropus europäus (alalus)*. (Krausse, 79).

52. Sterne, *Werden und Vergehen*, vol. 2, 324–25; and Bölsche, *Die Entwicklungsgeschichte der Natur*, vol. 2 (Berlin: Neudamm J. Neumann, 1894–1896), 105.

53. Meissner makes the connection between Max and Böcklin in "Gabriel Max," 19.

54. Stern, "Pithecanthropus Alalus," 56.

55. Siebenmorgen, "Gabriel von Max," 227–28. Artinger, "Der Beobachtete Mensch," 167, quotes a statement by Max's son Colombo. Max's association of life with misery is also evident in the paintings he did of his dead ape, titled *Schmerzvergessen* (*Forgotten Pain*). His embrace of Schopenahuer is discussed in an article by Adolf Kohut, which was based on notes provided by Max: "Gabriel Max," *Westermanns Monatshefte* 54 (1883): 173–85, esp. 174.

56. Information about Munich activities, and Max's involvement with them, can be found in Corinna Treitel, *A Science for the Soul: Occultism and the Genesis of the German Modern* (Baltimore: The Johns Hopkins University Press, 2004), 40–50 and 110–12.

57. Kubin was hypnotized and experienced visions, as did Hermann Obrist. Klinger and his friend Hermann Prell attended a private séance with the notorious Henry Slade in Berlin in December 1877. A detailed account of the evening was provided by Prell in his unpublished memoirs, "Annalen Meinen Lebens," vol. 1, 13–14. These are located in the Sächsisches Hauptstaatsarchiv in Dresden. Kubin's experience with hypnosis triggered hallucinations and suicidal impulses. See Alfred Kubin, *Aus Meinem Leben* (1911; reprint, Munich: Ellermann Verlag, 1974), 16–17. For an English translation, see Kubin, *Alfred Kubin's Autobiography*, trans. Denver Lindley (New York: Galerie St. Etienne and Crown Publishers, 1968), xxii–xxiv.

58. Schopenhauer, *Parerga and Paralipomena*, vol. 1, 266–68 and 299. Haeckel clearly thought otherwise and took pains to distinguish his monist research on animal souls from mystical beliefs and spiritualism in general, and from the "fraud" Slade and du Prey in particular. See Haeckel, "Zellseelen und Seelenzellen," 42, and *The Riddle of the Universe*, 304–305.

59. Nicolaus Mann, *Gabriel Max: Eine kunsthistorische Skizze* (Leipzig: J.J. Weber, 1890), 30, trans. and quoted in Richter, "Gabriel Max," 27. Mann was the pen name of Lehmann.

60. Illustrated in Richter, "Gabriel Max," 704.

61. See, for example, the Pterosaur in Klinger's *Glove* cycle from 1878 (Leipzig), the bat and beetle in Müller's two drawings, *Nightmares*, 1903 (Leipzig), and numerous hybrid monsters and reptiles in Kubin's hallucinatory visions, as in the drawing *Nightmare*, c.1904 (Dichand Collection, Vienna).

62. Haeckel, *The History of Creation*, vol. 1, 19–20.

63. Haeckel, *Monism as Connecting Religion and Science*, 73–74,

64. His comments on the scientist and philosopher can be found in Joseph Kraus, *Wilhelm Busch* (Reinbek bei Hamburg: Rowohlt, 2001), 32. For a discussion of Busch's work in the context of Darwin and monism, see David Kunzle, *The History of the Comic Strip* (Berkeley: 1990), University of California Press, 231–36.

65. Haeckel, *The Evolution of Man*, vol. 1, 112.

66. These parallels have also been noted by Harter, "Kunstliche Ozeane," 104, and Andrea

Linnebach, *Arnold Böcklin und die Antike* (Munich: Hirmer, 1991), 59–60. The painting's Darwinian associations are also discussed by Winfried Ranke in "Muss ein 'Deutsch-Römer' Idealist sein?" in *'In uns selbst liegt Italien': Die Kunst der Deutsch-Römer,* ed. Christoph Heilmann, 72–74 (Munich: Hirmer, 1988).

67. Bölsche, *Love-Life in Nature,* 295. Information and illustrations of the station, which was located on the coast, appeared in several newspapers and journals. Dohrn maintained close contacts with artists, purchasing sculptures by Adolf von Hildebrandt and commissioning Hans von Marées to paint murals in the library. Both Klee and Picasso visited it in the early twentieth century. For more on Böcklin and Dohrn, who is portrayed as a sea creature in Böcklin's painting *Play in the Waves* (1888), see Linnebach, *Arnold Böcklin,* 58–61; Harter, "Kunstliche Ozeane," 97–104; and *Anton Dohrn und die zoologische Station in Neapel,* ed. Hans-Reiner Simon (Frankfurt a. M: Edition Erbrich, 1980). This volume reprints original essays by Dohrn and letters from his scientific colleagues.

68. Unsigned article, "Centaurenkampf," *Ueber Land und Meer* 49 (1875): 972. quoted and translated in Hans Henrik Brummer, "The Böcklin Case Revisited," in *Kingdom of the Soul: Symbolist Art in Germany 1870–1920,* exh. cat. (Frankfurt a. M., Schirn Kunsthalle, 2000), 31.

69. Thomas Huxley, *Zoological Evidences as to Man's Place in Nature* (London: Williams and Norgate, 1863), 1; and Sterne, *Werden und Vergehen,* vol. 2, 327. Sterne discussed in detail the plausibility of hybrid animals in his article on Arnold Böcklin. See Sterne, "Arnold Böcklin's Fabelwesen im Lichte der organischen Formenlehre," *Die Gegenwart* 37 (1890): 21–25. Sterne cited medical reports by Greek military physicians recording army recruits with partially formed foot-hoofs. He also drew connections between Böcklin's hybrids, Dürer's images of dragons, and Goethe's poem "Metamorphosis of Animals."

70. Darwin, *The Descent of Man,* 524.

71. Haeckel, *The Evolution of Man,* vol. 2, 393–94.

72. Haeckel to Darwin, 10 August 1864, quoted in Di Gregorio, *From Here to Eternity,* 94.

73. Otto Julius Bierbaum, "Schacks Böcklin-Galerie. Bilder in Worten," *Das Magazin für Literatur,* 1893, translated in Brummer, "The Böcklin Case Revisited," 32, and Bölsche, *Love-Life in Nature,* vol. 1, 230. He wrote: "Is there actually a Böcklin man of the sea living in the depths of the crystal palaces of the ocean, who in his leisure moments makes bouquets of gay medusae to pin on the corsage of his green-eyed nixy love?"

74. Sterne, "Arnold Böcklin's Fabelwesen," 24-25, translated in Brummer, "The Böcklin Case Revisited," 32, and discussed in Linnebach, *Arnold Böcklin,* 56–57.

75. Haeckel, *Arabische Korallen* (Berlin: Georg Reimer, 1876), 1, 33, and 34. As mentioned earlier, he invariably described the medusa as having the female attributes of delicacy and beauty.

76. Heinrich Heine, *Elementary Spirits in Germany,* vol. 11, in *The Works of Heinrich Heine,* trans. Charles Godfrey Leland (New York: Croscup and Sterling, 1920), 149. For further discussion, see George S. Williamson, *The Longing for Myth in Germany* (Chicago: University of Chicago Press, 2004), 112–16. Heine derived much of his material on nature spirits from tales (*Deutschen Sagen*) published by the Brothers Grimm. The impact of Heine on Böcklin is explored by Linnebach in the second chapter of her book.

77. For an excellent discussion of these water-female images (including examples by

Heinrich Vogeler and Gustav Klimt) and their predecessors in German art and literature, read Jost Hermand, "Undinen-Zauber: Zum Frauenbild des Jugendstils," in *Jugendstil*, ed. Hermand, 469–94 (Darmstadt: Wissenschaftliche Buchgesellschaft, 1971).

78. The interest in these authors by Klinger and Kubin is well documented in statements by the artists and in the literature about them. Klinger based his etching *Future III* (from the series *Eve and the Future*) on a passage from Jean Paul, while Kubin later illustrated Hoffmann's stories *Nachtstücke* [*Night Tales*] in 1913.

79. Schopenhauer, *The World as Will and Representation*, 2 vols., trans. E. F. J. Payne, (1819; reprint, New York: Dover, 1958), vol. 2, 534; and Haeckel, *The Evolution of Man*, vol. 2, 394.

80. This passage is reprinted in German with English commentary in J. W. Smeed, *Jean Paul's Dreams* (London: Oxford University Press, 1966), 98. Jean Paul was also a favorite author of Böcklin's.

81. Heine, *Florentine Nights*, trans. Leland (London: Methuen and Co., 1927), 33.

82. Kubin wrote that he found Schopenhauer's book *Parerga und Parilapomena* "gripping" and his philosophy of pessimism comforting. After seeing Klinger's *Glove* etchings, Kubin experienced visions of terrifying hybrid human-animals. See Kubin, *Aus Meinem Leben*, 16, 24, and 26. For a discussion of specific paleontological sources of Kubin's images, see Alexandra Karl, "'Naturfreund' or 'Naturfeind'? Darwinism in the Early Drawings of Alfred Kubin," in *Unmapped Countries: Biological Visions in Nineteenth-Century Literature and Culture*, ed. Anne-Julia Zweirlein, 117–32 (London: Anthem Press, 2005).

83. Ibid., 33.

84. *Die Gartenlaube* is referenced in Reudolf Leopold and Romana Schuler, ed., *Alfred Kubin: Aus meinen Reich [From My Realm] Masterworks of Drawing from the Leopold Museum, Vienna* (Ostfildern-Ruit: Hatje Cantz, 2002), 28. Kubin collected nearly seventy books on natural history, few of which are well known today. These included ten volumes of Brehm, Haeckel's student Wilhelm Haacke's *Die Schöpfung der Tierwelt* (Leipzig: Bibliographisches Institut, 1893), and Gustav Jaeger's *Das Leben im Wasser und das Aquarium* (Hamburg: Vereinsbuchhandlung, 1868). A typed, three-volume inventory of Kubin's library, prepared by Alfred Marks, is in the archives of the Oberösterreichisches Landesmuseum in Linz Austria ("Inventar der Bibliothek Alfred Kubin im Kubin-Haus des Landes Oberösterreich in Zwickledt/Wernstein").

85. Kubin, *Aus Neinem Leben*, 35.

86. Thirty-two of these tempera paintings were exhibited in Munich in 1907. The review in the Augsburg *Abendzeitung* emphasized evolutionary references and also compared the pictures to the horrors of Jules Verne. This article is quoted in Annegret Hoberg, ed., *Alfred Kubin, 1877-1959*, exh. cat., (Munich: Städtische Galerie im Lenbachhaus, 1990), 269.

87. For an illustration and discussion of this work, which is in a private collection, see Gamwell, *Exploring the Invisible*, 201 and Wichmann, *Jugendstil Art Nouveau*, 89.

88. Haeckel, *The Riddle of the Universe*, 341.

CHAPTER 4

Protoplasmania

Huxley, Haeckel, and the Vibratory Organism in Late Nineteenth-Century Science and Art

ROBERT MICHAEL BRAIN

LIFE, the popular name for the activity peculiar to protoplasm. This conception has been extended by analogy to phenomena different in kind, such as the activities of masses of water or of air, or of machinery, or by another analogy, to the duration of a composite structure, and by imagination to real or supposed phenomena such as the manifestations of incorporeal entities. From the point of view of exact science life is associated with matter, is displayed only by living bodies, by all living bodies, and is what distinguishes living bodies from bodies that are not alive.

—"Life," in *Encyclopedia Britannica*, 1911 edition.

The protoplasm develops to a point where it becomes a being . . . Human beings wished to see, so developed eyes—to hear, so ears . . . to communicate, so vocal chords came.

—Edvard Munch, *Notebook*, 1906.

The history of nineteenth-century science often has been told as a tale of two ideas—energy and evolution—born in similar circumstances and leading parallel but separate existences. Yet in the late decades of that century, many scientists sought to bring together energy and evolution, proposing that the unified forces of the physical world fused in a nitrogenous, semi-fluid, elastic substance that could be found in the cells of all organisms: *protoplasm*. They reckoned that the gelatinous medium would prove itself to be uniquely suited to store physical forces and therefore to serve as the substratum of all vital processes, including heredity. But over several decades, protoplasm theories became integrated into wider patterns of signification, serving as crucial planks of a broader theoretical architecture, roughly equivalent to (and often directly connected to) theories of the ether in the physical sciences. Until roughly the eve of the First World War, protoplasm theories also played an enlivening role in aesthetic theories, which were soon adapted to budding early forms of modernism in the arts from Art Nouveau design to the Symbolist work of Munch and the machine-inspired paintings of Picabia.

The key progenitors of protoplasmania were Darwin's most ardent and influential supporters, the English biologist Thomas Henry Huxley (1825–1895) and the German naturalist Ernst Haeckel (1834–1919).[1] Although protoplasm had been the subject of three decades of laboratory investigation, Huxley's 1869 lecture, "The Physical Basis of Life," launched the fascination with protoplasm as the primordial medium of life. But it was Haeckel's 1875 treatise *Über die Wellenzeugung der Lebensteilchen oder die Perigenesis der Plastidule* that provided a comprehensive biological vision of the cell plasm. Haeckel's theory challenged the reigning molecular theory of heredity proposed by Charles Darwin with a "theory of the transmission of force" as the basis of heredity and indeed all of the phenomena of living organisms.[2] Darwin's "provisional hypothesis of pangenesis" held that cells shed small particles, called gemmules, which collect in the reproductive organs prior to fertilization, conferring a role for every cell in the organism in the constitution of offspring.[3] Although Darwin emphasized the genetic role of the gemmules, he nevertheless treated them as constitutive units of the cell. Haeckel found Darwin's hypothesis unsatisfying because it ignored important research in cell theory, physiology, and morphology—the laboratory sciences in which Germans excelled. Still, Haeckel, the leading proponent of Darwin's theories in Germany, admitted to some discomfort criticizing the scientist he revered.[4] Heredity was, he wrote, "the only matter about which I disagree with Darwin." Haeckel proposed instead that the jelly comprising the nonnucleate preponderance of the cell had the ability to receive and maintain the waveform vibrations of the external world and to pass these on to all cellular offspring. For the next two or three decades, the two theories of heredity—Darwin's pangenesis and Haeckel's perigenesis—stood, in the words of the British biologist Ray Lankester, in "the same relation as the emission and undulatory theories of light": competing ontologies of corpuscles and waves, to be sure, but also theories whose contentions were fought not simply on the grounds of evidence, but on their larger implications.[5]

Beyond the more special concerns of theories of heredity, these decades saw a flurry of enthusiasm for protoplasm engulf biologists, psychologists, philosophers, and artists, who embraced the primordial jelly as the *fons et origo* of all life and what C. S. Peirce called the "glassy essence" of human nature.[6] Protoplasm theories addressed questions important to all Darwinians—including questions that Darwin privately contemplated but did not publicly express, such as the "intimate relation of Life with laws of Chemical combination, & the universality of latter."[7] As an answer to the question "what lives?"

protoplasm located fundamental problems of the life sciences at the subcellular level.

The Physical Basis of Life

Although he became its prophet and most consequential theorist, Haeckel did not originate protoplasmania. After protoplasm had become an object of interest in the 1830s, Max Schultze captured the imaginations of biologists with his 1860 assertion that it made up the primordial substratum of vital activity in the tissues of all living organisms.[8] In 1869, Huxley proclaimed protoplasm the "physical basis of life" in a popularly controversial Sunday Evening lecture in Edinburgh.[9] Showing bottles of smelling salts and carbonic acid—the constituents of protoplasm—to his rapt audience, Huxley argued that all living things, algal mats and humans alike, are unified in sharing one basic kind of matter. The primary evidence for the protoplasm as the physical basis of life could be found in its chemical constitution: basically proteinaceous and subject to heat coagulation, with a cellular "catholicity of assimilation" that made it uniquely suited to store vital forces.[10] Protoplasm's suitability as a substratum for living processes was manifest in its contractility, evident in the "unceasing activity" that characterized the protoplasmic layer of nettle hair, in which "local contractions of the whole thickness of its substance pass slowly and gradually from point to point, and give rise to the appearance of progressive waves."[11] Huxley did not spell out what he thought the physical relations of these waves might be, but as with nineteenth-century wave theories of light that postulated a very thin elastic solid or "jelly" stretching across space, the protoplasm seemed to provide a medium both rigid enough to transmit rapid vibrations and fluid enough for ordinary matter to move through it.[12]

But more than simply a substratum for vital forces, Huxley boldly asserted that protoplasm showed the way to a physiological theory of heredity. Sensitive to external forces such as heat, light, and pressure, the material structure of the protoplasm appeared uniquely suited to carry the imprint of recurring actions. The granules became driven "through channels in the protoplasm which seem to have a considerable amount of persistence," though they sometimes coursed in new directions when "opposite streams come into direct collision, and, after a longer or shorter struggle, one predominates."[13] Huxley contended that in complex organisms the differentiation of function was accompanied by greater specialization of the protoplasm.[14]

Thanks to Huxley, protoplasm became a household word, especially in Britain. Huxley's thesis found immediate supporters and detractors, both philosophical and scientific. "Mr. Huxley changed the glory of God into—Protoplasm!" exclaimed one Presbysterian minister, contending that the *Urschleim* was the new Baal of materialism and atheism, with Huxley as its high priest. Others took a wholly positive view, finding "science almost sublimated into poetry" in protoplasm's "rushing and roaring" maelstroms within the cell.[15] Protoplasm even reverberated in Parliament, when Benjamin Disraeli remarked in a parliamentary speech, "This is essentially a material age. [. . .] We live in an age when young men prattle about Protoplasm, and when young ladies in gilded saloons unconsciously talk atheism."[16]

A more scientific objection came from Scottish philosopher James Hutchinson Stirling, who challenged the universal identity that Huxley imputed to the protoplasm. Stirling understood that Huxley's account of protoplasm buttressed Darwin's theory, even if Huxley did not say so explicitly in his essay. The contractility of protoplasm provided what Stirling called an "autoplastic living matter that, produced by ordinary chemical processes, is yet capable of continuing and developing itself into new and higher forms." This "would fairly enable Mr. Darwin, supplemented by such a life-stuff, to account by natural means for everything like an idea or thought that appears in creation."[17] In fact, this kind of materialist evolution—or any definitive position on the boundary between the organic and inorganic—was probably not of much concern to Darwin. But it was of importance to Huxley and Haeckel, the chief lieutenants of Darwin's battalion. Haeckel's attraction to protoplasm derived in part from the notion that the simplest and therefore phylogenetically most-primitive known animals, the moners, appeared to consist of nothing more than a "nonnucleate globule of protoplasm," yet displayed properties of sensibility normally attributed only to "organisms with a nervous system."[18]

Perigenesis der Plastidule and the Problem of Heredity

Whether such an eponymous *Urschleim* existed or not, the close similarity between cellular protoplasm and the morphology of protozoa convinced Haeckel of a necessary connection between cytology and evolutionary development. With his biogenetic law (ontogeny recapitulates phylogeny) in mind, Haeckel observed that even humans, placed at the apex of creation, exhibited a cell stage during ontogenetic development, which united them with the lowest of all forms, the moners. Protoplasm therefore seemed to provide the royal road to "a mechanical explanation of vital phenomena, and especially for a Monistic explanation of entire organic nature."[19] But most importantly, protoplasm offered an explanation of the problem of heredity, the central vital phenomenon to Darwinians. Although Darwin's theory of natural selection established the critical understanding of the general function of heredity, the English biologist's own account of the specific organic mechanism—his so-called pangenesis theory—failed to convince many biologists, including many of his most devoted supporters. Darwin's theory therefore took its place among a variety of competing proposals for the mechanism of heredity, including Francis Galton's stirps, Herbert Spencer's physiological units, Gregor Mendel's factors, August Weissman's ids—and Haeckel's plastidules.

Haeckel argued that the appeal of his waveforce theory of evolution rested in its broad compatibility with the mechanical and thermodynamic worldview predominate among nineteenth-century physical scientists. It also dovetailed perfectly with the thriving field of experimental physiology pioneered by German physiologists during the late 1840s.[20] The physiologists equipped their laboratories with newly invented graphical recording instruments to visualize and record physiological functions like circulation, respiration, and muscle contraction.[21] The graphic images rendered physiological actions in the script of physical forces, that is, in periodic or waveform curves laid out against an x,y coordinate grid. These graphical curves, which resembled the physicists' method for understanding displacements of force over time, came to be seen as representing the true periodic or waveform character of physiological function in complex organisms (figure 4.1).

As physiologists became accustomed to working with these images, they began to see all movements of life as a play of undulating lines. The innovation of Haeckel's perigenesis theory rested in the suggestion that the waveforces of complex organisms originated in the most primitive manifestations of life. The varied functions of complex organisms, each with their specific rhythms and periodicity, came about through the differentiation of function in the division of physiological labor.

But Haeckel's wave-theory did rather more than simply posit an energetic basis of life. In his account, the protoplasm itself acted as a kind of graphical recording device, receiving impulses from the milieu and storing them as active vibrations in its colloidal structures. It was a prime case of turning an "epistemic thing"—an object that is brought into existence by the experimental set-up, in this case the physiological graphic—into a feature of the natural world itself.[22] Sensations or impulses thus inscribed themselves on organic tissues in a form similar to the physiological graphics produced in laboratory instruments.[23]

Haeckel's approach to the mechanism of evolutionary heredity also mingled Darwinian assumptions with a reading of the physiologist Ewald Hering's much-discussed essay *Memory as a Universal Function of Organized Mat-*

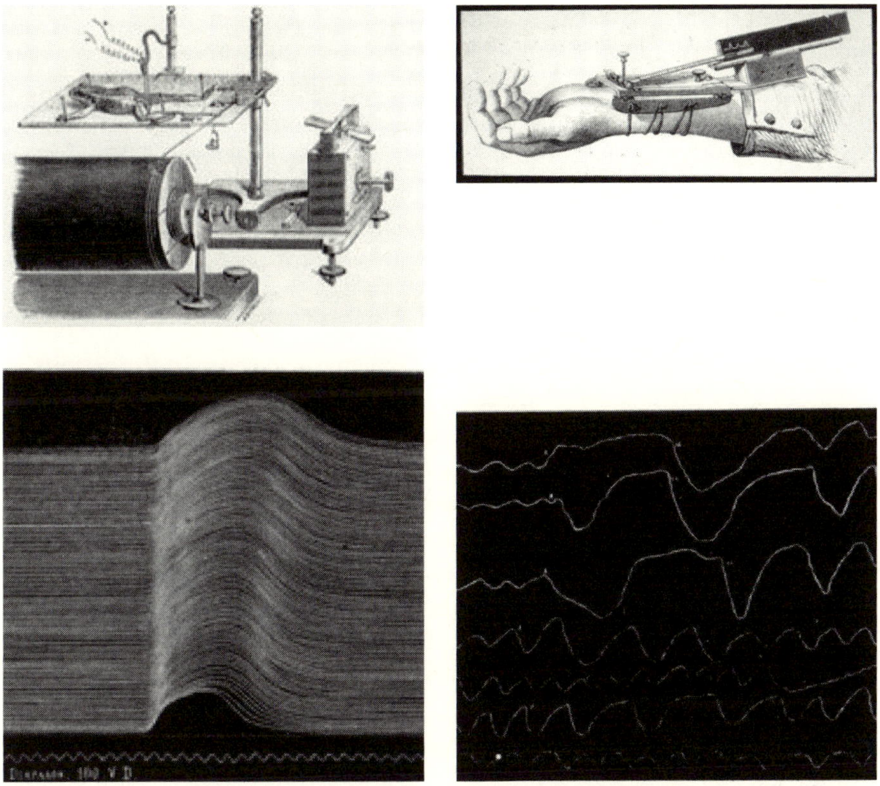

Figure 4.1 Graphical Recording Device: Instruments and Waveform Inscriptions. *Upper left*: Myograph, from E. J. Marey, *La méthode graphique en sciences experimentales* (Paris: G. Masson, 1878); *lower left:* Muscle contraction recordings by myograph, from E. J. Marey, *La méthode graphique en sciences experimentales* (Paris: G. Masson, 1878); *upper right*: Sphygmograph showing arterial pulse curve, from E. J. Marey, *La méthode graphique en sciences experimentales* (Paris: G. Masson, 1878); *lower right*: Pneumograph curve of respiration, from A. Tamburini and G. Seppilli, "Contribuzioni allo studio sperimentale dell'ipnotismo," *Rivista sperimentale di freniatria* VII (1881).

ter.[24] Hering suggested that there are close connections between the conscious memory of ordinary life and the phylogenetic "memory" transmitted through the inheritance of acquired characteristics.[25] Both were to be attributed to the effect of vibrations imparted to the organism from external objects: Vibrations that were repeated often enough passed from conscious memory to the unconscious inheritance of the organism. Although largely speculative, Hering's idea unleashed several decades of attempts to fix a theory of heredity and memory as the effect of traces or vibrations on organic tissues.[26]

In Haeckel's formulation, every "plastidule" (minute structures within the protoplasm) had a characteristic wave pattern as a result of its history and environment, which constituted memory for the organism and heredity for the species. "Adaptation," Haeckel explained, "is a modification of the plastidule's movement pattern, through which it acquires new characters."[27] These wave patterns are passed along by both the sperm and the egg, respectively, which combine at conception to produce a new wave pattern in the new organism's plastidules, which become further transmitted mechanically by cell division through the progressive differentiation of tissues and more complex organic forms. The wave-movement transfers the inheritance of its most immediate ancestor, but indirectly also the inherited characteristics of its earlier ancestors as well as their conditions of existence.

Haeckel illustrated his concept with a schematic diagram of the actions of the plastidules (figure 4.2). In this diagram, each simple cell is represented by a larger ball. The two cell offspring, the results of cell division, are shown by the two smaller balls. The wave-lines signify the vibrations of each individual cell with their unique plastidule-movement. The small bodies in various shapes represent the sum of the external conditions of existence, which influence the nutrition of the cell and alter the original plastidule-movement through adaptation. Thus the original plastidule-movement, transferred through heredity, is modified by the plastidule-movements contributed from each parent. In its unique periodicity, the wave-movement transfers the inheritance of its most immediate ancestor, but indirectly also the inherited characteristics of its earlier ancestors as well as their conditions of existence.

Haeckel argued that, at a broader level, branching wave-form movement could explain the divergence of characters that Darwin saw as the mark of evolution. The individuality of each cell or unicellular organism was signaled by its own unique waveform, which then reproduced itself in its own hereditary line. The unbroken continuity connected all persons, all living organisms with the great pattern that could be traced back to the beginning of life, a wave pattern that the organism recapitulated in individual development. Haeckel maintained that since the number of possible waveforms was incalculably large, this mechanism of heredity could generate an enormous amount of variation without trading in the assumption of continuity for discrete entities or any recourse to jumps or discontinuities. But the possible amount of variation was not unlimited. The length of the waves themselves was bounded, and their existence was confined to a specific place and location in the protoplasm.

Haeckel's description of the *Wellenzeugung* of protoplasm formed a complement to his well-known Descent-Tree. In his *Generelle Morphologie der Organismen* (1866), Haeckel presented a tree depicting the evolution of plants, protists, and animals, which could be read to support either the hypothesis of one moner as the source of all life, or the hypothesis that three or as many as

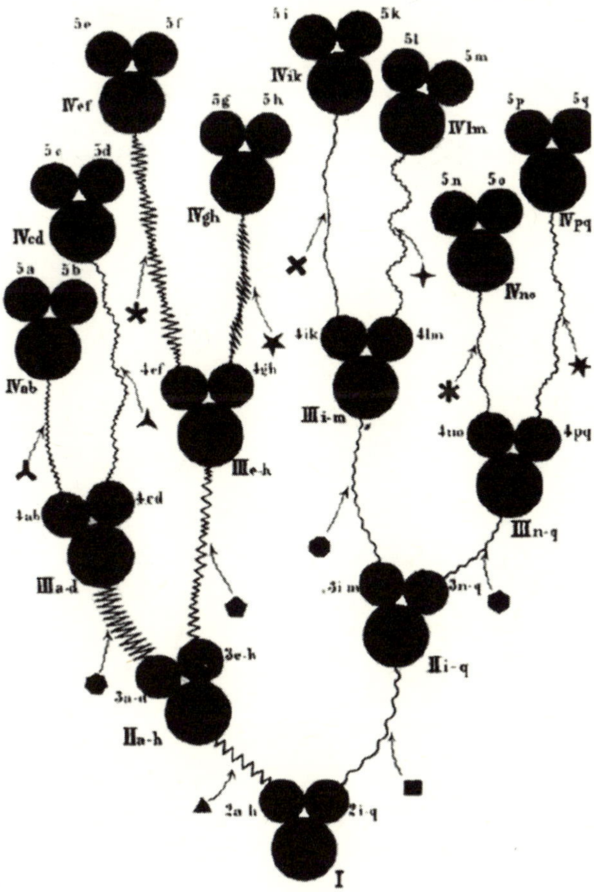

Figure 4.2 Haeckel's Schematic Diagram of the Inheritance of Different Wave Motions; With inherited wave-motions represented by divergent undulations emanating from each of the pair of smaller spheres in each generation. The small geometric figures intersecting the wave patterns represent different environments working their influence on each generation and modifying the wave-motions inherited by the next generation. *From Ernst Haeckel, "Über die Wellenzeugung der Lebensteilchen oder die Perigenesis der Plastidule," 1876.*

nineteen) different monera gave rise to the various phyla (figure 4.3).[28] In his *Wellenzeugung* essay, Haeckel reminded the reader that the grand movement depicted in the "tree of life" was primarily a story of protoplasm—the only organic substance shared (and preponderantly) by all living forms. Haeckel intended his perigenesis theory to apply equally to cells conjoined with other cells in organisms of all levels of complexity and to single-celled organisms composed preponderantly of protoplasm. He elaborated:

> The evolutionary movement presented by this series of our ancestors can be depicted simply by an undulating line in which the life of each individual corresponds to one wave. But we do not limit our view to the series of our direct ancestors: let us extend our vision and embrace the ensemble of our near relatives; we can express their relations very well in the form of a

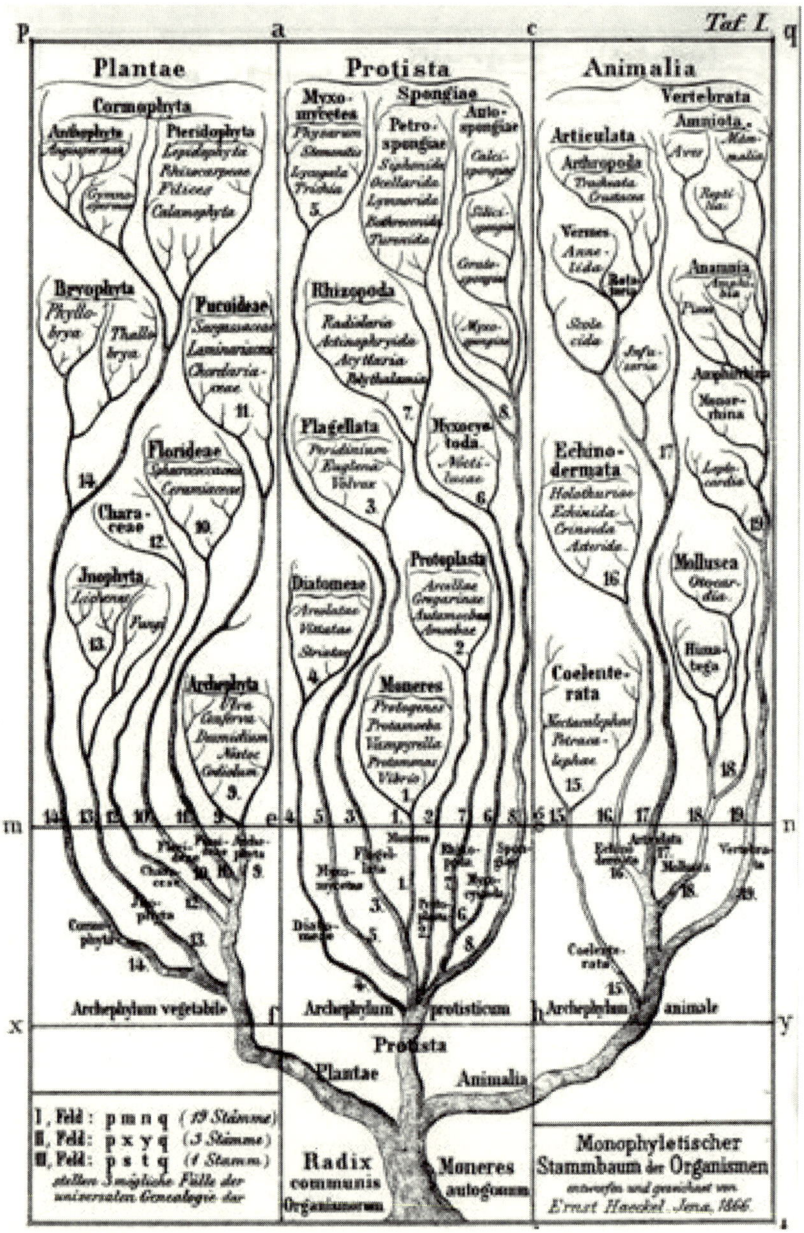

Figure 4.3 Haeckel's Descent-Tree of plants, protists, and animals; with *pstq* representing the hypothesis of one moneron as the source of all life; *pxyq* representing the hypothesis of three monera as the origin, respectively of plants, protists, and animals; and *pmnq* representing the hypothesis that some nineteen different monera gave rise to various phyla of plants, protists, and animals. *From Haeckel,* Generelle Morphologie der Organismen, *1866.*

> Descent-Tree. . . . The genealogical tree as a whole presents the image of *one ramified waveform movement*.[29]

Viewed through the lens of the perigenesis theory, the Descent-Tree depicted organic development as a summing of periodic waveforms, which stabilized at intervals into specific physiological functions, each with their own characteristic periodicity. The vibrations in the protoplasm of unicellular creatures congealed into functional motions, modified gradually by use or disuse, and in complex organisms differentiated themselves into more specialized organs and functions, following the principle of the division of physiological labor. In higher organisms, the branching wave-movement therefore produced the rhythmic, periodic characteristics of specific functions like circulation, respiration, and locomotion.

Haeckel thus ingeniously combined the idea of entwining and branching waveforms with the time-honored image of the genealogical tree, which represented in miniature "the development of every human family, the genealogy of every dynasty."[30] Haeckel's iconic tree of the ancestral lineage of humans offered the trunk as the *Ur* form, which gradually diversifies and ramifies through vast spans of time (figure 4.4). Yet, in Haeckel's Descent-Tree, time's arrow persists across vast shifts of scale, from the microscopic protoplasmic movements to the macroscopic directionality of phylogenic evolution. These continuous forces acting through time furnished the motive power of evolution, their natural graphics suggested "secret law, the divine riddle of Goethe's chorus of forms."[31]

From Protoplasm to Cell Psychology

Many artists working around the turn of the century were drawn to the invisible realm of the mind and for certain of them Haeckel's developing theory of "cell psychology" was of particular interest. In several essays written during the late 1870s, Haeckel argued that the perigenetic movements indicated not only physiological functions, but the presence of a *Seelenleben* with its seat in the protoplasm. Asking rhetorically "What is the Soul or Psyche?" Haeckel replied that "soul is the sum of a number of special cellular activities, among which feeling and will, sensation and involuntary movement are the most important and the most generally distributed."[32] Both cells and protozoa were "ensouled" and therefore amenable to psycho-physiological investigation using "mechanical" methods. Such an approach would, Haeckel insisted, overcome the shortcomings of the fledgling field of "psycho-physics" by placing its questions within the evolutionary history of psychological functions.[33] One

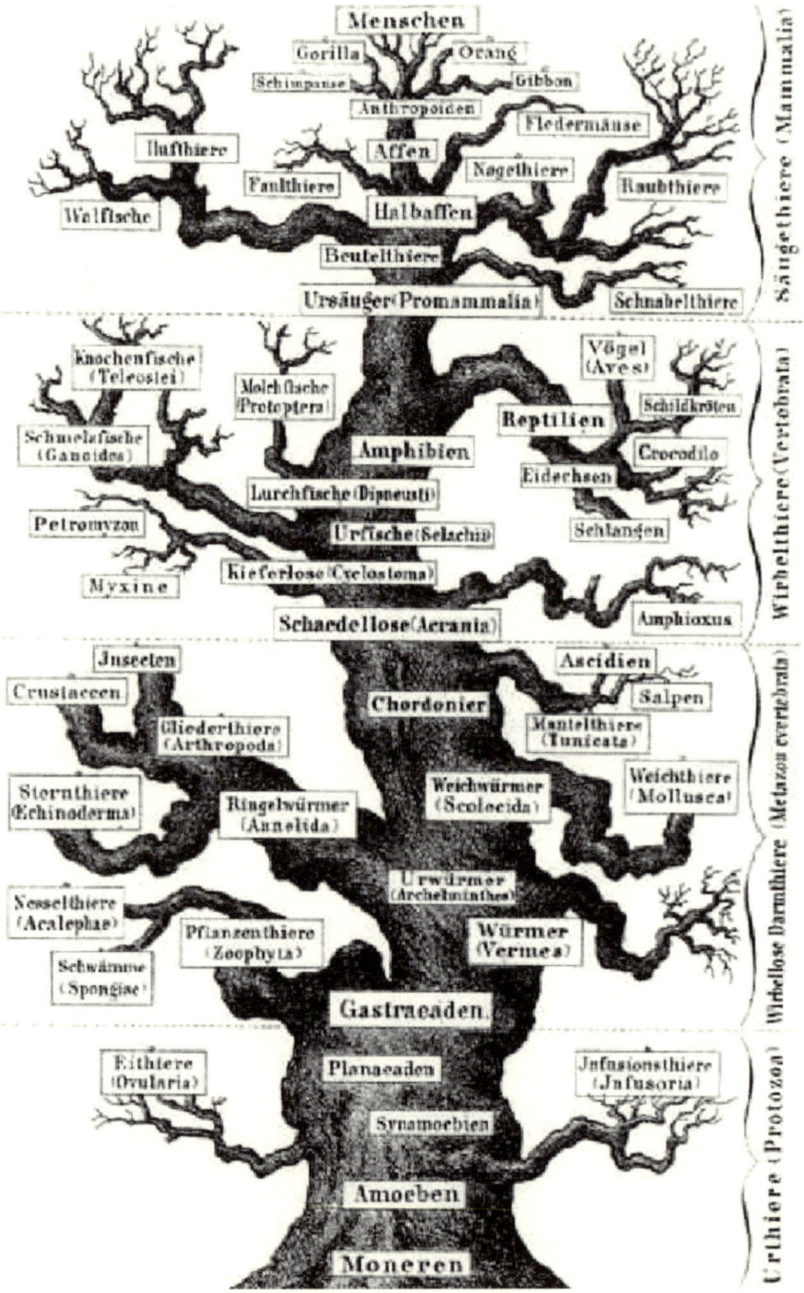

Figure 4.4 Haeckel's Descent-Tree of Human Descent. *From Haeckel,* Anthropogenie, *1874.*

would find that while every living cell possessed a "cell psyche" (*Zellenseele*), only higher animals and humans possess "psyche cells" (*Seelenzellen*), found in structures like the ganglia of the brain, which governed higher functions such as thought, representation, and consciousness.[34]

Haeckel's conjectures about the ensouled protoplasm kicked off a wave of experimental and speculative attempts to specify the elementary features of psychological life in both cellular protoplasm and in the movements of unicellular organisms. Judy Johns Schloegel and Henning Schmidgen have shown how Haeckel's description of the cell psyche inspired many talented young scientists internationally to conduct experimental investigations of the psychology of unicellular organisms or "protists."[35]

In France, similar studies on the "psychic life of micro-organisms" were conducted by the Haeckel psycho-physiologist Alfred Binet, who aimed to refute claims that mental and psychological functions were a relatively late development in evolution.[36] Binet's studies joined protoplasm investigations with a broader wave of French interests in the burgeoning field of psychophysiology. Binet published his results in the *Revue Philosophique*, a periodical edited by Théodule Ribot, one of France's leading exponents of the "psychology of movements," investigations of how "movements enter into the majority of our states of consciousness as a constitutive element."[37] Movements included involuntary motions like those studied by evolutionary physiologists, as well as voluntary actions and gestures in higher animals and humans. For Ribot and followers like Charles Richet, Charles Féré, Frédéric Paulhan, and Binet, feelings, thoughts, and ideas were generated by virtual movements set in motion from outside the organism (stimuli and sensation) and from real movements on the inside (ideas and internal sensations).

Binet's research on the psychology of micro-organisms sought to frame human psycho-physiology within a broader program of evolutionary development. One could show the essential unity of the psychological vibrations in the protoplasm of simple organisms with the rhythmicity of ideas and affects in the muscular sensations of humans. Binet's vision of a functional psychophysiology spanning unicellular organisms at one end and the human brain at the other paralleled the root and treetop of Haeckel's Descent-Tree (see figure 4.4). A photograph of Binet's laboratory conserved at the Archives Nationales in Paris (Pieron Collection) schematized this conception: Between the two poles set by images of infusoria and the human brain, respectively, stood the psycho-physiologists and their trusty graphical recording apparatus for investigating functional movements as the key to human psychology. The photograph iconically documents Binet's research program. It also promulgates a doctrine of the human mind shaped by what Marcel

Gauchet has called "the cerebral unconscious," a repository of inherited, primordial movements and automatisms.[38]

Protoplasm and the Politics of Synaesthesia

The new psychology of movements found eager reception among certain poets and artists associated in France with the Symbolist movement. Symbolist poets like Gustave Kahn and Jules Laforgue embraced the psychology of virtual and real movement as a theory of Symbol formation and the key to a new aesthetics of the externalization of the Idea. They learned their science largely through the theories of the mathematician and psychophysiologist Charles Henry, whose writings were also much admired among Neo-Impressionist painters.[39] Henry theorized works of art as extensions of sensory and motor functions of the creative artist. Paintings, music, and design of all kinds could thus be analyzed as physiological equivalents of force expressed in the formal elements of artistic media—line, color, tone, and rhythm—that Henry rendered through graphical recording methods. "The artist," Henry wrote, "is but an eye, an ear, a nervous system normally organized and developed" that senses a rhythm out of an "infinity of more or less invisible rhythms," realizes it virtually as an Idea, and produces it externally.[40] Seeking to extend the exciting new scientific apparatus of infravisibility to art and aesthetics, Henry developed technical instruments to capture these rhythms efficiently, thereby enabling artists and scientists to draw upon the entire evolutionary history of life expressed in rhythmic undulations. One found such rhythms and periodicities operating everywhere in nature with precise mathematical regularity, the physiologist Jenny Héricourt observed, from "the curves of Marey" to the design of beehives. He elaborated, "Among the waveform phenomena of life, nothing seems capable of escaping the rigors of the principles that [Henry] has established, from artistic productions to the beats of the heart. *A veritable mechanics of the protoplasm is thus revealed.*[41]

What made the Idea manifest in the Symbolist artwork was its capacity to make the primordial rhythms of biological life perceptible to the beholder. According to Henry, at the same time that we perceive an object, our "internal machinery" re-creates it in internal muscle sensations. In his version of the ideo-motoric theory of cognition, Henry observed that thanks to eye movements, to phenomena in our vascular and muscular systems, and to our breathing, "there is no idea without virtual, then real, movement." This, he added, was our "mécanique naturelle," the result of our long evolutionary history.[42] Our human appreciation of art was thus an unconscious recognition of the rhythmic movements and automatisms stored in the cerebral unconscious, the legacy of our branching waveform movements of protoplasm. Such a physiological aesthetics naturally made rhythm and its graphical representation as undulating line as the primary element of art and aesthetic language.[43]

But there was more. Héricourt argued that with Henry's physiological aesthetic, the memory archive of organic rhythms would enable artists and designers to engineer the built environment with exteriorized psycho-physiological states. It was easy to envision a landscape of everyday objects through which the human relation to the built environment could be modified at will, thus forging, in Lamarckian fashion, a new sensory milieu through which new humans of the future would take shape.[44] Henry and his Symbolist and Neo-Impressionist friends imagined this aesthetic engineering as a fusion of neo-Lamarkian evolution and the *Gesamtkunstwerk*, the aesthetic object "at once pictorial, symbolic, and poetic, of which [Richard] Wagner is said [. . .] to have dreamed."[45]

This fusion of monist protoplasm doctrines, psycho-physiological aesthetics, and Wagnerism found expression in French and Belgian Art Nouveau, and in German *Jugendstil*, where artists and architects externalized phylogenetically inherited psychic functions in what Robert Proctor has aptly called an "architecture of the cell-soul."[46] Some of the most influential examples could be found in the designs of the French architect René Binet, who looked to Haeckel's studies of radiolaria—a large class of microscopic unicellular marine animals that secreted unusual exoskeletons of silica—as an archive of natural form.[47] For Haeckel, the simple protoplasmic radiolaria provided a particularly important source of knowledge of evolution, because of the many thousands of different species that could be examined and classified into a linear sequence, while their physiological similarity and the very slight differences among species allowed the naturalist to trace the development of forms more closely than was possible with higher animals. Binet echoed that view, finding the incessant evolutionary movement a source for artists to find "the infallible secret of creations and transformations." In his *Esquisses décoratives*, Binet displayed designs of all manner of furniture, electric lamps, rings, and stairwells, using radiolarian motifs.[48] Binet's most famous work, however, was the famous Monumental Entry Gate to the 1900 Universal Exposition in Paris, commonly known as the Porte Binet, an arch that appeared as a giant radiolaran rising from the ground, with a tower to woman—*La Parisienne*—perched on top (figure 4.5). Fifty million visitors, including people from nearly every country in the world, passed under the gate, which critics deemed an "art nouveau," "supple and vital," whose "greatest apostle is Monsieur Binet."[49]

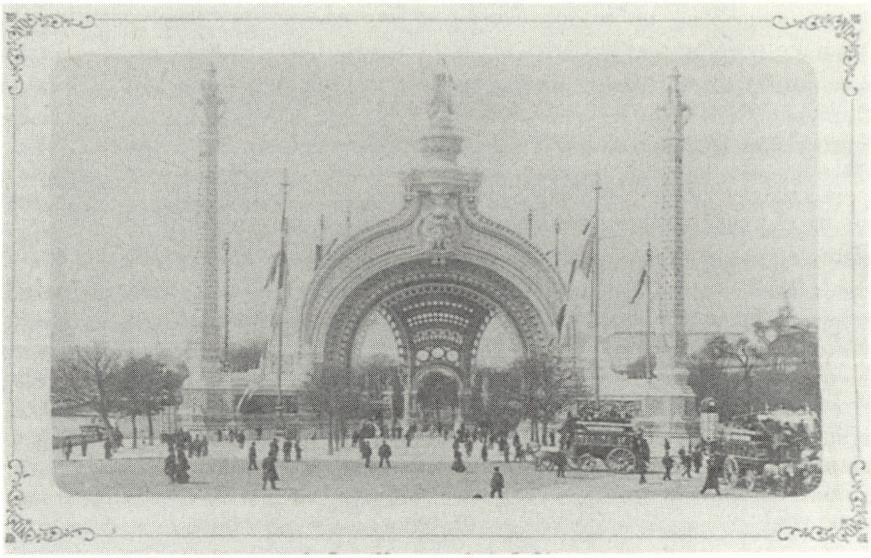

Figure 4.5 René Binet, Monumental Entry Gate to the 1900 Universal Exposition. *From the author's collection.*

Examples of the cell-soul architecture proliferated across Europe, from Hermann Obrist and August Endell's biomorphic whiplash lines, described in the language of psycho-physiological aesthetics, to Victor Horta's Tassel House in Brussels, for example, which featured pulsating and undulating lines suggesting the fluid energy of flagella, tendrils, neurons, and vines (figure 4.6).

The most auspicious point of contact between evolutionary psychophysiology and Wagnerian aesthetics could be found in questions of sensory modalities, especially synaesthesia, the sensory pathology *à la mode* around 1890. Wagner's ideal of the re-unification of the different forms of art, which he held come apart because of a division of artistic labor, also championed the convergence of the different sensory modalities associated with each artistic medium. Symbolist artists smitten with Wagner's ideal developed aesthetic techniques to produce fusions between senses, especially the eye and ear. The artists' fascination with sensory fusion encouraged scientists and medics to reconsider various pathologies of synaesthesia, especially so-called "color hearing." In this most frequent form of sensory confusion, sounds, or even the memory of sounds, awaken sensations of color or luminous images, which are always the same for the same letters, the same tone of voice or musical instrument. According to some, color hearing was a rare gift of exquisitely organized nervous systems; for others it was merely an accidental abnormal

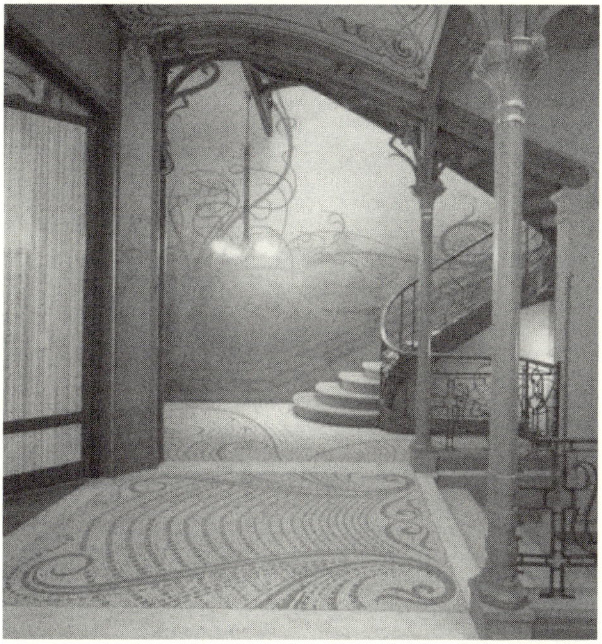

Figure 4.6 Victor Horta, Tassel House (main-floor entrance and landing), Brussels, 1893–95. *SOFAM, Brussels, Belgium. Photo credit: Bastin & Evrard.*

connection between the optic and acoustic brain-centers by means of nervous filaments. Because color hearing appeared to have a hereditary component, some scientists sought its source in evolutionary development, arguing that it was connected to an abnormal differentiation of sensory functions.

This explanation, however, did not cast any light on the larger animating question around the synaesthesia: Was its presence a sign of regression or evolutionary advance? After all, it might represent a heightened access to the unseen physical vibrations, a human faculty akin to the most advanced recording device, cathode ray tube, or spectroscope. The biologist Félix Le Dantec pointed out that this would make artists akin to scientific instruments—or to protoplasmic beings. "The living protoplasms, very complex colloides, are highly susceptible to imitate [. . .] colors and sounds." This happened through a condition of "resonance" that establishes itself "between a colloid and its ambience."[50] Raphaël Dubois, a comparative physiologist, provided what many took to be a firm foundation for this view with a "general theory of sensation" based on studies of an ancestral mollusk, the common piddock (*Pholas dactylus*, Fr. *Pholade dactyle*).[51] The piddock provided Dubois with the opportunity to investigate the primitive organism's modes of cognition of the ambient milieu. Unlike oysters, and other bivalve mollusks, the piddock possesses a proboscis or siphon, through which it is sensible to all external impressions: light, noise, touch, smell. Thus, in contrast to "higher animals in which the protoplasm is differentiated" and "nerves, ganglia, brain, and sense-apparatus are formed," this mollusk "sees, hears, smells, and feels with this one part of its body; its proboscis functions at once as a eye, ear, nose, finger, etc." For Dubois, this gave the study an important philosophical value in determining what is "fundamental in the play of organs and apparatus which perpetuate life and thought among humans."[52]

With graphical recording instruments, Dubois recorded the movements of the siphon. In "the amplitude and the velocity of the contraction of peripheral contractile segments," he wrote, the animal itself wrote its impressions of sensory stimuli. In effect, all senses were reduced to one, which he called "touch-vision" (*dermoptique*) but this did not mean that stimuli were undifferentiated. Different kinds of visual stimuli, odor, and pressure all resulted in different graphic curves. More remarkably, in response to different colors, the piddock produced curves whose amplitudes corresponded to the order of the solar spectrum: yellow, blue, violet, red (white produced a curve in the middle). Sound produced a similar range of responses in accordance with the rapidity and intensity of vibrations.

Around 1900, the Norwegian painter Edvard Munch figured among the many artists who pursued a synaesthetic ideal in his painting, after having drunk from the wellspring of protoplasmania in Paris and Berlin. Munch may have acquired this interest during his 1889 stay in Paris, where he mingled with Neo-Impressionist circles. Protoplasm was, in any event, an enduring passion by the early 1890s, after he had established himself in Berlin with the artists' group that gathered at *Zum Schwarzen Ferkel*. Many of Munch's closest friends—especially Swedish writer and painter August Strindberg and the Polish writer Stanislaw Przybyszewski—had some medical education and avidly read the latest in physiology and neuropsychiatry, and by every account Munch devoured the same texts.[53] One German member of the circle, the German biologist and physician Carl Ludwig Schleich, reports on the experimental activities of Strindberg around this time, including trials on the "electro-molecular vibration of the protoplasm" using chemical preparations and spectral analysis. Strindberg described these laboratory experiments in an essay entitled "Where are the Nerves of Plants?" in which he concluded that instead of nerves, energy in plants is "distributed—everywhere in the protoplasm."[54] Among the consequences that Strindberg drew from his alleged discovery, was the evolutionary basis of "sensory confusion," or synaesthesia, which he championed as the basis of a new art.

Przybyszewski, in his authorized critical writings on Munch's painting from the same period, reported on his friend's aspiration to paint unconscious sensations that effaced the gates of sense. Munch sought to find the "knotting-point" where "all impressions flow together, where the most heterogeneous things are sensed as equivalent" because individuality rendered them in the same emotional tone.[55] The result was synaesthesia: "color becomes line, scent becomes sound: les parfums, les coleurs et les son se repondent."[56] Przybyzewski marked Munch's originality in his having renounced all painting from direct observation of Nature, turning instead to congealed memories inscribed on his own sensorium, which he then rendered in form and line equivalents. The aim of painting was to recover that original protoplasmic unity in the higher form of the synaesthetic *Gesamtkunstwerk*. While these themes are evident throughout Munch's work, they appear in striking form in *The Scream* (figure 4.7).

There has been some disagreement among Munch scholars about when *The Scream* was painted, either in 1893, or later, around 1910. Munch's notebooks reveal an abiding interest in synaesthesia through both of these moments and beyond, which is almost always described as an effect of protoplasmic differentiation. In a notebook entry from around 1906—the year he audited the lectures of the physicist Felix Auerbach in the hopes of learning to paint sound—Munch wrote that the protoplasm "develops to a point where it becomes a being . . . Human beings wished to see, so developed eyes—to hear, so ears . . . to communicate, so vocal chords came."[57] Much later in life (1929), Munch described his method similarly, that "by painting colors and lines and forms that [he] had seen in troubled times—[he] wanted to let [those] sounds vibrate yet again like a phonograph."[58]

The general monist character of the painting has been remarked by scholars. Reinhold Heller, for example, writes, "the curving lines of the sky, echoed in the curves of the figure's body, dominate. It is as if, in their essential form and color there was no distinction between the landscape, sky, and figure, and that all were fused in the symbolic flatness of Munch's pictorial representation of Monistic unity." The monist unity of the painting might be said to concentrate around the melding of color and sound in the painting, underscored by one of Munch's inscriptions, "I felt the great Scream through nature." The receiver of this Scream—the humanoid person with cupped hands around the face—might be said to resemble typical period representations of cell plasmas with semi-permeable membranes.

Some of the clinical phenomena associated with synaesthesia suggested this question of the ambiguous boundaries of selfhood. Synaesthetics typically reported that they "heard colors" outside of themselves in an area just beyond the body rather than internally, the way most sense perceptions are experienced. The suggestion that synaesthesia marked a kind of projection in

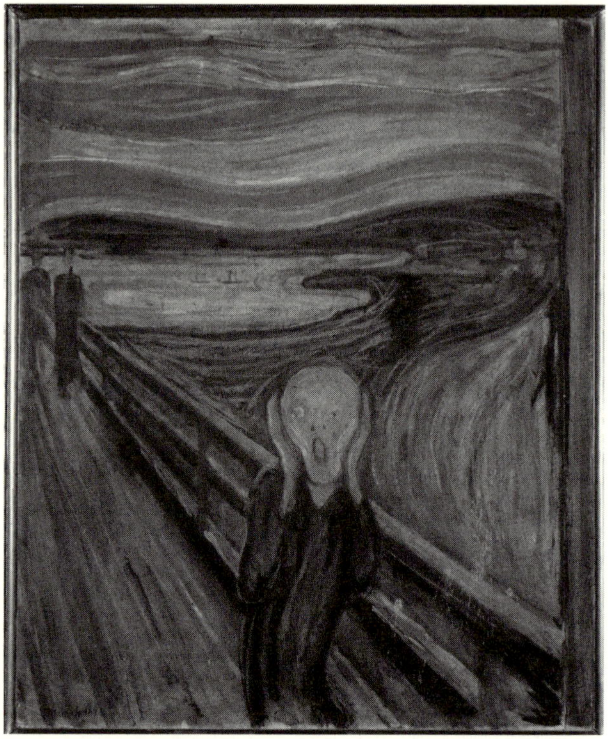

Figure 4.7 Edvard Munch, *The Scream*, 1893. Tempera and pastel on cardboard (91 × 73.5cm).*Nasjonalgalleriet, Oslo. ©2009 The Munch Museum / The Munch-Ellingsen Group / Artists Rights Society (ARS), New York. Photo credit: Erich Lessing / Art Resource, NY.*

auratic space confirmed its association with ambiguous boundaries of selfhood associated with protoplasm. For some contemporaries, like the English writer Edward Carpenter, there was a positive correlation between synaesthesia and the shaman in so-called "primitive societies," as well as homosexuals and other "deviant" sexual orientiations: all were examples of a fortunate failure of protoplasm to differentiate itself, a fate that conferred extraordinary powers upon the individual to perceive the world in its original condition of undifferentiated unity.[59]

These conditions were conventionally branded pathological, of course. One of Munch's inscriptions suggests this connection: "could have only been made by a madman." Yet for artists in Munch's circle, like Carpenter's homosexuals as modern shamans, certain forms of madness were the mark of superior gifts.

This supposition was fiercely attacked by Max Nordau, the Austrian neurologist turned French cultural jeremiah, in *Degeneration*, his notorious condemnation of decadence in modern art and culture.[60] Nordau insisted that the valorization of synaesthesia, the desire to exalt the perception of undifferentiated senses, presented a symptom of evolutionary regression or atavism, in short, of a will to return to a condition of the "protoplasm in the living cell."[61] Nordau observed that from Raphaël Dubois we know that primitive organisms like the piddock exist in a perfect condition of synaesthesia, the very state idealized by the French artistic avant-garde, who fail to see that is simply "evidence of diseased and debilitated brain-activity." Moreover, he concluded forcefully,

> It is a retrogression to the very beginning of organic development. It is a descent from the height of human perfection to the low level of a mollusk. To raise the combination, transposition and confusion of the perceptions of sound and sight to the rank of a principle of art, to see futurity in this principle, is to designate as progress the return from the consciousness of man to that of the oyster.[62]

Into this debate stepped the biologist Félix Le Dantec, anarchist and friend of the artistic avant-garde, to defend synaesthesia. Le Dantec maintained that in higher organisms there was a capacity—and a drive—to reunite the senses not in synaesthesia per se, but in a unification of the senses under the direction of vision. While each sense is by itself incapable of furnishing a complete picture of the external world, Le Dantec argued, the different senses exceed their boundaries to produce cooperatively a relatively full picture. But vision is unique in its capacity to largely supercede the other senses, especially through the prosthetic help of scientific instruments. According to Le Dantec, "The sense of vision encroaches very largely on the domains of all the other [senses] and, day by day, its efficacy grows by the invention of perfected apparatus; one can even wish that they will not arrive too late to give us a complete knowledge of the phenomena."[63]

Le Dantec's prime examples were graphical recording instruments, which translated all sensory modalities into vibrations and rendered them to the eyes in graphical form. The Edison phonograph, for example, "translates in one sinuous line inscribed on its cylinder, the piece of music which one plays before it, and we know that the sinuous line suffices to integrally reproduce the piece of music."[64] Similarly, pressure, heat, and even scent (as evidenced in a device constructed by M. Maneuvrier to determine the vintage of wine over the telephone line) could all be translated into the overarching sense modality of visuality though graphical inscription techniques, which Le Dantec liked to call "direct optics."[65] With the technical extensions of sense offered by recording apparatus, all senses were subsumed into one, the visual. Humans could be said to have overcome the sensory compartmentalization bequeathed by evolution and effectively recovered the original protoplasmic unity of sense celebrated in the common piddock. "Science will perhaps lead us one day to know all phenomena of the world with just one of our senses; and that will truly be *monism*."[66] Le Dantec's argument effectively restated the original assumptions of Haeckel's perigenesis theory: The protoplasm served as a kind of graphical recording apparatus, a medium for the inscription of forces acting in the organic world.

Le Dantec's prophetic announcement of the hegemony of vision beautifully foretold the modernist obsession with pure opticality. Under the hegemony of vision, the unification of the senses would enable the unification of the arts and of the sciences, respectively. In the case of science, the evolution of instrumental prosthesis was also on the verge of delivering a universal language, which would bring the end of "compartmentalized sciences."[67] Similarly, the opticalization of the arts would deflect any threat posed by the musicalization of painting or similar synaesthetic projects. On the contrary, it would reinforce and facilitate the interchange of sense modalities.[68]

These ideas inspired a rich new wave of aesthetic theorizing. The most influential came from Albert Cozanet, alias Jean D'Udine, who adopted Le Dantec's notion of imitation in the colloidal protoplasm to a full-blown theory of art. Beginning with his *De la correlation des sons et des couleurs en art* (1897), D'Udine developed a theory of art as the reproduction of synaesthetic waveforms on the model of the protoplasm. "Vivre, c'est vibrer," D'Udine asserted in the opening sentence of his 1910 work *L'Art et le Geste*, a work both dedicated to, and designed to unite the thought of, Cozanet's teachers Le Dantec and Emil Jaques Dalcroze, the famous inventor of the pedagogy of modern dance. The task of Jean D'Udine's book was to offer a "mechanical theory of artistic signs," joining Le Dantec's theory of "objective imitation" of external vibrations by colloidal compounds with Dalcroze's ideas of "rhythmic gymnastics" in which the acoustic sensation of duration has its basis in kinaesthetic memory. Life is movement, and underlying all feelings and states of mind are physiological rhythms, including those that are involuntary or hereditary. "What interests us," he wrote, "is the notion that the colloid particles which compose the human body are unified by complex relations, [. . .] our physiological modifications [. . .] by the presence of sonorous phenomena or colors, [. . .] rhythmic modifications at a very small scale.[69] D'Udine argued that through the hereditary memory stored in protoplasm, a rich archive of rhythmic pulsation has been bequeathed to all organic beings. The task of the artist is to learn to access this archive through the bodily practices of each artistic medium, be it dance, painting, music, or poetry. Artistic creativity, then, involves tapping these resources and representing them in inventive new combinations and sequences.

Each work of art is thus a series of signs of force capable of stimulating a condition of recognition in the beholder or recipient of the work. Because arrangements of sounds and colors, lines and gestures, produce modifications of physiological states, they are all effectively synaesthetic, although some are doubly or multiply so by virtue of the number of sense functions they engage. Yet D'Udine supported Le Dantec's claims for the hegemony of the visual sense, with its unique ability to govern and subsume the other senses. Since art is primarily a physiological phenomenon, the formal critical language of art or aesthetics should similarly be drawn from physiology, especially in its visually realized, graphical form.

The most successful implementation of Jean D'Udine's theories arrived in the work of French artist Francis Picabia, who met the aesthetician in 1909 and soon thereafter changed his style of painting.[70] While many of the so-called Simultanist painters of Paris in this period breathed in the ubiquitous biological philosophy of Henri Bergson's *Creative Evolution,* Picabia drew upon the aesthetic theory of *L'Art et le Geste*.[71] In a series of works initiated in 1913, just after returning from a voyage to New York, Picabia realized on canvas D'Udine's theories (figure 4.8). During his stay in the American metropolis, Picabia remarked on the dizzying array of sensations generated by New World modernity: the crowds, the immense vertical architecture, the electrically illuminated night, the Babel-like language-scape of "all tongues of the world" merging in a great chorus. In New York, Picabia thus found the themes of his European artistic comrades magnified to unprecedented scale: the Futurists' ecstasies of technological force and speed, the Simultanists's fascination with the mind's grasp of an infinitude of interrelated states of being.[72] In interviews, Picabia stated repeatedly that in the face of these modern realities the painter's task was not to optically render the directly observed world, but to allow the sensations to condense into memories that eventually would provide material for artistic creation.

The "Udnie" paintings are entitled with an anagram of D'Udine, the penname of his friend and theoretical inspiration, Albert Cozanet. The anagram, especially as used in the title of the painting *I See You Again in My Memory, My Dear Udnie,* underscored Jean D'Udine's notion of artistic creation as an imaginative combinatorics of affective and aesthetic signs drawn from personal and organic memory. The personal memory was probably of a Polish dancer whom Picabia met on the ship to New York, although some have suggested that it referred to Isadora Duncan, whose tragic death occurred around the time that Picabia was in America. Rather than a literal reference to one or the other, Picabia probably brought several memories together to demonstrate the overdetermination of meanings that can be generated by the kind of combinatoric invention championed by D'Udine.

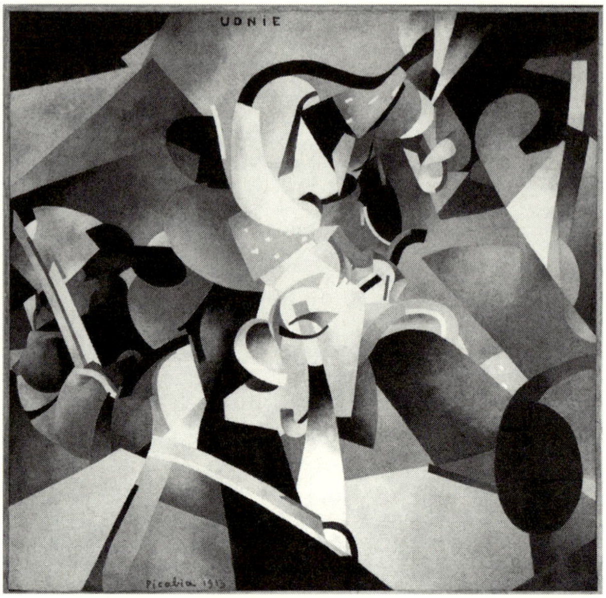

Figure 4.8 Francis Picabia, *Udnie (Young American Girl: Dance)*, 1913 (300 × 300cm). *Musée National d'Art Moderne, Centre Georges Pompidou, Paris, France © 2009 Artists Rights Society (ARS), New York / ADAGP, Paris. Photo credit: Erich Lessing / Art Resource. NY.*

Some later remarks of the poet Gertrude Stein regarding the paintings of Picabia during this period tend to confirm the theoretical orientation of Jean D'Udine.

> Picabia had conceived and is struggling with the problem that a line should have the vibration of a musical sound and that this vibration should be the result of conceiving the human form . . . in so tenuous a fashion that it would induce vibration in the line forming it. It is his way of achieving the disembodied.[73]

Stein explained that "the emotion of the object" creates a vibration that determines the character of the line. In 1913, Picabia was reported to have said that he was attempting to represent "the emotion produced in our minds by things," remarks very close to those of Stein, who became a close friend many years later. Elsewhere, Picabia spoke similarly of the analogy between painting and music, claiming that if a musician is inspired by a landscape, rather than describe it, "he expresses it in sound waves, he translates it into an expression of the impression, the mood. And as there are absolute sound waves, so there are absolute waves of color and form."[74]

These ideas were reinforced by the method of painting composition that Picabia developed for the New York paintings. He first improvised a linear structure based on an idea from memory, for example, of a dancer or, in another work, of African-American singers in a Harlem church. The lines captured the remembered experience as form, energy, and emotion, rather than suggesting a particular grouping or scene (as he previously had done as an Impressionist painter). Once the linear structure was in place, Picabia then began to improvise around it, building a composition out of form and color, which he believed could embody inner experience without recourse to the sphere of verbal consciousness. The improvisation proceeded by either affirming the areas bounded by the line, or breaking it down by continuing a color over a boundary, or fading one plane into the next. Picabia probably learned these techniques from his friends among the Cubist painters, like Marcel Duchamp, but in his hands they served his distinctive idea of the self-generating evolution of a painting out of the phylogentic and personal archive of organic memory. It was the painter's method of realizing what Jean D'Udine called imagination: "the faculty of creating new rhythms through the combination of rhythms previously recorded."[75] These were an artist's rendering of the myriad interrelated rates of physiological time through which Marey sought to understand the organism.

Picabia's painting technique hewed closely to the Dalcroze method in dance, as well as Jean D'Udine's generalization of it to a larger aesthetic principle. Dalcroze schools emphasized rhythmic gymnastics (eurhythmics) as the basis of all training, followed by solfege (ear training) and finally, improvisation. The emergence of dance as a key modernist art form around 1900 owed much to physiological aesthetics. For much of the nineteenth-century, physiologists had been fascinated by phenomena variously known as inner sense, organic, and visceral sensibility, which referred to those unclassifiable sensations that could not be traced accurately to one of the five known sense organs. By late century, these phenomena became linked with the original undifferentiated sensations of protoplasm. Close to these sensations were the phenomena of "muscle sense" or "kinaesthesia" (eventually best known as proprioception): the sense of movement, balance, the sense of weight and resistance to the force of gravity that give the body its sense of orientation in space. Kinaesthesia acquired the status of the "sixth sense" because of the ability of muscles to receive sensation and carry out movements, a sentience comparable to the ear and eye. The primacy of dance grew from the idea that kinaesthetic awareness functioned as a kind of primordial cognition, a touchstone for the unification of the differentiated senses and their corresponding special arts like painting or music. Eurythmic exercises became a touchstone for arts pedagogy of all kinds: a key to finding the thread of the *Gesamtkunstwerk* within the constraints of the specific arts.

In Jean D'Udine's aesthetic theory, kinaesthesia was represented by the primacy of the sense of touch as the primordial basis for the unification of the senses. "The sense of touch functions with us each time that life or a work of art interests one or another of our other senses, even when these appear to us impressed by the sensible phenomenon in isolation."[76] Touch was the educator of the other senses, the model for their function, much like the one developed in Raphaël Dubois's notion of "touch-vision." D'Udine's term for the sense of touch in the automatisms of art was "gesture." D'Udine situated this expanded sense of touch at the center of the synthaesthetic function in the arts, asserting that "gesture is the basis of all syanesthesia." [77] Touch or gesture, was, moreover, the educator of the four other senses. It followed that dance should take a correspondingly prime position as the touchstone for all other arts. D'Udine argued that this order of the arts recapitulated a long evolutionary course of aesthetic education. In the beginning, the simple movements of walking gave rise to the acoustic sense of duration, to rhythms, cadences. Then music, which was "able to find in our muscular sensations the notions of duration which served as its primordial element" was born "of bodily movements accomplished by the first representatives of our species."[78]

Following this aesthetic theory, dance figured as the constant theme of Picabia's paintings in these years. Among the New York paintings, besides *Udnie (Young American Girl: Dance)*, dance appeared in *Edtaonisl: Ecclesiastique*, whose title was an anagram for "etoile danseuse" and whose subtitle conjured the painter's amused recollection of the dancer performing before a portly Dominican priest. Besides the obvious contrasts of secular eroticized entertainment and traditional religious asceticism, the amusement deepens when one remembers that, according to Jean D'Udine's theory, the very purpose of art was to excite the memory of the affective rhythms within the observer through the micro-processes of inner imitation. Picabia's canvas would thus suggest the awakening of the memory of the pulsating spirit within the cleric. More generally, and even in secular observers, the dance paintings aim to provoke kinaesthetic self-awareness, calling attention to our orientation in space by techniques such as posing movements that develop in different directions at different speeds and flouting the principle of gravity. In *Culture physique* (1913), for example, Picabia made ribbon-like forms coil over one another while refusing any focus or point of rest, and effacing any distinction between form and space.

Conclusion

The path from Darwin, Huxley, and Haeckel to some early modernist painters might be surprising to those accustomed to thinking of either evolutionary theory or the arts in conventionally bounded ways. Yet it reminds us above all that the theory named after Charles Darwin became attached in the late nineteenth-century to the large and varied enterprise of the life sciences, and brought new ideas and practices to unexpected people and places. Huxley and Haeckel, Darwin's greatest defenders and popularizers and both towering biologists in their own right, showed the power of the English naturalist's theory for the much larger enterprise of biology. The protoplasm theory of inheritance and memory, staunchly allied with Darwinian ambitions yet in disagreement with Darwin's own conjectures about heredity, joined the late nineteenth-century mainstream of evolutionary theory along with a range of new questions of laboratory and field.

Protoplasm doctrines also brought to Darwinism the rich visual culture of these disciplines, above all the graphical methods and recording instruments that rendered evolution in the undulating lines and curves of energy. Waveform lines and curves became the primary visual language of this complex of scientific ideas and experimental questions. This visual idiom appealed to many artists, some of whom were drawn to the scientific phenomena they represented, others who might simply have sought a new aesthetic grammar of waves, energy curves, and rhythmic lines. For avid students of the new science like Edvard Munch and August Strindberg, for example, this visual idiom delivered the science in a familiar medium, close to their own work as artists, making the ideas more compelling and more easily transferred to their art.

But more than simply a visual style or grammar, protoplasm theories furnished a psycho-physiological doctrine that explained sensation and aesthetic perception, including the fashionable condition of synaesthesia as a product of evolutionary processes gone fortunately awry. In the hands of aesthetic theorists like Charles Henry, Félix Le Dantec, and Jean D'Udine, protoplasm underwrote full-blown doctrines of the creation and reception of works of art.

NOTES

1. For general accounts of the life and work of Huxley, see Adrian Desmond's two-volume biography: *Huxley: The Devil's Disciple* (London: Michael Joseph, 1994) ; *Huxley: Evolution's High Priest* (London: Michael Joseph, 1997); and Paul White, *Thomas Huxley: Making the Man of Science* (Cambridge: Cambridge University Press, 2003). On Haeckel, see Robert J. Richards,

The Tragic Sense of Life: Ernst Haeckel and the Struggle over Evolutionary Thought (Chicago: University of Chicago Press, 2008). For different views of Haeckel, see Mario Di Gregorio, *From Here to Eternity: Ernst Haeckel and Scientific Faith* (Göttingen: Vandenhoeck & Ruprecht, 2005); and Olaf Breidbach, *Visions of Nature: The Art and Science of Ernst Haeckel* (New York: Prestel, 2006). On the social context of Haeckel's cell theory in Germany, see Paul Weindling, "Ernst Haeckel, Darwinismus and the Secularization of Nature," in *History, Humanity, and Evolution: Essays in Honor of John C. Greene*, ed. James R. Moore, 311–28 (Cambridge: Cambridge University Press, 1989); and "Theories of the Cell State in Imperial Germany," in *Biology, Medicine, and Society, 1840–1940*, ed. Charles Webster, 99–155 (Cambridge: Cambridge University Press, 1981).

2. Ernst Haeckel, "Über die Wellenzeugung der Lebensteilchen oder die Perigenesis der Plastidule," in *Vorträge und Abhandlungen* (1876; reprint, Berlin: Henschel & Leipzig: Kröner, 1924), 86–142. See also E. Ray Lankester," "A Theory of Heredity: A Review of Haeckel's Pamphlet Entitled Perigenesis der plastidule. From *Nature*, 15th July, 1876," in *The Advancement of Science: Occasional Essays and Addresses* (London and New York: Macmillan, 1890), 280.

3. Charles Darwin, *Variation of Animals and Plants under Domestication*. Reprinting of the 2nd edition (1883), with a new foreward by Harriet Ritvo (Baltimore: Johns Hopkins University Press, 1998).

4. For a surpassing account of Haeckel's science and its relation to Darwin's, see Richards, *The Tragic Sense of Life*.

5. Lankester, "A Theory of Heredity," 286.

6. Ibid.

7. In his "Notebook C," (102), for example, Darwin wrote: "The intimate relation of life with laws of Chemical combination, & the universality of latter render—spontaneous generation not improbable." *Charles Darwin's Notebooks, 1836–1844*, ed. Paul Barrett et al., 269 (Ithaca, N.Y.: Cornell University Press, 1987).

8. Max Schultze, "Die Gattung Cornuspira unter den Monothamien und Bemerkungen über die Organisation und Fortpflanzung der Polythamien," *Archiv für Naturgeschichte* 26 (1860): 287–310; Gerald L. Geison, "The Protoplasmic Theory of Life and the Vitalist-Mechanist Debate," *Isis* 60, no. 3 (1969): 272–92; William Coleman, "Cell, Nucleus, and Inheritance: An Historical Study," *Proceedings of the American Philosophical Society* 109 (1965): 124–58.

9. Thomas Henry Huxley, "The Physical Basis of Life," in *The Fortnightly Review* n.s. 5 (1869): 129–45.

10. Desmond, *Huxley: The Devil's Disciple*, 367.

11. Huxley, "The Physical Basis of Life," 134.

12. Bruce J. Hunt, "Lines of Force, Swirl of Ether," *From Energy to Information: Representation in Science and Technology, Art, and Literature* (Stanford: Stanford University Press, 2002), 100.

13. Huxley, "The Physical Basis of Life," 137.

14. Ibid., 138. For Huxley, protoplasm represented the basis of the principle of the division of physiological labor postulated by Henri Milne-Edwards: One and the same portion of protoplasm may successfully take on the function of feeding, moving, or reproducing appa-

ratus. For Milne-Edwards, the principle of the division of physiological labor demonstrated the primacy of function over the development of organs to carry it out. He later described protoplasmic organisms (*sarcodaires*) as "workers without tools." Henri Milne-Edwards, cited in Yvette Conry, *L'Introduction du Darwinisme en France au XIXe siècle* (Paris: J. Vrin, 1974), 39. On Milne-Edwards' principle, see Camille Limoges, "Darwin, Milne-Edwards, et le principe de divergence," *XII Congrès International d'Histoire des Sciences* 8 (1968): 111–15.

15. Desmond, *Huxley: The Devil's Disciple*, vol. 1, 367.

16. Disraeli, quoted in Anonymous, *Protoplasm, Powheads, Porwiggles, and the Evolution of the Horse from Rhinoceros, Illustrating Professor Huxley's Scientific Mode of Getting Up the Creation and Upsetting Moses. A Guide for Electors* (London: Longmans & Co., 1875), 2. Two decades later, the dignitary Pooh-Bah (Lord High Everything Else) of Gilbert and Sullivan's comic opera *Mikado* would claim a staggering list of titles on the basis of his ability to trace his lineage to "a primordial protoplasmal atomic globule." W. S. Gilbert and Arthur Sullivan, *The Mikado or, The Town of Titipu* (Woodford Green, Essex, UK: International Music Publications, 1996). On the context of the opera, see Christopher Hibbert, *Gilbert and Sullivan and their Victorian World* (New York: American Heritage Pub. Co., 1976).

17. James Hutchinson Stirling, *As Regards Protoplasm in Relation to Professor Huxley's Essay on the Physical Basis of Life* (New Haven: Charles C. Chatfield & Co., 1870), 58-59.

18. Not long after Haeckel speculated that an amorphous albumen was the primordial living matter, Huxley received an inchoate jelly-creature retrieved from the depths of the English Channel from the diggers of the transatlantic undersea telegraph cable. Huxley christened it *Bathybius Haeckeleii*, a gesture that greatly enthused Haeckel. Huxley then speculated further about a pulsating film of protoplasm carpeting the "whole sea bottom from the Persian Gulf round Cape of Good Hope & away by St. Helena to England." Huxley, quoted in Desmond, *Huxley: The Devil's Disciple*, vol. 1, 365. See also Nicholas A. Rupke, "*Bathybius Haeckelii* and the Psychology of Scientific Discovery," *Studies in the History and Philosophy of Science* 7, no. 1 (1976): 53–62.

19. Ernst Haeckel, "Remarks on the Protoplasm Theory," *Quarterly Journal of Microscopical Science* 10 (1869): 223–29.

20. Timothy Lenoir, "Laboratories, Medicine, and Public Life in Germany 1830–1849: Ideological Roots of the Institutional Revolution," in *The Laboratory Revolution in Medicine*, ed. Andrew Cunningham and Perry Williams, 14–71 (Cambridge: Cambridge University Press, 1992).

21. Robert M. Brain and M. Norton Wise, "Muscles and Engines: Indicator Diagrams and Helmholtz's Graphical Methods," in *The Science Studies Reader*, ed. Mario Biagioli, 51–66 (London: Routledge, 1998); Soraya de Chadarevian, "Graphical Method and Discipline: Recording Instruments in Nineteenth-Century Physiology," *Studies in History and Philosophy of Science* 24, no. 2 (1993) : 267–91.

22. Hans-Jörg Rheinberger, *Toward a History of Epistemic Things* (Stanford: Stanford University Press, 1997).

23. Haeckel's was not the only attempt to describe organic tissues as a recording device. Étienne-Jules Marey, in a classic statement on neo-Lamarckian physiology, described how functional movements inscribe themselves as traces on different organs. "The bone sustains,

like soft wax, all of the deformations of the exterior forces imprinted upon it," Marey wrote, concluding that tissues and surfaces served as so many internal recording cylinders, each capturing the imprints of organic movements. Étienne-Jules Marey, "Le transformisme en physiologie," *Revue Scientifique*, 2nd series 35 (1 March) 1873: 818.

24. Ewald Hering, *Über das Gedächtnis als eine allgemeine Funktion der organisierten Materie*, 2nd ed. (Vienna: Gerold, 1876).

25. Ibid., R. Steven Turner, *In the Eye's Mind: Vision and the Hering-Helmholtz Controversy* (Princeton: Princeton University Press, 1994), 57–58.

26. Laura Otis, *Organic Memory: History and the Body in the Late Nineteenth and Early Twentieth Centuries* (Lincoln: University of Nebraska Press, 1994); E. S. Russell, "Samuel Butler and the Memory Theories of Heredity," in *Form and Function: A Contribution to the History of Animal Morphology* (1916; reprint, Chicago: University of Chicago Press, 1982); Samuel Butler, *Unconscious Memory*, 3rd edition (London: Cape, 1922); Richard Semon, *Die Mneme als erhaltendes Prinzip im Wechsel des organischen Geschehens*, 4th and 5th editions (Leipzig: Wilhelm Engelmann, 1920).

27. Haeckel, "Über die Wellenzeugung der Lebensteilchen," 122.

28. In the fifth edition of the *Origin of Species* (1869), Darwin proclaimed Haeckel's tree a bold and "great beginning" that showed "how classification will in the future be treated." Charles Darwin, *The Origin of Species by Charles Darwin: A Variorum Text*, ed. Morse Peckham (Philadelphia: University of Pennsylvania Press, 1959), 676. On Darwin's reception of Haeckel's tree-diagrams, see Richards, *The Tragic Sense of Life*, 136–142.

29. Haeckel, "Über die Wellenzeugung der Lebensteilchen," 129 (italics added for emphasis).

30. Ibid. On the biological tree diagram's many biblical and secular genealogical antecedents, see Mary Boquet, "Family Trees and Their Affinities: The Visual Imperative of the Genealogical Diagram," *The Journal of the Royal Anthropological Institute* 2, no. 1 (1996): 43–66. Richards, in *The Meaning of Evolution: The Morphological Construction and Ideological Reconstruction of Darwin's Theory* (Chicago: University of Chicago Press, 1992), 108, argues convincingly that well before Haeckel, Martin Barry's "Tree of Animal Development" (1837) placed at its roots "the germ, which was morphologically similar in all animals; and from this common ancestral monad the invertebrates branched off on one side, and vertebrates on the other, with fishes, mammals and finally man ramifying through progressively higher branches of the tree."

31. Haeckel, "Über die Wellenzeugung der Lebensteilchen," 129.

32. Ibid., 238.

33. Ibid.

34. Ernst Haeckel, "Zellseelen und Seelenzellen," in *Vorträge und Abhandlungen*, 162–95; Haeckel, "Zellseele und Zellularpsychologie," part IV of: "Freie Wissenschaft und freie Lehre," in *Vorträge und Abhandlungen*, 236–46; and Haeckel, *Essais de psychologie cellulaire*, trans. Jules Soury (Paris: Baillière, 1880).

35. Judy Johns Schloegel and Henning Schmidgen, "General Physiology, Experimental Psychology, and Evolutionism: Unicellular Organisms as Objects of Psychophysiological Research, 1877–1918," *Isis* 93 (2002): 614–45.

36. Alfred Binet, *The Psychic Life of Microorganisms: A Study in Experimental Psychology* (Chicago: Open Court, 1897). Binet's research took part of a wave of French enthusiasm for

Haeckel's cell psychology following Jules Soury's translation of Haeckel's key essays on the subject. See especially Soury's introduction to Ernst Haeckel, *Essais de psychologie cellulaire*, trans. Jules Soury (Paris: Baillière, 1880).

37. Théodule Ribot, "Les mouvements et leur importance psychologiques," *Revue Philosophique* 8 (1879): 383.

38. Marcel Gauchet, *L'Inconscient Cerebral* (Paris: Seuill, 1992).

39. On Henry's relations with Neo-Impressionist painters, see Robert L. Herbert, "'Parade de cirque' de Seurat et l'esthétique de Charles Henry," *Revue* de *l'art* 50 (1980): 9–23; William Innes Homer, *Seurat and the Science of Painting* (Cambridge, Mass.: MIT Press, 1964); and Michael Zimmerman, *Les Mondes de Seurat* (Paris: Albin Michel, 1991).

40. Charles Henry, *Rapporteur ésthétique* (Paris: G. Seguin, 1888), 15.

41. J.[enny] Hericourt, "Une théorie mathematique de l'expression. Le contraste, le rythme et la mesure d'après les travaux de M. Charles Henry," *Revue Scientifique* 44 (1889): 593.

42. Charles Henry, "Introduction à une ésthétique scientifique," *La Revue Contemporaine* 2 (1885): 442.

43. The roots of rhythm are varied, of course; but the physiological aesthetics described here anchored rhythmicity in the primordial legacy of evolution and offered methods for producing lines and movements that could claim to reflect that primordial reality.

44. This was a neo-Lamarckian (and anthropocentric) version of what neo-Darwinian biologists today call an "extended phenotype," in Richard Dawkins's words, "the extension of the action of the genes beyond the outermost boundaries of the organism." See Dawkins, *The Extended Phenotype: The Long Reach of the Gene* (Oxford: Oxford University Press, 1982). In a fascinating development of this thesis, J. Scott Turner, *The Extended Organism: The Physiology of Animal Built-Structures* (Cambridge, Mass.: Harvard University Press, 2000), examines how hives, burrows, termite mounds, galls, plastron, and the houses of caddis flies function as extensions of the physiology of the organisms that build them.

45. Charles Henry, undated letter to Félix Fénéon, Sorbonne University Library archives, Paris.

46. Robert Proctor, "Architecture from the Cell-Soul: René Binet and Ernst Haeckel," *Journal of Architecture* 11 (2006): 407–24.

47. Haeckel's great two-volume study of radiolaria gathered on the *Challenger* expedition was the work that first earned him the admiration of Charles Darwin. On Haeckel's radiolarian studies, and Darwin's reception of them, see Richards, *The Tragic Sense of Life*, 1, 3, 63–67, 74–77, 336–47.

48. Very few copies of the *Esquisses décoratives* exist, but many of the plates have been reproduced in René Binet, *From Nature to Form*, with essays by Robert Proctor and Olaf Breidbach (Munich: Prestel, 2007).

49. Jacques Desroches, "La Porte monumentale de l'Exposition," *Revue illustrée de l'Exposition universelle*, 25 June 1900, 127. On the Porte Binet, see also Phillipe Julien, *The Triumph of Art Nouveau: Paris Exhibition in 1900* (New York: Phaidon, 1974), 56–57; and Deborah Silverman, *Art Nouveau in Fin-de-Siècle France: Politics, Psychology, and Style* (Berkeley: University of California Press, 1989).

50. Jean D'Udine, *L'Art et le geste* (Paris: F. Alcan, 1910), 116.

51. Raphaël Dubois, *Anatomie et physiologie compares de la pholade dactyle. Structure, locomotion, tact, olfaction, gestation, vision, dermatoptique, photogenie, avec une théorie générale des sensations* (Paris: Masson, 1892).

52. Ibid., Jules Soury, "Anatomie et physiologie compare de la pholade dactyle," *Revue Philosophique* 40 (1893): 541–51.

53. Stanislaw Przybyzewski, *Errinerungen an das literarische Berlin* (Munich: Winkler, 1965). On Munch's engagement with physiology and medicine, see Shelly Wood Cordulack, *Edvard Munch and the Physiology of Symbolism* (London: Associated University Presses, 2002).

54. August Strindberg, "Wo sind die Nerven der Pflanzen?" in *Verwirrte Sinneseindrücke* (Amsterdam: Verlag der Kunst/OPA, 1998), 190. Other essays in this volume report related experiments with protoplasm, especially "Das Seufzen der Steine" (141–74) and "Die Spectral-analyse" (113–16).

55. Stanislaw Przybyzewski, *Das Werk des Edvard Munch: Vier Aufsätze* (Berlin: Fischer, 1894).

56. Ibid., 2. The French words were an unacknowledged quotation from Charles Baudelaire's *Les Fleurs du mal* (1857).

57. Edvard Munch, unpublished notebook (1906), Munch T 2785, Munch Manuscript Collection, Munch Museum, Oslo.

58. Edvard Munch, *Livsfrisens tilblivelse* (Oslo, 1929), cited in Cordulack, *Edvard Munch and the Physiology of Symbolism*, 44.

59. Edward Carpenter, The *Art of Creation: Essays on the Self and its Powers* (London: George Allen, 1900), 2–7. See also Carpenter, *Intermediate Types among Primitive Folk: A Study in Social Evolution* (New York: Mitchell Kennerley, 1914); and Carpenter, *Love's Coming of Age* (London: Methuen, 1896).

60. Max Nordau, *Degeneration*, translated from the second edition of the German work, introduction by George L. Mosse (Lincoln: University of Nebraska Press, 1968); Sander L. Gilman and Edward J. Chamberlain, eds., *Degeneration—the Dark Side of Progress* (1892; reprint New York: Columbia University Press, 1985); Daniel Pick, *Faces of Degeneration: A European Disorder, c. 1848–1918* (Cambridge: Cambridge University Press, 1989).

61. Nordau, *Degeneration*, 142. On Nordau's critique of synaesthesia, see also Pascal Rousseau, "Confusion des sens: Le débat évolutionniste sur la synesthésie dans les débuts de l'abstraction en France," *Les Cahiers du Mnam* 74 (2000–2001): 5–33.

62. Nordau, *Degeneration*, 142.

63. Félix Le Dantec, "L'intuition," *Les Arts de la vie* 1 (1904): 31.

64. Ibid., 32.

65. Ibid., 30–32.

66. Ibid., 32.

67. Ibid., 33.

68. Rousseau, "Confusion des sens," 14–15.

69. D'Udine, *L'art et le Geste. . .*, 115. The links between Picabia and Jean D'Udine have been made convincingly by Arnaud Pierre, *Francis Picabia: La Peinture sans Aura* (Paris: Gallimard, 2002), 102–105.

70. Maria Lluïsa Borràs, *Picabia* (London: Thames and Hudson, 1985).

71. Bergson's theories of memory, evolution, and time drew heavily on the protoplasm literature as well. See Yvette Conry, *L'Évolution Créatrice d'Henri Bergson: Investigations critique* (Paris: L'Harmattan: 2000), 75–90.

72. On the Paris and New York contexts of Picabia's turn to nonfigurative painting, see the fine study by Virginia Spate, *Orphism: The Evolution of Non-figurative Painting in Paris 1910–1914* (Oxford: Clarendon Press, 1979).

73. Gertrude Stein, *The Autobiography of Alice B. Toklas* (New York: Random House, 1961), 210.

74. Francis Picabia in *New York Tribune* (1913), quoted in Spate, *Orphism*. . . . , 320.

75. D'Udine, *L'Art et le Geste*, 6.

76. Ibid., 118.

77. Ibid., 234.

78. Ibid., 245.

CHAPTER 5

Framing Darwin

A Portrait of Eugenics

FAE BRAUER

In July 1912, nearly one thousand scientists, politicians, and delegates from every European capital, as well as from eugenics societies in America, Australia, and New Zealand, flocked to the First International Eugenics Congress in London.[1] Presided over by Charles Darwin's son, Major Leonard Darwin, it was strategically timed in June to coincide with the British Parliament's second reading of the Mental Deficiency, Inebriates, and White Slave Traffic bills.[2] Thirty-three papers in five languages examined "the great Darwin's doctrines" in relation to Francis Galton's theories of heritability, eugenic procreation, and miscegenation of "the feeble-minded," as well as the asylumization, segregation, and sterilization of "defectives, degenerates and criminals."[3] These papers were visually corroborated, if not compounded, by the eugenic images assembled from America, Australia, France, Germany, and all parts of the United Kingdom for the first International Eugenics Exhibition.[4] While the ancestral and professional relationship between Charles Darwin and Francis Galton was constantly emphasized throughout the Congress, they were both "framed" by their pedigrees (see figures 5.1 and 5.2) and jointly exhibited portraits (see figures 5.5 to 5.8) at this exhibition as not just the pioneers but linked progenitors of eugenics. Far from being an isolated event, this "framing" appeared in the first volume of Karl Pearson's massive biography of Galton, *The Life, Letters and Labours of Francis Galton* (see figure 5.7).[5] It also appeared in the subsequent International Eugenics Exhibitions held in 1921 and 1932 (see figures 5.2 and 5.8), as well as in the spate of books, journals, and magazines published on eugenics. "It is really on Darwin's work that the modern society of eugenics is based, and it owes its beginning to Darwin's cousin, Francis Galton," explained Paul Popenoe and Roswell Hill Johnson in their popular college textbook, *Applied Eugenics*.[6] Yet due to the "shadow" cast over eugenics by its association with genocide and the Holocaust, the relationship between the so-called "father" of eugenics, Francis Galton, and his cousin, Charles Darwin, became expunged, while any linkages between Darwin's evolution theory and Galton's eugenics were severed.[7]

"After the second World War," Daniel Kevles observes, "eugenics" became a word to be hedged with caveats in Britain and virtually a dirty word in the United States, where it had long been identified with "racism."[8] That this sanitization persists is illustrated by the exhibition of memorabilia of Darwin and his family at Down House, there being no reference to Galton, let alone eugenics, despite Darwin's son Leonard having presided over the British Eugenics Society for nearly thirty years.[9] Yet not only does this process of whitewashing the stigma of eugenics deny the relationship forged by Darwin and Galton over thirty years. It also represents the antithesis to ways in which leading academics, artists, scientists, eugenic societies, and the press all called attention to their closeness. Through an interplay of text and image at international eugenics conferences and exhibitions, as well as in books, journals, and newspaper articles devoted to Darwin and Galton, their relationship was constantly highlighted. Through these visual cultures, eugenics was presented as not only the ingenious outcome of a family of genius, but also the next natural step to be taken in "selection" after Darwin. Contrary to the post-Holocaust segregation of Darwin from Galton, this chapter will first establish their closeness, before revealing how their theoretical differences became elided. Through an examination of Galton's theories of heredity and ability in relation to visual cultures of pedigrees, silhouettes, and generic portraits at the First International Eugenic Exhibition and in the first major book published on Galton, it will reveal how these two men of science were jointly "framed" as the founding "fathers" of eugenics.

Hereditary Genius: The Darwin, Galton, and Wedgwood Pedigree

It was the launching of *Origin of Species* that consolidated the relationship between the half-cousins, Charles Darwin and Francis Galton.[10] Even fifty years after first reading *Origin*, Galton could still vividly recall its impact, especially Darwin's statement: "We cannot suppose that all the breeds were suddenly produced as perfect and as useful as we now see them; indeed in many cases, we know that this has not been their history. The key is man's power of accumulative selection: nature gives successive variations; man adds them up in certain directions useful to him."[11] In his introduction to *Hereditary Genius*, Galton posited eugenics as the next logical step to be taken after *Origin*.[12] "Natural ability" operated in culture, according to Galton, in much the same way as "natural selection" functioned in nature. "Every long-established race has necessarily its peculiar fitness for the conditions under which it has lived," he explained, "owing to the sure operation of Darwin's law of natural selection."[13] Elaborating the term Darwin had used in the fifth edition of *Origin*, "survival of the fittest" to "survivorship of the fittest," Galton argued that those races best able to survive culture were equivalent to those species best able to survive nature.[14] Only those with "intellect and disposition" would have sufficient zeal, according to Galton, to overcome hindrances strewn along "the path to eminence."[15] Consistent with his genderism and Anglocentricism, Galton considered the British male best able to overcome the great number of cultural obstructions strewn in their career paths to produce far more "first-class works of literature, philosophy, or art" than any American or European.[16]

By focusing upon families of British men in which their members had achieved eminence as judges, statesmen, commanders, writers, and scientists, Galton endeavored to prove that "men who are largely aided by social advantages, are unable to achieve eminence, unless they are endowed with high natural gifts."[17] Darwin's theory of pangenesis was singled out to validate this deduction.[18] If Darwin's theory of pangenesis were true, Galton hypothesized that the average characteristics of descendants and their deviations could be predicted not just in a family but an entire population.[19] "This theory," he concluded, "is of enormous service to those who inquire into heredity. It gives a key that unlocks every one of the hitherto unopened barriers to our comprehension of its nature."[20] To corroborate this theory, Galton chose the Darwin family.

Due to his "great vigour, humour and geniality," as well as his progeny, Galton located Erasmus as the starting point of the Darwin family's eminence.[21] Galton highlighted the achievements of his sons and his grandsons, particularly "the illustrious modern naturalist" who had achieved eminence for his "theory of natural selection."[22] Following his hereditary model, Galton then singled out two of Charles' sons, one of whom, he pointed out, was "second wrangler at Cambridge, 1868" (George) while another (Leonard, who became the first President of the Eugenics Education Society) was "second in the Woolwich examination of the same year."[23] While the Darwins' judicious marriages were compared to the astute coupling in nature described by Darwin, Galton considered that "natural ability" became cumulative through heredity, each successive generation becoming increasingly exceptional. This was not just demonstrated by the example of Charles but supposedly corroborated by his theory of "natural selection": "The sons of gifted men are decidedly more precocious than their parents . . . I do not care to quote cases, because it is a normal fact, analogous to what is observed in diseases and in growths of all kinds, as has been clearly laid down by Mr. Darwin."[24] With the Darwin family seeming to clinch his thesis, Galton concluded that regardless of circumstances, a man of "natural ability" would succeed while a man of moderate ability would fail.

So convinced was Galton of his hereditarian thesis that even when challenged by the environmental counterthesis posed by the Swiss botanist Darwin praised, Alphonse de Candolle, he was undeterred.[25] Galton circulated a questionnaire on the background and education of scientists—a new form of survey for its time—and began tabulating the results. As 56 out of the 91 scientists he surveyed claimed their scientific aspirations and talent were innate rather than environmentally determined, Galton felt vindicated. In *English Men of Science: Their Nature and Nurture*, Galton singled out the Darwin family to corroborate his theory of their "natural history" as hereditary and cumulative.[26] Again he posited Erasmus Darwin as the source of this "pedigree."[27] Galton pointed out that by the third generation, the progeny was even more remarkable as proven by "the Aristotle of our days," whom "all scientific men reverence and love": Charles Darwin.[28]

Nearly forty years later, in *Noteworthy Families (Modern Science)*, published by the Eugenics Record Office in collaboration with Darwin's loyal publisher, John Murray, Galton tried to show how the Darwin and Galton generation following Charles had achieved eminence, as was demonstrated by George Howard Darwin and Major Leonard Darwin.[29] The entries in *Hereditary Genius*, *English Men of Science*, and *Noteworthy Families* then became transmuted into the visual cultures of pedigrees as illustrated by *The Inheritance of Ability, as exemplified in the Darwin, Galton and Wedgwood Families* (figure 5.1). This pedigree became one of the prize exhibits for the first and succeeding International Eugenics Exhibitions. This is illustrated by its elaboration into ten generations with twenty-two photographs of the extended family, particularly of Charles Darwin and Francis Galton, for the Third International Eugenics Exhibition in New York in 1932 (figure 5.2).

"Charts, pedigrees, photographs, and specimens illustrative of Heredity, especially in man" were announced as the prime objective of the First International Eugenics Exhibition.[30] When the methodology of eugenics was elaborated from 1900 until 1920, this period represented, according to Pauline Mazumdar, "the age of pedigrees."[31] In *Natural Inheritance*, Galton had likened their articulation to "a necklace," the main line of heredity being comparable to its "chain," the personalities appearing like "pendants attached to its links."[32] For being able to convey the network of relationships at a glance without contentious interpretations, they were highly valued by Director of the Biometric Laboratory, Karl Pearson.[33] In looking like "rivers flowing steadily on wide fronts, carrying on their surface patches of refuse," they were lauded by Leonard Darwin for also revealing undesirable heredity.[34] So prized were they for exposing dominant and recessive modes of transmission by the American Mendelian eugenicist, Charles Davenport, and such British Mendelians as William Batesman that Mendelism became, in Mazumdar's words, "almost entirely visual: a matter of the inspection of pedigrees."[35] The First International Eugenics Exhibition appeared "dominated by pedigrees of all kinds."[36]

At this exhibition, there were pedigrees showing the inbreeding of such royal families as the Archduchess Maria of Tuscany, Kaiser Wilhelm II, and the Hapsburg dynasty over twelve generations, as well as Cleopatra.[37] The literary, musical, commercial, and agricultural abilities inherited by a polygamous Utah family who had married amongst themselves were exhibited by the Agricultural College of Utah in a spectacular 147-foot-long chart.[38] By contrast, sixteen pedigrees collected by eugenic fieldworkers in America were displayed alongside charts and statistics to illustrate Mendelian recessive heredity in the American Breeders Association exhibition curated by E. J. Lidbetter and Davenport.[39] A system for making pedigree records was even exhibited.[40] Despite their differences, Mazumdar surmizes, "the pedigree represented the most convincing demonstration of the basic hereditarian claim that like produces like."[41]

Some pedigrees exhibited the risk of extinction when pedigree was disrupted through dislocation, miscegenation, or inbreeding as purportedly verified by Charles Darwin's *Variation of Animals and Plants under Domestication.*[42] The most ominous of these exhibits was devised by the German Archiv für Rassen und Gesellschafts Biologie. Its huge diagrams to illustrate the inheritance of progressive muscular atrophy, tuberculosis, and such "taints" of "moral imbecility" as alcoholism, madness, and "abnormality of character" culminated in the pedigree of the Zero von Jorger family.[43] Pictured as a huge spider's web with a spiral curving inwards, this pedigree was designed to illustrate the gradual extinction of this Mannheim-based family from 3,081 to 543 in one hundred years due to degeneration and miscegenation.[44] Quick to play upon the surname "Zero" in order to sensationalize its probable extinction, the British press headlined it as the "Worst Family in the World."[45] By contrast, the British press lauded the Wedgwood, Darwin, and Galton pedigree for demonstrating the opposite (see figure 5.1).

"Relics of Charles Darwin, Sir Francis Galton, and Gregor Mendel" had been announced as the other main mission of the First International Eugenics Exhibition.[46] While not a relic, *Chart Showing the Inheritance of Ability*

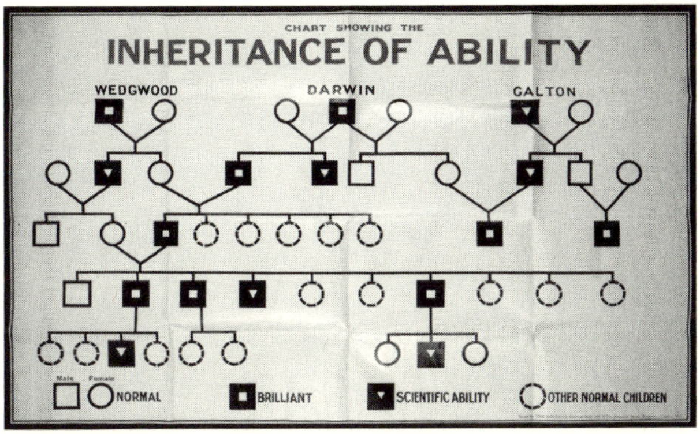

Figure 5.1 Chart showing the Inheritance of Ability, as exemplified in the Darwin, Galton and Wedgwood Families (After Whetham and Marshall). *Paper poster exhibited and issued by the Eugenics Education Society, Exhibit O 5, The First International Eugenics Exhibition, 1912; Galton Institute, SA/EUG/G.34; Wellcome Library, London.*

(figure 5.1) seemed able to straddle both exhibition aims. Devised by Cambridge physicists W. C. D. Whetham and C. G. Marshall, this chart was featured regularly in science journals, particularly the *Journal of Heredity* to which Whetham and Marshall regularly contributed.[47] It was designed to diagramize Galtonian eugenics, both Whetham and Marshall being members of Cambridge University's Eugenics Society, as were Francis, Horace, and George Darwin. Displayed in the Eugenics Education Society installation of pedigrees, this chart was surrounded by examples of Mendelian inheritance in peas, mice, and blue Andalusian fowls.[48] Those adjacent to it were three pedigrees designed by Galton. The first, "Standard Scheme of Descent," was designed to show how regression to the mean population occurs; the second, "Descent of Qualities in a Population," and third, "Mr. Booth's Classification of All London with the Normal Classes," were designed to reveal how pauperism was linked to the transmission of defect.[49] By contrast, *Chart Showing the Inheritance of Ability* was designed to reveal how the opposite could be achieved through heredity and judicious marriage as demonstrated by Darwin's and Galton's ancestry.

While Mendelian pedigrees generally traced only two filial generations, Galtonian pedigrees revealed vaster kinship networks. Following Galton's analysis of *Hereditary Genius*, this chart showed that in the first generation of Wedgwood, Darwin, and Galton families, only two out of the three males and four females proved to be brilliant, with only one of the males revealing exceptional scientific ability. By the second generation of four males and six females, the males with scientific ability had trebled, while by the third generation, the brilliant males had doubled. Although the fourth and fifth generations show how the figures seemed to have stabilized, nevertheless they disclosed how brilliance and scientific ability had continued unabated without any trace of the defects associated with pauperism, let alone the criminals,

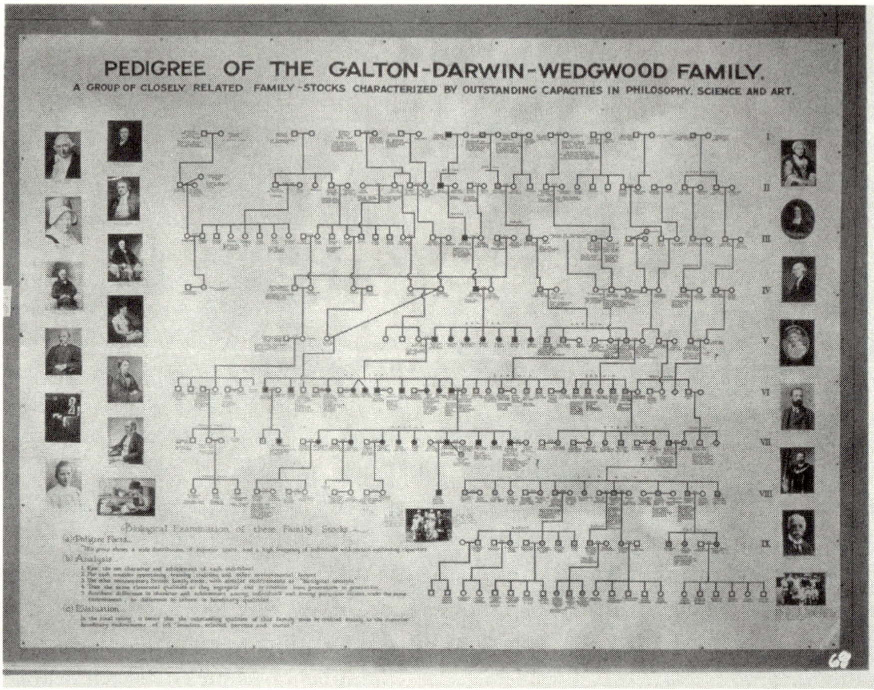

Figure 5.2 Pedigree of Galton-Darwin-Wedgwood Family, Third International Eugenics Conference, 1932. *The Harry H. Laughlin Papers, Truman State University, Blk photo 1,19; copyright Cold Spring Harbor Laboratory.*

lunatics, and feeble-minded persons that had tainted the Zero von Jorger family. Instead of the hereditary downfall signified by the vortex model of the Zero von Jorger family, the diachronic pedigree of the Wedgwood, Darwin, and Galton pedigree showed the efflorescence of these families with every generation. These differences were highlighted by the London press.

"In the course of time," the London *Pall Mall Gazette* declared of the Zero von Jorgers, "this family has burdened the sound and fit with taxation amounting to hundreds of thousands of pounds."[50] By contrast, the Wedgwood, Darwin, and Galton families, they claimed, had enriched the sound and fit with their brilliance and scientific genius.[51] Their prudent cultivation of heredity had culminated in producing the founding fathers of eugenics.[52] Yet as the books *Hereditary Genius, English Men of Science, Noteworthy Families,* and *Kantsaywhere* indicate, long had Galton disseminated this view and contributed to its discursive formation. Rarely did he hesitate to link his abilities not just to the Darwin family but to those of Charles specifically. Even in his speech at the Royal Society dinner on being awarded the Gold Medal in 1886,

Galton provided an analysis for his heredity that seems like a textual equivalent to its delineation in the diachronic chart:

> I can assure you as a specialist in heredity, that I am not speaking without reason when I say that qualities which I seem to have inherited through two of my grandparents yielded precedence to those that I certainly inherited from the other two. . . . Again, as regards biology, I am sure there is a similarity between the form of the bent of my mind and that of my mother's father, Dr. Erasmus Darwin. The resemblance chiefly lies in a strong disposition to generalize upon every-day matters that commonly pass unnoticed. I have myself attempted some of the very inquiries to which he had drawn attention, in complete unconsciousness that he had done so. It was owing to this hereditary bent of mind that I was well prepared to assimilate the theories of Charles Darwin when they first appeared in his "Origin of Species."[53]

In purportedly practicing eugenics well before its scientificization to ensure the inheritance of ability and its proliferation, the Wedgwood, Darwin, and Galton families were hailed as the eugenic model for all other families to emulate. Through the display of this pedigree, together with the exhibition of their portraits, both Darwin and Galton appeared well and truly framed as the progenitors of eugenics.

"Hereditary Improvement" and Pangenesis: Photography and Silhouettes

From Darwin's hypothesis of pangenesis, Galton developed his theory of heredity. Working from aspects of Darwin's theory not involving the transportation of hereditary particles, he hypothesized that the fertilized ovum contains a large number of hereditary elements that he called "stirps" (see chapter 4), the latent parts of which could be transmitted to the next generation, as indicated in *Natural Inheritance*.[54] This was the premise for his theory of hereditary improvement.[55] Following Darwin's theory in *Descent of Man*, Galton considered that even though the improvement of a race should be a national duty, civilization had "spoilt" it.[56] By establishing a network of regional record offices to register the pedigree, measurements, and photographs of gifted families, Galton claimed the nation-state could foster "survival of the fittest" and breed a "favoured race"—a process he called "viriculture."[57] By encouraging gifted families to proliferate while prohibiting ungifted ones from doing so, Galton envisaged that the latter would be extinguished in much the same way as Darwin described the extinction of "barbarians" on contact with "civilized nations."[58] After three generations, the selected race would bear "purer blood," he maintained, but only after six generations would inferior reversions stop.[59]

The same month that "Hereditary Improvement" was published in 1873, the *Times* published Galton's letter provocatively entitled "Africa for the Chinese," in which he speculated on a comparable result arising if the Chinese were to outbreed "the Negro" in Africa.[60] Far from dismissing Galton's breeding proposals, George Darwin eagerly embraced them in his article, "On Beneficial Restrictions to Liberty of Marriage."[61] Immediately, the Catholic comparative anatomist, St. George Mivart, denounced both Galton and George Darwin for encouraging licentiousness and held Charles Darwin directly responsible for his son's views (see chapters 2 and 8). No doubt Mivart's fit of pique had already been fueled by what Darwin called "the tremendous stir-up" ignited by Galton's "excellent" article, "Statistical Inquiries into the Efficacy of Prayer."[62] Praising his son's scheme as "a good omen for the future," Charles Darwin severed all connection with St. George Mivart.[63] It was at this contentious moment in Darwin and Galton's professional lives when visual culture became a crucial component in their research for very different reasons.

One year before Galton had recommended that in "Hereditary Improvement," photography become an essential component of human data, Darwin had deployed photography along with other visual cultures in *The Expression of the Emotions in Man and Animals*.[64] Darwin was "one of the first scientists," as Phillip Prodger points out, "to attempt to use photography to record moments of activity previously invisible to the human eye," his *Expression of the Emotions* being one of the first photographically illustrated scientific texts.[65] Of its twenty-nine photographic illustrations and numerous engraved plates from illustrations, three were photographs from Dr. G.-B. Duchenne de Boulogne's 1862 *Mécanisme de la physionomie humaine*, four were photographs that Darwin had commissioned from the Swedish-born, British-based photographer Oscar Gustave Rejlander, and three were by the Hamburg photographer Herr Kindermann.[66] In his introduction, Darwin readily acknowledged his close collaboration with Rejlander.[67] So important were Rejlander's and Kindermann's photographs to Darwin that no expense was spared in turning them into heliotype illustrations, three of which were fold-outs.[68] Not only did Darwin value them as "the best photographs in my collection," he also stressed that the heliographs of these photographs were "faithful copies" and "much superior for my purpose to any drawing, however carefully executed."[69] Their seeming fidelity and accuracy was lauded by Darwin: "That the expression is true, may be inferred from the fact that out of fifteen persons, to whom the original was shown, without any clue as to what was intended being given them, fourteen immediately answered 'despairing sorrow', 'suffering endurance', 'melancholy', and so forth."[70] Yet given the incapacity of photographic technology at that time to capture expression instantaneously, paradoxically Rejlander's photographs were simulations rather than documentation of "expressions" that were "true."[71] That Darwin recognized that their truth was contrived if not doctored, did not deter him from ranking the factual authenticity of photography above life drawing, as did Galton, but for very different reasons.[72]

Not only did the Council of the Anthropological Institute approve Galton's proposal to collect measurements of heights and weights of school students, they also approved his proposal to collect photographs. Three years later, when Director-General of Prisons, Sir Edmund du Cane, commissioned Galton to undertake a comparable study of criminals, modelled upon those conducted by Cesare Lombroso, Galton began his investigation with drawings and photographs.[73] While Darwin may have planned for *The Expression of the Emotions* to act as a corrective to Lavater's *Essay on Physiognomy*, Galton seems to have planned to elaborate Lavater's thesis and apply it to criminals.[74] Darwin's rejection of treatises on physiognomy and phrenology seemed as staunch as Galton's acceptance of them as a premise for his methodology.[75] His mission seemed to stem from Immanuel Kant's succinct definition of Lavater's physiognomy as "the art of judging what lies within a man, whether in terms of his way of sensing or of his way of thinking, from his visible form and so from his exterior."[76]

In his lectures and articles, Galton often showed or referenced Lavater's profiles from the *Physiognomische Fragmente*.[77] Just as Lavater had invented instruments for measuring parts of the face and calculating proportional differences between profiles, so did Galton.[78] Yet, while Galton's calculations were complemented by photography, Lavater's were complemented by the art of creating portraits with scissors facilitated by his invention of a *machine for drawing silhouettes*.[79] Disseminated by *The Pocket Lavater*, so popular did Lavater's "science" become that silhouettes burgeoned. During Dr. Erasmus Darwin's and Tertius Galton's lifetimes, they were the most prominent form of portraiture and one to which they both subscribed. Not only did Dr. Erasmus Darwin commission silhouettes of his wife and himself but also of his son and himself playing chess, while Tertius Galton commissioned portraits of himself with his children, Adèle, Erasmus, Emma, and Bessie (figures 5.3 and 5.4). Following Lavater's semiotics, the prominent aquiline noses, long receding foreheads, and curvular craniums crisply delineated in these silhouettes, without any sign of "weak" concavities, would have revealed the immense strength and high intelligence of the Darwin and Gal-

Figure 5.3 Anon., *Erasmus Darwin (left) and his Father, Dr. Erasmus Darwin (right) at Chess. From a silhouette at Claverson in the possession of Mr. Wheeler Galton; Karl Pearson,* The Life, Letters and Labours of Francis Galton, *vol. 1 (London: Cambridge University Press, 1914), Plate IV; Wellcome Library, London.*

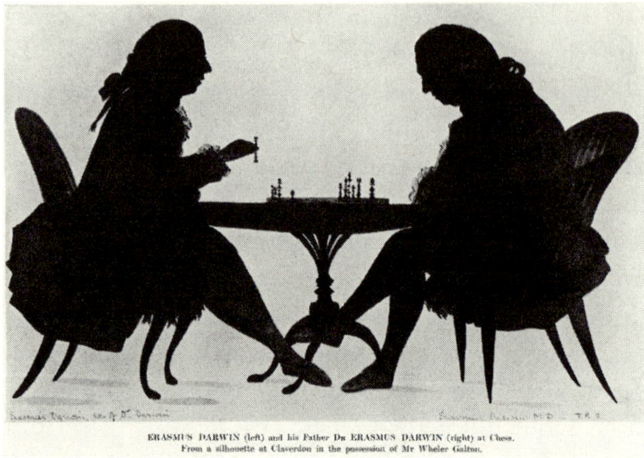

ton family.[80] Furthermore, the very projection of Dr. Erasmus Darwin's nose and its continuous line with the slope of the forehead, following Lavater's nasal index, would have signified that he was not only brilliant but also commanding. As these silhouettes displayed the heredity of ability in the Darwin and Galton families, this was no doubt why they were chosen for display alongside the chart and the portraits in the First International Eugenics Exhibition.

While Lavater divided the profile into nine sections, he did not calculate their differences, claiming that such a project would need "a Mathematical Physiognomist of the next age."[81] His prophecy seemed to be fulfilled with Galton, who used the very instrument that would deal a deadly blow to silhouettes. Ironically, as Galton pointed out in 1887, photography was also the instrument best able to redeem them, particularly once it was realized how silhouette photography could facilitate profile measurement.[82] By overlaying full-face and profile photographs onto a single plate, Galton explained that he was able "to obtain with mechanical precision a generalized picture; one that represents no man in particular, but . . . possessing the average features of any group of men."[83] His and Darwin's use of photography crystallized their differences.

For Darwin, photography was instrumental in freeing physiognomy from its moral and religious roots and for taking to task those natural theologians, like Charles Bell and William Paley, who claimed that humans were unique in their capacity for expressing their feelings through facial muscles due to the hand of God.[84] Since expression occurred at times through the movement of tissue in response to nerves preparing for fight or flight, for Darwin it was adaptive behavior that proved that evolution by natural selection with atten-

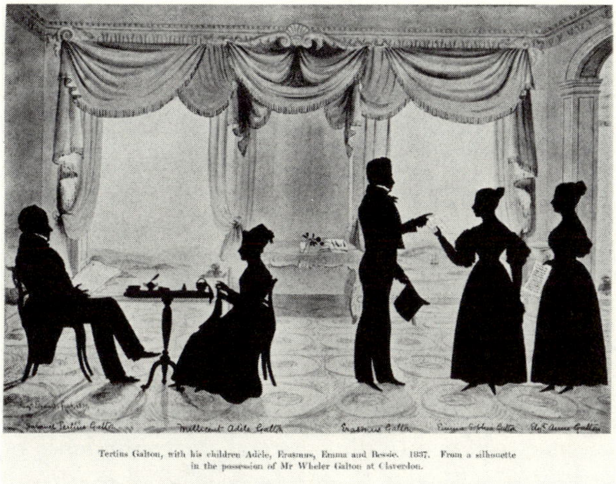

Figure 5.4 Anon., *Tertius Galton, with his children, Adèle, Erasmus, Emma and Bessie, 1817. From a silhouette at Claverson in the possession of Mr. Wheeler Galton; Karl Pearson,* The Life, Letters and Labours of Francis Galton, *vol. 1 (London: Cambridge University Press, 1914), Plate XXXIV; Wellcome Library, London.*

dant emotions occurred in humans as much as in animals. As Darwin pointed out: "Even insects express anger, terror, jealousy, and love by their stridulation."[85] In revealing how cats, dogs, hens, swans, porcupines, primates, and humans share expression, the photography and drawing in Darwin's treatise were seminal in proving that "man is derived from some lower animal form" and that "various races are due to inheritance from a single parent-form."[86] Instead of photography drawn from composite printing processes being used to demonstrate racial unity and the human continuum of animal life, Galton adapted composite processes of photography to demonstrate differences in race, hereditary, ability, and psychology, as exemplified by his composite portrait of eight skulls of male Andaman Islanders exhibited at the British Association in 1881.[87]

Just as Lavater believed that physiognomy could lay bare character and morality concealed by signs of human status, so Galton considered that composite photography could lay bare character "type" and intelligence concealed by fashion, particularly as he believed that mentality, like heredity, left its mark on physical features. Just as Lavater subscribed to what Ernst Gombrich called the "physiognomical fallacy," so did Galton, but instead of equating physical beauty with moral goodness, he equated it with eugenic fitness.[88] Such faith did he have in his invention that Galton believed composite photography could give everyone the skill of Lavater's connoisseur physiognomist. "A composite portrait represents the picture," he explained, that would rise before the mind's eye of a man who had the gift of imagination in an exalted degree."[89] This was why composite photography became integral to his theory of eugenics.

The Death of Darwin: The Birth of Eugenics and Composite Photography

On no other occasion in his life did this reserved and diffident man express himself so emotionally affected as upon Darwin's death, as illustrated by the letter Galton wrote to Emma Darwin.

> I feel at times quite sickened at the loss of Charles Darwin. I owed more to him than to any man living or dead; and I never entered his presence without feeling as a man in the presence of a beloved sovereign . . . The world seems so blank to me now Charles Darwin is gone. I reverenced and loved him thoroughly.[90]

By no means was his reverence confined to his personal correspondence or confidences, as illustrated by Galton's speech on being awarded the Royal Society's Gold Medal for his statistical contributions to biology in 1886. At the dinner in his honor held by the Fellows of the Royal Society, Galton openly admitted to this prestigious assembly that a hereditary hand, especially that of his cousin's, had "moulded" his scientific career.[91] It was, in the words of John C. W. Waller, "a moment of extraordinary catharsis."[92] Galton's interest in biological investigations markedly declined, according to Pearson, and increasingly he devoted himself to quantitative and psychometric analyses.[93] On the death of Darwin, he began to use the term eugenics.

In his *Inquiries into Human Faculty and Its Development,* Galton provided the definition of eugenics that became the mission statement of the Eugenics Education Society and the crest of the First International Eugenics Congress: "Eugenics is the study of agencies which, under social control, have for their object the improvement of the physical and mental qualities of future generations."[94]

To gain anthropometric data for his quest, in 1883 Galton published "Medical Family Registers," in which he requested the support of doctors and families.[95] In his pamphlet *The Record of Family Faculties,* Galton offered incentives for doing so, prizes of 500 pounds being awarded to those doctors who best succeeded. Once his Anthropometric Laboratory was installed at the Royal Horticultural Society in South Kensington for the International Health Exhibition in May 1884, he vastly extended his database. By the time the exhibition closed in 1885, he had compiled data on 9,337 individuals, measured in seventeen different ways. Continuing to operate the laboratory at his own expense in the Science Galleries of the South Kensington Museum, Galton collected statistics on 3,678 people over three years. He also collected individual portraits of members of families that proved instrumental to his composite photography.

Composite photography, as Galton first explained in 1878, "enables us to compare the average features of the produce with those of the parent." To clarify its value for eugenics, he added: "Composites . . . would undoubtedly aid the breeders of animals to judge of the results of any proposed union, better than they are able to do at present."[96] From individual portraits of members of families, Galton produced family composites to examine the hereditary transmission of physiological character and, in keeping with eugenics, predict the incidence of physiological and psychological characteristics between generations. These results were published in 1889 in his highly influential book, *Natural Inheritance*, designed, as its play upon words indicates, to act as the next step to "natural selection."[97]

To reveal features that supposedly typified different groups of criminals, Galton was commissioned by the Director General of Prisons to examine photographs of criminals, which he rephotographed onto the same photographic plate. From this experiment, he deduced that if physical features reflected specific behavioral or racial traits and if these were inherited, composite photography would provide a rapid means of identifying these characteristics. It could provide a means of detecting the potential criminal and preventing crime. Galton also experimented with the process to produce composite portraits of Jewish boys and, with the help of Leonard Darwin, to produce composite portraits of officers. However, after commissioning hundreds of photographs of patients with tuberculosis at Guy's Hospital, Galton turned to phthisical patients at London's lunatic asylums, discovering from his composites that no firm correlation could be established between particular physiognomic characteristics and a predisposition to insanity. "The results lend no countenance to the belief that any special type of face predominates among phthisical patients," Galton admitted, "nor to the generally entertained opinion that the narrow, void or tubercular face is more common in phthisis than among other diseases. Whether it is more common than among the rest of the healthy population we cannot at present say."[98] Nevertheless, he insisted that it was still possible to distinguish between a particular physiognomic type that predominated among the mentally ill and criminal population. Galton maintained that composite photography could not only expose the eugenically unfit but could also prove that mental, moral, and physical difference amongst individuals, classes, and races were transmittable by inheritance. This was supposedly proven by his composite portraits of academicians, geologists, naturalists, mathematicians, and American scientific men.[99] While maintaining that scientific and artistic ability could be enhanced through heredity, conversely disease, disability, alcoholism, and pauperism could be avoided, he claimed, with the assistance of composite photography.

"What Nature does blindly, slowly, and ruthlessly," Galton explained in his *Essays in Eugenics*, "man may do providently, quickly, and kindly."[100]

To pursue his vision, Galton persuaded the University of London to provide rooms in University College London for a Eugenics Record Office. In bequeathing a huge annuity of 45,000 pounds to endow a chair in eugenics, he enabled Pearson to become the first Galton Professor of Eugenics. Galton also bequeathed 500 pounds each year to the Francis Galton Laboratory of National Eugenics as well as his immense collection of photography, including his composites. Galton's use of photography inspired publication by Pearson from 1909 until 1958 of *The Treasury of Human Inheritance*. Not only was photography used in these books to demonstrate the heredity of ability, particularly among Western races, but in order to mobilize paranoia of degeneration during the British quest for National Efficiency, it also was used to highlight the prevalence of degeneracy, particularly among non-Western races.[101] Its juxtaposition of photographs of the "normal" and "degenerate" face and body proved central to curation of the First International Eugenics Exhibition, as did pedigrees and portraits of Darwin and Galton. It was at this Exhibition that the tools that Galton had developed for judging a generic portrait were turned upon portraits of himself and his cousin.

Every Portrait Tells a Pedigree: Framing Charles Darwin and Francis Galton at the First International Eugenics Exhibition

While the Eugenics Education Society had been planning an international congress and exhibition on eugenics since its inception in 1907, Galton's death in 1911 provided the catalyst. As a tribute to Galton's contribution to the field of visual cultures, this exhibition was dominated by portraits as well as pedigrees. While anthropologists employed portraiture to distinguish race typology, Galton had deployed it to identify what Huxley called the "generic portrait" and to distinguish between mental types. Dividing the profile into forehead, nose, lips, and chin, Galton mapped his criteria for judging the portrait onto Lavater's, although his analyses extended well beyond the slope of the forehead and projection of the nose. In 1888, it entailed measuring parts of the face with the help of a prism, pinhole scheme, mechanical selector, or even the silhouette device in reverse—strongly lit profiles photographed against a black background.[102]

To lexiconize portraits and reduce measuring time, in 1907 Galton refined this criteria to six cardinal features: First, the tip of the chin; second and third, the lower and upper lip; fourth, the hollow between the upper lip and the nose; fifth, the tip of the nose; and sixth, the hollow between the nose and the brow.[103] "On that basis a collection of 1,000 profiles from brow to chin could be lexonised and searched with great ease," he explained. "In 667 cases each portrait would have a clearly distinctive formula."[104] As these measurements were all based on progressions or regressions from the average, one profile could have, for example, a number 3 forehead, number 31 nose, number 26 lips, and a number 8 chin. Once these measurements were aggregated, they were correlated to a particular number in a catalogue that would indicate heredity, ability, and even personality in terms of good, bad, or neutral temper.[105] Galton's formula was applied in the First International Eugenics Exhibition Gallery of Portraits and the Gallery of Silhouettes.

Exhibiting thirteen photographic copies of portraits by artists of distinguished historical personages of the sixteenth century, the British physician, Frederick Adams Woods attempted to show how the facial bone structure, particularly the distance between the eyes and the nasal projection, had evolved. Among the portraits he selected from the National Portrait Gallery, Queen's Collection, and the Louvre, were Mary, Queen of Scots, Francis I, Holbein's portraits of the Bishop of London, Duke of Norfolk, Henry VIII and Jane Seymour, plus Lorenzo Lotto's Portrait of the Apostolic Juliano.[106] By comparing the facial symmetry depicted in these portraits with Classical Greek statues, a biometrical aesthetics of facial beauty was minutely calculated: The nose projecting no more than 47.8 millimetres; 62.7 millimetres being the correct measurement between the pupils; 19 millimetres for the lips; 50.8 millimetres from the lips to the chin.[107] Unimpressed, the *Pall Mall Gazette* quipped: "There is a whole gallery of portraits and silhouettes . . . championing the cause for the betterment of the race, but none is so interesting as the photograph of Charles Darwin on his horse Tommy."[108] This photograph was displayed in what the British press unanimously proclaimed as the most important of all galleries at the beginning of the exhibition.

Flanking the opening to this exhibition were portraits of Charles Darwin and Francis Galton. The first two galleries introducing visitors to eugenics were devoted entirely to portraits of Charles Darwin and Francis Galton. The exhibition opened with the portrait of Sir Francis Galton by Charles Furze, executed in 1903, in Gallery A organized by E. G. Wheeler (figure 5.5). In the exhibition curated by William and Leonard Darwin in Gallery B were several portraits of Charles Darwin. The first of these portraits was by the Royal Academician, W. W. Ouless, painted in 1875, currently housed in Christ's College at Cambridge University. The second was the photograph by Maull and Polyblank taken in 1855. The third was Leopold Flameng's engraving of the portrait by Huxley's son-in-law, John Collier, commissioned by the Linnaean Society (figure 5.6).[109] According to Darwin's third son, Francis: "The portrait repre-

Figure 5.5 Charles Wellington Furze, *Portrait of Sir Francis Galton*, oil on canvas, 762 mm × 20753 mm, 1903. *National Portrait Gallery NPG 3916.*

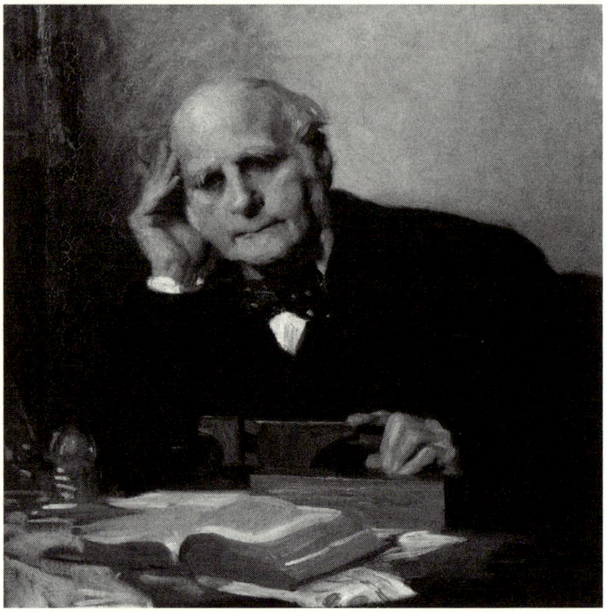

sents him standing facing the observer in the loose cloak so familiar to those who knew him and with his slouch hat in his hand. Many of those who knew his face most intimately, think that Mr Collier's picture is the best of the portraits and in this judgement the sitter himself was inclined to agree."[110]

In keeping with the primacy of heredity, this exhibition included such portraits of their antecedents as the silhouettes of Mrs. Erasmus Darwin, Dr. Erasmus Darwin with his son and Tertius Galton with four of his children (see figures 5.3 and 5.4). It also included the portrait of Erasmus Darwin executed after Joseph Wright of Derby in 1770, hung with a didactic explaining that he was "the common grandfather of Charles Darwin and Francis Galton." These portraits and their didactics appeared to be displayed to illustrate Galton's creed: "That a man's natural abilities are derived by inheritance, under exactly the same limitations as are the form and physical features of the whole organic world." That this exhibition was curated to illustrate Galton's theory of "natural inheritance," not Darwin's theory of "natural selection," was reinforced by the huge "Inheritance of Ability" poster charting the pedigree of the Wedgwood, Darwin, and Galton families (see figure 5.1). That "natural inheritance" framed the way in which they were to be ingested is confirmed by the analysis accompanying Pearson's juxtaposition of photographs of Darwin and Galton taken when they were both aged fifty (figure 5.7).

"These two photographs in much the same attitude indicate the degree of resemblance between the two grandchildren of Erasmus Darwin," stated

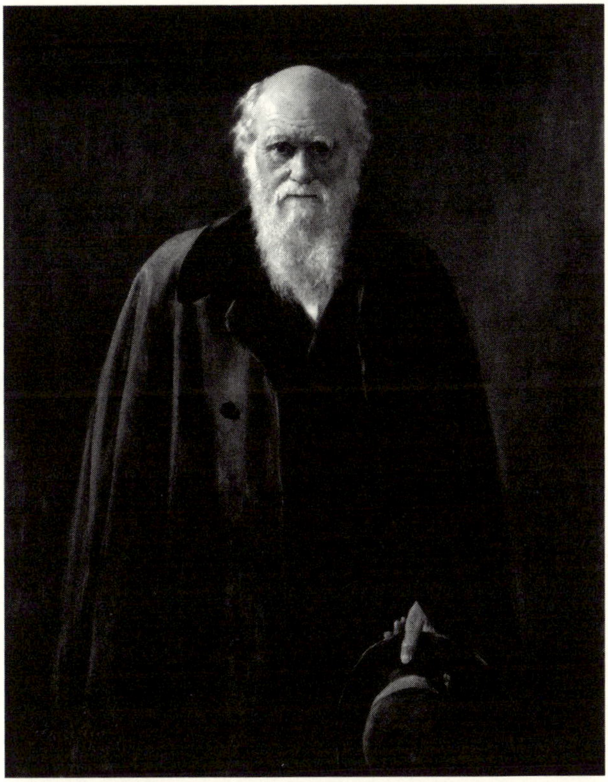

Figure 5.6 John Collier, *Portrait of Charles Darwin*, oil on canvas, 1257 mm × 965 mm, 1883. *National Portrait Gallery NPG 1024*.

Pearson. Furthermore, Pearson maintained that Galton seemed to resemble the Darwin family more than he did his own kin. Using tools well-gleaned from Galton's study of generic images, Pearson explained why. It was due to the "resemblances in the rather firm lips, the strong chin, the heavy brow and luxuriant eyebrows, the slightly receding forehead and the apparent absence of marked occipital development." Yet Pearson also considered "the greatest likeness" lay in their "mental characters." These characteristics seemed to be derived from Pearson's application of Galton's six cardinal features to these portraits. Both were, he deduced, "even tempered," sympathetic, "ascetic," adventurous, moral, steadfast, humorous, mechanical, numerical, observant with a "clinical instinct" that was extraordinarily scientific. Like so many other eugenicists Pearson considered that both had proved instrumental to achieving the "science" of eugenics. In ranking them as paradigms of the Western race fast disappearing, Pearson was able to stress the need for eugenics:

> If on the average only one in four brothers of distinguished stock reaches first-class eminence, can we not quite well understand how Charles Darwin

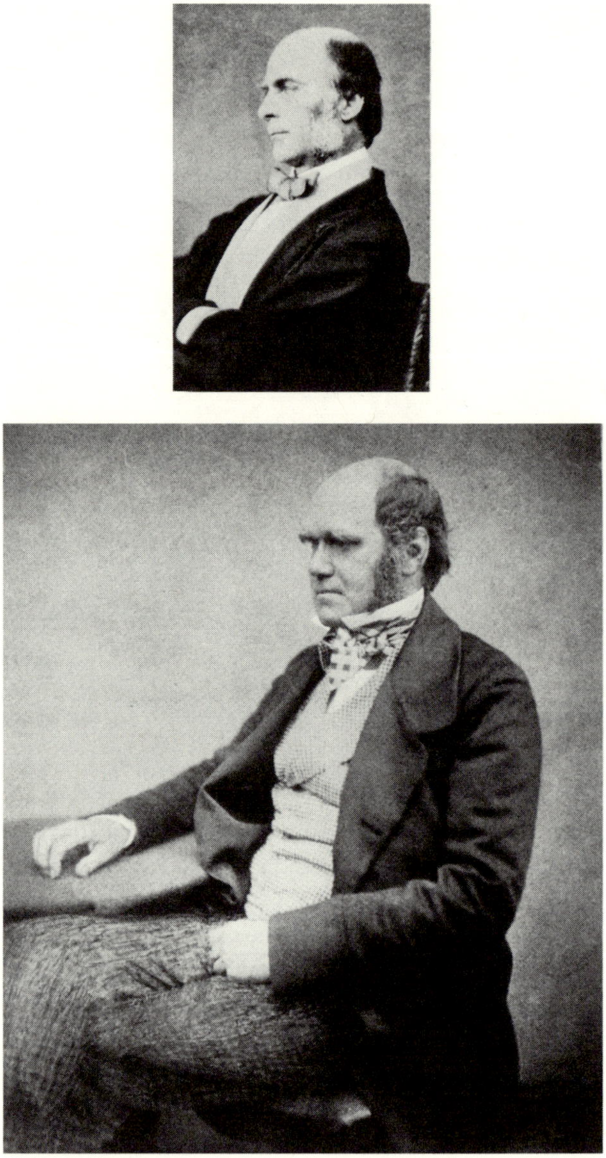

Figure 5.7 Maull and Fox, Charles Darwin photographed aged fifty-one (*top*); *Galton Laboratory*. Francis Galton photographed aged fifty (*bottom*): "These two photographs in much the same attitude indicate the degree of resemblance between the two grandchildren of Erasmus Darwin." *Karl Pearson,* The Life, Letters and Labours of Francis Galton, *vol. 1 (London: Cambridge University Press, 1914), Plate XXXVII; Wellcome Library, London.*

and Francis Galton stand alone, but also appreciate how greatly the chances of perpetuating ability are reduced, when men of able stocks leave in modern conditions but one or two children to preserve their name? . . . with our modern views as to parental responsibility neither Charles Darwin nor Francis Galton would have been born! . . . Herein lies . . . the key to Francis Galton's demand that Eugenics should pass as rapidly as possible from the laboratory to the market place.... One able leader, inspirer and controller of men, is worth thousands of everyday workers to the race.[111]

Through the interplay of such texts and visual cultures, Darwin and Galton were clearly framed as the joint progenitors of eugenics. Ironically, given Darwin's constant agonizing over his "wretched" health and that of his family, he was also hailed as a model of Galton's "survivorship of the fittest," rather than "survival of the fittest," to which eugenicists should aspire. As illuminated by the conjunction of Pearson's text with the portraits in his publication, as with the didactics and portraits in the exhibition of Darwin and Galton, they were appropriated as propaganda for the popularization of eugenic marriages, and the breeding of large, intelligent families in order to produce "first-class eminence." Yet far from being the only eugenic exhibition in which Darwin was twinned with Galton and "framed" as one of the "fathers" of eugenics, this exhibition provided a model for all subsequent International Eugenics Exhibitions. This is illustrated by the huge busts of Darwin and Galton flanking the entrance to the Third International Eugenics Exhibition at the Natural History Museum held in New York in 1932. There, Darwin was identified on the plinth below his bust as a theorist primarily concerned with "racial evolution" and "the possible improvement in human-family stocks" (figure 5.8).[112]

The First International Eugenics Exhibition and the Mental Deficiency Act, 1913

After publication and commemoration of Galton's "survivorship of the fittest," Darwin posited "grade" of civilization as crucial.[113] After publication of Galton's law of deviation from averages showing male preeminence, Darwin considered man's intellectual capacity superior to woman's.[114] While citing *Hereditary Genius* as Galton's "great work," Darwin had acknowledged Galton, along with W. R. Greg and Wallace, as the source for his remarks about "survival of the fittest" in savages.[115] While "the weak in body or mind" were eliminated among savages, Darwin then pointed out that through interventions within "civilized" societies, "the weak members propagate their kind."[116] Once Galton had established eugenics as a science, it could have almost been Galton himself who wrote the following words by Darwin:

> No one who has attended to the breeding of domestic animals will doubt that this must be highly injurious to the race of man. It is surprising how soon a want or care, or care wrongly directed, leads to the degeneration of a

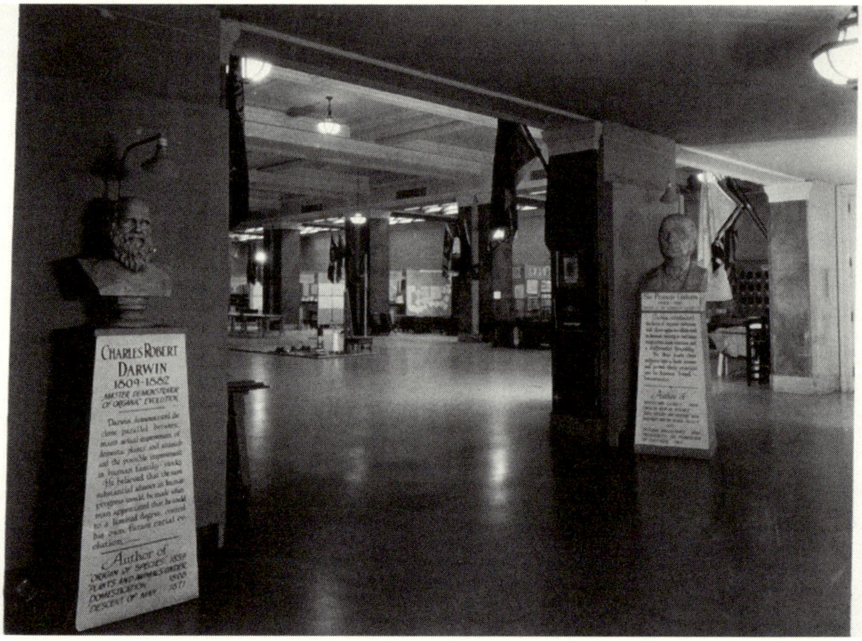

Figure 5.8 Anon., Busts of Charles Darwin and Francis Galton, black and white photograph, Third International Eugenics Congress and Exhibition, 1932. *Natural History Museum, New York, The Harry H. Laughlin Papers, Truman State University; Blk photo 1058; copyright Cold Spring Harbor Laboratory.*

> domestic race; but excepting in the case of man himself, hardly any one is so ignorant as to allow his worst animals to breed.[117]

Like Galton, Darwin considered conscription of the strongest men, granting the weakest a greater chance of propagation, a eugenic absurdity. Like Galton, he considered how the children of short-lived parents deficient in health have a greater opportunity to propagate. Like Galton, Darwin pointed out how this was held in check by the weaker and inferior members of society not marrying as freely as the sound.[118] Like Galton, he predicted that if the converse occurred, the inferior would supplant superior members of society.[119] Like Galton, he deduced that "this check might be indefinitely increased by the weak in body or mind refraining from marriage."[120] Like Galton, he conceded the dysgenic effects of civilization through development of asylums, hospitals, and poor-laws:

> With savages, the weak in body or mind are soon eliminated; and those that survive commonly exhibit a vigorous state of health. We civilised men, on the

> other hand, do our utmost to check the process of elimination; we build asylums for the imbecile, the maimed and the sick; we institute poor-laws; and our medical men exert their utmost skill to save the life of everyone. Thus the weak members of civilised societies propagate their kind.[121]

Yet unlike Galton, Darwin considered that "sympathy" for the weak and helpless constituted "the noblest part" of human nature.[122] Its neglect would, he emphasized, lead to an "overwhelming present evil." Hence, unlike Galton, he concluded: "We must bear the undoubtedly bad effects of the weak surviving and propagating their kind."[123]

Nevertheless, due to Galton's valorization of the Darwin and Galton families and the "framing" of Darwin and Galton within visual cultures as "the fathers of eugenics," this crucial difference became effaced. Despite Darwin's horror of the "evil" consequences that he envisaged would arise from eugenics, he was "framed" as one of its sources as epitomized by the First, Second, and Third International Eugenics Exhibitions. His incrimination was not only reinforced by three of his sons' membership in eugenic societies, but also by Leonard's presidency of the Eugenics Education Society, as well as of the First International Eugenics Conference and Exhibition. The very name, Darwin, lent legitimacy to the eugenic quest, particularly for the Mental Deficiency Act.

In Major Leonard Darwin's 1911 Presidential Address to the Eugenics Education Society, he had announced: "A nation would become decadent if inferior classes were survived by more children than superior classes, leading to the proliferation of the feeble-minded."[124] Legislation for the feeble-minded was therefore urgently required, he declared. Just before this congress, Major Darwin had circulated a card asking politicians and delegates, including Winston Churchill, if they would support measures to discourage parenthood by the feeble-minded and other degenerates.[125] By the end of the congress, Churchill, one of its vice-presidents and Home Secretary in the Asquith government, spoke for the majority.[126] While the thousands of feeble-minded in Britain deserved, "all that could be done for them by a Christian and scientific civilization," he surmised, "that now they were in the world they should be segregated so that their curse died with them and was not transmitted to future generations."[127] With an overwhelmingly affirmative response, the Eugenics Education Society and the National Association for the Care of the Feeble-Minded drafted the Feeble-Minded Control Bill and presented it to Parliament.[128]

Framed as the doyens of those who had inherited ability, "the able leader, inspirer and controller of men, worth thousands of everyday workers to the race," Darwin and Galton were both hailed in the International Eugenics Exhibition as the paradigm to which others should aspire, especially in the British quest for National Efficiency. By contrast, the exhibition of images of "degenerates" at the First International Eugenics Exhibition was designed to mobilize post-Darwinist phobia of devolution and to compound national fears of a "feeble-minded" implosion. As the attainment of "healthy" and "civilized" subjectivity is, according to Julia Kristeva, conditional upon expulsion of the unclear and the disorderly, their embodiment of difference then needed to be not just monitored and surveyed, projected, and exhibited, but ultimately contained—if not expunged.[129] Those suffering androplasic dwarfism or rickets, hysteria or epilepsy, deafness or cataracts, alcoholism or even migraines were then not distinguished from one another, let alone sympathetically accepted as suffering an isolatable and curable illness. They were objectified as "mentally deficient" and phobicly repulsed as an invasive pollutant.

Due to the huge lobbying force galvanized by the First International Eugenic Congress and this exhibition, the Mental Deficiency and Inebriates bills immediately passed their second readings at the House of Commons, while comparable legislation was drafted in France, Germany, and America.[130] When the government's bill passed with only three dissenting votes one year later, this meant that those who were either paupers, syphilitics, epileptics, or alcoholics; either on poor relief or pregnant with an illegitimate child; either unable to advance from school education or look after themselves, were defined as "mentally deficient."[131] Once officially categorized as "mentally deficient," they could be removed from their families, institutionalized, and segregated to prevent multiplication of the unfit. Outside Parliament, the "last of the Radicals," Josiah Wedgwood, a descendant of the Darwin family who captured the egalitarian ethos of Charles, endeavored to galvanize opposition to the working-class dimension of the bill, which he called "the first essay in legislation of the Eugenist school."[132] "It looks like a harmless proposal for segregating idiots in the crime of being inefficient," he wrote. "It really is a first essay in the scientific breeding of the poor."[133]

Given the seminal roles played by this Congress and Exhibition in lubricating eugenic legislation, and the leading roles within them assigned to Darwin and Galton, both seemed to be sources for this act. Due to the misframing of Darwin in pedigrees, portraits, and photographs as a progenitor of eugenics, he appeared to validate its practice and to legitimate its application to the "mentally deficient." Hence paradoxically these visual cultures endorsed the very violation of human ethics that Darwin so abhorred. Instead of enhancing "sympathy" for those Darwin called "the imbecile, the maimed and the sick," these visual cultures led to their inferiorization, social segregation, and brutal incarceration. Far from eliciting "the noblest part" of human nature, they lad to their sterilization in twenty-four American states. Once the Third Reich Law for Euthanasia and the Prevention of Genetically Diseased Offspring was passed in Nazi Germany, ultimately they led to the realization of the "overwhelming present evil" that Darwin long dreaded.

NOTES

1. *First International Eugenics Congress* (London: Charles Knight & Co., Ltd., 1912); Wellcome Trust Eugenic Society Archives, SA/EUG/B.1.

2. Herbert Davey, *The Law Relating to the Mentally Defective: The Mental Deficiency Act, 1913*, 2nd ed. (New York: Da Capo Press, 1981). The Mental Deficiency Bill was first read as a Private Member's Bill in the House of Commons on 16 May 1911, by Gresham Stewart. The three Bills were scheduled for their second reading in the House of Commons on 27 July 1912.

3. *Problems in Eugenics, Report of Proceedings of The First International Eugenics Congress* (London: Eugenics Education Society, 1913), vol. II, 8. Director of the United States Eugenics Record Office, C. B. Davenport, was amongst many to deliver a paper on "Eugenics and Marriage." Reporting "on the best practical means for cutting off the defective germ plasm in the human population," Chairman of the Committee of the Eugenic Section of the American Breeders' Association, Bleeker Van Wagenen, examined the results of sterilizing thousands of "defectives, degenerates and criminals" in California, Connecticut, Indiana, Iowa, Nevada, New Jersey, and Washington.

4. "International Eugenics Congress," *British Medical Journal*, 13 July 1912: "Many interesting exhibits have been received from America, Australia, France, Germany and all parts of the United Kingdom. Professor von Guber has sent over from the International Race Hygiene Congress held in Dresden in 1911, a collection of exhibitions . . . and the American Record Office, as well as the State Epileptic Colony, New Jersey, are sending exhibits."

5. Karl Pearson, *The Life, Letters and Labours of Francis Galton*, vol. I (London: Cambridge University Press, 1914).

6. Paul Popenoe and Roswell Hill Johnson, *Applied Eugenics* (New York: The Macmillan Company, 1918), 20. From 1913, Popenoe edited the *Journal of Heredity*, devoting several issues to eugenics and social hygiene in the United States before opening the first marriage clinic in Los Angeles in 1930. Roswell Hill Johnson was a university professor.

7. J. C. Waller points out, in "Ideas of Heredity, Reproduction and Eugenics in Britain, 1800–1875," *Studies in History and Philosophy of Science*, Part C: *Biological and Biomedical Sciences* (September 2001): 457–89, due to the intense study of heredity throughout the nineteenth century, by no means does Galton deserve the appellation, "father" of eugenics. Nevertheless, this was how Galton was popularized in eugenic cultures.

8. Daniel J. Kevles, *In the Name of Eugenics, Genetics and the Uses of Human Heredity* (Cambridge, Mass., 1985; 1995), 251. Denial has also proved a common response, as pointed

out by William H. Schneider, *Quality and Quantity: The Quest for Biological Regeneration in Twentieth-Century France* (Cambridge: Cambridge University Press, 1990), 3–7; see also Fae Brauer and Anthea Callen, eds. *Art, Sex and Eugenics: Corpus Delecti,* (Aldershot, U.K., and Burlington, Vt.: Ashgate, 2008).

9. In 1911, Major Leonard Darwin was elected President of the Society, remaining in this position until 1938.

10. Charles Darwin, *On the Origin of Species by Means of Natural Selection, or the Preservation of Favoured Races in the Struggle for Life* (London: John Murray, November 1859).

11. Ibid., 287. In *Memories of My Life* (London: Methuen & Co., 1908), 2, Francis Galton recalled: "The publication in 1859 of the Origin of Species by Charles Darwin made a marked epoch in my own mental development, as it did in that of human thought generally. Its effect was to demolish a multitude of dogmatic barriers by a single stroke, and to arouse a spirit of rebellion against all ancient authorities whose positive and unauthenticated statements were contradicted by modern science."

12. Francis Galton, *Hereditary Genius: An Inquiry into Its Laws and Consequences* (London: MacMillan and Co., 1869), 1: "I propose to show in this book that a man's natural abilities are derived by inheritance, under exactly the same limitations as are the form and physical features of the whole organic world. Consequently . . . it would be quite practicable to produce a highly-gifted race of men by judicious marriages during several consecutive generations."

13. Ibid., 336.

14. Janet Browne, *Darwin's Origin of Species: A Biography* (Sydney: Allen & Unwin, 2006), x. Galton, *Hereditary Genius,* 337: "Under even a very moderate form of material civilization, a vast number of aptitudes acquired through the "survivorship of the fittest" and the unsparing destruction of the unfit, for hundreds of generations, have become as obsolete as the old mail-coach habits and customs."

15. Ibid., 33.

16. Ibid., 35.

17. Galton, *Hereditary Genius,* 38. This data was garnered from the 1865 edition of *Dictionary of Men of the Time* and from *The Times* obituaries.

18. Galton, *Hereditary Genius,* 349, with reference to Charles Darwin, *The Variation of Animals and Plants under Domestication,* (London: John Murray, 1868). Ruth Schwartz Cowan, "Nature and Nurture: The Interplay of Biology and Politics in the Work of Francis Galton," *Studies in the History of Biology* 1 (1977), maintains that so impressed had Galton been by Darwin's theory of cellular "gemmules" that Galton's copy of *The Variation of Animals and Plants* was literally covered in his notes.

19. Galton, *Hereditary Genius,* 371–72: "The immediate consequence of the theory of Pangenesis is somewhat startling. It appears to show that a man is wholly built up of his own and ancestral *peculiarities* . . . I do not see why any serious difficulty should stand in the way of mathematicians, in framing a compact formula, based on the theory of Pangenesis . . . foretelling the average distribution of characteristics among a large multitude of offspring whose parentage was known."

20. Ibid., 350.

21. Ibid., "Men of Science," 202–203.

22. Ibid.

23. Ibid., 203. In J. B. Innes letter to Charles Darwin, 30 January 1868, he congratulates him on George Darwin's success at Cambridge University. In "Cambridge Drops Senior Wranglers," *New York Times*, 6 June 1909, Charles Darwin's grandson was featured as the last Senior Wrangler. Their explanation seems to emanate from Galton's *Hereditary Genius*: "The Darwin family is an extraordinary instance of the heredity of talent. Erasmus Darwin, the grandfather of the great biologist, was a scientist, and all of Charles's sons achieved fame, while his grandson is one of the more promising competitors for the distinction of being the last of the Cambridge Senior Wranglers."

24. Galton, *Hereditary Genius*, 320.

25. Alphonse de Candolle, *Histoire des Sciences et des Savants depuis Deux Siècles* (Geneva: 1867). Switzerland had produced over 10 percent of the great scientists over the past two centuries, with less than 1 percent of the population of Europe. In a letter to de Candolle, Galton maintained that Darwin's view "confirms mine in every particular." G. de Monsier, "Unpublished Correspondence between Alphonse de Candolle (1806–1893) and Francis Galton (1822–1911)," *Gesherus* 29 (3): 143. Nevertheless, Galton was unaware that Darwin had already written to de Candolle saying: "I have hardly read anything more original and interesting than your treatment of the causes which favour the development of scientific men." See R. E. Fancher "Alphonse de Candolle, France Galton, and the Early History of 'Nature-Nurture Controversy,'" *Journal of the History of the Behavorial Sciences* 19 (4): 341–52.

26. Francis Galton, *English Men of Science: Their Nature and Nurture* (London: Macmillan & Co., 1874).

27. Ibid., 45: *First generation.* (1) Erasmus Darwin, M.D., F.R.S., physician, physiologist, and poet.

28. Ibid., 47. Despite privileging Charles, Galton did point out that there were many in this generation with talent. Since few had reached "mature manhood" in the fourth generation, Galton only mentions George and Leonard.

29. Francis Galton and Edgar Schuster, *Noteworthy Families (Modern Science): An Index to Kinships in Near Degrees between Persons Whose Achievements Are Honourable, and Have Been Publicly Recorded*, vol. 1 of the Publications of the Eugenics Record Office of the University of London (London: John Murray, 1906), 17, 19, 22.

30. *Programme of the Exhibition*: "The Committee desires to make the Exhibition as fully representative as possible to the present state and past history of the science of Heredity and Eugenics." Wellcome Trust Eugenic Society Archives, SA/EUG/B.1.

31. Pauline M. H. Mazumdar, *Human Genetics and Human Failings: The Eugenics Society, Its Sources and Its Critics in Britain* (London: Routledge, 1992); see particularly chapter 2, 58–95.

32. Francis Galton, *Natural Inheritance* (London: Macmillan, 1889), 19–21.

33. Karl Pearson, *The Grammar of Science* (London: Walter Scott, 1892).

34. Mazumdar, *Human Genetics*, 87.

35. Ibid., 60.

36. Ibid., 95.

37. First International Eugenics Congress, University of London, *Catalogue of the Exhibition* (London: Charles Knight & Co., 1912), Exhibit C.

38. Ibid., H.25, 58; also N 1; see Fay Brauer, "Eradicating Difference: The Bioethics of Imaging 'Degeneracy' and Exhibiting Eugenics" ("Art and Ethics," *Australian and New Zealand Journal of Art* 1 (2004): 139–66.

39. *Catalogue of the Exhibition,* Exhibits N and P 1–P 10.

40. Ibid., G 1, assembled by Dr. Raymond G. Pearl.

41. Mazumdar, *Human Genetics,* 95.

42. *Catalogue of the Exhibition,* 1912, 17, Exhibit C 45–C 46: "In particular, Chs. Darwin has collected facts of this kind in his 'Variation of Animals and Plants under Domestication.' For civilized peoples it is a matter for reflection that with animals even slight deviations from their customary 'natural' mode of living may lead to such serious consequences."

43. Ibid., 4–7, Exhibit C 11–C 21.

44. Ibid., 6.

45. "Worst Family in the World: Interesting and Curious Exhibition. Pedigrees of the Great," Pall Mall Gazette, 29 July 1912, 1.

46. *Programme of the Exhibition.*

47. A Fellow of Trinity College, Cambridge, W. C. D. Whethem was a Council Member and Officer of the University of Cambridge Eugenics Society. At its First Annual Meeting, 23 November 1911, Whetham delivered a paper entitled "The Influence of a Colonial Empire on Race Evolution." The anthology of essays edited by A. C. Stewart, *Darwin and Modern Science,* published by Cambridge University Press in 1909 in commemoration of the centenary of the birth of Charles Darwin and of the fiftieth anniversary of *Origin of Species,* included "The Evolution of Matter" by Whetham. At the First International Eugenics Congress, the joint paper given by Whethem and his wife advanced the theory that the supremacy of Western nations depended upon the tall, blue-eyed, fair-haired members of a community predominating over short, dark-haired ones. The exhibition catalogue lists their installation, I 1–3.

48. *Catalogue of the Exhibition, Exhibited by the Eugenics Education Society, Mendelism,* O 1a–O 1f, 1912, 75.

49. Ibid., O 2–O 4.

50. *Pall Mall Gazette,* 29 July 1912.

51. Ibid.

52. Ibid.

53. "Galton's speech at the Royal Society dinner after receiving the Gold Medal of the Society," Report, *The Times,* 1 December 1886.

54. Michael Bulmer, "The Development of Francis Galton's Ideas on the Mechanism of Heredity," *Journal of the History of Biology* 32, no. 2 (September 1999): 263–92.

55. Francis Galton, "Hereditary Improvement," *Frazers Magazine* 37 (January 1873): 116–30; Francis Galton letter to Charles Darwin, December 1869: "I wonder if you can help me. I want to make some peculiar experiments that have occurred to me in breeding animals and want to procure a few couples of rabbits of marked and assured breeds."

56. Galton, "Hereditary Improvement," 117.

57. Galton, *English Men of Science,* 129.

58. Ibid.: "the non-gifted would begin to decay . . . in the same way as inferior races always disappear before superior ones."

59. Ibid.

60. Francis Galton, "Africa for the Chinese," *The Times*, 5 June, 1873.

61. G. H. Darwin, "On Beneficial Restrictions to Liberty of Marriage," *Contemporary Review* 22 (1873): 412–26.

62. Francis Galton, "The Efficacy of Prayer," letter to *Spectator*, 24 August 1872, 1073.

63. Letter 8997, C. R. Darwin to G. H. Darwin, 2 August 1873.

64. Charles Darwin, *The Expression of the Emotions in Man and Animals* (London: John Murray, November 1872). It is clearly stated on the title page of this edition: "With photographic and other illustrations." For an outstanding analysis of Darwin's use of photography in this treatise, see Phillip Prodger, "Illustration as Strategy in Charles Darwin's 'The Expression of Emotions in Man and Animals,'" in *Inscribing Science: Scientific Texts and the Materiality of Communication*, ed. Timothy Lenoir, 139–81 (Stanford, Calif.: Stanford University Press, 1998).

65. Ibid., 141.

66. Darwin, *The Expression of the Emotions*. Two drawings were from Henle's *Handbuch der Systematischen Anatomie des Menschen* and fifteen were animals, including a "disappointed and sulky" chimpanzee, drawn from life mostly by Mr. J. W. Wood.

67. Ibid., 23: "I must have the pleasure in expressing my obligations to Mr. Rejlander for the trouble which he has taken in photographing for me various expressions and gestures."

68. The heliotype process was one of the earliest methods to retain the authenticity of the photographic image in large runs, without resorting to the cost of hand-mounting hundreds of original prints. The first, second, and sixth of these heliographs were fold-outs.

69. Darwin, *The Expression of the Emotions*, note, p. 148: "The best photographs in my collection are by Mr. Rejlander, of Victoria Street, London, and by Herr Kindermann, of Hamburg. Figs. 1, 3, 4, and 6 are by the former; and figs. 2 and 5, by the latter gentleman"; note at the end of "List of Illustrations."

70. Ibid., 24.

71. Prodger, "Illustration as Strategy," 141.

72. Ibid., 173–79. This paradox is highlighted, as Prodger reveals, by "Ginx's Baby." Despite being "hailed as one of the first 'momentary' images," which "appeared to have succeeded in capturing the child's appearance while his face and body were in vigorous movement," as Prodger identifies, "it was a photographic copy of a drawing *after* an original photograph."

73. Martin Brookes, *Extreme Measures: The Dark Visions and Bright Ideas of Francis Galton* (New York and London: Bloomsbury Publishing, 2004), 210.

74. Johann Caspar Lavater, *Essay on Physiognomy Designed to Promote the Knowledge and Love of Mankind*, 5 vols. (First published Zurich, 1772; London: John Murray, 1789–1798).

75. Darwin, *The Expression of the Emotions*, 5: "Many works have been written on Expression, but a greater number on Physiognomy . . . With this latter subject I am not here concerned."

76. Immanuel Kant, *Anthropology from a Pragmatic Point of View*, ed. Mary Gregor (The Hague: Martinus Nijhoff, 1974), 160.

77. Francis Galton, "Personal Identification and Description," *Weekly Evening Meeting*, 25 May 1888, 847.

78. In *Ape to Apollo: Aesthetics and the Idea of Race in the 18th Century* (London: Reaktion Books, 2002), 98, David Bindman refers to the *frontometer* invented by Lavater for measuring foreheads.

79. Johann Caspar Lavater, "A Sure and Convenient Machine for Drawing Silhouettes," *Essay on Physiognomy*, vol. 2, 179.

80. Ibid., 105–106. In *Ape to Apollo*, Bindman points out that in contrast to Winckelmann's ideal of the vertical profile running continuously from forehead to nose exemplified by the *Apollo Belvedere*, Lavater's ideal was the prominent nose and receding forehead embodied by Goethe.

81. Lavater, *Essay on Physiognomy*, vol. 2, 201.

82. Francis Galton, "Photography and Silhouettes," *The Photographic News*, 8 July 1887, 429: "This art was superceded by photography, and is now temporarily extinct; but I want to show that it might . . . be advantageously re-introduced by the help of the very agency that extinguished it."

83. Francis Galton, "Composite Portraits," *Nature*, 23 May 1878, 97. Galton was most insistent that an exact profile be photographed from the right side of the face.

84. Anthea Callen, "Mediating Madness: Expressions of Insanity from Charles Bell to Charles Darwin," in *Contesting the Body: Art, Sexualities and Biogenetics*, Conveners, Fae Brauer and Anthea Callen, 33rd Annual Conference of the Association of Art Historians, University of Ulster, Belfast, 12–14 April 2007: "Crichton-Browne's interest in photography was brought to the attention of Charles Darwin when he was writing The Expression. He approached Crichton-Browne, perhaps because he had been a student at Edinburgh with his father. Crichton-Browne sent him drawings and 37 photographs of facial expression in his psychiatric patients, one of which Darwin had engraved for publication."

85. Darwin, *The Expression of the Emotions*, 353–54.

86. Ibid., 369, 364.

87. Michael Bulmer, *Francis Galton: Pioneer of Heredity and Biometry* (Baltimore: The Johns Hopkins University Press, 2003), 34.

88. E. H. Gombrich, *Meditations on a Hobby Horse* (London: Phaidon, 1963), 51: Francis Galton, *Memories of My Life*, 315–16. After collecting data for a beauty map of the British Isles, Galton declared: "I found London to rank highest for beauty; Aberdeen lowest."

89. Galton, "Composite Portraits."

90. Pearson, *The Life, Letters and Labours of Francis Galton*, vol. 2, 198.

91. "Galton's speech," *The Times*, 1 December 1886, 236: "I owe more of my later scientific impulses to the influences of Charles Darwin that I can easily express. I rarely approached his genial presence without an almost overwhelming sense of devotion and reverence, and I valued his encouragement and approbation more, perhaps than that of the whole world besides."

92. John C. W. Waller, The Social and Intellectual Origins of Sir Francis Galton's (1822–1911) Ideas on Heredity and Eugenics (PhD. thesis, University College, London, 2001), 119.

93. Pearson, *The Life, Letters and Labours of Francis Galton*, vol. 1, 202.

94. Francis Galton, *Inquiries into Human Faculty and Its Development* (London: Macmillan, 1882).

95. Francis Galton, "Medical Family Registers," *Fortnightly Review* 34 (August 1883): 244–50.

96. Galton, "Composite Portraits," 100.

97. Francis Galton, "Natural Selection," in *Natural Inheritance*, 119–24.

98. D. W. Forrest, *Francis Galton: The Life and Work of a Victorian Genius* (London: Elek, 1974), 141.

99. *Science*, 8 May 1885, Francis Galton Archives, University College London.

100. Francis Galton, *Essays in Eugenics* (London: The Eugenics Education Society, 1909), 42. Galton was bowled over by his cousin Charles Darwin's *Origin of Species*; it proved the catalyst for his eugenic crusade to determine how human beings could accelerate the process of evolution.

101. Fae Brauer, "Incriminating Evidence: Bodies, Skulls and Statistics in the Francis Galton National Eugenics Laboratory," in *Figurations of Knowledge*, 5th Biannual Europeans Conference of the SLSA, Zentrum für Literatur-und Kulturforschung, Berlin, 2008.

102. Francis Galton, "Personal Identification and Description," *Proceedings of the Royal Institution* 12 (1888): 346–60: "The parts consisted of the slope of the nose to the tip, tip of the nose to base, the concavity of notch between the brow and nose, the radium of circle of curvature between the nose and upper lip, the curve of the upper and lower lips and even the markings of the iris."

103. Francis Galton, "Classification of Portraits," *Nature* 76, 17 October 1907, 617.

104. Ibid., 618.

105. Francis Galton, "Numeralised Profiles for Classification and Recognition," *Nature* 83 (31 March 1910): 127–30.

106. First International Eugenics Congress, University of London, *Catalogue of the Exhibition:* S9 Queen of Scots (National Portrait Gallery)—the naso-orbital region is typical of the northern races during the 16th century; S5 the Bishop of London, Dr. Stokesley, drawn by Holbein—eyes far apart; broad upper part of nose.

107. "Les Conditions de la beauté," *Les Nouvelles*, 16 October 1912, 1.

108. "Worst Family in the World: Interesting and Curious Exhibition; Pedigrees of the Great," *Pall Mall Gazette*, 29 July 1912, 1.

109. The portrait in the National Portrait Gallery, London, is a copy of the original for the Linnean Society according to Charles Saumarez Smith, *The National Portrait Gallery: An Illustrated Guide* (London, 2000), 145. In his 1896 letter to Lionel Cust, William Erasmus Darwin explained: "The picture is a replica of the one in the rooms in the Linnean Society and was made by Collier after the original."

110. Smith, *The National Protrait Gallery*, 145.

111. Pearson, *The Life, Letters and Labours of Francis Galton*, vol. 1, Plate XXXVII.

112. Eugenic Archives, Cold Spring Harbor Laboratory, 3d International Eugenics Conference, 1932, Image 1058.

113. Charles Darwin, *The Descent of Man and Selection in Relation to Sex* (London: Penguin Books, 2004), 212: "When civilized nations come into contact with barbarians the struggle is short. . . . The grade of their civilization seems to be a most important element in the success of competing nations."

114. Ibid., 629.

115. Ibid., 159.

116. Ibid.

117. Ibid.

118. Ibid., 160.

119. Ibid., 688.

120. Ibid., 160.

121. Ibid., 168.

122. Ibid., 169.

123. Ibid.

124. Major Leonard Darwin, "Presidential Address to the Eugenics Education Society," *Eugenics Review,* 1911.

125. A copy of this letter exists in the Wellcome Institute, Contemporary Medical Archives Centre, SA/EUG/B.1.

126. Winston Churchill's views were fully endorsed by the Eugenics Education Society. Buoyed by the success of the congress, the Eugenics Education Society launched a huge public drive to train social workers and schoolteachers in elementary eugenics and started organizing a Eugenics Education Conference.

127. Harvey G. Simmons, "Explaining Social Policy: The English Mental Deficiency Act of 1913," *Journal of Social History* 2 (1978): 396–97. Kevles points out that privately Churchill described the proliferation of the mentally deficient to Asquith, combined with the "restriction of progeny among all the thrifty, energetic, and superior stocks" as a "very terrible danger to the race." Arthur Balfour, a fellow Member of Parliament, called for a social standard of fitness.

128. Ibid. In its letters canvassing support for this bill (held in the Wellcome Trust eugenic archives, SA/EUG/B.1), the Eugenics Society wrote: "The group to be dealt with consists of those persons who, though not held to be lunatics, idiots, or imbeciles, are nevertheless, owing to their mental defects, a source of danger to themselves or to others, and who, by reproducing their kind, may inflict lasting injury onto their race. These are the feeble-minded; and amongst them there are many individuals who, for their proper care, require to be placed under the control of authorities, armed with legal powers not at present conferrable. . . . mental defects make them act . . . unsocially, or to be . . . mischievous to themselves . . . The evidence of mental defect and of the need for powers of detention is to be certified by two medical practitioners, and the recent order is to be made by a magistrate. The powers to be created by the Bill are to be entrusted to the existing Lunacy Commission."

129. Julia Kristeva, *Powers of Horror: An Essay in Abjection,* trans. Leon S. Roudiez (Paris: Éditions de Seuil, 1980; New York: Columbia University Press, 1982).

130. By 27 July 1912, the White Slave Traffic Bill, the Inebriates Bill, and the Mental Deficiency Bill had passed their second reading at the House of Commons. All three addressed eugenic issues, according to the *Daily Chronicle,* 27 July 1912: "The Inebriates Bill and the White Slave Bill both strike at what are called racial poisons, which we now know to be capable or originating degeneracy in previously healthy stocks."

131. Lindsay Farrell, *Origins and Growth of the English Eugenic Movement, 1865–1925* (Ann Arbor, Mich.: UMI, 1970), 244.

132. C. V. Wedgwood, *The Last of the Radicals: Josiah Wedgwood MP* (London, 1951); Mathew Thompson, *The Problem of Mental Deficiency: Eugenics, Democracy, and Social Policy in Britain c. 1870–1959* (Oxford: Clarendon Press, 1998), 47.

133. Josiah Wedgwood, "The Crime of Being Inefficient," *Nation,* 15 June 1912, 390–91.

CHAPTER 6

"One of a long row only"

Sexual Selection and the Male Gaze in Thomas Hardy's *Tess of the D'Urbervilles*

JAMES KRASNER

It may be said metaphorically that natural selection is daily and hourly scrutinizing, throughout the world, the slightest variations; rejecting those that are bad, preserving and adding up all that are good; silently and insensibly working, *whenever and wherever opportunity offers*, at the improvement of each organic being in relation to its organic and inorganic conditions of life.

—Charles Darwin, *The Origin of Species by Means of Natural Selection*

In the same manner as man can give beauty, according to his standard of taste, to his male poultry—can give to the Sebright bantam a new and elegant plumage, an erect and peculiar carriage—so it appears that in a state of nature female birds, by having long selected the more attractive males, added to their beauty. [. . .] What reason, then, can be assigned why similar results should not follow from the long-continued selection of the most admired women by those men of each tribe who were able to rear the greatest number of children?

—Charles Darwin, *The Descent of Man*

Sexual Selection and the Male Gaze

In the passages quoted above, Charles Darwin describes the two engines of evolutionary development: Natural selection and sexual selection. At the center of each lies a visual act: Natural selection "scrutinizes" nature with its sharp, pragmatic eye, resulting in "improvement"; men involved in sexual selection "admire" potential mates, resulting in greater "beauty."[1] While Darwin personifies natural selection as a force with individual agency, he consistently portrays sexual selection as a compilation of particular aesthetic choices by individual female animals or male humans. This implies an idiosyncratic, even arbitrary, standard, resulting in "elegant plumage" or a "peculiar carriage," rather than the harshly practical operation of natural selection.

Yet when Darwin addresses the "extremely improbable" notion that animals have "powers of discrimination and taste," he demonstrates a certain anxiety about his aesthetic claims for sexual selection.[2] The "sense of beauty" that animals possess is, he explains, only comparable to "that in the lowest savages, who admire and deck themselves with any brilliant, glittering, or curious object." Animals and savages are capable only of the roughest aesthetic discrimination, which involves the most vivid, visual variations. While natural selection seems to have a visual power of its own, "daily and hourly scrutinizing throughout the world, the slightest variations," sexual selection can operate through variable choices and can be exercised by aesthetically unsophisticated animals. Darwin thus establishes a dual identity for sexual selection relative to civilization: It is at once primitive and aesthetic, savage and refined, with one foot in the jungle and the other in the art museum.

Darwin goes on to suggest that, even among humans, beautiful features must be fairly "extreme" to be selected. "The men of each race prefer what they are accustomed to; they cannot endure any great change; but they like variety, and admire each characteristic carried to a moderate extreme."[3] While Darwin regards the sensibilities of civilized humans as sophisticated enough to make aesthetically refined choices, nevertheless he considers that sexual selection must even then be played out at on a visually spectacular canvas. Civilized women "delight in decorating themselves with all sorts of ornaments . . . They borrow the plumes of male birds, with which nature has decked this sex, in order to charm the females."[4] What Darwin implies is that Victorian ladies, like peacocks and hornbills, must be vivid enough to attract attention.

In order to make sexual selection relevant to human evolution, moreover, Darwin transfers the power of agency from the female to the male, which he accomplishes through a deft invocation of masculine force and intellect:

> Man is more powerful in body and mind than woman, and in the savage state he keeps her in a far more abject state of bondage than does the male of any other animal; therefore it is not surprising that he should have gained the power of selection.[5]

This passage has overtones of political and cultural coercion that are borne out in Darwin's portrayals of men selecting beautiful women. In his description of Hottentot standards of beauty, Darwin describes Somali men choosing wives by "ranging them in a line and by picking her out who[se backside] projects furthest a tergo."[6] This scene involves both careful attention to the variation of a particular body part, and a fully organized social process by which such variations can be detected. Without "ranging them in a line," the Hottentots could not engage in sexual selection. The scenario offers a schematic representation of the "abject state of bondage" that has granted men the "power of selection." Darwin's portrayals of human sexual selection typically are enacted in scenarios of social control and public spectacle.

While animal mating also can be ritualized and spectacular, Darwin's portrayal of human sexual selection places much greater emphasis on examples of organized coercive power exerted by males over females. This contrast is apparent in a comparison between bird and human mating rituals that Darwin uses to justify his claim that female birds choose their mates.

> If an inhabitant of another planet were to behold a number of young rustics at a fair courting a pretty girl, and quarrelling about her like birds at one of their places of assemblage, he would, by the eagerness of the wooers to please her and to display their finery, infer that she had the power of choice.[7]

What is so striking about this passage is that Darwin is *not* portraying human sexual selection here, but using a human scenario in order to illustrate sexual selection among birds. The playful, eager quarrelling of the "young rustics" occurs in the bird world, while Darwin's portrayal of sexual selection in Somali culture emphasizes order and control. Moreover, in this scene, women are choosing men. For the comparison between humans and birds to be rhetorically effective, Darwin's reader must recognize this rustic mating ritual as something that might actually take place in the English countryside. Yet Darwin goes on to argue that such a mating scene would not take place in the human world, where men choose women, and where their choices occur through the social systematization of female beauty.

In his reference to the "well known" Hottentot standard of beauty, Darwin may also have in mind the exhibition of Sarah Baartman from 1810, which many current scholars, notably Sander Gilman, have analyzed in terms of racialized sexuality.[8] The striking thing about Darwin's use of the example is how it conflates Hottentot culture with the sort of ethnographic exhibition in which Baartman was displayed before the English public. Darwin asks us to imagine that sexual selection in Hottentot society looked a lot like ethnographic exhibits in London. Female bodies are displayed for public evaluation; the selection process is neither individual nor spontaneous, but a highly structured social activity in which public showmanship organizes erotic desire.

During his discussion of culturally relative standards of Western white beauty in the conclusion of chapter 19 in *The Descent of Man*, Darwin portrays another scenario in which men review a strictly controlled array of similar beauties. Rather than a scene of savage society, however, Darwin here casts sexual selection in the realm of art appreciation at its most civilized.

> As the great anatomist Bichat long ago said, if every one were cast in the same mould, there would be no such thing as beauty. If all our women were to become as beautiful as the *Venus de' Medici*, we should for a time be charmed; but we should soon wish for variety; and as soon as we had obtained variety, we should wish to see certain characters in our women a little exaggerated beyond the then existing common standard. [9]

Beauty must be defined against a "common standard" that Darwin imagines as a classical statue. The standard woman would be "cast" in the "mould" of a classically perfect type (the *Venus de' Medici*), and sexual selection would be based on the intensification of one or more of her standard features. The passage presents reproduction as whimsical public craftsmanship, in which men mold and remold female beauty to fit their changing tastes and exaggerate those traits deemed most desirable. Sexual selection is an artistic practice undertaken by a coercive male community. "*We* should for a time be charmed" by the standard, Darwin wrote, but "*we* should soon wish for variety" in "*our* women" and work together until "*we* had obtained" the desired female body. While the passage evokes the artist's studio, it also gestures toward industrial manufacture.

Daryl Ogden unequivocally associates the male, sexually selecting gaze with female subjugation, arguing that, for Darwin, "men control procreation and inheritance through the power of their eyes and that power's relationship to sexuality. . . . [the] enhanced beauty of women came about as a result of being, in effect, sexually enslaved by men."[10] I would add that Darwin often represents this elision between visual and social power through the figure of the artist. In his discussion of inherited beauty from chapter 20 of *The Descent of Man*, for example, Darwin links art to the social management of female beauty.

> [T]he priestesses who attended the temple of Venus Erycina at San-Giuliano in Sicily, were selected for their beauty out of the whole of Greece; they were not vestal virgins, . . . the women of San-Giuliano are now famous as the most beautiful in the island, and are sought by artists as models. [11]

The word "selected" in the first sentence clearly refers to a socially engineered process, in which the "whole of Greece" engages in selection. This is followed, several generations later, by another public selection process, this time an explicitly artistic one, in which models are chosen for their inherited beauty. Strangely, the stages in the progression from priestess to model that Darwin *does not* represent are the intermediate ones, which actually involve sexual selection of one mate by another. We see the socio-religious pageant of the priestesses, and the aesthetic spectacle of the artists' models, but we never see an individual man choosing a wife. The mating practices of the priestesses of Venus are, ironically enough, more societal than sexual. Darwin portrays sexual selection of women by men as a highly controlled and aestheticized marketplace.

Edwin Long's painting *Babylonian Marriage Market* (1885), explicitly represents the visual dynamics of sexual slavery in an eroticized market for women (figure 6.1). The painting investigates the operation of the male gaze, both in apprehending women's beauty as an "existing common standard," and in selecting them for specific physical traits.[12] The woman at the apex of the scene is being sold, or selected, in a public spectacle clearly ordered and controlled by men. The auctioneer on the left points to her, while his assistant manipulates her clothing, rendering her body a fully objectified commodity. Yet the viewer does not share the perspective of the purchasers, but is focused on the array of women waiting to be sold in the foreground. The exhausted, disempowered postures of these women and the flagrant coerciveness of the scene suggest that, at least to some degree, Long means to critique male ocular power. By arraying them in a line before us, however, Long simply offers a different inflection of that same coercive gaze. Despite minor differences, the similarities among their bodies, dress, and hair rob these women of individual identity, and their strictly linear placement in the painting's composition reifies their enslavement. By rendering this public exhibition artistically, Long allows the viewer to participate in it. The two acts of arrangement and selection depend upon each other, enacting complementary visual erotics.

In the discussion that follows, I would like to investigate how this Darwinian visual aesthetic of standardization and selection operates in one late-Victorian text, Thomas Hardy's *Tess of the d'Urbervilles*, and in the illustrations that accompanied its first publication. I will argue that, in the novel, Hardy represents sexual selection through social spectacles that resemble those portrayed by Darwin. The illustrations that accompany the text serve to reinforce the dual processes of standardization and selection such spectacles require. Both the novel and its illustrations place the reader in the position of a male spectator, participating in the process of sexual selection.

Standardization and Selection in *Tess of the D'Urbervilles*

Thomas Hardy read *Origin of Species* when he was nineteen years old, and remained profoundly influenced by Darwin's ideas throughout his writing career. In particular, Hardy was interested in the impact of sexual selection on love and marriage, believing that "topics traditional to the novel—courtship,

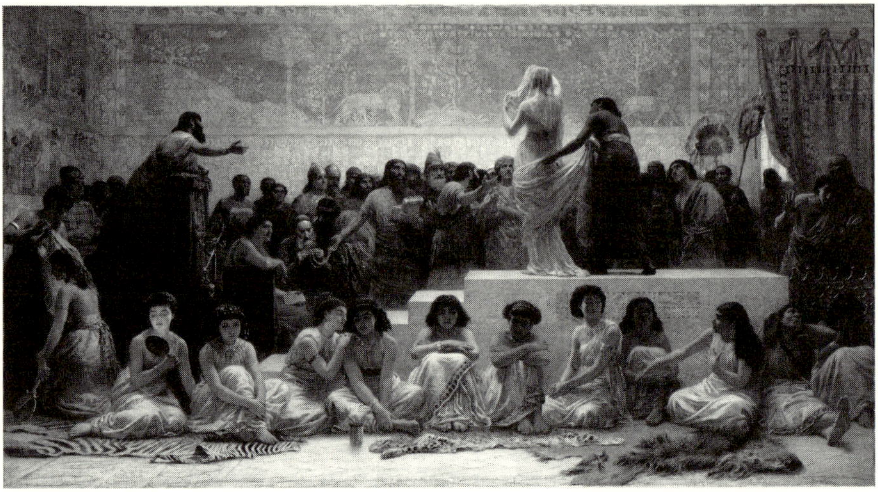

Figure 6.1 Edwin Longsden Long, *Babylonian Marriage Market. From the Picture Collection, Royal Holloway, University of London.*

sensibility, the making of matches, women's beauty, . . . became charged with new difficulty in the wake of the publication of *The Descent of Man*."[13] Darwin's influence on Hardy's thought in general, and on the discourses of nature and sexuality in particular, have been analyzed in great depth by writers such as Gillian Beer and George Levine. Following Laura Mulvey's analysis of the male gaze in film, critics such as Dianne Sadoff, Penny Boumhela, Rosemarie Morgan, and Kaja Silverman have investigated Hardy's narrative scopophilia, particularly in *Tess of the D'Urbervilles*, arguing that its heroine is "mastered by the masculine gaze as figuration, split as subject, and submitted to the oscillation such instability produces . . . the narrator's fantasies of penetration and engulfment violate Tess as fully as do Alec's actions."[14] These analyses have been elaborated by Jules Law and Jeff Nunokawa, to demonstrate the power of the gaze to fix and control Tess's body in relation to history and culture, as well as gender.

However, the relationship between the male gaze and Darwinian sexual selection remains somewhat unclear. Daryl Ogden, Richard A. Kaye, and Jennifer Gerstel emphasize Hardy's depiction of female-driven sexual selection, particularly in *Far from the Madding Crowd*. Angelique Richardson addresses gender politics outside the text, convincingly arguing that Hardy's use of the language of eugenics was part of a "struggle for expression" between male and female authors resulting in the "late nineteenth-century biologization of aesthetics."[15] In her analysis of *Tess*, Lisa Sternlieb focuses on male-driven sexual selection, asserting that "It is difficult to think of the work of another Victorian novelist in which the laws of sexual selection are so starkly set forth."[16] Nevetheless, she attends primarily to Hardy's use of biblical allusion rather than scopophilia. I hope to add to this discussion by arguing that the aesthetic of standardization and selection that Darwin enunciates in *The Descent of Man* parallels the operation of the male gaze in *Tess*.[17] Like Darwin, Hardy represents the aestheticization of female beauty through public rituals of selection that standardize and control women's bodies in spectacular arrays, thus placing the reader in the position of sexually selecting Tess.

Throughout the novel, Hardy portrays Tess as one of a series or group of nearly identical female figures, then identifies the particular feature (her mouth, her eyes, her hair) that draws the viewer's eye to her. "She was a fine and handsome girl—not handsomer than some others, possibly—but her mobile peony mouth and large innocent eyes added eloquence to colour and shape."[18] Hardy asks us to envision Tess as a typical "country girl," or "an almost standard woman," like Darwin's "existing common standard," only to single out the "certain characters" (here her mouth and eyes) that appeal to the male viewer because they are "a little exaggerated."[19] The reader is thus asked to imagine Tess's beauty through a two-part process: First we see her as one of a homogeneous group or array, then we select her from that group by focusing in on one distinctively beautiful bodily feature.

We first see Tess walking with her women's club at a May-Day celebration; all the women wear the same clothes and accessories, and walk in a double line. The reader's perspective is aligned with that of Tess's future husband, Angel Clare, who leans over a gate to observe the girls and, like the Hottentot men, makes his selection.[20] Hardy demonstrates how the standardization of the group allows the beauty of each particular variation to emerge.

> The banded ones were all dressed in white gowns . . . In addition to the distinction of a white frock, every woman and girl carried in her right hand a peeled willow wand, and in her left a bunch of white flowers. . . . The young girls formed, indeed, the majority of the band, and their heads of luxuriant hair reflected in the sunshine every tone of gold, and black, and brown. Some had beautiful eyes, others a beautiful nose, others a beautiful mouth and figure.[21]

When the narrative finally focuses upon Tess, it dwells on the specific features that attract the eye, her "mobile peony mouth and large innocent eyes."[22] Her "pouted-up deep red mouth" receives special attention: "her lower lip had a way of thrusting the middle of her top one upward, when they closed after a word."[23] Hardy's close attention to anatomical detail recalls Darwin's description of secondary sexual characteristics in chapter 19 of *The Descent of Man*.

> [T]he fleshy appendages about the head of the male Tragopan pheasant (Ceriornis Temminckii) swell into a large lappet on the throat and into two horns, one on each side of the splendid top-knot; and these are then coloured of the most intense blue which I have ever beheld.[24]

Like Darwin, Hardy wants the physiological basis of sexual selection to be clear. We do not simply focus in on Tess because she is erotically appealing in some inchoate way, but because of her specific bodily features.

Hardy begins this scene by associating the narrator's perspective with that of a "tourist or landscape-painter."[25] Kaja Silverman argues that Hardy's employment of the male artist's gaze both aestheticizes and eroticizes Tess as a figure standing out against the background of the other women.[26] Jeff Nunokawa, who emphasizes the tourist rather than the landscape painter, places the scene within the context of Victorian travel writing, suggesting that Clare, who is on a walking tour when he pauses to observe the club walkers, "first encounters 'the visionary essence of femininity' as a tourist attraction."[27] In both cases, the male gaze exerts power through an eroticized spectacle. I would argue that the subjugating gaze that Nunokawa and Silverman identify in tourism and painting, for Hardy, would both have been subsumed in Darwinian sexual selection. In Darwin's discussion of the beauties of San-Giuliano, the public ceremonial whereby the priestesses were "selected for their beauty out of the whole of Greece" corresponds to the May-Day "Cerealia" in *Tess*, in which the women are displayed for "public scrutiny."[28] The contemporary artists who select individual women as models, moreover, are clearly tourists, drawn to this particular town in Sicily by its reputation for beautiful young women who, like Tess, embody an eroticized history.[29] When Darwin states that they "are now famous as the most beautiful in the island," he is participating in just the same sort of eroticized travel-guide discourse, or "scopophilic pastoral," that Nunokawa attributes to Hardy.[30]

In his description of Tess mowing in chapter 14, Hardy also indulges in such erotic pastoral, once again implicating the reader in the two-part process of sexually selecting Tess. The chapter begins with a panorama of field-women walking to work together, moving their bodies in unison, and wearing similar clothing: "drawn cotton bonnets with great flapping curtains to keep off the sun, and gloves to prevent their hands being wounded by the stubble."[31] Hardy proceeds to expound on the aesthetic appeal of such female uniformity.

> But those of the [female] sex were the most interesting of this company of binders, by reason of the charm which is acquired by woman when she becomes part and parcel of outdoor nature. . . . A field-man is a personality

> afield; a field-woman is a portion of the field; she has somehow lost her own margin, imbibed the essence of her surrounding, and assimilated herself with it.[32]

There is an erotic charge to their disempowerment through physical labor, which men do not exhibit. Patricia Murphy describes Tess's "absorption into the landscape" as unification with the female essence of Nature that takes on a "sexualized cast."[33] This essentialist invocation of the feminine is consistently linked, for Hardy, with Tess's social disempowerment: Absorption becomes elided with abjection. Throughout the novel, Tess's agricultural work increasingly places her in an "abject state of bondage," and Hardy's portrayal of these field-women, I would suggest, elides their disadvantaged social position with their standardized beauty.

Once the reader has perceived Tess as part of a group, Hardy focuses the narrator's eye upon her.

> This morning the eye returns involuntarily to the girl in the pink cotton jacket, she being the most flexuous and finely-drawn figure of them all. . . . Perhaps one reason why she seduces casual attention is that she never courts it, . . . one can see the oval face of a handsome young woman with deep dark eyes and long heavy clinging tresses, which seem to clasp in a beseeching way anything they fall against. The cheeks are paler, the teeth more regular, the red lips thinner than is usual in a country-bred girl.[34]

The reader's attention gradually hones in upon the hair, lips, teeth, and cheeks that make Tess distinctive; Hardy's narration enacts sexual selection by directing our gaze toward the features that meet the "usual" standard of a "country-bred girl" but are sufficiently different—"paler," "more regular," "thinner"—to make her stand out. While Hardy renders such selection as a form of powerlessness, in which the male eye is "seduced" and moves "involuntarily" toward Tess, the whole passage operates as an elaborately controlled pageant, in which women are dressed, paraded, and arranged against an appealing backdrop, so that the best one can be singled out. As Nunokawa puts it, "[t]o subjugate a woman in *Tess of the d'Urbervilles* is to enlist her for display."[35]

Hardy's aesthetic of selection, like Darwin's, relies upon the erotic potential of *both* standardization and selection. Human sexual selection, for Darwin, operates through societal rituals, enforced by men's physical domination of women, in which women are made comparable through socially organized visual arrays, so that their preferable characteristics can be identified easily. Lacking the omnipresent precision of natural selection, which can choose the "slightest variation," men need the aid of beauty pageants, religious spectacles, and artistic exhibitions to help them "admire each characteristic carried to a moderate extreme."[36] Women's beautiful attributes must be moderate enough that they match the prevailing standard, but extreme enough that men, who are more sophisticated than animals but still much less perceptive than natural selection, can discern them. The oxymoronic quality of the term "moderate extreme" demonstrates that Darwin, like Hardy, locates sexual selection in the oscillation between two forms of perception: The charm of perceiving a uniform array of standardized female bodies, and the pleasure of focusing in upon the eyes, hair, or lips.

The Specular Power of Sexual Selection: The Illustrated *Tess*

The importance of visual spectacle to the dramatization of sexual selection, particularly given its greater accessibility to visual representation than natural selection, was well recognized by Darwin. This is demonstrated by his choice of illustrations for *The Descent of Man*. As Jonathan Smith has shown, Darwin sought out new illustrations for the second edition of *Descent* that would more vividly represent the process, rather than simply the product, of sexual selection by "showing secondary sexual characteristics *in use*."[37] When *Tess of the D'Urbervilles* was first published in serialized form in *The Graphic* in 1891, it was accompanied by twenty-five illustrations. Many of these illustrations emphasize the process of sexual selection, either by directly portraying Tess's selection by Angel, or by encouraging the reader to select her visually from an array of similar figures.

The Graphic gave the commission for the *Tess* illustrations to its regular staff illustrator, the well-known painter, Sir Hubert Von Herkomer.[38] In an unusual step, Von Herkomer collaborated with three of his students: E. Borough Johnson, Joseph Syddall, and Daniel A. Wehrschmidt. While Hardy had previously published serialized novels with illustrations, the use of multiple illustrators was unprecedented. The absence of synchronicity in their collaboration was only intensified by the four illustrators working largely in isolation of one another.[39] As a result, the illustrations portray Tess as a series of variations on a physiological theme. From plate to plate, she alters slightly in height, hair color, figure, and facial structure. At times she seems a society lady, at others a ragged, working-class woman.

Johnson's Tess has a distinctly heart-shaped face, pronounced lips, and tendency to wear fashionable clothing. Wehrschmidt's Tess seems taller, older, and more Amazonian than the rest. Von Herkomer used one particular model for his Tess, while the other illustrators either used different models or none at all. The ultimate effect is to give the viewer the impression of multiple, slightly varied images of Tess parading past. Rather than establishing Tess's elusive appearance once and for all, as a single illustrator might have done, the combination of text and illustrations unwittingly renders Tess as a generalized "fine and handsome girl" or "almost standard woman."[40]

Jennifer Wicke analyses Hardy's use of the language of industrial standardization in *Tess*, noting his tendency to portray Tess as at once type and variation. "Both relative and practical standards are continually invoked by Hardy's text to position her, to deliver her to us not as a species of goods but a Standard—a 'Tess' with relative ('the best') and practical ('flexuous' etc.) Tess-ness."[41] The artistic effect of this, Wicke argues, is that Tess herself becomes imaginatively multiplied in the reader's mind, like an industrialized product. "*All* products in the age of labeling, trademarking and standardization are copies of a standard, copies of themselves."[42] By publishing the novel in an illustrated serial form, Hardy insured that *Tess* would be received in combination with multiple reproduced images of its title character's body.[43]

The illustrations themselves encourage the viewer to select Tess from an array of similar figures, in the same way that Hardy's text does. In "'I don't know about ghosts,' she was saying," Wehrschmidt portrays a scene from chapter 18 in which Angel, attracted by the beauty of Tess's voice, attempts to locate her among the dairymaids sitting at the kitchen table (figure 6.2).[44] In Wehrschmidt's illustration, Tess is one of seven figures, five of them dairymaids, who are almost identical in dress and general features. Our perception recapitulates Angel's, who is portrayed at the edge of the scene, in the process of selecting Tess from the other women, just as he does in the May-Day scene that starts the novel. Angel faces straight out toward the viewer, establishing the bond between the two more directly. Describing the cinematic version of the same scene portrayed by Wehrschmidt, Dianne Sadoff argues that Polanski's film recapitulates Hardy's narrative strategy, as it "constitutes Tess's sexuality through a relay of gazes by characters, camera and spectator."[45] This "relay of gazes" occurs in Wehrschmidt's illustration through a process of mirroring.

Wehrschmidt positions Angel so that Tess has her back to him; at this moment, he still seems uncertain about which woman to choose. Our identification of Tess is somewhat easier, as she is slightly taller than the rest, and her dark hair stands out against a lighter background, but when we do settle on her, we notice that directly across from her, with her back to us, is a woman who has the same figure and hairstyle, and holds her arm at a similar angle. This, we realize, must be the view Angel has of Tess, especially since our viewpoint is roughly a mirror-image of his (the curve of a shelf in the foreground

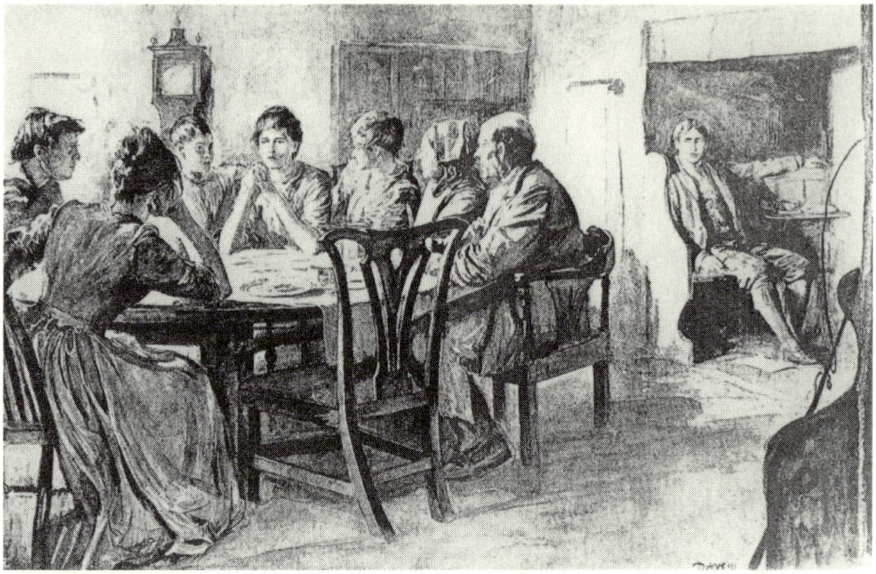

Figure 6.2 D. A. Wehrschmidt, "'I don't know about ghosts,' she was saying." The Graphic *(London), 15 August 1891, 192.*

even seems like a reflection of the curve of the bench he sits on). On either side of Tess are two other dairymaids whose postures also mirror one another. Thus Wehrschmidt's illustration implicates us in Angel's selection of Tess by forcing us to recognize our own gaze mirrored in Angel's. Edwin Long employs a somewhat similar mirroring effect in *Babylonian Marriage Market*, whereby the participants in the slave auction gaze out at us, allowing us to view our own scopophilic gaze looking back upon itself.

Picking Tess out is also a challenge in Von Herkomer's illustration. In "'This here stooping do fairly make my back open and shut,' exclaimed the dairy man," she is depicted as one of eight laborers lined up across a field (figure 6.3). The eye runs back and forth, as in a police line-up or scientific array, the selection further complicated by the sightlines of the figures in the engraving, most of whom are looking at Dairyman Crick.

Most evocative of Hardy's portrayal of sexual selection are the illustrations portraying Tess with her fellow dairymaids. Lisa Sternleib has argued that Hardy uses Angel's selection of Tess from the other three dairymaids, Izz, Retty, and Marian, to demonstrate Darwinian sexual selection. Throughout the novel, Hardy represents the four women as a group. When Angel encounters them on their way to church, for example, he perceives them as a "rosy-cheeked, bright-eyed quartet . . . clinging to the roadside bank like pigeons on

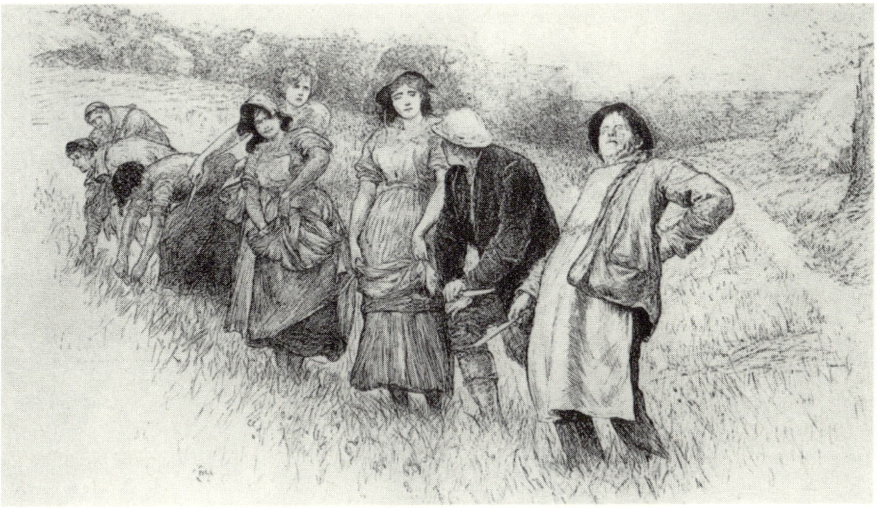

Figure 6.3 Hubert Von Herkomer, "'This here stooping do fairly make my back open and shut,' exclaimed the dairy man." The Graphic *(London), 29 August 1891, 245.*

a roof-slope."[46] When Tess announces that Angel has chosen to marry her, the other three women stare at her, "like a row of avenging ghosts."[47] In his illustration of "'You be going to marry him?' asked Marian," Von Herkomer represents this moment (figure 6.4). The illustration distinguishes Tess's new status within and outside the group, and emphasizes the emotional consequences of sexual selection. The three dairymaids encircle Tess (who stands with her hand in her pocket), their identical hair and clothes making them look somewhat like disheveled triplets. Tess can be clearly distinguished from the rest, with her distinct clothing and hairstyle, and her face vividly profiled against the dark background. But the similar folds of their clothing, the overlapping of their bodies, and the hand one of Tess's companions has placed on her arm shows that she retains her identification with the group. The women gaze directly at her, as though they are surrogates for Angel's gaze, guiding the viewer's eye toward her. While the other plates emphasize the standardization preceding selection, as does Hardy's description of the club-walkers or field-women, this one focuses our central attention on Tess. This illustration echoes Hardy's narrative eye zeroing in on the girl in the pink jacket. Yet an ominous quality is added to the scene. The heavy beam hanging overhead, and the darkness all around, suggests the inevitably tragic results of this selection.

This unease is also apparent in the following illustration by Wehrschmidt, which portrays Tess and Angel's departure after their wedding (figure 6.5).

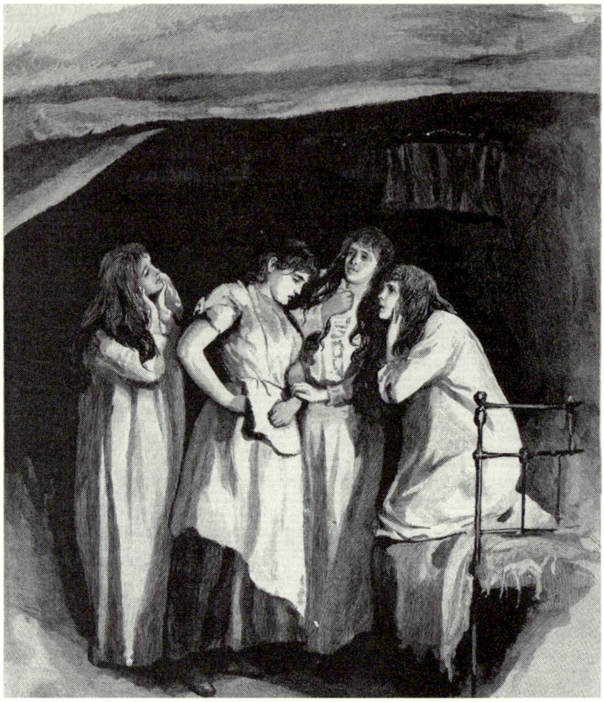

Figure 6.4 Hubert Von Herkomer, "'You be going to marry him?' asked Marian." The Graphic *(London), 3 October 1891, 389. Brown University Library.*

Angel is shown pausing to kiss each of the other dairymaids who are lined up on the left side of the church door, while Tess waits on the right, in the shadows. While the newly married Tess is marked as different from the group she has just left, Wehrschmidt makes us recognize her physical similarity to them, and their nearly interchangeable resemblance to one another. Surprisingly, the focus of the picture is the row of dairymaids, particularly the farthest left (apparently Marian), who is standing in the light. The sun reflects brilliantly from Marian's dress for, ironically, she is dressed in white on Tess's wedding day, while Tess herself appears in dark traveling clothes. Besides the brightness of Marian's dress, there are no clear distinctions among the three unmarried women. As in "'I don't know about ghosts,'" Tess is positioned opposite a mirroring female figure, the center of the three, whose posture and figure match hers. Behind Tess, and in exactly the same pose, stands the barely visible Mrs. Crick, who appears as a dark silhouette with a death-like visage. Both Tess and Mrs. Crick, as the married women in the scene, have been selected by men, yet both Angel and the dairyman turn away from them to focus on the line of available maids. The plate is entitled "As he passed them he kissed them in succession where they stood." It demonstrates how, even

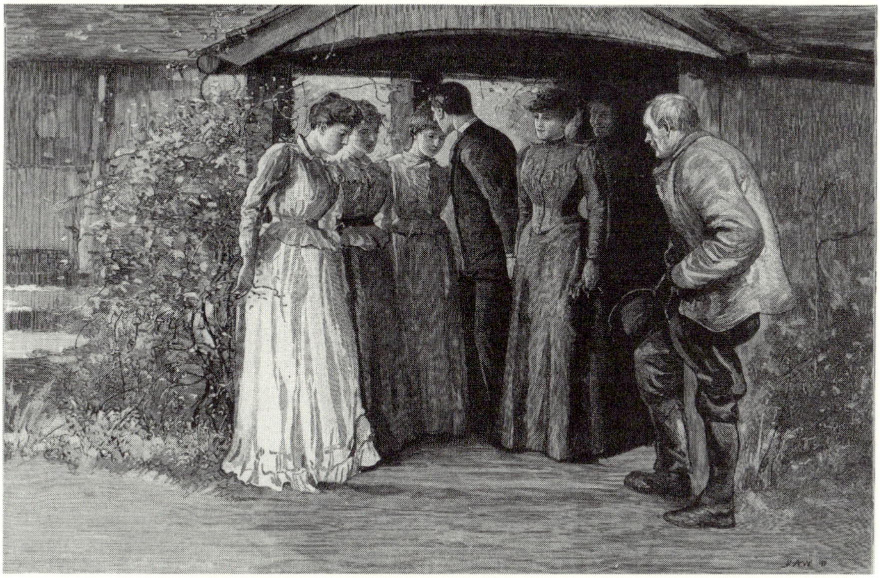

Figure 6.5 D. A. Wehrschmidt, "As he passed them he kissed them in succession where they stood, saying 'Good-bye' to each as he did so." The Graphic *(London), 10 October 1891, 421. Brown University Library.*

after his marriage, Angel continues to view the dairymaids as a standardized group. Angel, who was selecting Tess from this same group in the earlier illustration, is still focused on the line of available women, rather than on the shadowy bride behind him. He seems to have married them all, or to wish he had. (Indeed, later in the novel he abandons Tess and attempts to marry Izz.) Here, the viewer's point of view roughly parallels Angel's; we see the dairymaids in the same array as he does, and, initially, look to find Tess there. The illustrations thus implicates the viewer in the process of sexual selection, while also suggesting, as Hardy does in the novel, that this sort of scopophilia is more likely to lead away from monogamous marriage than toward it.

When asked by Angel if she wants to learn about history, Tess demures, saying "what's the use of learning that I am one of a long row only . . . making me sad, that's all."[48] Tess thus enunciates the emotional toll of the sort of scopophilic sexual selection that Hardy adopts from Darwin. This may become clearer by returning to Darwin's comparison between mating birds and "young rustics at a country fair courting a pretty girl."[49] Hardy's novel begins with just such a country fair, but, as in Darwin's scenes of sexual selection in *The Descent of Man*, it is an orderly, somewhat dreary social pageant, in which the women are arrayed before Angel who "glanced them over, and attempted some discrimination."[50] If, as Darwin whimsically suggests, "an inhabitant of another planet" were to arrive at such a fair, he might well see sexually empowered women in an eager, chaotic mating scene. Yet a male visitor from a nearby town on this planet, such as Angel Clare, sees only "a processional march of two and two round the parish."[51] Moreover, Angel is not the only male presented with a choice of women from the beginning of the novel; it is the reader and spectator who Hardy places in the position of sexual selector. Darwin and Hardy, in granting the power of sexual selection to human males, also grant them the power of displaying the female bodies they view. In both *Tess of the D'Urbervilles* and *The Descent of Man,* human sexual selection is thus characterized as much by men's ability to range women in a line as to pick them out of one.

NOTES

1. Charles Darwin, *The Origin of Species by Means of Natural Selection or the Preservation of Favored Races in the Struggle for Life,* 6th ed. (London: John Murray, 1880), 65–66; Darwin, *The Descent of Man and Selection in Relation to Sex,* 2 vols. (London: John Murray, 1871), vol. 1, 259, vol. 2, 371.

2. Darwin, *Descent of Man,* vol. 1, 259.

3. Ibid., vol. 2, 354.

4. Ibid., 371–72.

5. Ibid., 371.

6. Ibid., 346.

7. Ibid., 122.

8. Sander L. Gilman, "Black Bodies, White Bodies: Toward an Iconography of Female Sexuality in Late Nineteenth-Century Art, Medicine, and Literature," in *Race, Writing and Difference,* ed. Henry Louis Gates (Chicago: University of Chicago Press, 1992).

9. Darwin, *Descent of Man,* vol. 2, 354.

10. Daryl Ogden, *The Language of the Eyes: Science, Sexuality, and Female Vision in English Literature and Culture, 1690–1927* (Albany: State University of New York, 2005), 121, 124.

11. Darwin, *Descent of Man,* vol. 2, 357.

12. Ibid., 354.

13. Gillian Beer, *Darwin's Plots: Evolutionary Narrative in Darwin, George Eliot and Nineteenth-Century Fiction* (London: Routledge, 1983), 213.

14. Dianne Sadoff, "Looking at Tess: The Female Figure in Two Narrative Media," in *The Sense of Sex: Feminist Perspectives on Hardy,* ed. Margaret R Higonnet, 149 (Chicago: University of Illinois Press, 1992). Linda Shires attempts to complicate the notion of the "monolithic

patriarchal male gaze" (167) in her reading of *Far from the Madding Crowd*, pointing out that various men gaze differently and that the gaze can be linked with both male disempowerment and female empowerment. Similarly, Jennifer Gerstel argues that, in *Far from the Madding Crowd*, "[p]ower relations . . . tilt and change with looking and the consciousness of being looked at" (234).

15. Angelique Richardson, "'How I mismated myself for love of you!': The Biologization of Romance in Hardy's *A Group of Noble Dames*," *Thomas Hardy Journal* 14, no. 2 (1998): 64, 68.

16. Lisa Sternlieb, "Three Leahs to Get One Rachel: Redundant Women in *Tess of the d'Urbervilles*," *Dickens Studies Annual* 29 (2000): 359.

17. This is not to say that precisely the same dynamic of sexual selection operates in all of Hardy's novels. Jennifer Gerstel convincingly argues that, in *Far from the Madding Crowd*, Hardy wishes to complicate Darwin's portrayal of female passivity. Bathsheba Everdene, she suggests, negotiates a "flurry of male attention, not merely as a passive object, but as an active selector, a sort of interesting combination of both peahen and peacock" (210). In *Tess*, however, Hardy significantly limits female power, and focuses almost entirely on male selection, thus adhering more closely to Darwin's portrayal of male selection than he does in other novels.

18. Thomas Hardy, *Tess of the d'Urbervilles*, ed. Scott Elledge (New York: Norton, 1991), 8.

19. Ibid., 71; Darwin, *Descent of Man*, vol. 2, 354.

20. It can reasonably be argued that Angel does not actually select Tess in this scene, as he does not end up dancing with her, and only makes his appearance after the narrative eye focuses in on her. As Silverman, Nunokawa, and Law suggest, however, the narrative gaze clearly is overlayed upon Angel's gaze over the course of the chapter: "Tess's nomination as a subject worthy of narrative attention . . . constructs at the same time an ideal viewer: the discriminating consumer of aesthetic effects. . . . And in the paragraph immediately following the delineation of the 'phases of her childhood,' the embodied representative of the narrator emerges (Angel)." Jules Law, "Sleeping Figures: Hardy, History, and the Gendered Body," *ELH* 65, no. 1 (1998): 247–48.

21. Hardy, *Tess*, 6.

22. Ibid., 7.

23. Ibid., 8.

24. Darwin, *Descent of Man*, vol. 2, 72. In chapter 19 of *Descent*, Darwin dwells at length on lip extension in his discussion of ornamentation through bodily mutilation. While Hardy is addressing structure rather than ornament here, Tess's large, projecting lip, which is associated with her "native" dialect, seems to gesture toward Darwin's description of primitive ornamentation.

25. Hardy, *Tess*, 5.

26. Kaja Silverman, "History, Figuration and Female Subjectivity in Tess of the d'Urbervilles," *Novel* 18 (1984): 6.

27. Jeff Nunokawa, "*Tess*, Tourism and the Spectacle of the Woman," in *Rewriting the Victorians: Theory, History, and the Politics of Gender*, ed. Linda M. Shires, 75 (New York: Routledge, 1992).

28. Darwin, *Descent of Man*, vol. 2, 357; Hardy, *Tess*, 6, 7.

29. See Jules Law's discussion of Tess's "temporally-sedimented body," "Sleeping Figures," 248.

30. Nunokawa, "*Tess,* Tourism," 72.

31. Hardy, *Tess,* 68–69.

32. Ibid., 69.

33. Patricia Murphy, *Time is of the Essence: Temporality, Gender, and the New Woman* (Albany: State University of New York Press, 2001), 103.

34. Hardy, *Tess,* 69.

35. Nunokawa, "*Tess,* Tourism," 71.

36. Darwin, *Origin of Species,* 65; Darwin, *Descent of Man,* vol. 2, 354.

37. Jonathan Smith, "Picturing Sexual Selection: Gender and the Evoution of Ornithological Illustration in Charles Darwin's *Descent of Man,*" in *Figuring It Out: Science, Gender and Visual Culture,* ed. Ann B. Shteir and Bernard Lightman, 102 (Hanover: Dartmouth College Press, 2006).

38. In 1869, when Hubert von Herkomer (1849–1914) first exhibited at the Royal Academy, he also began working as an illustrator for the newly founded London newspaper, *The Graphic.* By the time "Tess of the d'Urbervilles: A Pure Woman Faithfully Presented" was published by *The Graphic* in weekly installments from 4 July until 26 December 1891, von Herkomer was a Royal Academician. In 1907, he was knighted by King Edward VII.

39. Arlene M. Jackson, *Illustration and the Novels of Thomas Hardy* (Totowa: Rowman and Littlefield, 1981), 57.

40. Hardy, *Tess,* 8, 71.

41. Jennifer Wicke, "The Same and Different: Standards and Standardization in Thomas Hardy's *Tess of the d'Urbervilles,*" in *Tess of the d'Urbervilles,* ed. Jon Paul Riquelme, 580–81 (Boston: Bedford Books, 1998).

42. Ibid., 586.

43. Diane Sadoff notes intriguing parallels between the market pressures that led to Hardy's revisions of the novel for its publication in the *The Graphic* and the cinematic market pressures influencing Polanksi's film Sadoff, "Looking at Tess," 166–67.

44. Darwin identifies women's voices as a trait developed through sexual selection: "Women are generally thought to possess sweeter voices than men, and as far as this serves as any guide, we may infer that they first acquired musical powers in order to attract the other sex." *Descent of Man,* vol. 2, 337.

45. Sadoff, "Looking at Tess," 152.

46. Hardy, *Tess,* 112.

47. Ibid., 155.

48. Hardy, *Tess,* 99.

49. Darwin, *Descent of Man,* vol. 2, 122.

50. Hardy, *Tess,* 9.

51. Ibid., 6.

CHAPTER 7

Darwin's Sexual Selection and the Jealous Male in Fin-de-Siècle Art

BARBARA LARSON

Jealousy and *The Descent of Man*

One of the most pervasive images in Symbolist art is that of the *femme fatale*, a lascivious, looming, beastly woman who is thought to signify by turns the unwelcome empowerment of the turn-of-the-century female who seeks suffrage or a male-dominated career, or the disease-carrying prostitute, all considered as central to socially urgent issues that posed a threat to masculinity. Bram Dijkstra elaborates on the varying types of fatal women to be found in turn-of-the-century art in his wide-ranging *Idols of Perversity*, focusing in part on the fallout of Darwin's *Descent of Man, and Selection in Relation to Sex*. He contends that the generally accepted Darwinian argument that women were less evolved and intellectual furnished the scientific proof that women could be considered as animal-like and prepared through evolution to be thought of primarily in terms of their biological instinctive nature, thus the fusion of animals or fish and women as hybrids who seek to entrap men or the Judiths holding bloody male heads as virtual castrators found in art of the period.[1] Whether sadistic or merely erotic, they represent women whose overt sexuality is to be contrasted with art that depicts the more appropriate demure mothers and children that bond in natural settings, equally representative of Darwinian ideas.[2] However denigrating images of the *femme fatale* are to women, they represent a different choice than the less-exploited, masculinized Amazons that also formed the iconography of powerful women at the turn of the century. They are voluptuous objects of display primarily designed to titillate a male audience. These overwhelmingly fleshy women were depicted by modern male artists at a time when artists were considered by the general public and oftentimes by themselves to be weak and degenerate, unlikely to win a prize female against virile rivals in a Darwinian schema of sexual selection. The *femme fatale* may often represent a different side of dreaded power than that Dijkstra primarily explores: personal, psychological effects of rejection by the most desirable of women at a time when Darwin's interpretation of the rationale behind mate choice was much discussed. This chapter examines how the popularization of the theory of sexual selection informed imagery of jealousy or powerlessness and how certain artists like Munch and Kokoschka personally identified with the suitor who must inevitably lose out to a more dominant male, doomed to be consumed by the emotion of jealousy.[3]

Sexual selection refers to an individual of one gender making a choice between two or more potential mates of the opposite gender. Darwin brought up sexual selection in his ground-breaking *On the Origin of Species* (1859), but by the time of the publication of *The Descent of Man, and Selection in Relation to Sex* (1871), he had come to attach tremendous significance to the role played by sexual selection in evolution. He considered it to be responsible for the primary human racial and gender differences, both physical and mental.

The first chapter of *Descent of Man* introduced similarities among all living organisms, arguing for general descent and made the daring connection between apes and humans, noting how they shared many of the same structures, diseases, and even courtship rituals. Chapter 2 was devoted to similarities in mental faculties and emotions between humans and other creatures. Among shared instincts are self-preservation, sexual love, and love of the mother for her offspring.[4] Much of volume 1 of *Descent of Man* was devoted to explaining how a moral sense in humans evolved from social instincts in other creatures. In volume 2, Darwin built his argument on sexual selection by devoting no less than eleven chapters to reproductive behavior in insects, birds, and mammals before discussing humans. He introduced the unpopular idea that females selected mates almost exclusively and did so largely through appreciation of "beauty."[5] Thus, for example, the spectacular colors and patterns of certain male birds as opposed to the drab plumage of the females of the species could be explained by female choice in favor of the most magnificent. In many instances, males engaged in combat with one another, which Darwin referred to as "the law of battle" to drive off rivals. Competition among males for reproductive access to females resulted in significant evolutionary developments and accounted for dimorphism of secondary sexual characteristics.

While *Descent of Man* was devoted to establishing continuity between humans and other living creatures, when it came to sexual selection among *Homo sapiens*, Darwin gave males the power of choice. Nevertheless, he maintained that females of all species were generally more passive and coy and males more sexually aggressive. Darwin defended his transition in this way:

"Man is more powerful in body and mind than woman, and in the savage state he keeps her in a far more abject state of bondage than does the male of any other species; therefore it is not surprising that he should have gained the power of selection."[6] Healthy, virile men are the evolutionary result of subsequent generations of men fighting men for the pick of women. As Darwin elaborated, "the greater size, strength, courage, and energy of man, in comparison with the same qualities in woman, were acquired during primeval times, and have subsequently been augmented, chiefly through the contests of rival males for females."[7] Through the centuries, he had become larger and more muscular, and more courageous, energetic, inventive, and sexually assertive than woman. Although physical combat was no longer common in gaining a woman's attention in the present day, the continued necessity of defending and feeding offspring favored the ongoing development of intelligence. Women had evolved to be more nurturing, reclusive, and altruistic than men. According to Darwin, women's principal attraction to men lay in cultural standards of beauty (thus, the differing characteristics of the races), "mental charm," and ornamentation.

In order to strengthen his argument on sexual selection and "beauty," Darwin augmented the role of rivalry in sexual selection beginning with the second edition of 1874.[8] He had compared *Homo sapiens* to apes and argued that humans were originally monogamous or polygamous, largely due to male jealousy, female fear of reprisal and dependency, and had never engaged in general promiscuity or polyandry as certain contemporary anthropologists argued.[9] Males who were not as strong would tend to lose mates and would be perceived as less desirable. There was little room for explanations of innocent romantic love in Darwin's world, for nature's ultimate game plan was always reproduction. In the second edition, he quoted Schopenhauer, a favorite of the Symbolists: "the final aim of all love intrigues, be they comic or tragic, is really of more importance than all other ends in human life . . . it is not the weal or woe of any one individual, but that of the human race to come, which is here at stake."[10] Schopenhauer's pessimism regarding human behavior was in alignment with Darwin and is one of the reasons that Symbolists were prepared to accept the scientist's ideas. They embraced Schopenhauer's theory that the "will to live" (not unlike Darwin's "struggle for survival") is motivated by irrational forces at work in nature, including the urge towards sexual reproduction, which masks as romantic love.[11] For Schopenhauer, love affairs could lead to insanity, suicide, or murder.

Darwin's demystification of love in *Descent of Man* made him one of the founding theorists of sexology, a field of study that also influenced artists' interest in the psychology of sex. Sexual selection was the stimulus for Havelock Ellis's *Man and Woman: A Study of Secondary or Tertiary Sexual Characteristics* (1894) and *Studies in the Psychology of Sex,* volume four (1908) being specifically on sexual selection in humans. Freud's studies of Darwin date to the 1870s and the evolutionist strongly influenced Freud's theories of humans as driven by unconscious forces like passion, pleasure, reproduction, and survival.[12] For this most influential of psychologists of the twentieth century, sexual motivations were central. Called the "Darwin of mental life" by his biographer and pupil Ernest Jones, Freud credited Darwin with dealing a "biological blow" to human narcissism and proving that "man is not a being different from animals or superior to them; he himself is of animal descent."[13] Sexologist Otto Weininger, a strong influence in Viennese circles in which Kokoschka participated, quoted Darwin on men's superior intellectual gifts and discussed women as possessed by their sexuality.[14]

Wife Capture

At a time when mate selection was under the microscope of science, the origins of marriage were being theorized by anthropologists. One of the arenas of investigation that influenced Darwin and was picked up in popular culture involved wife capture. Darwin cited John Lubbock's *The Origin of Civilization and the Primitive Condition of Man: Mental and Social Conditions of Savages* (1870) and John McLennan's *Primitive Marriage: An Inquiry into the Origins of the Form of Capture in Marriage Ceremonies* (1865). Both posited that wife capture was an important part of the history of civilization, but disagreed about the advance of civilization before this point. Wife capture was an important focus for Darwin since it was through this brutal act that men held women in "an abject state of bondage," which in turn ultimately gave them full advantage in sexual selection. Jealousy was at the root of the crucial stage that eventually would lead to the ritual of marriage.

The prehistoric brute that fought for and dragged off a young woman became a popularized aspect of sexual selection in the late nineteenth century, and accounts were given in many novels of the period and in art such as Paul Jamin's *An Abduction—the Stone Age* (figure 7.1). Because of the blurred lines between anthropoid and man in Darwin's history, the possessor could be ape, Neanderthal, or *Homo sapien.*[15] Prehistoric romances were popular in the West in the wake of *Descent of Man.* Women are carried off by savage victors in J. H. Knight-Adkin's *The Woman-Stealers* (1905), J. H. Boex's [Rosny the elder] *Vamireh* (1892) and *Nomaï, Amours lacustres* (1911), Robert Bennet's *Romance of the Polar Pit* (1901), Jack London's *Before Adam* (1906), and Peter McCord's *Wolf: Memories of a Cave Dweller* (1908), among others.[16] In Élie

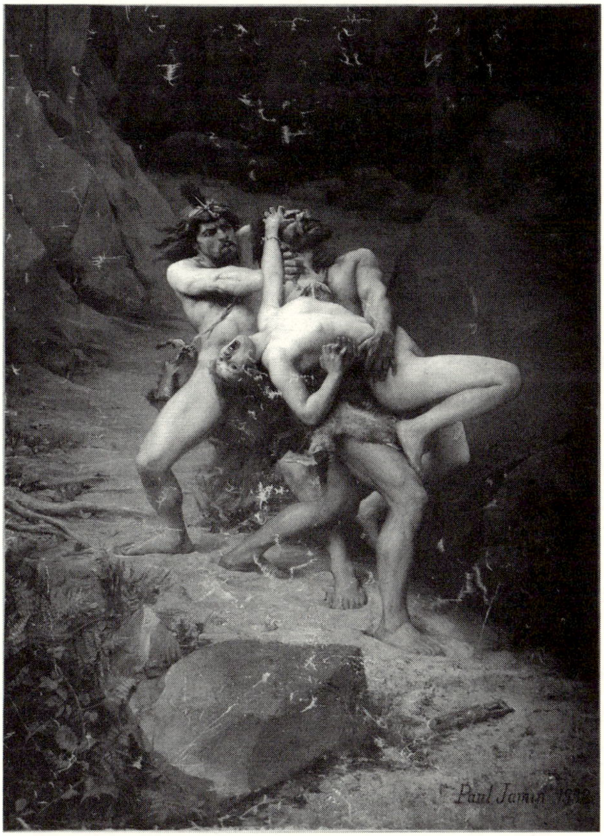

Figure 7.1 Paul Jamin, *An Abduction—The Stone Age,* 1889, oil on canvas. © *Musée des Beaux-arts de la ville de Reims.*

Berthet's *Romans Préhistoriques: le monde inconnue* of 1876 (republished as *Paris avant l'histoire* in 1885), the young woman Deer dwells in a cave in what would become Montmartre in the north of Paris during the Old Stone Age; she is admired by the relatively genteel Fair Hair, who carves ivory and bone into animal shapes that demonstrates that "despite the coarseness of the work the maker was an artist of the first rank for the time." However, it is the hairy, Herculean brute Red who carries Deer off after killing her father, keeping her subjugated by clubbing her. Fair Hair's only chance of rescuing Deer is through cunning. He is ultimately successful, but Red is so strong that even an arrow to the throat and heart leave him standing for a time and it remains uncertain that Fair Hair will prevail. When at last Red falls to the ground, the jealousy and rage experienced by Fair Hair now shifts to the ape-like brute who is only able to watch the newly formed couple. Fair Hair has gained advantage through a superior weapon and the ability to plan an attack. These advances, plus an artistic ability not central to survival, suggest that he has greater intelligence than Red; he seems able to lead history to a new stage and will be the one likely to propagate. What has propelled him forward at a crucial moment has been the emotions of jealousy and possessiveness, the results of which will affect the next generation.

A decade after the first publication of Berthet's novel, another monstrous kidnapper of a lovely young woman in Paris threatened to carry the day. Though pierced in the side by an arrow, Emmanuel Frémiet's popular *Gorilla Carrying Off a Woman* bares his fangs at the viewer, a struggling nude held under one arm (figure 7.2). The positive reception of Frémiet's *Gorilla*, which won a medal of honor at the salon of 1887, demonstrates the widespread acknowledgment of Darwin's direct connection between humans and apes and the study of rudimentary states of instinctive sexuality, jealousy, and capture by the end of the century. A similar sculpture, *Gorilla Abducting a Negress*, had been entered into the salon of 1859 by Frémiet with less official and public success. Although the artist had identified the 1859 ape as a female through an inscription on the sculpture's base, it was generally understood as male. Hidden behind a curtain in the entrance foyer, it was nevertheless something of a sensation and the critic Baudelaire wrote of it, "The orang-outang carrying a woman into the woods (a refused work, which naturally I haven't seen) is very much the product of a sharp mind. Why not a crocodile, a tiger, or another beast likely to eat a woman? Why not? Remember, he has no interest in eating her, but in raping her. For the lone ape, the gigantic ape, at once more and less than a man, has sometimes shown a human appetite for woman."[17]

Baudelaire's commentary demonstrates that sexual connections between humans and apes were already familiar territory in the year that Darwin published his *Origin of Species*, which only hints at human evolution. Frémiet noted that the sculpture was created at a time when there was much discussion about the relationship between apes and humans.[18] Its appearance coincided with the establishment of the Société d'Anthropologie in that year by physical anthropologist and evolutionist Paul Broca, eventual disseminator of Darwinian ideas. Broca made the study of similarities between human skeletons and apes central to his work. At Paris's museum of natural history a revived interest in early nineteenth-century French evolutionists Étienne Geoffroy Saint-Hilaire and Jean-Baptiste Lamarck at midcentury was contributing to the embrace of transformism.

Shocking though *Gorilla Abducting a Negress* may have seemed in 1859, stories of African women coupling with apes already circulated in the eighteenth century and were referred to by Buffon, who had precociously treated the chimpanzee as part of a continuity between humans and animals.[19] Carl

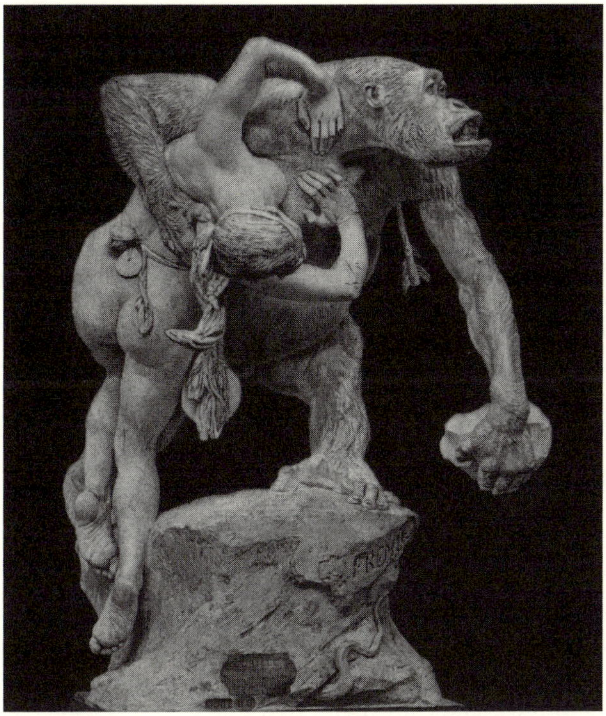

Figure 7.2 Emmanuel Frémiet, *Gorilla Carrying Off a Woman*, 1887, plaster. Reproduced in Gustave Ollendorf, *Salon de 1887* (Paris: L. Baschet, 1887), opposite 82. *Photo credit: The New York Public Library / Art Resource, NY.*

Linnaeus illustrated an orangutan carrying off an African woman in his *Genuine and Universal System of Natural History* (1795). By the late 1840s, the naturalist Richard Owen had begun publishing reports on the gorillas of Gabon who supposedly showed an interest in abducting native women.[20] Frémiet's interest in this newly identified species, the largest of the great apes, is not surprising since he was attached to Paris's museum of natural history, eventually becoming Master of Zoological Drawing there in 1875.[21] By 1849, the Paris natural history museum received a gorilla skeleton and in 1851 two bodies, a male and an infant, preserved in alcohol. The donor of the skeleton perpetuated stories of gorillas' lust for women.[22] That the similarity and purpose of the emotions of jealousy and possession among apes and humans was commonly understood by the late nineteenth century is further suggested in a published rumor that circulated after the exhibition of the second version of *Gorilla*. Marek Zgorniak noted that a story was told of a married man who thought he recognized the features of his wife, a one-time fiancée of Frémiet, in the unfortunate woman and something of his own in the gorilla.[23]

While the 1859 sculpture was destroyed in 1861 and existing photos do not clarify the representation of the genitalia, the 1887 piece is decidedly male. In this version, Frémiet is more daring in the potential for collapsing the categories of human and ape and indeed European and ape. This female is white and a snake slithers up the rock beneath the ape's feet, undercutting the Judeo-Christian account of origins and the fall from innocence; a related drawing was inscribed "the first Adam."[24] Frémiet's gorilla carries a crude chipped tool, an evolutionary hint at the incipient human within simian ancestry.

Contemporary romances were often recast in light of natural history and novelists examined males' passion, jealousy, and combativeness. The flirtation novels of Paul Bourget and Paul Hervieu, Edith Wharton's *The Choice* (1916), and William Dean Howells, *Their Wedding Journey* (1894) are all examples. In Henry James' *The Bostonians* (1886), the feminist heroine is carried off by brute force.[25]

The Symbolists and Sexual Atavism

Modern artists also created images of prehistoric males battling for females as well as of contemporary men and women engaged in similar pursuits. These scenes had a personal side since modern artists were thought of as part of the peripheral degenerate population, whose fantastic way of representing the world was tied to overly stimulated nervous systems and negative heredity.[26] The antithesis of the robust, vigorous males that Darwin envisioned as winners in the contest over women, modern artists by default would be the likely loser when it came to the most desirable of women. Inventive artists might be thought of as geniuses, but this term carried negative associations in the late nineteenth century, for artistic genius was thought of as a particular form of degeneration.

Symbolists tended to agree that they were touched by madness and had overly stimulated nervous systems, but this gave them access to unusual insights. These ideas were not new, but recent work in neurology and the influence of Cesare Lombroso's *Man of Genius* (1863) popularized the notion of the "mad genius" afresh. He argued that certain forms of mental illness were a stimulant to genius, but genius led to weakness of sexual and muscular activity and eventually to sterility. His disciple, the physician Max Nordau, took things further in his notorious text *Degeneration* of 1892. He connected modern art to "visual derangements." He devoted an entire chapter to Symbolist writers whose work was often close to that of artists. Of the artists he wrote:

> The Symbolists, so far as they are honestly degenerate and imbecile, can think only in a mystical, i.e., in a confused way. The unknown is to them more powerful than the known; the activity of the organic nerves preponder-

ates over that of the cerebral cortex; their emotions overrule their ideas. When persons of this kind have poetic and artistic instincts, they naturally want to give expression to their own mental state.[27]

The Symbolists Max Klinger, Franz von Stuck, Alfred Kubin, and Arnold Böcklin in Germany all created scenes of competition, struggle, and death informed by Darwinian ideas (see chapter 3 of this anthology). Ernst Haeckel, Karl Vogt, and Wilhelm Bölsche were influential supporters and popularizers of Darwin in Germany. The biologist and evolutionist Haeckel had himself made comparisons between humans and apes in advance of Darwin in his *General Morphology* (1866), acknowledged in *Descent of Man*. He invented the name *Pithecanthropus alalus* for a transitional ape-man yet to be discovered and illustrated his theory of the relatedness of tribal populations with close simian kin in his *Anthropogenie* (1874).[28] This idea of racial hierarchy with Blacks at the bottom of the ladder just next to their ape kin was widely accepted (see figure 3.3).

One of the main themes in the work of Franz von Stuck is the battle of the sexes. The artist noted, "In choosing my themes, I set out to treat only the purely human, the eternally valid, such as the relationship between man and woman. 'He' and 'she' are present in most of my paintings."[29] Like his compatriot Böcklin, von Stuck made use of fighting mythical creatures to suggest primal drives, often contrasting battling male centaurs or fauns with a lone woman who passively awaits the outcome. Like many of the Symbolists, he explored not only the animal side of the jealous male, but separate imagery of *femme fatales*, especially portrayed as sphinxes.

Max Klinger had read Darwin as early as the 1870s and an early sketchbook of the period is filled with scenes of aggressive sexuality.[30] His social concerns, coupled with readings of Schopenhauer and Nietzsche, gave him a bleak outlook on the human potential to rise above immediate simian ancestry. As an advocate of women's equality, part of his explorations of sexuality concerned ways in which female oppression could be envisioned. A huge lobster with an enormous pincer that rapes a woman in his *Nightmare* of 1878 recalls Darwin's contention that the male lobster's overly large pincer was the result of sexual selection, but it is also a horrific sexual aggressor, whose size makes attempts at escape impossible. Jealousy used to determine the outcome of sexual pairing without female choice occurs in "Rivals" from *A Life* of 1882, where two men fight over a prostitute, and "In Flagranti" from *Dramas*, where a husband kills his wife's lover, among other examples.

Alfred Kubin, inspired by Klinger, pursued graphic work, much of which was based on dark instincts and prehistory. In *Lust* of 1900, an enormous ape with an erect penis regards a nude woman who cowers in a corner. In *One for All* (1900/1901), a mob of apes approach a chained woman. Also drawn to Schopenhauer and Nietzsche, and emphasizing Schopenhauer's materialistic "Will" in nature, Kubin's perspective was even darker than that of Klinger.

František Kupka, best known for his Symbolist works and abstractions in the early twentieth century, worked as an illustrator in turn-of-the-century Paris. Interested in the sciences and mysticism, he thought of the reproductive instinct and selection as part of the vital force of nature. From 1896 to 1900, he created a series of monkeys with human characteristics in crayon, pastel, and watercolor. In *Anthropoïdes* of 1902, two apes fight perhaps to the death over a passive female who holds a flower (figure 7.3). Women traditionally have been associated with nature, especially flowers, long before Darwin gave a scientific underpinning to the natural female.[31] In this case, the reference may also be to Darwin's claim that animals share with humans an aesthetic sensibility, sometimes caricatured during this period as monkeys gazing appreciatively at flowers. It may also allude to Darwin's considerable attention to the development of color and sexual mechanisms in the evolution of flowers.

In 1904, Kupka was commissioned to illustrate his uncle Élisée Rèclus's study of geography and history *L'Homme et la Terre* (1905–1908). The artist included scenes of apes and anthropoids meant to demonstrate behavioral roots of humankind. In the plate *Origines: La Succession des ages est pour nous la grande école*, an anthropoid family sits together, the mother nursing an infant. In *Progrès: Le Vrai progress est la conquête du Pain et de l'instruction pour tous les hommes*, a working man who reaches out to the viewer is juxtaposed next to an ape with a rudimentary tool. His *Rapt: Conquête de la femme* shows the now-familiar trope of a brute (this time a man) stepping from a simple boat carrying an unconscious nude female in his rugged arms. For the anarchist uncle and nephew, this is a socially critical image of the makings of patriarchy.[32]

Symbolists whose projects included the exploration of atavistic sexual roots of human behavior often identified with the victimized and powerless female or the hopeless condition of a future inextricably bound to a brutal, prerational past. Their position differs from Naturalists like Jamin or Frémiet whose work represents the public side of scientific or anthropological currents. It demonstrates an antithetical stance to social Darwinists who used natural and sexual selection to rationalize and uphold ideologies of progress with an unsympathetic stance towards the "weak" who are best winnowed out. Introspective Symbolists were not necessarily blind participants in antifeminist fin-de-siècle culture that historians like Dijkstra maintain them to

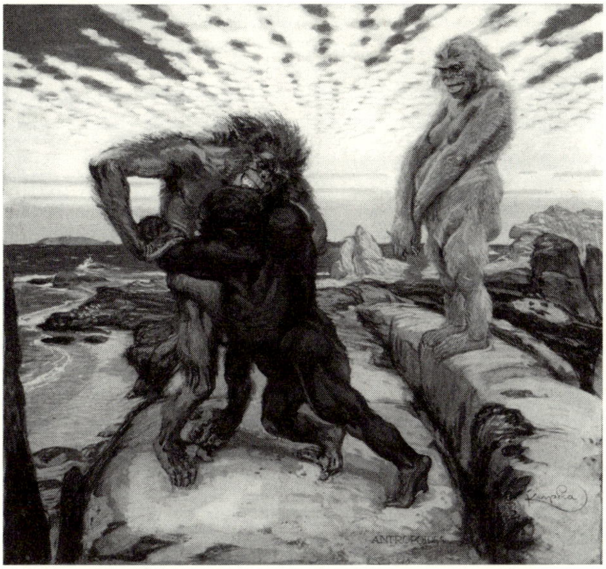

Figure 7.3 František Kupka, *Anthropoïdes—Fight for a Woman,* 1902, gouache on paper, 59.5 × 62 cm. *Courtesy Jiri Svestka Gallery, Prague.*

be. For some, hopelessness and loss in selection would be central to deeply personal imagery of life experience.

Jealousy and Loss in the Work of Munch and Kokoschka

Edvard Munch devoted much of his oeuvre to the wounding experience of sexual jealousy and loss. He never married and obsessed over the women who left him. Munch perceived himself as a degenerate, tainted by negative heredity. In his journal he wrote the much-referenced: "Two of mankind's most horrible enemies were granted to me as an inheritance. An inheritance of tuberculosis and mental illness. . . . A mother who died young gave me a weakness for tuberculosis; an overly nervous father, so pietistically religious as to be almost insane, the descendent of an ancient family, gave me the seeds of insanity."[33] When Munch adopted a Symbolist style, he was cast as a degenerate by critics. Andreas Aubert wrote of him in 1890, "Among our painters, Munch is the one whose entire temperament is formed by the neurasthenic. He belongs to the generation of fair, sickly sensitive people that we encounter more and more frequently in the newest art. And not seldom they find a personal satisfaction in calling themselves Decadents, the children of a refined overly civilized age."[34] Munch would be accused of degeneracy by critics and the public thereafter.[35] At the age of forty-three, he committed himself to a sanatorium in Copenhagen for the treatment of nervous exhaustion and alcoholism; the proprietor Dr. Daniel Jacobson specialized in treating artists. Throughout his life, Munch maintained that his perpetual state of suffering and his nervous disorders were central to his creativity as an artist, not an unusual stance for a Symbolist.

In the 1880s, Munch was a member of the Kristiania Bohème, a group of Naturalist artists and writers that included the painter Christian Krohg. Interested in psychological motivations, Krohg shared with his close friend Klinger an interest in Darwin's work.[36] In 1889, he painted *Struggle for Existence*, which depicted a mob fighting over a crust of bread, meant as a criticism of those who promoted social Darwinism.

Krohg advocated free love, which the group practiced sometimes as a veritable scientific experiment. He was involved in a love triangle that included Hans Jaeger, the leader of the group, and the young painter Oda Lasson. Krohg ended up as the temporary victor, marrying Oda, and Jaeger published his journal entries as *Perverse Love* in 1889. Munch noted that the weakness of this practice was jealousy, which he recalled in the print *From the Kristiania Bohème II* (1895). Reinhold Heller interprets the print with its lovely *femme fatale* and male members of the bohemian group gathered around a café table as a single male jealous of the ghosts of the lovers of his young wife.[37]

In 1892/93, Munch did a series of studies on the subsequent love triangle of Krohg, Oda, and her young lover Jappe Nilssen. In the painting *Melancholy* (also known as *Jealousy* or *The Yellow Boat*), Nilssen is depicted hand to face in the iconic pose of melancholia. Behind him, the Krohgs are on a dock near a boat, seemingly unconcerned with his brooding thoughts. The primordial sea, birthplace of all life, was a common setting in Munch's depictions of dark human emotion. This painting inspired a series of others that would represent the major effort of his mature period, first known as *Studies for a Series on Love* and later as the *Frieze of Life*. His own elusive love interest in Kristiania was the married Milly Thaulow, and it was upon learning of her divorce and remarriage that he executed *Melancholy*. In 1893, his friend the novelist/medical student Stanislaw Przybyszewski wrote of it: "the painting is nothing more than the visualization of the suffering felt in natural selection [sic] ... This is the way that a landscape is pictured in the mind of a male who has lost a female he had chosen to someone else; the wild, prehistoric battle for the female has been transformed into a cultured, *triste*, cowardly, resigned brooding."[38] In 1904–1908, Munch wrote the play *The City of Free Love*, a satire of the bohemian involvements that had caused him so much psychological distress.

Munch used an image based on *Melancholy* to illustrate the book of poems *Alruner* for his friend the Danish poet Emanuel Goldstein in 1892. Similarly, the poems were based on loss and jealousy. Alruner itself is a reference to *alrune* or a mandrake root used in a love potion. In 1892, Goldstein wrote to Munch in reference to the woman who had rejected him:

> I recently met the heroine of my poems again. Now she is married. I told her that if I had not already dedicated the collection of poems to you there would be no reason why it could not be dedicated to her . . . Just think about the women we loved, Munch! That is to say those that betrayed us, we owe many a beautiful impression to them. Just imagine what would have happened had they not betrayed us.[39]

The last time Munch took up this motif was in 1902, when the artist had a final break with his last major love Tulla Larsen.

As a young *enfant terrible* in 1892, Munch exhibited in Berlin where his controversial Symbolist works gave him immediate notoriety. The exhibition was closed down in less than a week at the behest of Kaiser Wilhelm on behalf of a seemingly outraged public. In protest, a group of young artists formed the Free Association of Berlin Artists, the beginning of the Berlin Secession. Munch moved to Berlin in 1893 and became involved with a group of international writers, artists, and scientists who were interested in Symbolism, Nietszche's connection between eroticism and death, psychology, evolution, and sexual selection. Here he met the Swedish novelist Ola Hansson, who had written *Sensitiva Amorosa* (1887) on the principal importance of sexual love; the German poet Richard Dehmel, who would make human passion his major theme as in his scandalous *Woman and World* (1896); and the Norwegian sculptor Gustav Vigeland, who based many of his pieces on the sex drive. Munch became close to the playwright August Strindberg, who frequently explored Darwinian ideas in his plays. Przybyszewski, who specialized in neurology, was here as well. He wrote the treatise *Concerning the Psychology of the Individual Neurasthenic* in 1892, but like many of the Symbolist generation connected creativity with pathology; he declared degeneration genius.

Jealousy at a personal level was no less pervasive among this community than it had been with Krohg's group. In 1893, Munch courted a young student named Dagny Juell, desired by many of the men of the Berlin circle. Jealousy was such that in a few short months this fraternity was torn apart. Although Juell played one man off against another, Przybyszewski emerged as Munch's main rival. In Munch's *Jealousy* of 1895, the features of the man in the foreground are those of Przybyszewski, while a couple reenacts the biblical scene of temptation in the background (figure 7.4). The fatal woman is posed as Eve plucking fruit while a dark-haired man is the willing victim. Her red robe is open and the entire body and clothing form the shape of a vaginal opening.

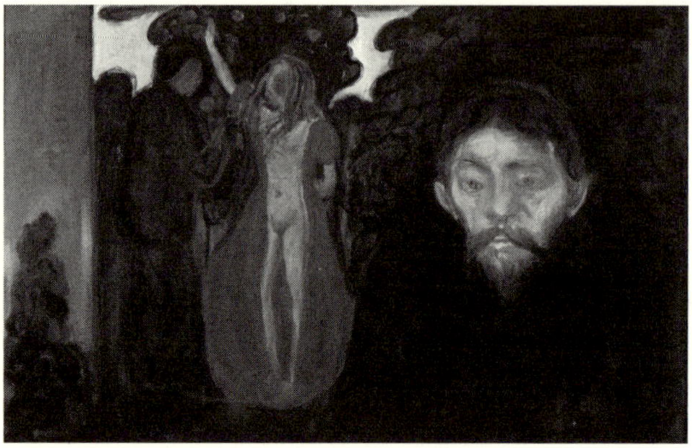

Figure 7.4 Edvard Munch, *Jealousy*, 1895, oil on canvas, 67 × 100 cm. *Historical Museum, Bergen, Norway. Photo credit: Scala / Art Resource, NY. © 2008 The Munch Museum / The Munch-Ellingsen Group / Artists Rights Society (ARS), New York.*

Przybyszewski's beard and moustache pictured in *Jealousy* may represent more than a personal choice in appearance. Darwin believed that facial hair on men was an alluring secondary sexual characteristic, a vestige of the primitive past in which men were selected by women for their beauty and ornamentation. In November of 1892, Munch grew a mustache and maintained it the entire time he was in Berlin. Darwin also listed long hair in women as a universal secondary sexual characteristic. Munch's *femme fatales* often have long hair that can take on a life of its own, sometimes gravitating toward and even encircling men. In *Jealousy*, a few of the woman's tresses fall over her lover's arm.

Przybyszewski eventually married Juell and he wrote a trilogy on the cruelty of love entitled *Homo Sapiens*, featuring two jealous males, himself and Munch, published in 1896. In the first part, "Overboard," Munch is the thinly disguised Makita who arrives in Berlin and presents his beloved fiancée to his best friend Falk, who claims her. Makita is driven to the brink of insanity, bitterly observing, "Woman is a breeding animal, but man loves. Woman never loves, never. It's enough for her to breed."[40] He pursues the couple, who depart Berlin, and hallucinates, seeing an imagined fight between two bucks:

> Two elks were fighting. They struck at each other with their large horns, separated, and made another terrific lunge. Their horns interlocked. In great leaps they tried to disentangle themselves, turning round and round. There was a crunching of horns. . . . And near the fighting animals a female elk was pasturing unmindful of the savage struggle of the passion-mad males.[41]

Makita's vision is reminiscent of the work of contemporary German animal painters like Richard Friese, who depicted various creatures according to Darwinian ideas of sexual selection, such as *Fighting Moose* of the 1890s, in

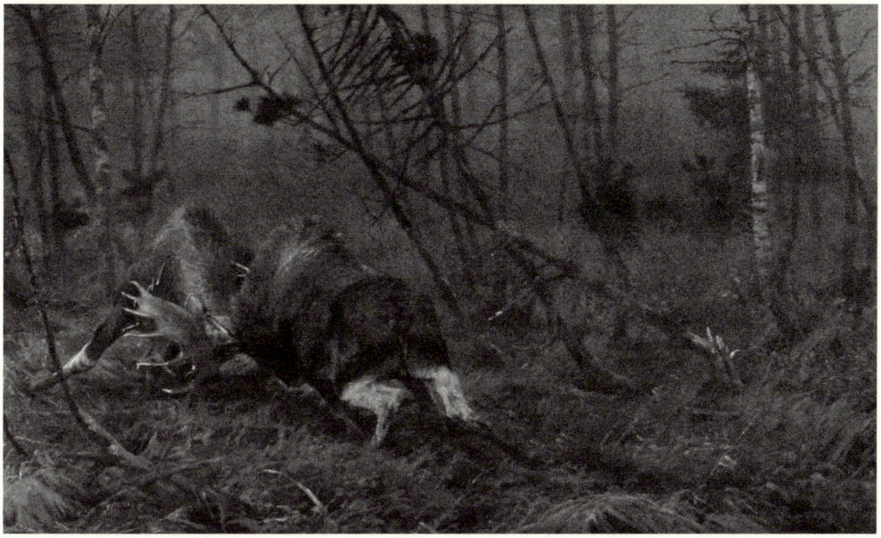

Figure 7.5 Richard Friese, *Two Bull Moose in Combat, with Cow Moose in the Background*, n.d., oil on canvas, 124.4 cm × 226 cm, inv. nr. 0195. *Collection Rijksmuseum Twenthe, Enschede (photography R. Klein Gotink).*

which females passively await the outcome of two battling males (figure 7.5). The secondary sexual characteristic of unnecessarily large horns alluded to by Makita was a favorite example of Darwin's to demonstrate the cumulative effect of sexual selection:

> The development . . . of certain structures—of the horns, for instance, in certain stags—has been carried to a wonderful extreme which, as far as the general condition of life is concerned, must be slightly injurious to the male. From this fact, we learn that the advantages which favored males derive from conquering other males in battle or courtship and thus leaving a numerous progeny, have been in the long run greater than those derived from rather more perfect adaptation to the external condition of life.[42]

Dagny Juell was also featured as the desired female of a love triangle by the infatuated and mentally unstable Strindberg, who is haunted by Juell and Przybyszewski in his novel *Inferno* of 1897.

In the mid-1890s, Munch executed a cycle of ink washes as studies for etchings (that never came to fruition) on the theme *The First Human Beings*. Munch would go back to these studies in 1908 when he entered Jacobson's clinic, after six years of obsessing over Tulla Larsen; at the same time, he worked on a series of writings beginning in 1902 called "The Diary of a Mad Poet." The illustrations eventually were produced as *Alpha and Omega*. This

Adam and Eve are prehistoric humans who inhabit an island. Connecting sexuality with the animal world, Munch follows the unfaithful Omega, who indulges in sexual liaisons with animals. She disappears across the water on a buck, then returns again. In a fit of jealous rage, Alpha kills Omega, while her hybrid children in turn murder him.

Kokoschka, who greatly admired Munch, is another artist who dwelt on the battle of the sexes and rejection. His play *Murderer, Hope of Women* of 1909 was inspired by Strindberg's celebrated Darwinian play *The Father*, originally produced in 1888. However, unlike Darwin, who rejected the idea of a period of matriarchy in advance of male domination in the evolution of civilization, Kokoschka was interested in this idea, explicated in Bachofen's *Mother Right*. *Murderer* is a prehistoric drama of love and death in which men and women have a violent clash to establish supremacy. The female leader is animal-like and sexual. In the end, in an allusion to male dominance and female weakness, the male leader kills everyone including his would-be Amazon adversaries. The psychological violence of disparities between the sexes and jealousy continued in plays like the adulterous *Sphinx and the Strawman* of 1913.[43]

Kokoschka, like Munch, cultivated the state of loss. One of his first major works was an illustrated book *Dreaming Boys* (1908) written after a bitter break-up with Lilith Lang, who worked for the Wiener Werkstätte.[44] The theme is a sexual coming-of-age story of a young couple in which the boy experiences the "werewolf" within. Arguably his most prolific and important period occurred during his doomed relationship with Alma Mahler and its aftermath. The affair began in 1912 shortly after the death of Mahler's husband, the composer Gustav Mahler. In 1915, Alma left Kokoschka for the architect Walter Gropius. The jealous and devastated artist spent the next several years attempting to revive her interest. He was wounded in the Great War in 1915 and was left on the battlefield for four days, an event he recalled later that year in the painting *Knight Errant*. In this painting, he lies helpless in a watery domain with Alma Mahler as a sphinx in the distance. He is also the suffering Christ; in the sky above appear the letters E.S. next to a tiny self-portrait. The letters refer to Christ's final words "My god, my god, why hast thou forsaken me?"

Unable to regain Alma's affections, Kokoschka had a large, nude, stuffed doll made in her likeness down to details of her private parts, which he lived with and painted for a number of years (figure 7.6). He had the doll waited on, dressed, and served tea by a maid, and stories circulated about the Mahler doll being taken on outings by the artist. By 1918, he was known publicly as "the mad Kokoschka," another example of a deranged modern artist.

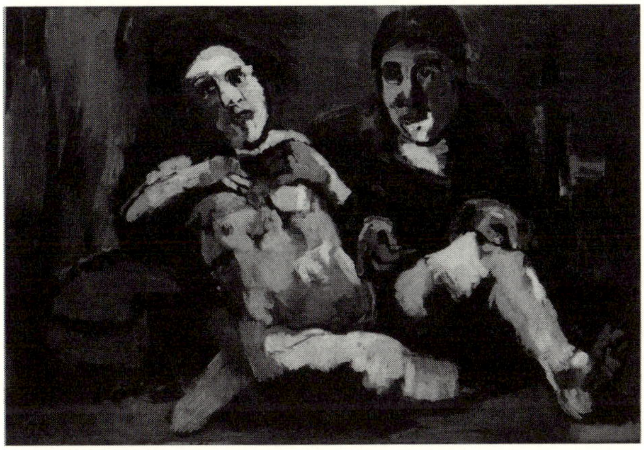

Figure 7.6 Oscar Kokoschka, *Man with a Doll,* 1922, oil on canvas, 80 × 120 cm., Inv. B 1058. *Nationalgalerie, Staatliche Museen zu Berlin, Berlin, Germany. Photo credit: Bildarchiv Preussischer Kulturbesitz / Art Resource, NY. Photo: Joerg P. Anders. © 2008 Artists Rights Society (ARS), New York / Pro Litteris, Zurich.*

Feathers and Gems

Another kind of elusive prize female also influenced the visual culture of the turn of the century: the woman dressed in gems and feathers. In one of his most transparent allusions to the authority of his own class and period of time, Darwin tied the fashion of Victorian feather hats and jewelry made of precious stones to sexual selection. He believed that, given the aesthetic sensibility of all creatures, the remarkable patterns or colors that might attract a female to a male in nonhuman species now transferred gender. According to Darwin, "Our women, both civilized and savage, deck their heads with borrowed plumes and use gems which are hardly more brilliantly colored than the naked skin and wattle of certain birds."[45] Women, he believed, perfectly aware of the power of their beauty in selection, "delight in decorating themselves."

Darwin had spent many chapters of *Descent of Man* discussing sexual selection in birds, which he thought of as most closely connected with humans in terms of a sense of beauty and song. He insisted, "they have nearly the same sense of the beautiful that we do."[46] In his discussion of birds, Darwin had used the extraordinary case of the peacock to demonstrate the extent to which sexual selection might overshadow natural selection, since the brilliant colors and enormous fan of the male peacock would make him vulnerable to predators. It was this example that especially appealed to Symbolists of elegant beauties like the young woman portrayed in Edgar Maxence's *Profile with Peacock* or Edmond Aman-Jean's *Young Girl with a Peacock.* In a lithograph by Munch based on *Jealousy* (Munch museet, Oslo), the Edenic tree is transformed into a peacock's tail, while "Dagny" sensually yet coyly reveals but a single breast. In Gauguin's *Te Nave Nave Fenua* (*Tahitian Eve*, 1892), a nude with vestiges of two extra toes reaches out to pluck flowers that resemble peacock feathers.[47] Gustav Klimt, who was much influenced by Darwin, created shimmering, patterned, elegant clothing of gold and bright colors that suggest gem inlays and sumptuous jewelry for his portraits of society women and voluptuous aquatic beauties.[48] This unabashed womanizer (his many affairs included the young Alma) may have excused himself as hopelessly driven by sexual urges.

Many turn-of-the-century modern artists, whose work involved personal introspection, were affected by materialist explanations of mate choice and infidelities, much of which was based in Darwin's view of the unforgiving nature of sexual selection. The pessimism of the period, in which misunderstandings of the nature of heredity led to concerns with degenerate family lines and the potentially lethal effects of accumulating bad habits, put modern artists in a vulnerable position. Some modernists, conditioned to consider themselves as physically tainted and socially peripheral, explored their own states of loss or inescapable atavistic behavior surrounding the sex drive.

NOTES

1. See Bram Dijkstra, *Idols of Perversity: Fantasies of Feminine Evil in Fin-de-Siècle Culture* (New York: Oxford University Press, 1986), especially chapter 6, "Evolution and the Brain," 160–209. More generally on Darwin and women see Evelleen Richards, "Darwin and the Descent of Women," in *The Wider Domain of Evolutionary Thought*, ed. David Oldroyd and Ian Langham, 57–112. (Dordrecht: R. Reidel Publishers, 1983). A number of other recent studies have expanded on Victorian cultural aspects of the way that Darwin framed women. On the biologizing of female nature, see Cynthia Russett, *Sexual Science: The Victorian Construction of Womanhood* (Cambridge, Mass.: Harvard University Press, 1989); and Ruth Hubbard, *The Politics of Women's Biology* (New Brunswick: Rutgers Press, 1990).

2. The bond between mother and child was an example cited by Darwin to demonstrate close continuities between humans and their animal kin.

3. On the gifted, degenerate male artist, see Patricia Mathews, *Passionate Discontent: Creativity, Gender and French Symbolist Art* (Chicago: University of Chicago Press, 1990), especially chapter 3, "The Ecstasy and the Agony," 46–63.

4. For a discussion of the structure of *Descent of Man*, see Robert Richards, *Darwin and the Emergence of Evolutionary Theories of Mind and Behavior* (Chicago: University of Chicago Press, 1987), 190–218.

5. For a discussion on the controversy over beauty in selection among nonhumans, see Helena Cronin, *The Ant and the Peacock: Altruism and Sexual Selection from Darwin to Today* (Cambridge: Cambridge University Press, 1991); and chapter 2 of this volume.

6. Charles Darwin, *The Descent of Man, and Selection in Relation to Sex*, 2 vols. (1871; reprint, Princeton: Princeton University Press, 1981), vol. 2, 371.

7. Ibid., vol. 2, 373.

8. Jonathan Smith argues that the many added illustrations of sexual selection in practice was meant to demonstrate how display and competition actually works, making his theories more immediate and acceptable. "Picturing Sexual Selection: Gender and the Evolution of Ornithological Illustration in Charles Darwin's *Descent of Man*," in *Figuring it Out: Science, Gender and Visual Culture*, ed. Ann B. Shteir and Bernard Lightman, 85–109 (Hanover: University Press of New England, 2006).

9. Rosemary Jann, "Darwin and the Anthropologists: Sexual Selection and its Discontents," in *Sexualities in Victorian Britain*, ed. Andrew Miller and James Adams, 79–95 (Bloomington: Indiana University Press, 1996).

10. Darwin found this quotation in an 1871 article by David Asher, "Schopenhauer and Darwinism," *Journal of Anthropology* (January 1871): 323. Cited in *Descent of Man*, 2nd ed. (London: John Murray, 1874), 586.

11. In *Parerga and Paralipomena*, 2 vols., trans. E. F. J. Payne (1851; reprint, Oxford: Clarendon Press, 1974), Schopenhauer had written that "women exist in the main solely for the propagation of the species" and "live more for the species than the individual." He also speculated about the relationship between humans and apes.

12. See Lucille B. Ritvo, *Darwin's Influence on Freud: A Tale of Two Sciences* (New Haven: Yale University Press, 1990).

13. Sigmund Freud, *The Standard Edition of the Complete Psychological Works*, 24 vols. ed. James Strachey, (London: W. W. Norton & Co., 2000), vol. 17, 140–41.

14. Otto Weininger, *Sex and Character* (London: William Heineman, 1906), 71, 88.

15. Darwin used anthropomorphic descriptions of mating in quadrumana, including the use of the terms "marriage" and "wives." Darwin, *Descent of Man*, vol. 2, 361.

16. On prehistoric fiction of the period, see Claude Cohen, *L'Homme des Origines: savoirs et fictions en préhistoire* (Paris: Editions de Seuil, 1999); and Marc Angenot and Nadia Khouri, "An International Bibliography of Prehistoric Fiction," *Science-Fiction Studies* 23, no. 8, pt. 1 (March 1981): 38–53.

17. Charles Baudelaire, *Ecrits sur l'art*, with an introduction by F. Moulinat (1859; reprint, Paris: Le Livre de Poche, 1992), 314: "L'orang-outang entrainant une femme au fond des bois (ouvrage refusé, que naturellement je n'ai pas vu) est bien l'idée d'un esprit que naturellement je n'ai pas vu), est bien l'idée d'un esprit pointu. Pourquoi pas un crocodile, un tigre, ou toute autre bête susceptible de manger une femme? Non pas! Songez bien qu'il ne s'agit pas de manger, mais de violer. Or le singe seul, le singe gigantesque, à la fois plus et moins qu'un home, a manifesté quelquefois un appétit humain pour la femme." Baudelaire's error in assuming the creature was an orangutan had to do with its longer yet equally sensationalistic appearance in France. A live orangutan had been illustrated by Frémiet's instructor at the natural history museum, Jacques-Christophe Werner, in 1824 and in 1836 another was put on exhibition there,

inspiring speculation about the proximity of man to ape. When it died in 1837, it was stuffed and put on exhibition at the museum in the Ape Room in the Galeries de Zoologie, where it was visible to the public for decades to come.

18. Frémiet in Thiébault-Sisson, "Au jour le jour, une vie d'artiste, Emmanuel Frémiet" (*Le Temps*, 2–3, Maan, 1896), reprinted in Catherine Chevillot, *Emmanuel Frémiet, 1824–1910: Le main et le multiple*, exh. cat. (Dijon: Musée des Beaux-Arts, 1988), 187.

19. Noted in Sander Gilman, "Black Bodies, White Bodies: Toward an Iconography of Female Sexuality in Late Nineteenth-Century Art, Medicine and Literature," in *Race, Writing, and Difference*, ed. Henry Gates, Jr., 231 (Chicago: University of Chicago Press).

20. The gorilla was first reported by the American physician Thomas Savage and Jeffries Wyman in 1847 and named *Troglogytes gorilla (Savage)*.

21. Frémiet had worked at the museum as an illustrator beginning when he was sixteen years old. Here he became familiar with animal anatomy and then successfully transferred his training to the human body in his subsequent work for the dean of the Faculty of Medicine in Paris, Mateu Josep Bonaventura Orfila i Rotger. He also studied in the sculpture studio of Francois Rude and thus, had a dual background in science and art. For additional information on Frémiet's background, see Thiébault-Sisson, "Au jour le jour," 187; and T. H. Bartlett, "Emmanuel Frémiet," *American Architect and Building News* 31, no. 788 (31 January 1891): 72–73; 32, no. 805 (30 May 1891): 129–31.

22. Noted in Ted Gott, "Clutch of the Beast: Emmanuel Frémiet, Gorilla-Sculptor," in *Kiss of the Beast, from Paris Salon to King Kong* (South Brisbane: Queensland Art Gallery, 2005), 32.

23. Marek Zgomiak, "Frémiet's Gorillas: Why Do They Carry Off Women?" *Artibus et historiae* 27, no. 54 (2006): 219.

24. Reproduced in Hélène Lafont-Couturier et al., *Vénus et Caïn: Figures de la Préhistoire 1830–1930* (Bordeaux: Musée d'Aquitaine, 2003), figure 10.

25. Landmark studies on contemporary fiction and Darwin's sexual selection include Gillian Beer, *Darwin's Plots: Evolutionary Narrative in Darwin, George Eliot and Nineteenth-Century Fiction* (Cambridge: Cambridge University Press, 1986); Bert Bender, *The Descent of Love: Darwin and the Theory of Sexual Selection in American Fiction, 1871–1926* (Philadelphia: University of Pennsylvania Press, 1996); Richard Kaye, *The Flirt's Tragedy: Desire without End in Victorian and Edwardian Fiction* (Charlottesville: University Press of Virginia, 2002); and Joseph Carroll, *Literary Darwinism: Evolution, Human Nature, and Darwinism* (New York: Routledge, 2004).

26. See Mathews, *Passionate Discontent*. Also see J. E. Chamberlain and Sander L. Gilman, *Degeneration: The Dark Side of Progress* (New York: Columbia University Press, 1985) and Marijke Gijswijt-Hofstra and Roy Porter, *Cultures of Neurasthenia from Beard to the First World War* (Amsterdam: Rodopi, 2001).

27. Max Nordau, *Degeneration* (1892; reprint, New York: G. Moose, 1968), 118.

28. Vogt also supported the ape-human relationship in his *Lectures on Man*, 1863.

29. Quoted in Edwin Becker, *Franz von Stuck: Eros and Pathos* (Amsterdam: Van Gogh Museum, 2002), 12.

30. On Klinger, see Marsha Morton, "Impulses and Desires: Klinger's Darwinism in Nature and Society," *Nineteenth-Century Art Worldwide* 2, no. 2 (Spring 2003).

31. On this history, see Ludmilla Jordanova, *Languages of Nature: Critical Essays on Science and Literature* (New Brunswick: Rutgers University Press, 1986).

32. For a discussion of Kupka's illustrations for the Rèclus volumes, see Marie-Pierre Salé, "Rèclus et Kupka. L'homme est la nature prenant conscience d'elle-même," in *Vers des temps nouveaux Kupka oeuvres graphiques 1894–1912*, exh. cat. (Paris: Musée d'Orsay, 2002), 106–23.

33. Quoted in Reinhold Heller, *Munch: His Life and Work* (Chicago: University of Chicago Press, 1984), 14–15.

34. Ibid., 69.

35. On the history of accusations of degeneracy, see Patricia Berman, "Edvard Munch's *Self-Portrait with Cigarette*: Smoking and the Bohemian Persona," *Art Bulletin* 75, no. 4 (December 1993): 627–46.

36. Klinger dedicated his lithographic series *Eve and the Future* to Krohg and exhibited the series in Kristiania in 1880.

37. Reinhold Heller, *Munch: The Scream* (New York: The Viking Press, 1973), 37–38.

38. Heller, *Munch: His Life and Work*, 56.

39. Ibid., 86.

40. Stanislaw Przybyszewski, *Homo Sapiens: A Novel in Three Parts* (1896; reprint, New York: AMS Press, 1970), 122.

41. Ibid., 116.

42. Darwin, *Descent of Man*, vol. 2, 279.

43. For a discussion of sexual jealousy as the organizing component of Kokoshka's plays, see Carol Diethe, *Aspects of Distorted Sexual Attitudes in German Expressionist Drama* (New York: Peter Lang), 146–79.

44. The relationship is discussed in Sherwin Simmons, "Ornament, Gender, and Interiority in Viennese Expressionism," *Modernism/Modernity* 8, no. 2 (2001): 254–55.

45. Darwin, *Descent of Man*, vol. 2, 39.

46. Ibid.

47. *Tahitian Eve* was put on exhibition in Paris in 1893 when Gauguin returned from Tahiti. Strindberg saw it there and may have commented on it to Munch. The "flowers" also appear as illustration in Gauguin's *Ancien Culte Mahorie* (13 and back cover). The image was distributed through translation into prints as Gauguin attempted to familiarize the public with his work. The critic Thièbault-Sisson referred to the woman in evolutionary terms as a *quadrumene*. Gauguin accepted the description and commented, "She is Eve after the Fall, still able to go about unclothed without being immodest, preserving all her animal beauty as in the first day . . . Like Eve, the body is still an animal thing. But the head has progressed with evolution, thought has developed subtlety, love has impressed an ironical smile on her lips. . . ." For a discussion on Gauguin and evolution, see Martha Lucy, "The Evolutionary Body: Refiguring the Nude in Post-Darwinian French Art," Ph.D. dissertation, New York University, 2004.

48. On Klimt and Darwin, see Emily Braun, "Ornament as Evolution: Gustav Klimt and Berta Zuckerkandl," in *Gustav Klimt: The Ronald S. Lauder and Serge Sabarsky Collections*, ed. Renée Price, 144–69 (New York: Neue Galerie, 2007). Braun connects Klimt's use of real mother-of-pearl to his interest in evolution.

CHAPTER 8

Wild Beasts and Tame Primates

"Le Douanier" Rousseau's Dream of Darwin's Evolution

FAE BRAUER

"I don't believe anyone will laugh this year," wrote Guillaume Apollinaire about Henri Rousseau's exhibition at the 1910 Salon des Indépendants.[1] Having suffered years of public jeering and press insults, it would seem Rousseau finally exhibited a painting that commanded respect: *The Dream* (figure 8.1). As if an odalisque, a naked ivory-skinned woman identified by the artist as a former lover of Polish descent was posed on a divan placed in front of an ebony-skinned flute-player. Unlike so many "Orientalist" odalisques displayed at the Salon des Peintres Orientalistes held in Paris every year from 1893, the usual signs of exoticism and eroticism do not frame her.[2] Instead, an impenetrable jungle of tropical plants surrounds her, albeit those found in Parisian hothouses at the Jardin des Plantes rather than in Amazonian rain forests. Instead of being pampered by maids and masseurs, she seems beset by lionesses, elephants, snakes, birds, apes, and monkeys. The long, black, hairy arms behind the ferns also imply that a gorilla may be charging in her direction. Nevertheless, unlike the "wild beasts" in Rousseau's "survival of the fittest" paintings, these animals do not attack. Mesmerized by the music playing on a still, moonlit night, human and animal seem to coexist as if in a dream of mutual harmony beyond the social divisions wrought by French technologized capitalism and the conflicts unleashed by colonization—the Foda Cabbah's Rebellion, the Franco-Tukolar, Franco-Dahomey, and Franco-Siamese riots, together with the Third Asante and Madascar War all erupting during the very time Rousseau was painting his "wild beasts" and "tame primates." It is as if they recognize that they are integral, interdependent parts of the same life force having long evolved from the same rudimentary species. It is as if their existence in a dream of a primordial time and space is an exotic twist on Charles Darwin's famous "entangled bank" analogy in his conclusion to *Origin of Species*:

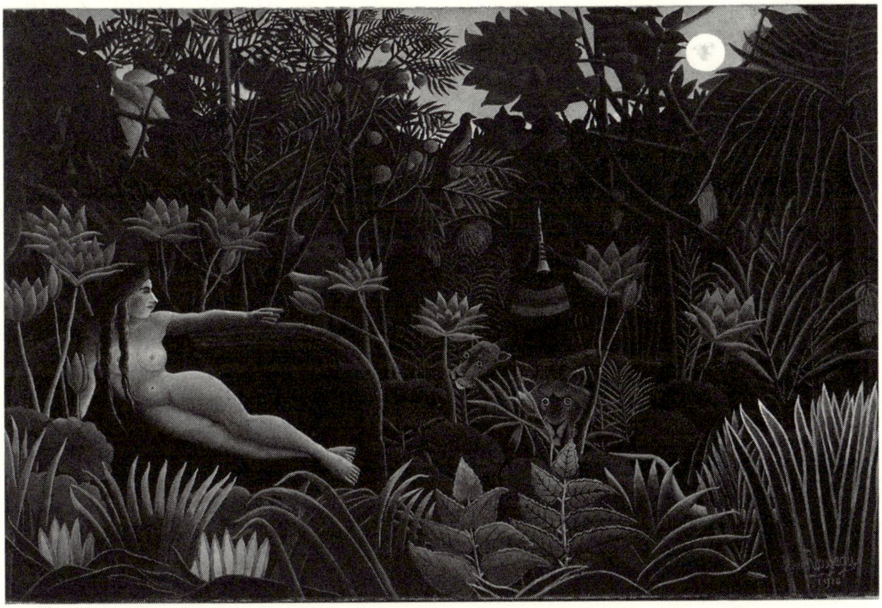

Figure 8.1 Henri Rousseau, *The Dream*, 1910. Oil on canvas, 204.5 × 298.5 cm. *Gift of Nelson A. Rockefeller. © 2008. Digital image, The Museum of Modern Art, New York / Scala, Florence.*

> It is interesting to contemplate an entangled bank, clothed with many plants of many kinds, with birds singing on the bushes, with various insects flitting about, and with worms crawling through the damp earth, and to reflect that these elaborately constructed forms, so different from each other, and dependent on each other in so complex a manner, have all been produced by laws acting around us . . . There is grandeur in this view of life, with its several powers, having been originally breathed into a few forms or into one; and that, whilst this planet has gone cycling on according to the fixed law of gravity, from so simple a beginning endless forms most beautiful and most wonderful have been, are being evolved.[3]

However, the very notion that this painting, like some fifty others by Rousseau of "wild beasts" and "tame primates," may be perceived in terms of Darwin's theories of evolution and their rearticulation in France, especially by anarchists, naturalists, and scientists, has not been entertained.

By focusing upon this painting and three others of Rousseau's with "wild beasts" and "tame primates," this chapter will explore the French cultural mediation of Darwin's theories upon Rousseau's art. To do so, it will begin by examining the prime sources of Rousseau's "wild beasts" and "tame primates," the Jardin des Plantes, Jardin d'Acclimatation, and Muséum national d'histoire naturelle, alongside the pre-Darwinian curation of evolution by Jean-Baptiste Pierre Antoine Monet de Lamarck, Étienne Geoffroy Saint-Hilaire, and Isidore Saint-Hilaire. To unravel the genre of "animal art" and evolutionism, it will investigate the long relationship of "les artistes animaliers" to the Jardin des Plantes and Muséum national d'histoire naturelle. It will then survey the groundwork laid for Darwin's theories before considering how the "lost Lamarck was vindicated by Darwin," while Darwin's theories were mediated through the conduit of Neo-Lamarckism. By scrutinizing the impact of Darwin and Neo-Lamarckism upon the Jardin des Plantes and Muséum National d'histoire naturelle, particularly under the directorship of Henri Milne-Edwards, Alphonse Milne-Edwards, and Edmond Perrier, it will analyze how Rousseau's paintings rearticulated their curation of evolution. After examining the roles of stuffed beasts at the Zoology Galleries, it will consider their relationship to Rousseau's "survival of the fittest" paintings. This will in turn unravel why, despite the similarities in their quest for mutualism, Rousseau neither bestialized *Homo sapiens* like the Fauves and Henri Matisse nor "primitivized" them in the same way as Pablo Picasso so much as anthropomorphized animal species. Finally, by focusing upon *The Merry Jesters, The Equatorial Jungle,* and *Exotic Landscape* (see figures 8.6, 8.7, and 8.8), this chapter will illuminate the relationship of Rousseau's "tame primates" to Darwinist socialism, anarchism, and "evolution by symbiosis." It will then return to his "dream of Darwin's evolution" to re-read it in light of Gilles Deleuze's and Félix Guattari's concept of "becoming-animal."[4]

Curating Evolution: Buffon, Lamarck, Cuvier, and Saint-Hilaire at the Jardin des Plantes and Muséum national d'histoire naturelle

"I don't know if you're like me," Le "Douanier" Rousseau told the critic Arsène Alexandre, "but when I go into the glass houses and I see the strange plants of exotic lands, it seems to me that I enter into a dream."[5] The glass houses that Rousseau frequented were those in the Jardin zoologique d'acclimatation and the Jardin des Plantes. While Napoléon III opened the Jardin zoologique d'Acclimatation in 1860, the Jardin des Plantes, along with the Muséum national d'histoire naturelle, were opened long before and were intertwined inextricably with the development of evolutionism in France.[6] First established as a medicinal garden by Louis XIII, the Jardin des Plantes was developed as a national menagerie by Louis XIV.[7] After Louis XV appointed Georges Louis Leclerc, Comte de Buffon, as Keeper of the Jardin de Roi in 1739, it came under the direction of a series of French naturalists who endeavored to theorize evolution and whom Darwin acknowledged as seminal to his conception of "natural selection."

During his fifty years as keeper, Buffon had enlarged the Jardin de Roi with trees and plants acquired from French expeditions to Africa, America, China, India, and Southeast Asia. He also converted it into a research center with a Cabinet d'Histoire Naturelle. From 1749, he had written his thirty-six-volume *Histoire naturelle, générale et particulière,* in which he argued, much to the horror of the Catholic Church, that the age of the Earth was 75,000 years and that Noah's Ark could never have happened.[8] Under similar climatic conditions, he deduced that fundamentally similar species would generate spontaneously on any planet. In his fifteenth volume, Buffon even speculated upon the similarities between humans and apes and the evolutionary origin of analogous species from common ancestral types.[9] Not only were his theories seminal to the next generation of naturalists, but also to Darwin. After crediting Aristotle with foreshadowing the concept of "natural selection," in his foreword to the sixth edition of *Origin of Species* Darwin stated that "the first author who in modern times has treated [evolution] in a scientific spirit was Buffon."[10]

A symbol of the scientific republic, in June 1793 the Jardin du Roi was reconstituted by decree of the First Republic Convention as the Jardin des Plantes, while the Cabinet d'Histoire Naturelle became the Muséum national d'histoire naturelle. To create the first public zoo, a Muséum menagerie was endorsed, together with the establishment of two new chairs of zoology.[11] In 1788, Buffon's successor had created a position for Lamarck as keeper of the herbarium of the Royal Garden.[12] In 1793, he assumed the Chair of Invertebrate Zoology and Professor of Natural History responsible for insects and microscopic animals.[13] While the mineralogist, Étienne Geoffroy Saint-Hilaire, assumed the Chair of Vertebrate Zoology responsible for the study of quadrupeds, cetaceans, birds, reptiles, and fish, he also became Director of the menagerie at the Jardin des Plantes. In treating animals as wonders of nature with scientific and utilitarian value, the Jardin des Plantes offered, according to Nigel Rothfels, "a pivotal moment in the history of keeping exotic animals in captivity."[14] Three years later, when Saint-Hilaire appointed Georges Cuvier as Assistant Professor of Comparative Anatomy, the menagerie was conceived as a living museum curated according to Saint-Hilaire's model of the universal "unity of type" as signified by homologous structures.[15] So significant was Saint-Hilaire's theory to Darwin's conception of evolution that in the first edition of *Origin of Species,* Darwin wrote:

> What can be more curious than that the hand of a man, formed for grasping, that of a mole for digging, the leg of the horse, the paddle of the porpoise,

> and the wing of the bat, should all be constructed on the same pattern, and should include the same bones, in the same relative positions? Geoffroy St. Hilaire has insisted strongly on the high importance of relative connection in homologous organs: the parts may change to almost any extent in form and size, and yet they always remain connected together in the same order.[16]

Despite the different trajectory taken by Cuvier and his son, Frédéric, under the directorship of Étienne Geoffroy Saint-Hilaire and Isidore Saint-Hilaire, and most of all of Lamarck, the curation of the museum exhibits and the display of animals in the Jardin menagerie appeared increasingly evolutionist.

To provide the study of new species, Lamarck, Saint-Hilaire, and Georges Cuvier ensured that the Jardin and Muséum contained the most important animal and fossil collection in Europe.[17] Once Cuvier became its director in 1826, his long-established Cabinet d'anatomie comparée was expanded into a special hall of comparative anatomy in which skeletons of four anatomical types could be compared with human skulls, embryos, and fossil vertebrates.[18] To illustrate the structural affinity between man and feline, this included the life-sized, plaster model of a flayed lion's foreleg sculptured by Jacques-Nicolas Brunot, which acted as a source for the humanized drawings of lions by Eugène Delacroix.[19] So great was the impact of Cuvier's hall that it remained untouched until the end of the nineteenth century and attracted hoards of artists, including, most notably in terms of Modernist history, Odilon Redon and Rousseau.[20]

The very year that Erasmus Darwin had published *Zoonomia* in which he hypothesized that the evolution of an organism was determined by the environment, Cuvier presented two papers on extinction. [21] The first to do so, Cuvier endeavored to account for the large number of extinct species that he encountered in his research through "the existence of a world previous to ours, destroyed by some kind of catastrophe." His "catastrophism" was vehemently attacked by Lamarck. From his investigations of the production of the simplest forms of life, Lamarck deduced that all other forms of life could be produced and altered by nature in terms of organic mutability and organic diversity. Lamarck's counter-theory that extinction arose through the gradual transmutation of species was affirmed by Darwin.[22]

After years of classifying vertebrates at the Muséum d'histoire naturelle, Lamarck had abandoned his commitment to the fixity of the species.[23] During this period, he developed his evolutionary theory about the spontaneous generation of life through the influence of the natural environment known as "transformism."[24] Premised upon adaption to the environment as the prime determinant of organic change, encapsulated by his term, *"l'influence des cir-*

constances," Lamarck's theory entailed the dual principles of use and disuse of an organ: The more an organ is used, the more it is strengthened and improved and vice-versa.[25] Lamarck's evolutionism also entailed the development of characteristics through adaption to an environment that could be passed on to descendants.[26] In the sixth edition of *Origin of Species*, this theory was also affirmed by Darwin: "I think there can be little doubt that use in our domestic animals strengthens and enlarges certain parts, and disuse diminishes them; and that such modifications are inherited."[27] Using a tree diagram not dissimilar to Darwin's to demonstrate the order in which he believed animals had come into being, Lamarck showed a close relationship between Cirripedia and Crustacea, which was confirmed by Darwin thirty years later.[28] As early as 1802 in his biological treatises, Lamarck had also outlined how man might have arisen from a "less perfect" animal.[29] This was readily acknowledged by Darwin in *The Descent of Man*: "The conclusion that man is the co-descendant with other species of some ancient, lower and extinct form, is not in any degree new," he wrote. "Lamarck long ago came to this conclusion."[30]

Despite being humiliated by Cuvier and dying a pauper, it was Lamarck's theories of evolution that were sustained.[31] After his death, Lamarck's views exerted a decisive influence upon the scientific and art community, particularly upon the curation of evolution at the Muséum and the Jardin des Plantes, as well as on *les artistes animaliers* who came to study there. "There is no doubt," Pietro Corsi writes, "that in early and mid-nineteenth century Europe the debate on Lamarck—however interpreted—constituted a key factor in the formation of the broad pro-evolutionary culture that greatly influenced, and often misdirected, the reception of Charles Darwin's *Origin of Species*."[32] The very appropriation of exotic beasts by French science and agriculture was, according to Michael A. Osborne, "embedded in a larger scientific discourse centering on theories of transformism and the appropriation and assimilation of exotic peoples and lands."[33] While it was through Lamarckism that evolution was curated when such *artistes animaliers* as Antoine-Louis Barye flocked to the Jardin des Plantes and Muséum national d'histoire naturelle, it was through Neo-Lamarckism in terms of a fusion of Darwin and Lamarck that evolution was curated when Frémiet and Rousseau began drawing there. These shifts in curating evolution are conveyed by their artwork.

Les Artistes Animaliers and Lamarckism: Capturing Wild Beasts in Paris Jungles

To authenticate his paintings of exotic fauna and flora, throughout his life Rousseau feigned to have visited tropical forests in Mexico while serving as a soldier with Napoleon III's expeditionary forces.[34] Yet not only did he, like the illustrious *artiste animalier* Barye never set foot outside France, but also, according to Arsène Alexandre, he never "travelled beyond the glass houses of the Jardin des Plantes."[35] By the time Rousseau frequented the Jardin des Plantes, the display of its zoo animals had been transformed into living tableaux, according to Eric Baratay.[36] Although inauthentic memoires of African and South American jungles, nevertheless Rousseau's paintings like Barye's sculptures, are authentic souvenirs of the Jardin des Plantes and Muséum national d'histoire naturelle.[37]

"Often on Sunday," recalls the Baroness d'Oettingen writing under her pen-name of Roch Grey, he would "walk in the Jardin des Plantes or the Jardin d'Acclimatation."[38] His Sunday promenades were far from being merely recreational. In the zoo at the Jardin des Plantes, Rousseau would watch the "wild beasts" and "tame primates" for hours before picking up his pencil or stick of charcoal to sketch them vigorously. On returning to his studio, he would pin these drawings up on his walls and transpose parts of them onto canvas.[39] By no means was he alone in so doing. Each spring, more than three hundred cards were issued by the Muséum to permit artists to set themselves up in front of the cages before the Jardin was opened to the public, as captured by the magazine illustrator Fortunino Matania in 1902 (figure 8.2).[40] The painters clustered in the foreground, easel to easel, paint-brush in one hand, palette in the other, together with the sculptor standing in the background who has just removed a moisturizing handkerchief from his clay *maquette,* seem to converge upon the "fauverie" of lions and tigers at the Jardin des Plantes. By no means were they the first "animaliers" to try to capture "wild beasts" in Paris at the Jardin and Muséum. As Alphonse Milne-Edwards reminded politicians in 1891, "Barye, Cain, Frémiet and many others were able to make studies there from which they were able to profit."[41]

By the time Barye began drawing directly from live animals at the Jardin des Plantes, Lamarck had become the Muséum Curator and Professor responsible for insects and worms, while Saint-Hilaire was Professor of Vertebrate Zoology and Cuvier was Professor of Comparative Anatomy. At five o'clock each morning, a sympathetic keeper gave Barye access to the animal cages.[42] Two years after Lamarck's death in 1829, Antoine-Louis Barye won a salon medal for *Tiger Devouring a Gavial* and for the first time, he was called an "animalier": A maker of animals.[43] Yet it was not until the 1851 Salon that Barye's exhibits, particularly his *Jaguar Devouring a Hare,* were commended. This led to Barye's appointment as Keeper of Plaster Casts at the Louvre, and in 1854, as Professor of Zoological Drawing at the Muséum.[44] That year, the Société zoologique de l'acclimatation was founded, with a zoo added six years

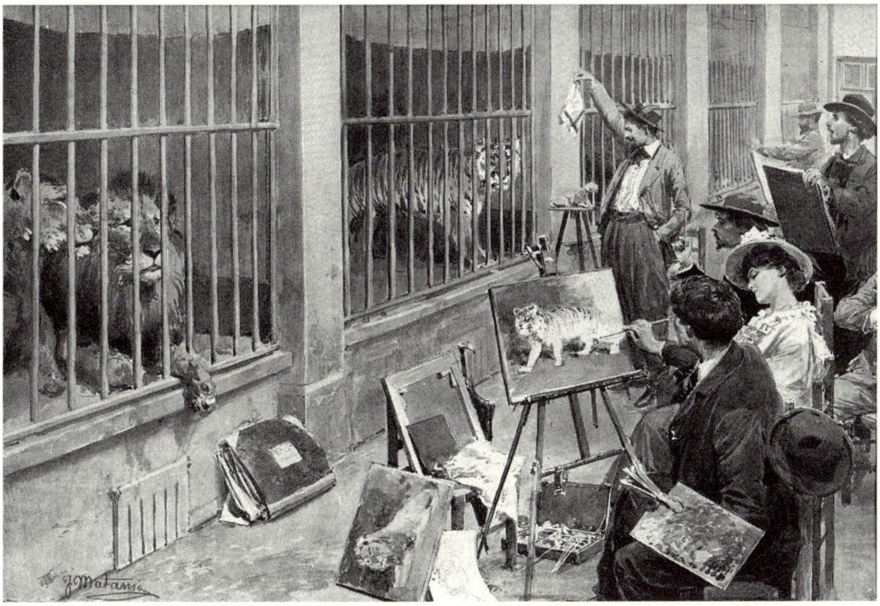

Figure 8.2 F. Matania, *Les artistes animaliers au Jardin des Plantes (Animal Artists at the Jardin des Plantes)*, oil on canvas, 30 × 40 cm. L'Illustration, *no. 3101, 2 August 1902; courtesy of the author.*

later under the direction of Isidore Geoffrey Saint-Hilaire, through which, following Lamarckian theory, exotic animals and plants were to become acclimatized to France. As Michael A. Osborne points out, "the scientific ideas which informed and animated this group, especially the notion of acclimatization, are rooted in Buffonian and Lamarckian ideas of biological transformism."[45] No species seemed to portray transformism more than primates.

In 1824, an orangutan had been illustrated by the principal painter at the Muséum d'histoire naturelle, Jacques-Christophe Werner, while in 1836, a male orangutan had been installed at the Jardin des Plantes.[46] Soon after discovery of the gorilla in 1847, it entered the Muséum, together with image and text demonstrating its closer proximity to *Homo sapiens*. In 1849, Werner produced the first images in France of the skeleton of a female gorilla and of gorilla skulls after their arrival at the Muséum.[47] A student of Werner, Emmanuel Frémiet may have not only viewed the gorilla skeleton and skulls but have also been commissioned to draw them.[48] In light of Barye's success and increasing validation of Lamarckism, Frémiet became a part of a new generation of animal artists who not only had access to the remains of primates but who also could participate in dissecting animal corpses.[49] This generation of *animaliers* included Henri Alfred Jacquemart, whose bronze sculpture, *Lion and Corpse*, mounted by the rue Cuvier entrance of the Jardin des Plantes, acted as a source for Rousseau's 1897 painting, *The Sleeping Gypsy*, a precursor to *The Dream*.[50]

While animal sculptures had begun to be welcomed by Salon juries, as illustrated by Barye's success, when Frémiet submitted his larger-than-life plaster, *Gorilla Abducting a Negress (Gorille enlevant une négresse)*, the very year when *Origin of Species* was first published, it was immediately expelled. Even though Frémiet engraved the words "gorille femelle" prominently on the base of his sculpture, the prospect of humans having sexual contact with primates, let alone evolving from them, was deemed outrageous.[51] Even when Second Empire Arts Minister, Comte de Nieuwerkerke, intervened, Frémiet's *Gorilla* could only be glimpsed at the 1859 Salon behind heavy green velvet curtains.[52] Nevertheless when Frémiet's new life-sized plaster of this subject was submitted to the 1887 Salon des Artistes Français, it was greeted with the opposite reception (see figure 7.2). Not only was Frémiet awarded the Salon Medal of Honour and his new gorilla sculpture acquired for the French State's art collection; it also was shown at the 1889 Exposition Universelle and the state permitted Frémiet to edition bronze versions in a reduced size.[53] This dramatic shift in receptivity occurred after Darwin's theories had been translated and transmuted into Neo-Lamarckism.

Fusing Darwin and Lamarck: Neo-Lamarckism in the Third Republic

In 1862, Guillaumin published Clémence Royer's French translation of *Origin of Species* with her inflammatory antireligious introduction.[54] When it was republished in 1869, Royer translated "survival of the fittest" from Darwin's 1869 edition as either "la lutte pour la vie" or "concurrence vitale": "The struggle for life" or "vital competition."[55] That this struggle or competition was "the fatal law" of animals as it was of humans evolved from animals was elaborated in Royer's 1869 book, *Origine de l'homme et des sociétés:* "The social question for every human organism is in reality simply another name for the universal struggle," Royer explained, "the struggle for life of Charles Darwin."[56] Royer's translation and subsequent publications galvanized scientific and nonscientific interest across France.

Members of the Société zoologique de l'acclimatation, Société d'Anthropologie, particularly its head, Paul Broca, welcomed Darwin's new treatise, as did the historian and philosopher of science at the Collège de France, Ernest Renan, and the naturalist philosopher, Hippolyte Taine, appointed as professor of Aesthetics and the History of Art at the École des Beaux-Arts in 1865.[57]

While before the Franco-Prussian War, Taine constructed his courses from the perspective of "natural selection," during the Third Republic he did not hesitate to use *The Descent of Man* to link the Commune to degeneration and devolution.[58] Following Darwin's statement that "extinction follows chiefly from the competition of tribe with tribe, and race with race," he also questioned whether the French race was threatened by extinction.[59] To prepare for the Rougon-Macquart series of novels that seemed to fictionalize Taine's philosophy of France's extinction, Émile Zola read *Origin of Species* during the 1860s and created many characters influenced by Darwin. To formulate his theories of heredity, Zola's character *Le docteur pascal* had studied Darwin, Haeckel, and Galton, while Octave Mouret in *Au Bonheur des Dames* constantly strove to triumph over rivals in the "struggle for existence." Yet despite this range of interest, Darwin was concerned that Royer's translation had "injured the book," her "juvenile ardour," as *Le Temps* put it, proving less useful than moderation.[60] So important was a more accurate and less controversial translation to Darwin that he enlisted the well-established French translator, J.-J. Moulinié, and negotiated with the French publishing house of C. Reinwald to forego his royalties on their publication of his translation.[61] Throughout the Franco-Prussian war, Moulinié also translated *The Descent of Man*.

At the outbreak of the Franco-Prussian war on 5 July 1870, Darwin had finished all but the last chapter of *The Descent of Man*. Just before the Battle of Sedan, his publisher John Murray had sent the manuscript to the printer. Within three weeks, Darwin began correcting what he called the "accursed proofs" that took him until signing of the Armistice in January 1871. Yet well before he had finished, his corrected sheets were despatched to his Dutch, German, Italian, and Russian translators, as well as to Moulinié in Paris. At the height of the Franco-Prussian war, hostilities raged around Moulinié and Darwin's German translator, Victor Carus, while they worked. The Russian translator, Vladimir Kovalevsky, carried his proofs through the Prussian lines into a besieged Paris, where he began his translation. By 15 February 1871, *The Descent of Man* was published in twin volumes and much to Darwin's delight, "selling like Mad."[62] Less than a month later, when the Communards took control of Paris, it was reprinted.

In its two-day review, the [London] *Times* insisted that the timing of such hypotheses was not opportune. Less than a fortnight after the Paris Commune had been established by those the *Times* denounced as utterly subversive was not the time to publish such "disintegrating speculations."[63] By demonstrating that reason and morality was not the exclusive domain of the human species but shared with animals ranging from chimpanzees and baboons to bees and ants, the *Times* considered that Darwin had acted perniciously. Not only had he abolished the intellectual barrier separating humans from animals, but more perilously, he had blurred the distinction between morality and brute instincts. In not establishing that moral absolutes were separate from instincts and required to curb them, the *Times* predicted that Darwin's treatise would lead to "the most murderous revolutions."[64] Already their views had been anticipated by the Darwinian apostate St. George Mivart, as indicated in chapter 5. Divorcing morals from religious "rewards and punishments," he warned Darwin, could cause a social and moral catastrophe, just as "Frenchmen are now paying for [it] in blood and tears."[65] This did not deter Reinwald from publishing Moulinié's translation of *The Descent of Man* (*La Descendance de l'homme*) in 1872. This was followed by their publication of Moulinié's translation of *Origin of Species* in 1873 (*L'Origine des espèces au moyen de la séléction naturelle, ou la lutte pour l'existence dans la nature*), Edmond Barbier's translation of it in 1876, translations of *The Expression of the Emotions in Man and Animals* in 1874 and 1877, and until 1882, nine of Darwin's other books.[66] This spate of publications reflects the re-evaluation of Darwin wrought by the new generation of biologists and zoologists who held the major positions in French science during most of the Third Republic.

For Alfred Giard, Marie-Yves Delage, Jean de Lanassan, Félix Le Dantec, and Edmond Perrier, *The Descent of Man* provided a valid theory to account for France's defeat, its declining natality, and escalating degeneracy.[67] It also provided important tools to determine evolution and regeneration of the French race, especially when fused with Lamarckism.[68] Due to publication of Darwin's treatises, Lamarck was chauvinistically reinstated by these French scientists as the "greatest" of all evolutionists who had guided Darwin.[69] In France, as, Stuart M. Persell surmises, "Darwin vindicated the lost Lamarck."[70] This was crystallized by the inscription on the statue of Lamarck erected in 1908 outside the Muséum d'histoire naturelle: "Founder of the doctrine of evolution."[71] Yet those who developed Neo-Lamarckism, according to Stephen Jay Gould, "reread Lamarck, cast aside the guts of it (continuous generation and complicating forces) and elevated one aspect of the mechanisms—inheritance of acquired characters—to a central focus it never had for Lamarck himself."[72] As distinct from Royer's emphasis upon "la lutte pour la vie" and "concurrence vitale," Lamarck's "transformism" struck a quixotic chord among Republican Progressists and Solidarists striving for cooperation rather than competition, altruistic association rather than egotistical rivalry, and the transmutation rather than elimination of low forms into higher species.[73] In its emphasis on association, cooperation, and the need for individuals to cohere in social groups like a living collective, this new interpretation of Lamarckism justified Republican Solidarism. While Lamarck was mythologized for conceiving of a Solidarist vision, he was also lauded for providing the pathway to an evolving culture in which humans could control evolution by controlling the environment. Neo-Lamarckism then seemed optimistic in its prospects for change, democratic in its applicability to all, and republican in confirming the need for health and social reform corroborated by Lamarck's oft-quoted statement in his *Power of Life*: "active life, results from the action of a stimulating cause that excites them."[74] Offering a theory explaining how psychological changes of habit, physiological reuse of organs, and recontrol of the environment could lead to biological evolution and cultural transformation, Neo-Lamarckism was latched onto by Radical Republicans as positivist justification for their programs of secularization, scientificization, and corporeal regeneration. Despite a challenge to its viability posed by August Weismann in 1883 and the apparent validation of germ plasm heredity in 1900 by rediscovery of Mendel's Laws, Neo-Lamarckism in the form of "transformism" remained the dominant model of evolution throughout the Radical Republic.[75]

This institutional shift in French science was symbolized, according to Persell, by the successful efforts of Giard and his mentors, Henri Lacaze-Duthiers and Camille Dareste, to establish a zoological station at Wimereux in the Pas-de-Calais in 1874. In 1875, the station became associated with the École pratique des hautes études. After 1877, the emergent Republican victory included Lamarckian transformists whose very professional lives depended on expansion.[76] By 1890, Neo-Lamarckians reigned within the faculties of the Sorbonne as they did at the Muséum d'histoire naturelle. Such "museum science" figures as Henri Milne-Edwards and Isidore and Albert Geoffroy Saint-Hilaire, directors of the Jardin zoologique d'Acclimatation from 1865, were replaced in 1893 by the Neo-Lamarckians Alphonse Milne-Edwards and Perrier. While Isidore and Albert Geoffroy Saint-Hilaire had situated the Muséum and Zoo within the theory of Lamarck, Alphonse Milne-Edwards and Perrier situated them within Neo-Lamarckism.[77]

These Neo-Lamarckians insisted that their interpretation and application of Darwin to achieve peace and solidarity constituted the antithesis of the Neo-Darwinists in Germany, following Haeckel (see chapters 3 and 4), as explained by Perrier:

> The Prussianized Germans have fixated upon the second principle of Darwin: The struggle for life. In the ferocious naivety of their conceptions, immediately they translated it as the oppression and destruction of the weakest by the strongest, and in this natural philosophy . . . Its cult of force, the eluciations of

> Treitsche, Waldersee, Bernardi, Nietzsche and other apologists for crime, provide only indirect commentaries on the second principle of Darwin.[78]

This French Neo-Lamarckian quest for peace and solidarity seems captured by Rousseau's painting in 1907, *The Representatives of Foreign Powers Coming to Greet the Republic as a Sign of Peace.* The opposite of his 1894 painting, *War,* in which the figure of battle in Nordic mythology, the Valkyrie, rides horseback across a decimated landscape littered with corpses, this painting shows representatives from countries as diverse as Ethiopia, Greece, Persia, and Serbia joining France and its colonies to commemorate peace. That this peace could only be achieved by "harmonious coordination" and "association," as exemplified by animal communities, was expounded by Perrier in *Les Colonies animales.*[79] At the same time, Perrier was aware that in the *concurrence vitale* of colonialism, animals had become vulnerable.

Jungle Fever: The Exotic Masking of Colonial Carnage

It is no coincidence that Frémiet's success occurred when Neo-Lamarckian evolutionary theory had reached its zenith. Possessing a chiselled cutting tool, his *Gorille enlevant une femme* appears to have evolved one step toward the human condition (see figure 7.2). Yet only in "the struggle for life" does this tool seem to have been grabbed in self-defence. Wearing a gorilla's jawbone as a hair adornment, the woman carried by Frémiet's *Gorilla,* unlike the Negress in his 1859 sculpture, seems to be hardly an innocent victim. A stone-age predator, she would have been part of a prehistoric hunting party that had been attacking the gorilla as edible prey. Far from the hunter of his 1859 sculpture, Frémiet's *Gorilla* seems to be recast as the hunted, just like the bear in his 1885 bronze, *Bear Cub Hunter.* This shift is equivalent to the difference between the frontispieces of Paul du Chaillu's 1861 *Explorations and Adventures in Equatorial Africa,* and Alexander Sokolowsky's 1908 *Observation on the Psyche of the Great Apes* in which a menacing ape was replaced by a menaced ape with an "unmistakable expression of" anxiety and helplessness in its "worriedly introspective eyes."[80] That Frémiet's gorilla was to turn its accusatory gaze on human spectators at the Salon as at the museum was only affirmed by Frémiet's request to the National Gallery of Victoria "to display this work so that when the public come in the first thing they see is the ape staring straight at them."[81]

Coinciding with Jules Ferry's expansionist policy of "colonialism by investment," this was a time when the exoticized imagery of fauna and flora proliferated in the popular visual culture of "jungle fever." While the covers of magazines were illustrated with tigers and lions attacking humans, photographs of wild beasts featured in newspapers and *L'Illustration*.[82] Even the exclusive department store, Galeries Lafayette, published a book of two hundred illustrations amenable to framing entitled *Bêtes Sauvages*, these images of the "dangerous exotic" proving to be one of Rousseau's most exploited jungle picture sources.[83] "As this heady mixture of the real and the imagined filtered down to a popular audience," explains Nancy Iverson, "the jungle started to become entertainment, the dangers of the unknown a source of excitement."[84] Yet these images exoticizing the cruelty of wild beasts and the cannibalism of indigenous peoples both masked and justified the violence of colonial conquest. "Science, politics and entertainment united," surmises Vincent Gille, "to defend and promote the racist theories that accompanied and justified the colonial enterprise."[85] "Jungle fever" acted as an exotic façade for colonial carnage, deflecting attention away from the slave trade and widespread slaughter of wild beasts that occurred during "the scramble for Africa."[86] This slaughter was unveiled by Joseph Conrad's novel, *Heart of Darkness*, in which European colonizers were portrayed as exercising far greater savagery than any African beast or tribe, darkness lying at the heart of the euphemistically dubbed *mission civilisatrice*: "civilizing mission."[87]

One year after joining the Salon des Artistes Indépendants, Rousseau would have seen Frémiet's *Gorilla* at the Salon des Artistes Français. While still working as a custom's officer, he could have seen it exhibited at the 1889 Exposition Universelle. He would have viewed the huge retrospective of Barye's animal sculptures and paintings timed to open at the École des Beaux-Arts for this Exposition Universelle.[88] One year after retiring to paint full-time in 1893, he could have attended the inauguration of the monument to Barye at the Île Saint-Louis and have heard the dedication to this *animalier* delivered by Eugène Guillaume. He could have also seen Delacroix's *Lion and Snake* at the vast École des Beaux-Arts Delacroix retrospective held in 1885. This was the cultural context in which Rousseau became an *artiste animalier*, Delacroix's *Lion and Snake* becoming a model for his first successfully received animal painting shown at the 1891 Salon des Artistes Indépendants, *Tiger in a Tropical Storm (Surprised!)* (figure 8.3).[89]

"His tiger surprising its prey should not be missed," wrote Félix Vallotton. "It's the alpha and omega of painting and so disconcerting that the most firmly held convictions must be shaken and bought up short by such self-sufficiency and childlike naivity."[90] While the "disconcerting" nature of the painting stressed by Vallotton relates to Rousseau's naïve two-dimensional rendering of a claustrophobic jungle closing in the pictorial space, it also pertains to the dangers of the jungle signified by the tiger on guard with its fangs bared. While appearing consistent with exoticizations of the tiger in "jungle fever," there are subtle differ-

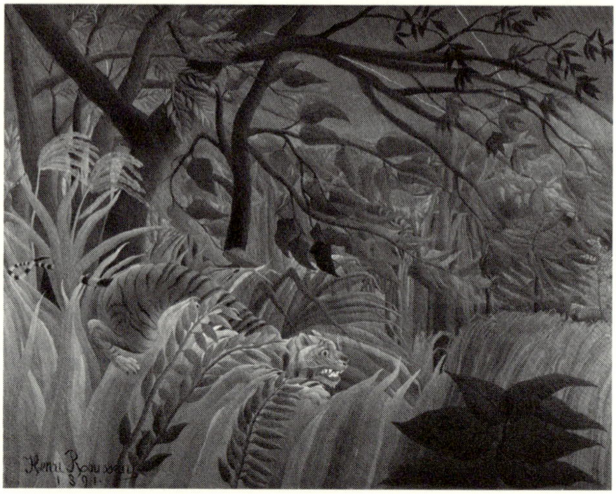

Figure 8.3 Henri Rousseau, *Tiger in a Tropical Storm (Surprised!)*, oil on canvas, 129.8 × 161.9 cm., 1891 Salon des Artistes Indépendants. *The National Gallery London* (NG6421).

ences. Even though the tiger-skin trade, like the ivory trade, became rampant during France's "scramble for Africa" and "colonialism by investment," images in the illustrated supplement of *Le Petit Journal* reveal an abundance of tigers massacring colonial settlers rather than being "surprised." Yet the team of indigenous trackers always included in these images together with their guns, rifles, and ample ammunition betray their colonial mission as wildlife stalkers and tiger-skin scalpers. "Surprised" by off-stage intruders that by implication become the human spectators at the Salon, Rousseau's *Tiger*, like Frémiet's ape, reveals that it was the "wild beast" that had become the prey of capitalist colonialists. From this time onward, the animals given one of two leading roles in Rousseau's paintings, as in Barye's sculpture, were the big cats (figure 8.4). Unlike Barye and his pre-Darwinian generation of *animaliers*, the other animals given a leading role were primates, particularly monkeys.

Rousseau's "Wild Beasts": Stuffed Beasts and "the Struggle for Life" at the Zoology Galleries

While the Jardin des Plantes had an impressive collection of lions and lionesses, tigers, jaguars, and panthers, it was impossible to see them perform as "wild beasts" either in their cages or their restricted outdoor enclosure. To try to capture their behavior in terms of "the struggle for life," in 1877 the Muséum began a project of stuffing dead animals and choreographing their bodies into movements and gestures typical of their species. In his mission to achieve the most life-like results possible, the chief taxidermist, J. Terrier, who led the animal stuffing, employed sculptors who had studied live animals in

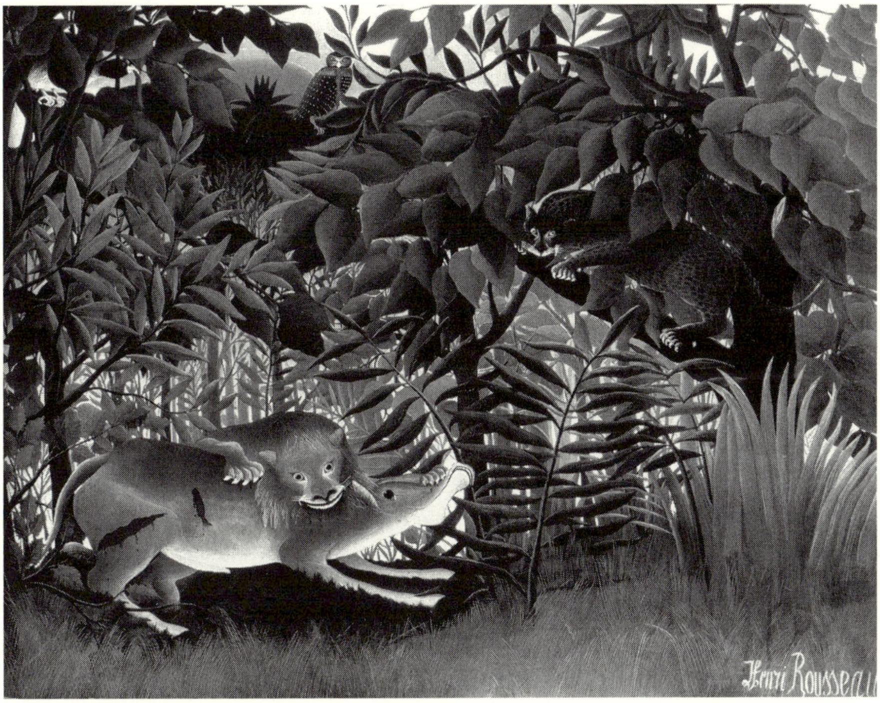

Figure 8.4 Henri Rousseau, *The Hungry Lion throws itself on the Antelope,* oil on canvas, 200 × 301 cm., exhibited at the Salon d'Automne, 1905. *Foundation Beyeler, Riehen/Basel.*

the Jardin as taxidermists. These sculptors included Frémiet, who had succeeded Barye as the Muséum Professor of Zoological Drawing. Frémiet's sculptures, especially *Gorilla,* were not only represented as the authentic product of first-hand examinations of stuffed animals in the Muséum collection but also as paradigms of the authenticity to which Terrier's sculptor taxidermists were told to aspire.

From the moment the Muséum's Zoology Galleries opened in 1889, these stuffed animals displayed in discrete groups proved to be a star attraction, particularly due to their authenticity. After the stuffed carnivores, the apes, and the monkeys in the long, lateral gallery of the new building were, according to the popular scientific weekly, *La Nature,* "magnificent new groups of panthers and tigers . . . admirably stuffed" in "lifelike attitudes."[91] These groups included *Senegal Lion Devouring an Antelope* (figure 8.5) by the taxidermists A. Quantin and Terrier, which acted as a source for Rousseau's painting, *The Hungry Lion Throws Itself on the Antelope* (figure 8.4). It was this painting that was exhibited alongside the discordantly colored, screeching artwork by Henri Matisse, André Derain, and Maurice de Vlaminck in the exhibition at

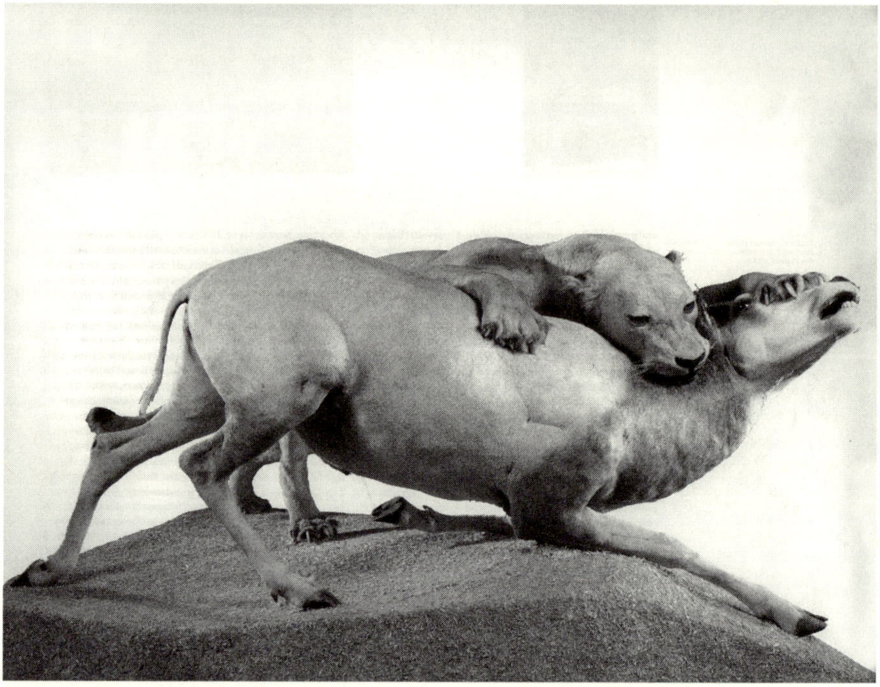

Figure 8.5 A. Quantin and J. Terrier, Taxidermists, *Senegal lion devouring an antelope*, 1886; stuffed animal display, tanned hide on wooden frame, built up with wood-shavings, modelled in plaster, prepared for the 1889 opening of the Zoological Galleries; Paris. *Muséum national d'histoire naturelle, Collections de Zoologie Mammifiéres et Oiseau.*

the 1905 Salon d'Automne. While likened by Vauxcelles to a "cage aux fauves," it was this painting that earned the group the pejorative appellation, "wild beasts," not without justification.

Instead of setting his "wild beasts" against a blank background, as illustrated by the photograph of *Senegal Lion Devouring an Antelope,* Rousseau sets the stuffed Senegal lion and antelope, together with his leopard in another painting drawn from a stuffed animal display in the Muséum, in their native situ: the jungle. To draw attention to the jungle savagery in the present and the future, his painting was accompanied by a plaque:

> The hungry lion throws itself upon the antelope, devours him; anxiously the panther awaits the moment that he too can claim his share. Birds of prey have torn a strip of flesh from the poor animal that is shedding a tear!

Unlike the restricted action of lions and panthers when viewed in a cage at the Jardin, as illustrated by figure 8.2, it is the savagery between animals that

Rousseau highlights in his text and spotlights in his painting as the central motif. In endeavoring to capture "the struggle for life" in its cruellest and most rapaciously parasitical form, his painting is equivalent to Darwin's vivid descriptions of "survival of the fittest." It is also an allegory for the predatory aspects of humans and "the struggle for life" that the Darwinist Anarchists, Élisée Rèclus and Pietr Kropotkin, as well as the Anarchist Rousseau perceived was taking place at this time in France and its colonies between capitalist industrialists and the worker, colonialists and indigenous people.[92] "After the Collectivist Revolution," declared Kropotkin, "instead of saying, 'twopence' worth of soap we shall say, 'five minutes' worth of soap."[93]

This is why, in this strange interplay of simulacra, Rousseau betrays that, unlike Terriers' sculptor taxidermists, he did not aspire to create authenticity. Instead, he positions these stuffed "wild beasts" as a theater designer would place props on a stage. From this perspective, it is possible to deduce that this painting does not act as a mere souvenir of Rousseau's experience of the Jardin des Plantes, as was mooted at the recent Rousseau exhibitions.[94] It was designed to act as a mis-en-scène able to display ways in which "the struggle for life" in terms of Darwin's "survival of the fittest" was being played out in the French Radical Republic, turning *Homo sapiens* into "wild beasts" without any compassion for those exploited and oppressed. Akin to the Darwinist Anarchism espoused by Rèclus and Kropotkin, Rousseau's paintings of "tame primates" seem to represent the antithesis to this savagery. At the same time, the knowledge Rousseau acquired of "tame primates" and the images he made of them reflect the didactic role that the Jardin des Plantes was designed to play in relation to evolution after Darwin.

Curating Evolution: Jardin des Plantes and Muséum national d'histoire naturelle after Darwin

When Georges Cuvier's younger brother, Frédéric, was appointed the first Superintendent to the public zoo in 1804, he was the first zoologist to take an interest in mammalian behavior. In his study of a young female orangutan, Frédéric Cuvier noticed her capacity to generalize, her intelligent forms of self-defense, and "senses as numerous and at least as delicate as ours."[95] Although he planned to write a survey of the causes of animal action, he died before its completion. Only a few weeks after Cuvier's death in 1838, Charles Darwin visited the London zoo and wrote in his notebook, "endeavoured to classify the expressions of monkeys."[96] After animals were brought back to France from Napoleon's expeditions, the Rotonde was built at the Jardin des Plantes especially to house elephants, followed by a bear ditch in 1805 and a

Fauverie in 1821 to contain predatory animals. Not until 1837 was the monkey house established. At the Jardin, as at the Muséum, "preserving, naming, classifying, displaying, interpreting, and otherwise deploying specimens went," according to Richard W. Burkhardt, "hand in hand with promoting scientific theories, and instructing the public."[97]

In 1854, Étienne Geoffroy Saint-Hilaire's son, Isidore Geoffroy Saint-Hilaire, established the Société zoologique de l'acclimatation to breed animals and plants favorable to the European climate. By 1855, Isidore Saint-Hilaire had drawn up a list of mammals and birds that could adapt to the French climate, leading to the Jardin zoologique d'Acclimatation being opened in the Bois de Bologne in 1860. To house the managerie's ferocious animals or "bêtes sauvages," it was divided into three squares for lions, tigers, panthers, and jaguars; elephants, camels, giraffes, hippopotamuses; monkeys to apes. To Europeanize these animals, if not to make them French, they were also taken to live in rural parts of France, yaks from China being made to graze in the Jura and the Cantal. The advent of Darwin's theory of evolution confirmed the role of the Muséum to find analogies and homologies between these species in order to consider how they were related through evolution. Yet it also led to a project to increase the collection of primates.

In 1884, the first living specimen of the great anthropomorphic ape, the gorilla, was imported to the Jardin from Gabon. It was brought in to study its intellectual faculties and to compare it with the orangutan and the chimpanzee. Those who studied the gorilla found him "savage, morose and brutal." Unsociable, he did not partake of games. "He never allowed himself to be touched without evidencing the greatest aversion, and for the most part he returned caresses by snappings," wrote Alphonse Milne-Edwards.[98] Only during Milne-Edwards' directorship and curation of their live and manmade collections in terms of Lamarckism and Darwinism did Rousseau begin to devise his "jungle paintings."

After studying medicine in Paris, Milne-Edwards became assistant to his father, Henri Milne-Edwards, at the Jardin des Plantes in 1859. In 1862, his father succeeded Isidore Geffroy Saint-Hilaire to the Chair of Zoology at the Muséum national d'histoire naturelle and sustained a long correspondence with Charles Darwin.[99] In 1864, Alphonse became a professor at the École supérieure de Pharmacie de Paris and from 1876, Professor of Ornithology at the Muséum d'histoire naturelle focusing upon fossil birds.[100] In 1870, he had dissected a giant panda, giving it a new genus name, and in 1878, corresponded with Thomas Huxley about the genus of a Madagascar crayfish.[101] After leading a scientific mission of exploration in 1881 of the Bay of Biscay, the Gulf of Gascony and the Canaries, the Cape Verde Islands and the

Azores, which was awarded the Royal Geographic Society Gold Medal, he was appointed Director of the Muséum in 1891. While director, he wrote on extinct species of birds represented in the collection, as well as publishing a natural history of animals.[102] He also lobbied government to increase the zoo budget.

To fund modernization, in 1891 Milne-Edwards presented a paper to the Minister for Public Instruction in Robert Arthur Talbot's government, arguing that the popularity of the zoo had proven a hindrance to development of its scientific research and the expansion of its collection.[103] To help build his argument, Milne-Edwards cited the outstanding research conducted by Georges and Frédéric Cuvier, Étienne and Isidore Geoffey Saint-Hilaire, and most of all, by Lamarck. Major breakthroughs in the understanding of comparative anatomy, animal behavior, hybridization, and the acclimatization of foreign species to European conditions, he maintained, had occurred only because the Muséum and zoo was at the center of a vast collecting and research program.[104] The Muséum's accent on precision in the categorization and description of animals, he continued, had spread across the literature of zoology and botany.[105] Milne-Edwards pointed out the role that the Muséum and zoo had played in contributing to the knowledge of evolution, following the "great Darwin," while endeavoring to develop new species, several types of antelope along with gnus having been released as "new game" into the forests around Paris.[106] For his ultimate point, he stressed that most of all they needed funding to be able to build up a collection of primates. Urgently, they needed to replace the deplorable monkey accommodation that, he said, had become so unhygienic that most of the monkeys became sad within weeks, before sickening and dying.[107] Virulent lobbying for the improvement of these conditions continued when Perrier became Director of the Muséum in 1900 and when as President of the Société zoologique de l'acclimatation, he insisted upon pursuing a policy dedicated to the protection and conservation of species.[108] In *The Merry Jester, The Equatorial Jungle, Exotic Landscape,* and his many other images with monkeys, Rousseau painted pictures of these "tame primates" free from the oppressive captivity of the Jardin des Plantes. By inverting the politics of vision at the Jardin des Plantes, the human spectator is implicated in Rousseau's paintings as the subject of his primate's gaze.

Rousseau's "Tame Primates": Solidarism, Darwinist Anarchism, and Evolution by Symbiosis

Almost every species of monkey represented by Rousseau is anthropomorphized. Following Henri Coupin's popularizing book describing monkeys, published in 1907, they are depicted as vivacious, charming, and caring, as epitomized by *The Merry Jesters*, *The Equatorial Jungle*, and *Exotic Landscape* (figures 8.6, 8.7, and 8.8).[109] Unlike the bloodthirsty behavior of Rousseau's "wild beasts" in which the only corporeal contact is to devour the other, whether it be antelope, tribal native, or a colonial trophy hunter, Rousseau's "tame primates" sensually rub up against one another, tenderly grooming each other's fur and readily tending to each other's needs for food and drink. They seem to illustrate Darwin's description in *The Expression of the Emotions in Man and Animals* of monkey's "delight in fondling and being fondled by one another."[110] "Touching each other with their much protruded lips," Darwin wrote, "they then mutually folded each other in their arms. Afterwards they stood up, each with one arm on the shoulder of the other, lifted up their heads, opened their mouths and yelled with delight."[111] They appeared capable of great seriousness, like old judges, according to Darwin, as exemplified by Rousseau's two bearded monkeys coupled in the foreground of *The Equatorial Jungle* (figure 8.7). They also were represented as models of sobriety, as in the amusing example cited by Darwin: "An American monkey, an Ateles, after getting drunk on brandy, would never touch it again, and thus was wiser than many men."[112]

Consistent with Darwin's descriptions of their chuckles, laughter, and playfulness, particularly their love of being tickled under the armpits, Rousseau's "tame primates" also appear as game players and mischief makers.[113] Seeming to act as surrogates for freedom from constraint, they peek out from behind frondes in *The Equatorial Jungle* and *Exotic Landscape*, while in *The Merry Jesters* they are pictured waving a back-scratcher while thrusting a milk bottle at the spectator. Mutually aiding one another sharing the fruit of nature rather than hoarding it or fighting over it, as illustrated by *Exotic Landscape*, they are shown able to live in harmonious communities.

Consistent with *Origin of Species* and *The Descent of Man*, Rousseau's "wild beasts" and these "tame primates" are pictured performing very different roles on his pictorial stage. Played off against one another, the destructive *bêtes sauvages* exemplify "survival of the fittest," while the primates are shown to be able to live in mutual harmony with one another and other species. In so doing, they seem to embody Republican Solidarism, as well as the Neo-Lamarckian espousal of association not rivalry, cooperation not competition, and harmonious social organisms.

In the wake of the Pasteurian revolution, Solidarism was posited by Minister and Prime Minister, Léon Bourgeois, as a means of negotiating the crisis of contagious disease and degeneration by cooperation and interdependence.[114] Extracted from the "scientism" of the chemists, Marcellin Berthelot

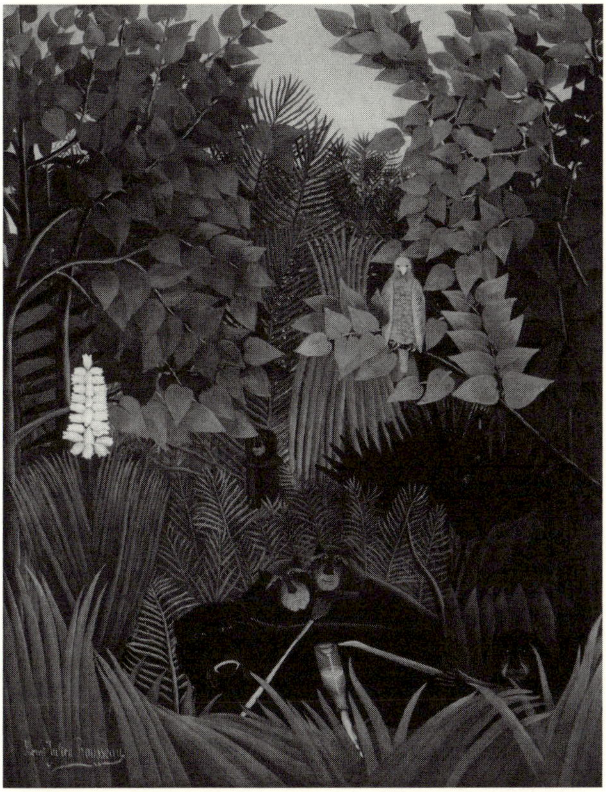

Figure 8.6 Henri Rousseau, *The Merry Jesters,* 1906, oil on canvas, 145.7 × 113.3 cm. *Philadelphia Museum of Art, The Louise and Walter Arensberg Collection.*

and Rudolf Virchow, Bourgeois' Solidarism was also derived from Alphonse Milne-Edwards' theories of the unification of organisms working together for the survival of the colony.[115] While the unification of organisms is captured in Rousseau's "tame primates," these paintings and their juxtaposition with "wild beasts" seem to embody more closely those political positions that engaged Darwinism. These positions were Darwinist Socialism and Darwinist Anarchism, as espoused in France by Rèclus in *L'Homme et la terre* and *Evolution and Revolution,* and by Kropotkin in his 1902 treatise, *Mutual Aid: A Factor of Evolution.*

Both Karl Marx and Friedrich Engels had warned against identifying "the struggle for life" with the class struggle. Both French Socialists and Anarchists appropriated Darwin as a proponent of "association for life" in human society. In his 1890 book, *Darwinism and Socialism,* Armand Boucher explained that Socialist Darwinism as distinct from Social Darwinism entailed acting in groups rather than as isolated individuals.[116] Founder of the French Socialist Party, Jean Jaurès expressed regret that because of Lamarck, French-

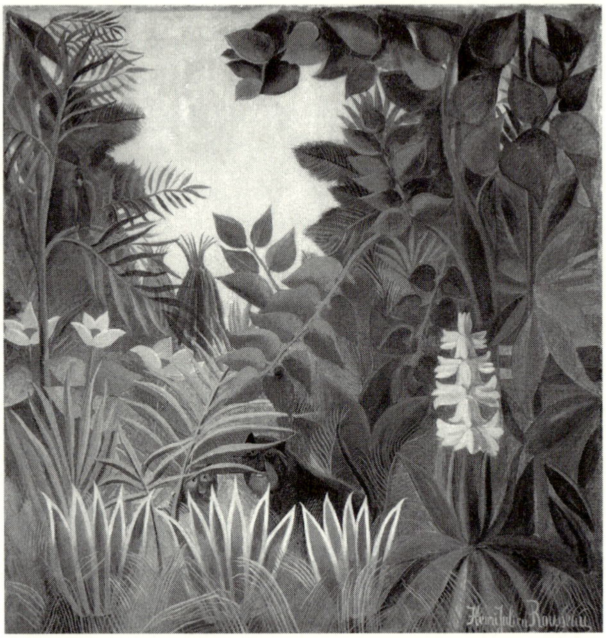

Figure 8.7 Henri Rousseau, *The Equatorial Jungle*, 1909, oil on canvas, 140.6 × 129.5 cm. *National Gallery of Art, Washington, Chester Dale Collection. Image courtesy of the Board of Trustees.*

men were long reluctant to recognize Darwin's greatness, misaligning his theories with capitalism. In 1895 in the Chamber of Deputies, Jaurès insisted that it was necessary "to substitute for the universal *lutte pour la vie*—which leads to universal struggle on the battlefield—a regime of social concord and unity."[117] Social Darwinism, French civilization, and colonization, Rèclus argued, should be replaced by "Darwinian evolution, the study of the conservation of energy and comparative sociology."[118] Fusing Proudhon's mutualism with Darwinism, Rèclus proudly confessed that he "embraced all animals in my affection for socialist solidarity" and insisted they be granted equal status in mutualist society.[119] Kropotkin's theory of animal and human survival also opposed "survival of the fittest."

In *The Descent of Man*, Kropotkin pointed out that Darwin had recorded that in numerous animal societies where there are sufficient resources, the struggle between individuals disappears and is replaced by cooperation. In such societies, the fittest are not the physically strongest or the most cunning, but those best able to provide mutual aid for the welfare of the community. "In the animal world we have seen that the vast majority of species live in societies, and that they find in association the best arms for the struggle for life," he wrote, "understood, of course, in its wide Darwinian sense—not as a struggle for the sheer means of existence, but as a struggle against all natural

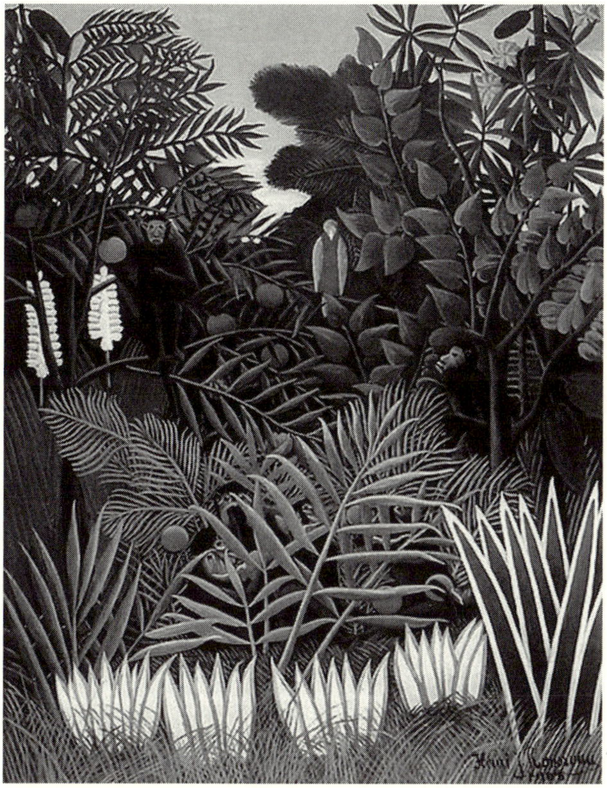

Figure 8.8 Henri Rousseau, *Exotic Landscape*, 1908, oil on canvas, 116 × 89 cm. *Private Collection, Public Domain.*

conditions unfavourable to the species."[120] He concluded that "the animal species, in which individual struggle has been reduced to its narrowest limits, and the practice of mutual aid has attained the greatest development, are invariably the most numerous, the most prosperous, and the most open to further progress."[121] As mutual aid, not rivalry, is posited as the key factor for survival, Kropotkin's theory is comparable to the endosymbiotic theory first articulated in 1905 by the Russian botanist, Konstanin Mereschkowski, and rearticulated by Lynn Margulis in her 1981 work, *Symbiosis in Cell Evolution*.[122] In their search for primitivist societies and their cultural manifestations of mutualism, these theories were just as significant for the Fauves and Picasso as they were for the art of Rousseau. They provide the discursive framing for rereading Rousseau's *Dream* (figure 8.1).

"The struggle for life" is conspicuous by its absence in this painting. Instead of an intractable conflict between humans and nature, as epitomized by Frémiet's 1887 *Gorilla* (figure 7.2), the struggle between individuals seems to have disappeared. Despite racial difference, humans are shown co-existing in harmony with one another, as well as with both "wild beasts" and "tame primates." Rather than being ranked and segregated as in the "great chain of being," humans and animals seem to be granted equal status. Despite the differences in tiger, lioness, elephant, bird, snake, gorilla, monkey, and human, when these species are placed together in the same jungle environment there appears, in keeping with Darwin and Neo-Lamarckism, a unity of living forms. This is not just portrayed by an affinity in physiognomy, comparable to Cuvier's anatomical comparisons of animal and human bone, muscle, leg, and claw. It is also portrayed by deeper affinities such as their common temperament, their mutual love of music, the way in which they all appear to be stilled and entranced by the magical notes. Instead of the fittest being the strongest and most cunning, in this community it is the one providing mutual aid for the welfare of all others: the snake charmer. Instead of the perpetual struggle of human against animal and their innermost selves, Rousseau's painting crystallizes the possibility of association without rivalry, cooperation without competition, peace without war, and harmonious coordination of the social organism long envisaged by Perrier in *Les Colonies animales*, as well as by Jaurès, Rèclus, Kropotkin, and, indeed, by Darwin. This possibility of animal and human affinity to the point of humans being released from repression and "becoming animal" was poetically captured during Ralph Waldo Emerson's epiphany at the Jardin des Plantes:[123]

> Here we are impressed with the inexhaustible riches of nature. The universe is a more amazing puzzle than ever, as you glance along this bewildering series of animated forms . . . Not a form so grotesque, so savage, nor so beautiful but is an expression of some property inherent in man the observer—an occult relation between the very scorpions and man. I feel the centiped in me,—cayman, carp, eagle and fox. I am moved by strange sympathies.[124]

This was then Rousseau's "Dream of Darwin's Evolution"—a dream of *Homo sapiens* and animals being able to live together in mutual wonder, empathy, and harmony.

NOTES

The author wishes to thank the curators of the exhibition *Henri Rousseau: Jungles in Paris*, which inspired this chapter. She also wishes to thank Christopher Green for encouraging pursuit of Rousseau's "Dream," and Vivian Van Blerk for his expert photography.

1. Guillaume Apollinaire, "Watch out for the Paint!," *L'Intransigeant*, 18 March 1910.

2. In 1893, the Société des Peintres Orientalistes was formed with fourteen members under the Presidency of Curator of the Luxembourg Museum, Léonce Bénédite. Each year, it held its own exhibitions in association with the Salon des Artistes Français. Bénédite declared the society's mission "to inspire love for indigenous races, to penetrate and understand their civilisation, their customs, their history, their arts, which now belong to them [the society members] like so many provincial riches." See Roger Benjamin, *Orientalist Aesthetics: Art, Colonialism, and French North Africa, 1880–1930* (Berkeley: University of California Press, 2003).

3. Charles Darwin, *On the Origin of Species by Means of Natural Selection, or the Preservation of Favoured Races in the Struggle for Life* (London: John Murray, 1872; New York: Modern Library, 1993) 648–49.

4. Gilles Deleuze and Félix Guattari, *A Thousand Plateaus: Capitalism and Schizophrenia*, trans. Brian Massumi (Minneapolis: University of Minnesota Press, 1987).

5. Arsène Alexandre, "La vie et l'œuvre d'Henri Rousseau, peintre et ancien employé de l'Octroi," *Comœdia*, 19 March 1910.

6. For the Jardin zoologique d'Acclimatation, see chapter 4 in Michael A. Osborne, *Nature, the Exotic, and the Science of French Colonialism* (Bloomington: Indiana University Press, 1994).

7. The Jardin royal des Plantes médicinales was established in 1626.

8. Georges-Louis Leclerc, Comte de Buffon, *Histoire naturelle, générale et particulière*, 36 vols. (Paris: 1749–1778). Eight additional volumes were published after his death by Lacépède.

9. Ibid., vol. 15 (1767).

10. Charles Darwin, "Foreword," *The Origin of Species* (London: John Murray, 1872), iii. This edition was the final one; in *Darwin's Origin of Species: A Biography* (London: Atlantic Monthly Press, 2007), x, Janet Browne writes: "The sixth edition, issued in 1872, is usually regarded as the last that Darwin corrected."

11. Michael A. Osborne, "Applied Natural History and Utilitarian Ideals: 'Jacobin Science' at the Muséum d'Histoire Naturelle, 1789–1870," in *Recreating Authority in Revolutionary France*, ed. Bryant T. Ragan, Jr., and Elizabeth A. Williams (New Brunswick, N.J.: Rutgers University Press, 1992), 132.

12. Alpheus Spring Packard, *Lamarck, the Founder of Evolution: His Life and Work with Translations of His Writings on Organic Evolution* (New York: Longmans, Green, and Co., 1901), 36. To sever its connections with monarchy, in 1790 Lamarck had recommended changing the name of the Royal Garden from Jardin du Roi to Jardin des Plantes.

13. Vernon N. Kisling and James Ellis, *Zoo and Aquarium History: Ancient Animal Collections to Zoological Gardens* (Boca Raton, Fla.: CRC Press, 2001), 89–90. Lamarck's official title was Professeur d'Histoire naturelle des Insectes et des Vers, for which he received a salary of nearly 2,500 francs per year.

14. Nigel Rothfels, *Savages and Beasts: The Birth of the Modern Zoo* (Baltimore: The Johns Hopkins University Press, 2002), 19.

15. In his 1818 book *Philosophie anatomique*, Etienne Geoffroy Saint-Hilaire asked the question: "Can the organization of vertebrated animals be referred to one uniform type?"

16. Charles Darwin, *The Origin of Species by Means of Natural Selection, or the Preservation of Favoured Races in the Struggle for Life* (London: John Murray, November 1859).

17. Stephen Jay Gould, *The Structure of Evolutionary Theory* (Cambridge, Mass.: Harvard University Press, 2002).

18. Georges Cuvier, "Notice sur l'établissment de la collection d'anatomie comparée du Muséum," *Annales du Muséum d'Histoire Naturelle* 2 (1803): 411.

19. Eve Twose Kliman, "Delacroix's Lions and Tigers: A Link between Man and Nature," *The Art Bulletin* 44, no. 3 (September 1982): 460. I am grateful to Barbara Larson for bringing this article to my attention.

20. Redon's biographer, André Mellerio noted, "It was at the museum that he grasped Cuvier's great law regarding the correspondence of being"; see Barbara Larson, *The Dark Side of Nature: Science, Society and the Fantastic in the Work of Redon* (University Park: Penn State University Press, 2005).

21. Eramus Darwin, *Zoomania or, the Laws of Organic Life,* two vols. (London, 1794–1796). In 1796, when Cuvier read his first and second paleontological papers at the École Centrale du Panthéon, he argued that the skeletal remains of animals no longer extant proved extinction; see Georges Cuvier, *Mémoires sur les espèces d'elephants rivants et fossiles* (1808).

22. Jean-Baptiste Pierre-Antoine Monet de Lamarck, *Philosophie zoologique ou exposition des considérations relatives à l'histoire naturelle des animaux* (Paris: Dentu, vol. I, 1809; vol. II, 1830).

23. Richard W. Burkhardt, *The Spirit of System, Lamarck and Evolutionary Biology* (Boston: Harvard University Press, 1977).

24. Lamarck, *Philosophie zoologique.*

25. Ibid., First Law, 13: "In every animal which has not passed the limit of its development, a more frequent and continuous use of any organ gradually strengthens, develops and enlarges that organ, and gives it a power proportional to the length of time it has been so used; while the permanent disuse of any organ imperceptibly weakens and deteriorates it, and progressively diminishes its functional capacity, until it finally disappears."

26. Ibid., Second Law: "All the acquisitions or losses wrought by nature on individuals, through the influence of the environment in which their race has long been placed, and hence through the influence of the predominant use or permanent disuse of any organ; all these are preserved by reproduction to the new individuals which arise, provided that the acquired modifications are common to both sexes, or at least to the individuals which produce the young."

27. Darwin, *Origin of Species* (1872), 134.

28. David M. Damkaer, *The Copepodologist's Cabinet: A Biographical and Bibliographical History* (Philadelphia: American Philosophical Society, 2002), 117.

29. Jean-Baptiste de Lamarck, *Discours d'ouverture du Cours de l'An X* (Paris: Dentic, 1802). Lamarck insisted upon the need to go beyond classification and understand the process by which species are formed, transformed, and "perfected." He considered the modifications made to animals and plants through human domestication as a basis for inferring nature's own power to transform.

30. Charles Darwin, *The Descent of Man: Selection in Relation to Sex* 1871; (reprint, New York: Penguin, 2004), 19.

31. Even on Lamarck's death in 1829, Buffon used a eulogy as a forum to discredit Lamarck. In his *Elegy of Lamarck,* Cuvier did not hesitate to say that Lamarck's theory rested on two

spurious presumptions: That a nervous fluid exists with the power to mold organs and that use and disuse can effect changes in an organism's body type. After Lamarck's death, his family were so poor they had to apply to the Académie for financial assistance. While Lamarck's books and the contents of his home were sold at auction, he was buried in a lime-pit.

32. Pietro Corsi, *The Age of Lamarck: Evolutionary Theories in France 1790–1830* (Berkeley: University of California Press, 1988), 268.

33. Osborne, "Applied Natural History and Utilitarian Ideals," 136.

34. Robert Delaunay is the principal source, Rousseau's fabrications as told to a gullible Delaunay being published in Robert Delaunay, "Mon ami Rousseau" *Arts et lettres*, August–September 1952.

35. Ibid. It was only while watching the animals at the Jardin des Plantes that Barye (1796–1875) became an "animal artist."

36. Eric Baratay, *Zoo: A History of Zoological Gardens in the West* (London: Reaktion Books Ltd., 2002), 150.

37. This interesting point in relation to Rousseau's artwork is explored by Christopher Green, "Souvenirs of the Jardin des Plantes: Making the Exotic Strange Again," in *Henri Rousseau: Jungles in Paris*, ed. Christopher Green and Frances Morris (London: Tate Publishing, 2005), 28–47.

38. Roch Grey, "Henri Rousseau," *L'Action*, no. 7 (May 1921).

39. Green, *Souvenirs of the Jardin des Plantes*, 32. Green points out that the dealer-critic, Adolphe Basler, recalls Rousseau sketching there. The American painter Max Weber who introduced Rousseau to Picasso, recalls seeing sketches of the Jardin des Plantes in his studio, according to Sandra E. Leonard, *Henri Rousseau and Max Weber* (New York: Richard L Feign & Co., 1970), 39–40.

40. Alphonse Milne-Edwards, *Musée d'histoire naturelle: La menagerie. Rapport au ministre de l'instruction publique* (Paris: 1891), 12: "Enfin, j'ajouterai que les artises trouvent, parmi les animaux tenus en captivité, des modèles précieux pour leurs études de peinture ou de sculpteur."

41. Ibid., 12: "Barye, Cain, Frémiet et beaucoup d'autres ont trouvé là des renseignements qu'ils ont su mettre à profit."

42. William R. Johnston, "A Monument to Antoine Louis Barye," *Magazine Antiques*, October 2006, 1: "For the remainder of his career, Barye frequented the Jardin des Plantes to study and sketch both living animals and corpses. . . . Barye's numerous drawings in sketchbooks or on separate scraps of paper attest to both his scrupulous attention to detail and the acuteness of his observations."

43. It was during his training at the École des Beaux-Arts from 1818 that Barye began to draw animals at the Muséum national d'histoire naturelle. Following the success of his animal sculptures and paintings at the Salon, he established a foundry in 1845 to produce smaller, affordable animal sculptures in bronze. His success is confirmed by his election to the Academy in 1868.

44. Johnston, "A Monument to Antoine Louis Barye."

45. Osborne, *Nature, the Exotic*, 1.

46. Tedd Gott, "Clutch of the Beast: Emmanuel Frémiet, gorilla-sculptor," in *Kiss of the Beast: From Paris Salon to King Kong* (Brisbane: Queensland Art Gallery Publishing, 2005), 25.

47. Ibid., 26.

48. Ibid., 29. This is the interesting speculation made by Ted Gott.

49. On Barye's death in 1875, Frémiet was appointed Professor of Zoological Drawing at the Muséum; see Jane Horsell, *Les Animaliers* (London: Antique Collectors' Club Ltd., 1971); James Mackay, *The Animaliers: The Animal Sculptors of the 19th and 20th Centuries* (London: Wand Lock, 1973).

50. Green, *Souvenirs of the Jardin des Plantes*, 38: "His lion sniffs the bare foot of a buried human corpse . . . The confrontation is the trigger . . . for Rousseau's fantasy of the sleeping gypsy in mortal danger." Frances Morris, "Jungles in Paris," in *Henri Rousseau: Jungles in Paris*, 19.

51. That Frémiet's sculpture signified rape was discerned by Charles Baudelaire, as discussed in chapter seven. "Le Salon de 1859," in Charles Baudelaire, *Critique d'Art*, ed. Claude Pichois (Paris: Armand Colin, 1865), 371; see also Gott, "Clutch of the Beast," 16.

52. Gott, "Clutch of the Beast," 16.

53. Ibid., 44. Nevertheless, this was a pyrrhic victory, Frémiet's award-winning sculpture being consigned to the Musée des Beaux-Arts in Nantes while, as Gott points out, a copy of it was despatched in 1906 by Frémiet as a gift to the National Gallery of Victoria (p. 54).

54. In "The Darwin Effect: Introduction," *Nineteenth Century Art Worldwide* (Spring 2003), Linda Nochlin points out that Royer was a theorist of evolution and women's rights. She was the only woman member of the Société d'Anthropologie, a novelist, an advocate of unmarried motherhood, and a recipient of the Légion d'honneur in 1900. A radical, a scientist, and a popularizer of Darwinian ideas on a grand scale, Royer was, in the words of Ernst Renan, "almost a man of genius."

55. Ibid.

56. Ibid., 34. Clémence Royer, *Origine de l'homme et des sociétés* (Paris: Guillaumin, 1869).

57. Linda L. Clark, *Social Darwinism in France* (Tuscaloosa: University of Alabama Press, 1984), 21–25. Fusing Darwin with Hegel, Taine's philosophy of history entailed an interaction between "la race, le moment, le milieu" in which the "physical temperament" of a race was seen as playing a role equivalent to "natural selection." Following Darwin, he regarded the art of the fittest artists that had survived as being the best monitor to gauge how a race, due to their particular physical temperament or Darwin's "natural selection" had proven to be those best able to negotiate their specific environmental conditions.

58. Hippolyte Adolphe Taine, *La Philosophie de l'art*, 2 vols. (Paris: Hatchette, 1865–1869).

59. Hippolyte Adolphe Taine, *Les Origines de la France contemporain, 1871–1890*, reprinted as *The Origins of Contemporary France: The Ancient Regime, The Revolution, The Modern Regime*, ed. Edward T. Gargan (Chicago: University of Chicago Press, 1974).

60. Clark, *Social Darwinism in France*, reference to *Le Temps* (1864), 15. In his letter to Charles Lyell, *Life, Letters and Journals of Sir Charles Lyell: Edited by His Sister-in-Law Mrs. Lyell*, volume 2 (London: Adament Media Corporation, 2003), 255, Darwin complained that Royer's translation had "injured the book."

61. Clark, *Social Darwinism in France*, 16.

62. James Moore and Adrian Desmond, "Introduction," in Charles Darwin, *The Descent of*

Man, and Selection in Relation to Sex (New York: Penguin Books, 2004, l. The first edition was published in London by John Murray, 24 February 1871. The second edition, from John Murray, came in 1879.

63. Ibid., li.

64. Ibid.

65. Ibid.

66. Clark, *Social Darwinism in France,* 2. These books are listed on 193–94, n. 6.

67. The close associate of Louis Pasteur, Jean de Lanassan, was author of *Le Transformisme* published in 1883.

68. Stuart M. Persell, *Neo-Lamarckianism and the Evolution Controversy in France, 1870–1920* (Lewiston, Queenston, Lampeter: Edwin Mellen Press, 1999), 4: "Lamarckian biologists . . . dominated major scientific institutions in Third Republic France."

69. Ibid., 56: "Notre immortal Lamarck." See also Madeleine Barthélemy-Madaule, *Lamarck the Mythical Precursor: A Study of the Relations between Science and Ideology,* trans. M. H. Shank (Cambridge Mass., MIT Press, 1982).

70. Persell, *Neo-Lamarckianism,* 12.

71. Edmond Perrier, "Lamarck et le transformisme actuel," *Centenaire de la fondation du Muséum d'histoire naturelle* (1993): 670: "Fondateur de la doctrine de l'évolution."

72. Stephen Jay Gould, "Shades of Lamarck," reprinted in *The Panda's Thumb: More Reflections in Natural History* (New York: Norton, 1980), 77.

73. Ibid.

74. Richard W. Burkhardt, *The Spirit of System: Lamarck and Evolutionary Biology* (Boston: Harvard University Press, 1977), 152.

75. Fae Brauer, "Eroticizing Eugenics: The Body Stripped Bare during French Sexual Neoregulation and Neo-Lamarckism," in *Art, Sex and Eugenics: Corpus Delecti,* ed. Fae Brauer and Anthea Callen (Aldershot, Hampshire: Ashgate, 2008), 97–138.

76. Robert Fox and George Weisz, eds., *The Organization of Science and Technology in France, 1808–1914,* (Cambridge: Cambridge University Press, 1980).

77. Michael A. Osborne, "Naissance et développement d'une institution," in *Le Muséum au premier siècle de son histoire,* ed. Claude Blanckaert et al. (Paris: Éditions du Muséum National d'Histoire Naturelle, 1993), 152: "Isidore Geoffroy Saint-Hilaire et . . . Edmond Perrier, deux directeurs du Muséum se situant dans l'orbite de la théorie biologique de Lamarck."

78. Edmond Perrier, "Préface," in Pierre-Jean Achalme, *La Science des civilisés et la science allemande* (Paris: Payot, 1916), 173–74.

79. Edmond Perrier, *Les Colonies animales et la Formation des organismes* (Paris: G. Masson, 1881).

80. Rothfels, *Savages and Beasts,* 3–4.

81. Gott, "Clutch of the Beast," 54, n. 66, quoting from a letter written to Director of the National Gallery of Victoria, Bernhard Hall, 13 December 1906, accompanying consignment of the sculpture.

82. "Devoré par un lion," *Le Petit Journal,* 29 September 1895.

83. *Bêtes Sauvages, environ 200 illustrations amusantes de la vie des animaux avec texte instructif* (Paris: Grand Magasins aux Galeries Lafayette, 1890). This album, translated as "Wild Beasts,"

included photographs of animals in captivity. Many of Rousseau's monkeys, lions, gazelles, and antelopes can be traced directly to this book, as established by Yann Le Pichon, "Les sources de Rousseau révélées," *Arts,* no. 809, Paris, 15–21 February 1961.

84. Nancy Iverson, "Jungles in Paris," in *Henri Rousseau: Jungles in Paris,* 143.

85. Vincent Gille, "Illusion of Sources—Sources of Illusion: Rousseau through the Images of His Time," in *Henri Rousseau: Jungles in Paris,* 58.

86. Thomas Pakenham, *The Scramble for Africa: White Man's Conquest of the Dark Continent from 1872–1912* (New York: Avon Books, 1991).

87. Joseph Conrad, *Heart of Darkness* (London: Blackwood, 1902). Conrad began writing the story in 1898 and finished the first draft in February 1899, the date when his first instalment appeared in *Blackwood's Magazine.*

88. The exhibition catalogue lists 855 entries, 673 sculptures, and 111 paintings.

89. Morris, "Jungles in Paris," 16.

90. Félix Vallotton, *Le Journal Suisse,* 25 March 1891.

91. Gaston Tissandier, "Nouvelles Galeries de zoologie," *La Nature* 854 (12 October 1889): 311–14.

92. Robert Delaunay recalls Rousseau often saying to him: "Je suis Anarchiste"; see "Mon ami Rousseau," *Arts et lettres,* August-September 1952. The source for his Anarchism may have been Alfred Jarry, who in 1884 had commissioned a lithograph of Rousseau's *War* and who stayed with the artist in 1897.

93. Pietr Kropotkin, *La Conquête du Pain* (Paris: Stock, Bibliothèque sociologique, 1892).

94. Green, *Souvenirs of the Jardin des Plantes,* 32.

95. Richard W. Burkhardt, Jr., "A Man and His Menagerie," *Natural History,* February 2001, 3.

96. Ibid., 5.

97. Richard W. Burkhardt, Jr., "The Leopard in the Garden: Life in Close Quarters at the Muséum d'Histoire Naturelle," *The History of Science Society* 98 (2007): 675–94. See also Burkhardt, "La Ménagerie et la vie du Muséum," in Blanckaert, *Le Muséum au premier siècle de son histoire,* 481–508.

98. Alphonse Milne-Edwards, "The Young Gorilla of the Jardin des Plantes," *La Nature,* 5 June 1884; reprinted in the *New York Times,* 29 June 1884.

99. Henri Milne-Edwards, *Histoire naturelle des Crustacés, comprenant l'anatomie, la physiologie et la classification de ces animaux,* 3 vols. (Paris: Roret, 1834–1840); Henri Milne-Edwards, "Observations sur les affinités zoologiques et la classification naturelle des Crustacés," *Annales des Sciences Naturelles (Zoologie)* 3d ser. 18 (1852): 109–66; Henri Milne-Edwards, *Rapport sur les progrès récents des sciences zoologiques en France* (Paris: Imprimerie Imériale, 1867).

100. The major ornithological works of Alphonse Milne-Edwards include *Recherches Anatomiques et Paleontologiques pour servir a l'Histoire des Oiseaux Fossiles de la France,* published in two parts in 1867 and 1872; *Recherches sur la Faune ornithologique etiente des iles Mascareignes et de Madagascar,* 1866–1874; and *Recherches pour servir à l'histoire naturelle des mammifères,* 1868–1874. His thesis, presented at the École supérieure de Pharmacie de Paris, was entitled *De la famille des solanacées* (Paris: E. Martinet, 1864).

101. T. H. Huxley to Alphonse Milne-Edwards, 17 and 28 April 1878, in Leonard Huxley, *The Life and Letters of Thomas Huxley,* vol. 2 (BiblioBazaar, 2006), 189.

102. Alphonse Milne-Edwards, *Notice sur quelques espèces d'oiseaux actuellement étientis qui se trouvent représentées dans la collections du Muséum d'Histoire Naturelle [Note on some currently extinct species of birds which are represented in the collections of the Natural history museum of Natural history]* (Paris: Imprimerie Nationale, 1893); Alphonse Milne-Edwards, *Histoire naturelle des Animaux [Natural history of the animals]* (Paris: Masson, 1897).

103. Milne-Edwards, *Musée d'histoire naturelle,* 13.

104. Ibid., 11.

105. Ibid., 12.

106. Ibid., 10.

107. Ibid., 22.

108. Osborne, *Nature, the Exotic,* 54.

109. Green, *Souvenirs of the Jardin des Plantes,* 46, n. 69.

110. Charles Darwin, *The Expression of Emotions in Man and Animals* (London: John Murray, 1872), 213.

111. Ibid.

112. Darwin, *The Descent of Man,* 24.

113. Darwin, *The Expression of Emotions,* 128–29, 198.

114. Larson, *The Dark Side of Nature,* 97.

115. Ibid., 97–98.

116. Armand Boucher, *Darwinisme et socialisme: Darwinisme socialiste* (Paris: Félix Alcan, 1890).

117. Jean Jaurès, Speech in the Chamber of Deputies, 7 March 1895, in *Oeuvres de Jean Jaurès. Textes rassemblés, présentés et annotés par Max Bonnafous,* vol. 4 (Paris: Rieder, 1931–1939), 88.

118. Elisée Rèclus, *Evolution et revolution* (Geneva, 1880; 1884; Paris: Bureau des Temps Nouveau, 1891; 7th ed. 1909).

119. Ibid.

120. Peter Kropotkin, *Mutual Aid: A Factor of Evolution* (London: William Heinemann, 1902).

121. Ibid.

122. Lynn Margulis, *Symbiosis in Cell Evolution* (New York: W. H. Freeman, 1981).

123. Gilles Deleuze and Felix Guattari, *A Thousand Plateaus* (orig. *Milles Plateaux,* 1980; reprint, Minneapolis: University of Minnesota Press), 1987.

124. Ralph Waldo Emerson, "Transparency in the Jardin des Plantes," *Journals and Miscellaneous Notebooks,* vol. 4 (1832), 199.

CHAPTER 9

Imag(in)ing Post-Revolutionary Evolution

The Taylorized Proletarian, "Conditioning," and Soviet Darwinism in the 1920s

PAT SIMPSON

After the Russian Revolution of 1917, the Bolsheviks demonstrated their commitment to Darwinism and the promotion of Darwinian science in many ways, including the publication of instructional pamphlets for use in Young Communist League clubs.[1] Enmeshed with this commitment was a belief, embedded in Bolshevik ideology even before 1917, that social revolution would bring about the evolution of a "new biologic type" of humankind—the New Person. This chapter explores the Darwinian implications of a dominant mode of visualizing the ideal, evolutionary, proletarian body in the early to mid-1920s, as a male "living labor machine."

Albeit variously articulated, the New Person was an ideal apparently subscribed to equally by Russian Bolshevik leaders, *Proletkul'tists*, and members of the pre-revolutionary literary and artistic avant-garde. Its most powerful manifestation, I suggest, was in the work and photographic records of Alexei Gastev at the state-funded Central Institute of Labor in Moscow. The evolutionary goal thus projected, I argue, was a "docile"—in the sense used by Foucault—mechanized, "Taylorized," male laboring body; tireless, efficient, and productive, whose evolution could be engineered by adaptation, through "conditioning" body disciplines and changes in sociocultural environment. Why and how was this apparently Lamarckian idea of evolution compatible with the Bolshevik espousal of Darwinism? What was its contemporary significance?

The first part of this chapter traces some of the main genealogical threads relating to Darwin and "Darwinisms" that were to become intertwined in the construct of the mechanized New Person. The starting point of the discussion is Darwin's ambivalence toward Lamarck's ideas on the inheritability of acquired characteristics, as leading to the possibility of a Lamarckian-style trajectory of "Darwinism" that had a strong following, both among pre-revolutionary Russian Darwinists, and in Bolshevik scientific thought. Within Russian Darwinism, two other elements seem to have been particularly compatible with post-revolutionary Bolshevik materialist and Marxist ideology: a materialistic approach to organisms as mechanisms, and a tendency to oppose the Malthusian aspect of Darwin's "struggle for existence" in relation to human society.

The latter chimed with a similar antipathy built into Bolshevism through the heritage of Marx's and particularly Engels' critiques of Darwin, which proposed purposive social organization, exertion of control over nature, increased productivity, and technological advance as the solution to the Malthusian population problem in a post-revolutionary society. These threads appear to have been variously brought together in the originary sources for the Bolshevik ideal of the New Person, the writings of Nikolai Chernyshevskii and Aleksandr Bogdanov. Their work helped to foster notions that the path to both social and human evolution lay in a new environment of increased technologization, intimately linked with changed habits through collectivized body discipline of the human mechanism. This idea was further reinforced, I suggest, by the popular theories of "Darwinist" behavioral psychologists Vladimir Bekhterev and Ivan Pavlov. Such "Darwinized" ideas—raised to the heights of utopian rhetoric—were propagated through the *Proletkul't* movement, and seem to have formed the basis for visual and textual invocations of the proletarian New Person in the early revolutionary years.

The second part of the chapter examines examples of the development of visualizations of the evolutionary proletarian ideal within the "leftist" artistic avant-garde during the early to mid-1920s. The discussion here considers images by Kasimir Malevich, Vera Ermolaeva, and El Lissitzskii relating to the opera *Victory Over the Sun*; poster drawings by Vladimir Krinskii; and photographs produced by Vsevolod Meierkhol'd and Alexei Gastev, with detailed emphasis on Gastev. While differing in many respects, these visualizations appear to have shared not only a basis in contemporary "Darwinized" notions of the technologized evolutionary ideal, but also a concern with the relationship of art to production, in particular, the utilitarian function of art in the production of the New Person's body. The robotic, geometricized imagery for *Victory Over the Sun*, for example, appears to have been underpinned by a belief—not very cogently articulated by Malevich—that Suprematism (his own invention), as the ultimate "evolutionary" form of art, offered new experiences and perceptions that would lead to physiological change in the spectators. By contrast, the poster drawings by Krinskii seem to have been more engaged with the evolution of the New Person's body at the less ambitious level of propaganda.

What Krinskii was supporting was the Bolshevik adoption of "scientific management" relating to the ideas of F. W. Taylor and other theorists of industrial efficiency, as the method of "conditioning" body discipline suitable for increasing productivity, and hastening social and human evolution. In response to this, Meierkhol'd and Gastev—to whom Meierkhol'd was largely indebted for his ideas—were drawn to engage with the production of the New Person's body at a more "scientific" and physiological level, importantly, supported by state funding that endured into the late 1930s.

A major linking factor between Meierkhol'd and Gastev, which differentiated their visualizations of the evolutionary New Person from those of the rest of the "leftist" avant-garde, was their use of photographic recording. Whereas visualizations of the mechanized New Person in graphic modes (including realizations in costume design) could only represent abstract invocations of a utopian ideal, the photographic records of Meierkhol'd and Gastev by their very nature might be seen not only as "realistic" representations of the process of realizing the ideal, but also as concrete evidence that this, "Darwinian," evolutionary process was already under way.

Within the contemporary Bolshevik context, Gastev's work was arguably the most significant for two main reasons, I suggest. While Meierkhol'd's "Taylorized" acting system of "biomechanics" only addressed the production of the actor-worker's body, Gastev's "art project" on the "psychotechnics" of labor engaged directly with the production of the industrial proletarian as "living labor machine," central to contemporary party and state concerns. Moreover, Gastev's analytical approach related more closely to Bolshevik engagement with empirical and materialist science, being more "scientific" and technological in making use of mathematics and measurement instruments, including chronocyclographic cameras, and was applied on a larger scale throughout the USSR. A key factor in the success and endurance of Gastev's, and to a lesser extent Meierkhol'd's, projects would seem to be the shared dependence, with the Bolsheviks, on Lamarckist-style understandings of the potentially inheritable elements of adaptation to environment, and operation of habit.

Darwin, Lamarck, and "Darwinisms"

Charles Darwin's *Origin of Species*, first published in 1859, both built on and challenged existing evolutionary theory, most particularly the ideas of Jean-Baptiste Pierre Antoine de Monet de Lamarck (1744–1829).[2] Darwin's theory, like Lamarck's, took a synthetic approach to natural science, using geological and fossil data to emphasise evolutionary "transformations" as occurring over vast tracts of time. It also linked humankind to animals in relation to the development of species, and, moreover, in ways that forged implicit and explicit connections to social theories—a shared aspect that was to be important in the Russian and Soviet contexts, especially in relation to the visualizations of the New Person. Additionally, for Darwin, as for Lamarck, species were perceived as mutable rather than as unique products of Divine Creation.[3] In this respect, Darwin went further than Lamarck in refusing to posit any source of original Creation, thereby gaining the approval of Karl Marx and Friedrich Engels for his materialist and nonteleological stance, and ensuring that "Darwinism" had a prime position in the pantheon of "atheistic" Bolshevik science.[4]

Perhaps most significantly in relation to the focus of this chapter, Darwin not only reinforced a notion of Lamarck as a primary source on evolution—apparently raising Lamarck's profile in post-1859 scientific debate—but also partly gave credence and continued possibility to Lamarck's ideas on adaptive evolution through habit in relation to environment, and on the inheritability of the characteristics thus acquired.[5] These ideas, as Jordanova has noted, were in any case commonly held by contemporary natural scientists. Indeed, despite various criticisms from the 1880s onward from supporters of genetics such as Weissmann, the ideas remained in the acceptable domain of biological science until the 1950s in Europe and the United States, and until the 1960s in the USSR.[6]

Darwin's challenges to Lamarck included an emphasis on the finality of species extinction, a rejection of Lamarck's ideas about the spontaneous generation of new organisms from nonorganic materials, and of Lamarck's idealistic progress model of all evolution as tending to increased complexity and, perhaps, perfectibility. Darwin also occasionally drew into scornful question Lamarck's ideas on the inheritability of acquired characteristics. But, while Darwin made derogatory comments about Lamarck's ideas in all versions of *Origin of Species*, in the final edition of 1872, the scorn for Lamarckian ideas on the inheritability of acquired characteristics in particular as unacceptable to contemporary science, was toned down to a suggestion that these ideas awaited scientific proof.[7] Moreover, in this edition of *Origin of Species*, Darwin seemed to continue to offer some evidence, not only of accepting the idea of inheritability of acquired characteristics, but also of including Lamarck's ideas of use and disuse of characteristics within the parameters of "natural selection."[8]

As a result, Darwin's ambivalence towards Lamarck, along with Lamarck's endurance as a canonical figure in evolutionary theory, appears to have enabled late nineteenth- and early twentieth-century European discourse on evolution to encompass, on the one hand, definitions of "Darwinism" that associated his ideas with emergent notions of genetics (Neo-Darwinism). On the other hand, these factors also implicitly supported definitions of "Darwinism," such as those offered by Spencer and Haeckel, that rejected genetic science and stressed the importance to Darwin of Lamarckian ideas on the inheritability of acquired characteristics and environmental adaptation.[9] The latter understanding of "Darwinism" seems to have been particularly prevalent within the Russian scientific community of the late nineteenth and early twentieth century, the community that was inherited and put to work by the Bolsheviks at the point of revolution in 1917. It was also favored by the Bolsheviks themselves, exemplified by the post-revolutionary orientation of the Timiriazev Institute and Communist Academy, and by the heroization of Kammerer in the 1920s, even after his international denunciation as a charlatan.[10]

Admittedly, this orientation was called into question during the so-called "Cultural Revolution" between about 1928 and 1932, in the debates over the role of genetics in Soviet, "Darwinian" science.[11] These resulted in a public renunciation of Lamarckism by the Communist Academy, and prosecutions and brief imprisonments for scientists such as Kuzin attached to the Timiriazev Institute.[12] Nevertheless, party orientation toward Lamarckian-style notions of Darwinism endured, reinforced by the apparent successes of Trofim Lysenko's experiments with the "vernalization" of wheat in the late 1920s and early 1930s.[13] With the benefit of hindsight, this orientation can be viewed as deeply unscientific, ultimately leading to disastrous consequences for Soviet agriculture. In the 1920s, however, it appeared to be both viable and credible, rooted in European and, most particularly Russian scientific exegesis of Darwin, as well as the writings of Marx and Engels.[14] As such, it was to have a decisive impact on the pre- and post-revolutionary construct of the New Person's evolution.

Russian Darwinism: A Special Case

Backtracking briefly, Russian interest in Darwin's work began in the 1840s. *Origin of Species* was first translated into Russian in 1864. Between 1864 and 1913, tremendous enthusiasm for Darwin was made evident, not only by the establishment of a Darwin Museum in Moscow in 1907 (the first of its kind), but also by a veritable spate of academic and popular publications, including multiple editions and translations of his major writings, with at least two separate publishers offering serial publications of Darwin's *Collected Works*.[15] The young evolutionary paleontologist Vladimir O. Kovalevskii went so far as to visit Darwin in 1867. The friendship thus established enabled Kovalevskii to publish a Russian translation of *The Variation of Plants and Animals under Domestication* some months before it came out in English in 1868, followed in 1872 by a translation of *The Expression of the Emotions*, the same year as the English version was published.[16] Darwin not only noted the intensity of Russian interest in his evolutionary theory in the final edition of *Origin of Species*, but also, in *The Descent of Man* (1871), cited observations made by both Vladimir Kovalevskii and by his brother, the embryologist Aleksandr Kovalevskii.[17]

The Russian orientation toward Darwin was identified in 1894 by the editor of *Science Review*, Mikhail M. Filippov, as "special" and involving a lack of differentiation between Lamarck and Darwin.[18] In relation to this, Vucinich has argued convincingly that in the pre-revolutionary period, Lamarckism and Darwinism were not treated by the Russians as separate sets of ideas. In contrast to the situation in France or Germany, there was no body of scholarship on Lamarck per se. In Russia, "Darwinism" appears to have become the umbrella heading for evolutionary theory, in which "submerged" elements of Lamarck's ideas on the inheritance of acquired characteristics and the influence of environment and training commonly were perceived as central tenets.[19]

Among those who supported this view was another Russian acquaintance of Darwin's, the plant physiologist Kliment Timiriazev (1845–1920), as well as the zoogeographer Mikhail Menzbir (1855–1935) and the physiological psychologist Ivan Sechenov (1829–1905).[20] These three were major pre-revolutionary translators and interpreters of Darwin, whose translations, significantly, were adopted by the Bolsheviks.[21] All three scientists favored a "monist," materialist and mechanical, physiological-chemical understanding of biological systems.[22] That is to say, they regarded organisms as mechanisms, making no division between mind—or brain—and body, and they located the evolutionary process firmly in relation to habit and environment. With the exception of Menzbir, they also shared with the majority of other Russian Darwinists and members of the late nineteenth-century Russian radical intelligentsia, a tendency to oppose the Malthusian element of Darwin's idea of the "struggle for existence," particularly as applied to human society.[23] Indeed, Timiriazev, in his *Short Essays on Darwin* (1865), pioneered an influential trend of approach to Darwin that stressed the need to differentiate between indirect competition, which might occur within a species, and direct struggle that was more linked to interspecies competition.[24] The Lamarckian-style emphasis on the role of environment and habit in the evolutionary process, the materialist approach, and the critical attitude to Darwin's Malthusian reference were all characteristics of Russian Darwinism that were ripe for Bolshevik colonization, in relation to the ambivalence of Marx and Engels to Darwin's original theory of evolution.

The main reason that the Bolsheviks were pledged to support Darwinism was the vague connection between Marxism and Darwinism forged initially in the writings of Marx, and most particularly Engels, which were subsequently repeated and elaborated by European Marxists including Lenin.[25] In Karl Marx's *Capital,* a copy of which he sent to Darwin, he identified *Origin of Species* as "epoch-making" for its materialist stance.[26] Engels reiterated this view, emphasizing the parallel to be drawn between the impact of Darwin's and Marx's theories in their own respective fields of natural science and sociology.[27] Despite their admiration, however, Marx and more particularly Engels identified Darwin's theory as problematic in its citation of Malthus's doctrine of population as a universal natural law, particularly in relation to the implications of Darwinism with regard to human society.

Thomas Malthus's theory proposed that populations expanded faster than food supplies, necessitating natural wastage, to counterbalance the working classes' propensity toward excessive procreation—unless this could be otherwise suppressed—since attempts to alleviate their conditions of existence through increased health care and education would increase the problem of subsistence for the whole of society.[28] Darwin had applied Malthus's notion of "struggle" to the process of "natural selection" in nature, where existed "no artificial increase of food, and no prudential restraint from marriage."[29] Unlike Malthus, Darwin used the idea of "struggle" as a factor within a theory of progressive evolutionary change in the natural worlds of plants and animals, but he did imply that it also operated within human society.[30] While this would fit with the Whiggish political context in which Darwin's theory was published, and to which Darwin himself belonged, for Marx and Engels, concerned with revolutionary improvement of working-class existence, this was pure, and unacceptable, capitalist theory.[31]

Engels, asserting that the "obstacle" to the development of population was not shortage of food but bourgeois society itself, declared "the pressure of population is not upon the means of subsistence, but upon the means of *employment*."[32] He further argued that the evolution of a "higher type" of society in the post-revolutionary era depended upon the "conscious organization of social production."[33] At the basis of Engels' argument was a belief, echoed by the Russian Darwinist Timiriazev, that, while the realms of plants and animals, being ruled by "blind agencies," were naturally subject to the "struggle for existence," the conscious and purposive realm of humankind was not.[34]

In *Capital,* Marx had drawn vague parallels between Darwin's ideas on evolutionary adaptation regarding the variation of parts for various functions in plants and animals, and the "evolutionary" development of specialized tools for particular facets of industrial production.[35] By this means, he implied not only that the development of the technologies of production followed an evolutionary process dictated by the demands of production, but also that the development of society itself could be understood as evolutionary adaptations to the conditions and technologies of production. On the basis of Marx's ideas, Engels identified the appropriation of the technological developments of "modern" bourgeois society, and the application of science and technology to agriculture, as potential means to increase efficiency and productivity in a socialist society.[36] The solution to the Malthusian population problem, according to Engels, was the development within post-revolutionary society of "means of production that will suffice to raise the productive power of each individual so that he is able to produce enough for two, three, four, five or six individuals."[37]

Engels' revision of Darwin offered a vision, fundamental to Bolshevism, of evolving post-revolutionary society evading the Malthusian population problem by focusing on a goal of increased productivity, which was achievable through conscious, purposive, technological improvement and social organization. It also potentially implied that social evolution included a new stage of organic human evolution: the evolution of the New Socialist Person. Russian Darwinism seemingly provided the Bolsheviks with a suitably materialist, anti-Malthusian, scientific basis for theorizing and imagining how the processes could be managed, with the additional promise that the evolutionary goals might be achievable in a relatively short time by means of the inheritance of acquired characteristics.

The Bolshevik Evolutionary Ideal of the New Person

The Bolshevik construct of the evolutionary New Person had two basic prerevolutionary sources of origin, which impacted in different ways on the imagining and imaging of this ideal after October 1917. One of these sources was Nikolai Chernyshevskii, a nineteenth-century Russian radical socialist, who initially engaged with materialist evolutionary science through Ernst Büchner's *Kraft und Stoff* (1855).[38] Although his anti-Malthusianism led him to reject Darwin in favor of Lamarck's "transformism," Chernyshevskii nevertheless shared the monist, mechanical approach to evolution characteristic of the Russian Darwinists Timiriazev, Menzbir, and Sechenov, with whom he was acquainted.[39] For Chernyshevskii, the evolution of a socialist social system depended on conscious, rational, and voluntary human self-transformation. Chernyshevskii's novel *What Is to Be Done? Tales about New People* (1864), set forth an ascetic model of this process based on body discipline, which was to provide precedents for concepts of the perfect revolutionary activist, and a basis for a wide range of "practical" attempts at "engineering" the New Person's evolution during the 1920s.[40]

Chernyshevskii's idea of the human body as a perfectible machine was developed further, with a more romantic, transcendental twist, and from a more Russian "Darwinist" stance, within the other basic source of the Bolshevik notion of the evolutionary New Person. This source projected a model of the New Person as a mechanized, collectivized proletarian, and theorized the post-revolutionary collective as eternal, all-powerful, and capable of victory over nature, perhaps even over death—at least in the sense that the individual might die but the collective would live on. The idea had been developed after the unsuccessful Russian revolution of 1905 as a suitable means to inspire and motivate the proletariat into self-sacrificial aspiration toward revolution.[41] At the time, the instigators were three figures destined to play major future roles in Soviet culture: Maxim Gorky, as primary literary figure, Anatolii Lunacharskii as the first Commissar for Enlightenment, and his brother-in-law, the physician Aleksandr Bogdanov, founder of the *Proletkult* movement and of the first Soviet blood transfusion research institute.[42] Ultimately, however, it was Bogdanov, via *Proletkult*, who had the most profound initial effect on early Soviet invocations and representations of the future New Person.

In parallel with Engels' revision of Darwin, Bogdanov associated social evolution with technological, industrial advances and took further the implications about human evolution by declaring that post-revolutionary society would generate a "new human type."[43] The notion that this type, collectively, could develop infinite powers may be seen as an inflated version of Engels' idea of social evolution as an extension of human power over nature through purposive, "conscious organization of social production." The implicit idea of evolution as a voluntary striving toward perfection might appear to be incompatible with an espousal of any sort of Darwinism, in the sense that it was an idea attributed to Lamarck first by Cuvier and then scornfully, by Darwin, and was not popular with pre-revolutionary Russian Darwinists.[44] Yet, its specific focus on humans can be linked to the differentiation between aspects of Darwinism applicable to the realms of the human and those of plants and animals, shared by Engels and Russian Darwinists such as Timiriazev.

For Bogdanov, psychology was the link between the biological and the social that held the key to understanding adaptive evolution.[45] This belief linked back to Russian Darwinism, both through the work of Sechenov on *Reflexes of the Brain* (1863) and that of the avowedly "Darwinist" founders of Russian behavioral psychology, Vladimir Bekhterev (1857–1927) and Ivan Pavlov, whose already influential ideas had a pervasive impact on post-revolutionary culture.[46] Bekhterev, an anti-Malthusian who had studied with Charcot in Paris, shared with the Russian Darwinists both their monist, mechanical approach to organisms, and the belief in adaptive evolution.[47] So did Pavlov, whose theory of "conditioned reflexes" was profoundly influenced by Sechenov's work, and who until about 1926 implied that "conditioned" changes of behavior might be organic and inheritable.[48] Their methodologies differed, Pavlov's being heavily inclined toward surgery. Both, however, eschewed Cartesian mind/body dualism and asserted that behavior could be changed by enforcing new, potentially inheritable habits and ways of thinking, through "conditioning" body disciplines and environmental change.[49] In relation to these ideas, the mythologization of the New Person seems to have been an element of psychological conditioning explicitly pursued in Bogdanov's formulation of *Proletkul't*.[50]

Proletkul't—the Organization for Proletarian Culture—was an agitational and educational organization intended to change working-class thinking and habits, by facilitating the development of art and literature within and by the proletariat, in contradistinction to the bourgeois culture of the past.[51] Set up in 1917, *Proletkul't* initially operated independently from the state- and party-controlled Commissariat for Enlightenment (*Narkompros*) headed by Lunacharskii (a co-theorist of the New Person), which was orientated toward Lenin's concern with utilizing aspects of past culture as the basis for educating the—largely illiterate—working classes. The independence, however, did not last long. Heavily and publicly criticized by Lenin in 1920, Bogdanov was removed from the control of *Proletkul't* in 1921 and returned to medical practice, while the *Proletkul't* organization was subsumed into *Narkompros* in 1922.[52] Nevertheless, its quasi-mystical vision of technologized post-revolutionary humankind, as an incarnation of the eternal, immortal spirit of the collective—evolving, as it were, to grasp infinite powers and capabilities of cosmic domination—was much invoked in the early revolutionary period in a variety of ways.

Predictably, *Proletkul't* poets, such as Alexei Gastev and the associated "Cosmist" and "Blacksmith" (*Kuznetsa*) groups, lyricized about the eternal collective, and expressed revolutionary fantasies of cosmic power that would be achieved by the new humans of the post-revolutionary world.[53] Such beings were, indeed, described by the sympathetic literary critic, Vladimir Friche, as sons "of light bringing Prometheus."[54]

These prophesies of the future, technologized humanity were echoed by members of the "leftist" literary and artistic avant-garde. The Futurist poet and critic, Sergei Tretiakov, for example, committed himself to "propaganda towards the forging of the new person," describing the individual in the new society as a "screw in the machine."[55] Meanwhile, Dziga Vertov, the radical film director, perhaps also inspired by Lenin's revolutionary slogan "Electrification plus the Soviets," prophesied the evolution of "the perfect electrical man . . . The new man freed from his clumsiness and incompetence, in possession of the precise and light movements of the machine."[56] Even Leon Trotsky, a leading Bolshevik who disapproved equally of *Proletkul't* and of the avant-garde's excesses of Futuristic fantasy, injected a similarly Promethean and technologistic ring into his own prediction of the evolution of a "new biologic type," armed with "technique," "scientific organization," "the machine," "planfulness," "will power," "courage," "speed," and "precision."[57] Moreover, Trotsky also declared that "the Revolution starts from the central idea that collective man must become sole master, and that the limits of his power are determined by his knowledge of natural forces and by his capacity to use them."[58]

"Darwinist" Visualizations of the Evolutionary Ideal

Mastery over nature was certainly the core theme of the vision of the ultimate evolutionary ideal embodied in the imagery produced by Vera Ermolaeva and El Lissitzsky for the performance of *Victory Over the Sun*. The performance was held at the newly Suprematist-dominated Vitebsk Art Institute—renamed UNOVIS—on 6 February 1920.[59] Originally staged in Luna Park, St. Petersburg, in December 1913, *Victory Over the Sun* was an opera, written by the Russian Futurist poet Alexei Kruchenykh, with libretto by avant-garde painter and composer Mikhail Matiushin. The somewhat incoherent storyline recounted the stabbing and capture of the Sun by a group of "strong men" of the future, and voiced a celebration of the endlessness of Futurist progress.[60] The initial Cubo-Futurist set and costume design had been done by Kasimir Malevich who, having effectively taken over the Vitebsk Institute after the revolution, closely directed the designs produced by Vera Ermolaeva, the Institute's official Director (figures 9.1 and 9.2).[61] An innovatory aspect of the reprised version of the opera was the inclusion of a "ballet" of new and very abstract two-dimensional images held up on placards by the students of UNOVIS. Lissitzskii's image of the *New Man* was one of these (figure 9.3).[62]

In its original context, the opera and imagery had referred to the Russian Futurists' concern with remaking the world and the human body, which has been argued to have had a vague engagement with the Darwinian evolution-

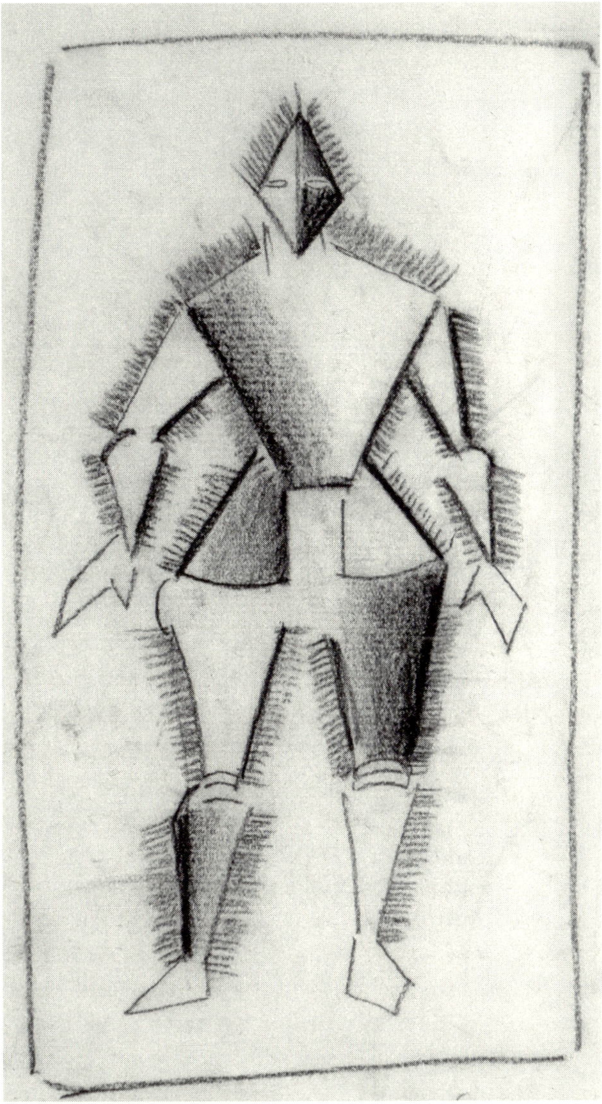

Figure 9.1 Kasimir Malevich, *The Athlete of the Future*, sketch of a costume for the opera *Victory Over the Sun*, 27 × 21 cm, paper, pencil, 1913. *St Petersburg State Museum of Theatre and Music, Russia. © 2008. Digital image, St. Petersburg State Museum of Theatre and Music.*

ary ideas that permeated pre-revolutionary Russian culture.[63] In 1920, these nuances were extended in response to the new context, partly as a vindication of the avant-gardists' belief that their ideas and work had somehow prefigured the Bolshevik social and political Revolution.[64] On one level, in this "electro-mechanical" performance the combination of a storyline that afforded the "men of the future" infinite powers over nature, and the abstract, geometricized, anonymised, and vaguely "robotic" representations of the figures,

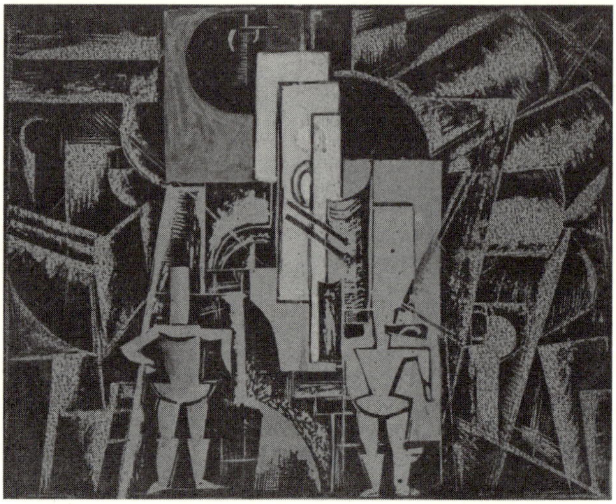

Figure 9.2 Vera Ermolaeva, sketch for set and costumes for *Victory Over the Sun*, 16.7 × 20 cm, woodcut with watercolor additions, Vitebsk 1920. *Museum of Modern Art, New York. Digital image © 2008 The Museum of Modern Art, New York / Scala, Florence.*

matched with Bogdanov's technologized, and mechanized concept of the collectivized evolutionary goal.[65] On another level, the images of the New Person, particularly Lissitzskii's, referenced deeply Idealistic and rather incoherent "evolutionary" ideas intrinsic to Malevich's post-revolutionary reformulation of Suprematism. In this sense, Ermolaeva's reprise of Malevich's 1913 imagery might be seen as alluding deliberately to an historic and prophetic moment in the development of Russian Cubo-Futurism that heralded the birth of Suprematism—invented by Malevich between 1915 and 1916—and exemplified in an evolved form in Lissitzskii's 1920 placard.

Malevich, acquainted with Pavel Filonov's ideas of "universal flowering," appears to have shared Filonov's view that art was organically involved with the general evolutionary process, having the power, through interaction, to assist in the transformation of the human body.[66] In 1920, Malevich stated the belief that "Suprematist forms have reached utilitarian perfection," apparently through a process of "genetic" mutation and modification involving both natural and artificial selection.[67] According to Malevich, Suprematism had already rendered the old culture redundant, and from its utilitarian, empirical, scientific basis in "Natural History," Suprematism offered a democratic new environment of experience and action, capable of drawing into being a new world and a new humanity.[68] Viewed from this perspective, Lissitzskii's image was not just a symbolic representation of the future perfected humanity, with a red square at its heart—perhaps standing for the symbiosis of Bolshevism and Suprematism—and a red star on its "head" similar to the insignia of the Red Army.[69] By its very style, the ultimate in artistic evolution, it

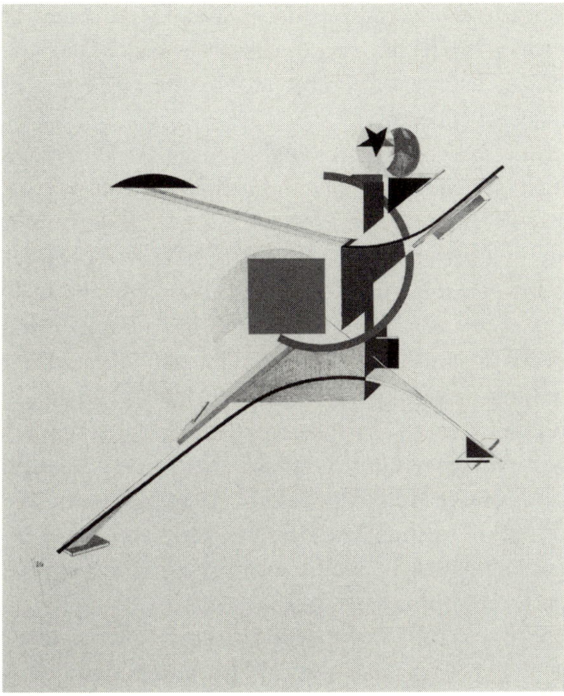

Figure 9.3 El Lissitzsky, *The New Man*, from *Victory Over the Sun*, 53.3 × 45.4 cm, lithograph, 1920. *Museum of Modern Art, New York. © DACS 2008. Digital image © 2008 The Museum of Modern Art, New York / Scala, Florence.*

offered the spectator a new visual experience that could lead to organic evolutionary change.

This assumption, implicit in Malevich's writings, was shared by Matiushin, the librettist of *Victory Over the Sun*, and by the ASNOVA group of "rationalist architects," which the architect and designer Lissitzskii eventually joined.[70] While far-fetched, the idea can be seen to link back to the Russian Darwinist construct of the organism as a physiochemical mechanism evolving through habit and response to environmental change. Most particularly, perhaps, it may be seen to connect with the currently influential extensions of this approach embedded in the two "Darwinist" trends of Russian behavioral psychology represented by Bekhterev and Pavlov and rooted in Sechenov's *Reflexes of the Brain*. In relation to this context of ideas, it might seem logical—to a nonscientist at least—that the production of new visual stimuli, affecting perception and thought, could engender permanent physiological as well as psychological change, especially if it was an intrinsic part of the conditioning effects of training to new habits in a new cultural environment such as that offered after the revolution. Indeed, such beliefs were to lead to the proliferation of "laboratory" studies in the "psychotechnics" of perception in the mid-1920s, respectively pioneered by Matiushin's Department of Organic Culture at Petrograd GINKhUK during the period of Malevich's directorship, and by ASNOVA, led by the architect Nikolai Ladovskii at VKhUTEMAS/VKhUTEIN in Moscow.[71]

The inclination of the "leftist" avant-garde toward framing art and visual culture in relation to scientificness, technologism, and utility derived, in part, from voluntary engagement with the new need for art to have a function in relation to building socialism, in a society where the art market had been replaced by the party, state, and trades unions. Much art discourse of the early 1920s circulated around ideas about the "rationalization" of art, concerning blurring the boundaries between art and labor—favored particularly by Bogdanov and *Proletkul't*—and taking art into production, associated particularly with the Constructivists and Productivists, and approached in a general sense by the discourse underlying the imagery of *Victory Over the Sun*. In relation to this, there were visualizations of the New Person that attempted to engage simultaneously with the production of the New Person's body, and more explicitly with contemporary issues relating to the renovation of industrial production as means to both social and human evolution.

One example of this approach was in the propagandist poster design work of Vladimir Krinskii (1890–1971), "leftist" architect and founding member of ASNOVA, who seems to have produced a vision of the collectivized New Person that came closest to illustrating Tretiakov's poetic idea of the collectivised worker as a "screw in the machine." This was illustrated by the undated poster drawing that was one of several similar works by Krinskii published in René Fülöp-Miller's anti-Soviet book *The Mind and Face of Bolshevism*, published in German in 1926 (figure 9.4). Krinskii's drawing, probably dating from the mid-1920s and executed in a style related to Russian Cubo-Futurism, seems to have been a celebratory invocation of something akin to Bogdanov's idea of the mechanized, collectivized worker. Another Krinskii drawing contrasting the old and new life, published in the same source, indicates the methods of "conditioning" through which the goal could be achieved (figure 9.5). The image pinpoints these means as the "scientific management" of industry—by reference to the grids used by Edweard Muybridge and Frank Gilbreth to "rationalize" physical motion, and by the exhortation to "Be an engineer of life. Reveal the mechanics of time."[72]

In 1918, Lenin, the Bolshevik leader, had insisted on the introduction of methods of "scientific management" in industry—known by the umbrella term "Taylorism" and also by the acronym NOT—including differential piecework rates for those workers who exceeded or failed to meet set production norms.[73] Before the revolution, Taylorism had been condemned by both

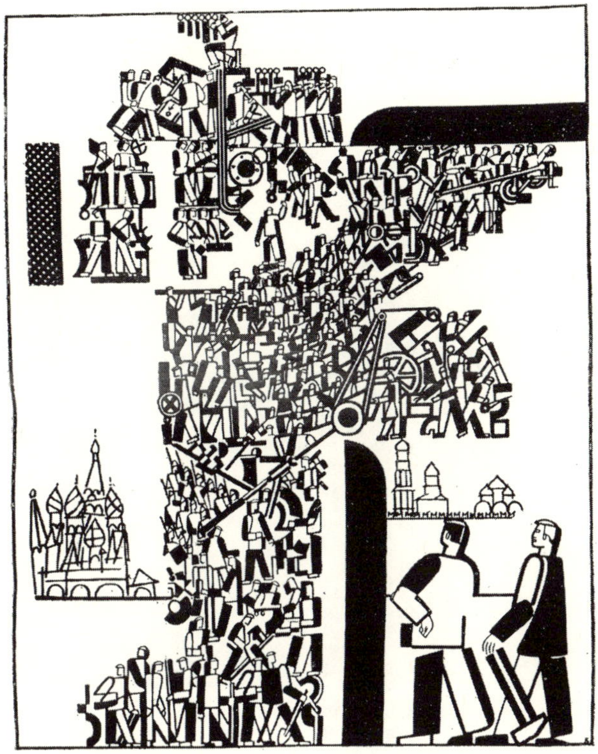

Figure 9.4 Vladimir Krinskii, *The Mechanized Individual Is Reduced to a Mere Component Part in the Mass Which Has Become the Machine*, poster drawing, 1920s. *Reproduced in René Fülöp-Miller,* The Mind and Face of Bolshevism *(London, 1927).*

Lenin and Bogdanov as an abhorrent, extreme form of exhaustive capitalist exploitation that treated workers as machines.[74] After the revolution, however, Lenin's decision was to adopt what was useful, modern, progressive, and "scientific" from such practices, in an attempt to improve the efficiency of the remaining vestiges of Russian industry.[75] Industrial technology itself also needed renovation to serve this end, and some attempt at this was made through the concessions to foreign capitalist investment within the New Economic Policy initiated in 1921.[76] In the aftermath of World War I and the post-revolutionary civil war, the renovation of industrial technology, however, was not only expensive, but also destined to take a long time, despite Stalin's introduction of five-year plans in the late 1920s.[77]

The initial needs were for the qualitative improvement, and eventually, the increase of the workforce, through changing the habits of the workers.[78] Contemporary notions of "conditioning," changed environment and body discipline deriving from Russian Darwinism and Chernychevskii's model of the New Person, held out the possibility of achieving these goals. They seemed to underpin major areas of body discipline promoted by the party and state, in

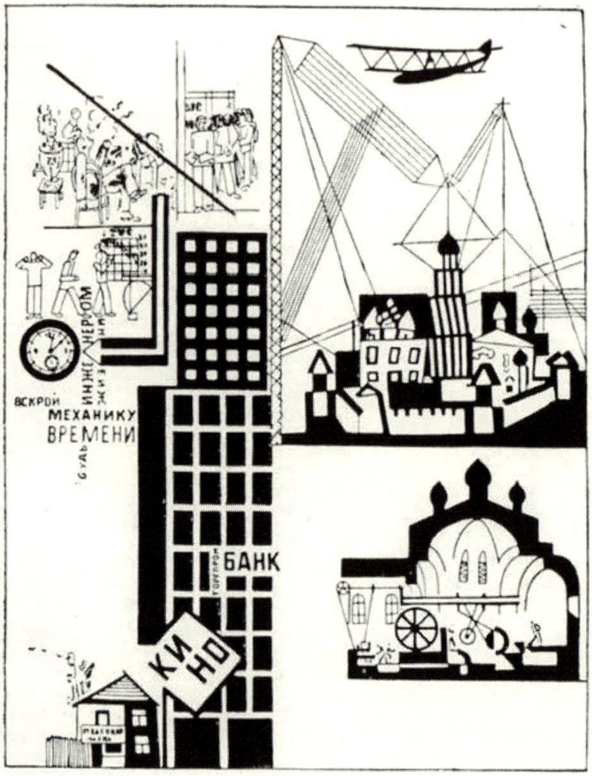

Figure 9.5 Vladimir Krinskii, *Constructivist-Symbolic Representation: "The New Epoch,"* poster drawing, 1920s. *Reproduced in René Fülöp-Miller,* The Mind and Face of Bolshevism *(London, 1927).*

relation to the redefinition of leisure as physical culture and the medicalization of women's bodies for "hygienic" reproduction.[79] The adoption of Taylorism, a subversion of modern capitalist industrial methods, which echoed Engel's "revision" of Darwin, offered a methodology for "conditioning" that focused specifically on increasing the productivity of the industrial proletariat by encouraging them to be more efficient. After the First All-Russian Conference on Scientific Management, organized by Trotsky in Spring 1921, Lenin authorized the creation of the Central Institute of Labor (TsIT) in August of that year, with a specific remit to Taylorize industrial production.[80] This was followed in 1923 (continuing until 1926) by the authorization of a "Time League," with a broader remit to encourage habits of timekeeping and efficiency throughout Soviet culture.[81]

Some members of the "leftist" avant-garde became intimately involved with promoting Taylorism, not only, as in the case of Krinskii—a member of the Time League—at the level of graphic propaganda, but also at a physiological level, using the medium of photography, both still and cinematographic, to record and study the process of engineering the physical evolution of the New Person.[82] One example of this, focused on blurring the boundaries between art and work, was the system of "biomechanics" invented by Vsevolod Meierkhol'd, radical theater director, member of the "Time League," and from 1921 Director of the State Higher Theater Workshops in Moscow.[83] Meierkhol'd proposed "biomechanics" as a "Taylorized" means to train the bodies of actor-workers, in order to make theater more efficient. It may be, as Edward Braun has implied, that Meierkhol'd's use of language was a timely (and successful) strategy to avert the closure of his theater.[84] Nevertheless, it squarely confronted the impetus of the time.

Meierkhol'd introduced the public to his acting system of "biomechanics" in a lecture on 12 June 1922, declaring that "the Taylorization of theater will make it possible to perform in one hour that which requires four at present."[85] The system comprised twenty-two movements, each corresponding with a state of mind, which, when learned, could apparently be speedily and automatically reproduced with Pavlovian "reflex sensitivity."[86] The photographs in figure 9.6 illustrate three of these movements, showing the actor's body nearly naked, thus emphasising the operation of the "conditioned" physiological mechanism. The location, outdoors rather than in a theater studio, seems a deliberate reference to the eugenic concern of the Commissariats for Health and Enlightenment with improving the worker's body by physical culture in contact with sun and air. Indeed, Meierkhol'd explicitly linked his system of thespian body discipline to this broader program of engineering the evolution of the New Person, prophesying that if a child was placed "in an environment in which gymnastics and all forms of sport are available and compulsory, we shall achieve the new man who is capable of any form of labor."[87] The photographs, by their commonly assumed nature as analogues of reality, offered evidence that this process was already under way in Soviet theater. [88]

In formulating "biomechanics," Meierkhol'd appears to have drawn on a variety of sources. One of these was the *Proletku't* blend of Chernyshevskii's body-discipline model of the pathway to the perfected New Person, with Russian "Darwinist" ideas of the body as inheritably trainable, favored throughout the Russian avant-garde. Another source was the theatrical theories of Jacques Dalcroze regarding the training and movement of the actor's body. Meierkhol'd also relied on a number of compatible sources relating to "scientific management."

In a general sense, "biomechanics" had some roots in the ideas of French ergonomist Jules Amar's writings on the "human motor."[89] More specifically, however, the idea of twenty-two motions seemed to echo the ideas of the

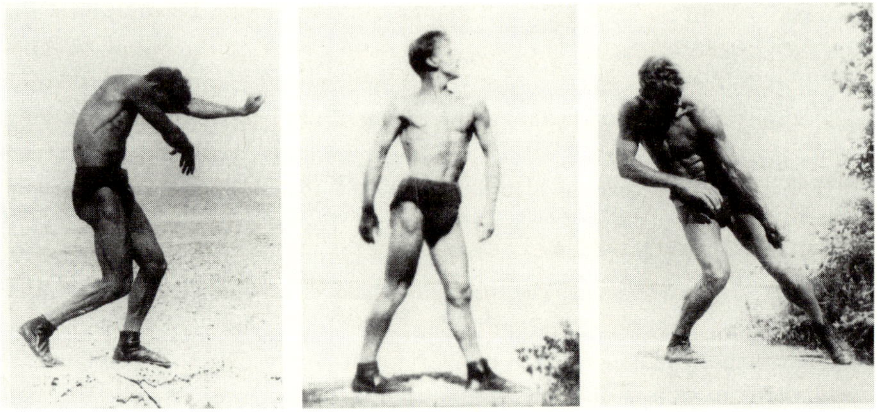

Figure 9.6 Vsevolod Meierkhol'd, biomechanics movements, photographs, 1921. *Reproduced in Konstantin Rudnitsky,* Russian and Soviet Theatre: Tradition and the Avant-Garde *(London, 1988). © 2008. Digital image, Cambridge University Library.*

American theorists of "scientific management," Frank and Lillian Gilbreth, regarding the possibility of there being a quantifiable number of industrial labor motions.[90] The most powerful reference point for Meierkhol'd, however, was the work of Alexei Gastev at TsIT, the Central Institute of Labor, perhaps the most extreme and significant example of taking art into production, focused on the simultaneous evolution of industrial production and of the New Person.[91]

Gastev was an extraordinary character who was simultaneously intimately connected with the "leftist" artistic and literary avant-garde, with *Proletkul't*, and with the Trade Unions as First Secretary of the All-Russian Metalworkers' Union.[92] In 1912, as a revolutionary trade unionist, he had worked at the Paris Renault factory when a disastrous attempt to introduce Taylorism had been made.[93] Yet, after the revolution he responded readily to Lenin's espousal of "scientific management." In 1919 for instance, as Commissar for the Arts in Kharkov in Ukraine, he organized a school of "social engineering," and then in 1920 formed an Institute of Labor in Moscow, supported by the All Russian Central Council of Trade Unions.[94] In addition, as representative of the metalworkers union, he had been instrumental in negotiating the pay differentials that were to form incentives for workers to engage with the principles of "scientific management."[95]

Lenin's 1921 Decree instituting TsIT effectively brought under party and state control Gastev's potentially syndicalist Institute of Labor, breaking its previous exclusive ties with the trade unions and amalgamating it with another similar organization. [96] Significantly, Gastev's project retained the support of the Bolshevik leadership until he was "purged" in 1938. Thousands of workers were trained by his methods.[97] Unusually, it was initially generously funded with convertible currency.[98] By 1924, there were eight hundred "cells" for the "scientific organization of Labor" all over Russia, as well as eight "laboratories" for the study of the "psychotechnics" of Labor—that is to say, the psychological and physiological aspects of industrial work.

The institute's purpose was to study, evaluate, and rationalize working procedures, and to offer short, three-to-six month training courses for semi-skilled industrial workers, enabling them to go back into industry as "instructors." The focal emphasis of these courses, accompanied by the use of a metronome to encourage adherence to strict timing, was to educate the proletariat to "work like a chronometer," as suggested in the drawing for a poster by Gastev in the 1920s, reproduced in Fülöp-Miller's book (figure 9.7). Reinforced by a portrait of Lenin in the top right-hand corner, the text of this Cubo-Futurist-style drawing states: "Let us take the storm of revolution in the USSR, unite it with the pulse of American life and do our work regulated like a chronometer."

The idea of "Soviet Americanism" advocated by Gastev's poster and his pamphlet *Vosstanie kul'tury* (1923), referred to a widespread European, as well as a Russian perception of America as the fount of economic dynamism successfully driven on by "scientific management."[99] This idea was alluded to, for example, by the prominent Bolshevik, Nikolai Bukharin, in 1922.[100] For Gastev, the idea was epitomized by the "inventors," Henry Ford—in relation to mass-production- and Frederick W. Taylor and Frank and Lillian Gilbreth—regarding "scientific management."[101] The Commissar for Enlightenment, Lunacharskii, expressed concern that emphasis on American business methods might distract the development of the New Soviet Person from revolutionary aims.[102] Gastev, apparently thoroughly engaged with Marx's and Engels' ideas on the connection between the evolution of industrial technology and that of society, and, potentially, of human beings, however, appeared confident that the adaptation of these methods to the Soviet economic context was the necessary evolutionary route.[103]

The goal, as imagined by Gastev in 1919 in the *Proletkul't* journal, when he was still in Ukraine, was of "mechanized collectivism" involving standardized and anonymous workers.[104] This vision eventually was toned down after 1921 in the publications emanating from TsIT, to include more concern with the welfare of individual workers and the problems of fatigue and "neurasthenia"—literally, nervous exhaustion—caused by contemporary pressure for increased productivity. The latter was a problem that became increasingly a topic on the Soviet medical agenda in the 1920s.[105]

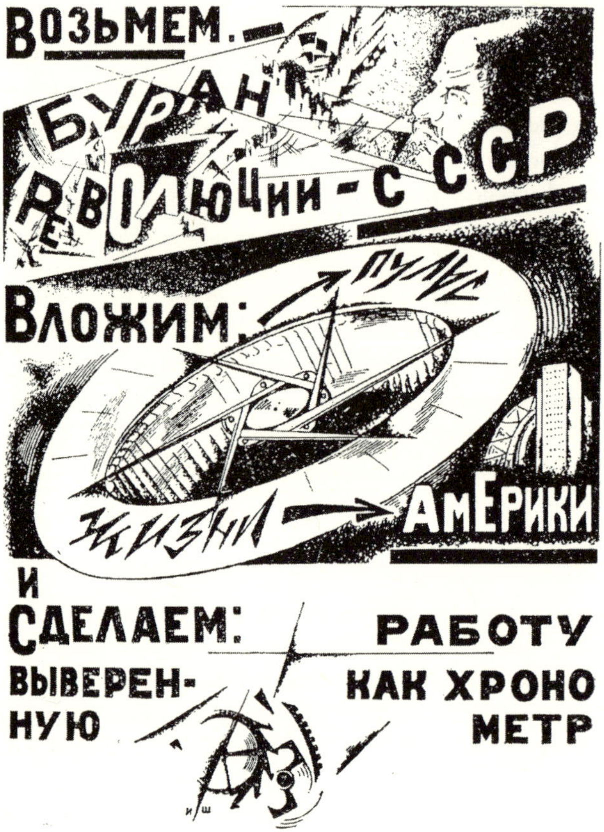

Figure 9.7 Alexei Gastev, *Let Us Take the Storm of Revolution in the USSR, Unite It with the Pulse of American Life and Do Our Work Regulated Like a Chronometer*, poster drawing, 1920s. *Reproduced in René Fülöp-Miller,* The Mind and Face of Bolshevism *(London, 1927).*

Solutions to the problem were often framed by medical authorities and experimenters in terms of so-called "rejuvenation" therapies, which seem to have represented in scientific and eugenic terms a halfway-house between "conditioning" and medical genetics in promoting the evolution of the New Person. These therapies included Steinach operations involving the attachment of monkey glands, and endocrine injections, both of which were studied and performed within the Moscow Eugenics Institute.[106] Blood transfusions were another method considered, and indeed, Bogdanov, prime theorist of the mechanized New Person's evolution, eventually became a victim of his own experiments with the rejuvenating effects of blood transfusions, dying in 1928.[107] TsIT, however, offered a different approach, partly based on the ideas of Jules Amar, whose theory of the "human motor" apparently had been developed in opposition to the version of Taylorism imposed on the Paris Renault factory in 1912, and who was concerned with rationalizing industrial labor in ways that would maintain workers' health and avoid the problems of fatigue and "neurasthenia."[108] Thus, TsIT's operations also included "control laboratories" to monitor "bio-engineering" in relation to the "organizational behavior" of the worker, bio-chemical aspects of fatigue, "functional diagnostics" of the "energy balance" of the worker's organism, and medicinal and anthropometric control of this organism.[109]

Gastev nevertheless continued to believe, along lines related to Bogdanov's *Proletkul't* ideal and Engels' revision of Darwin, that the introduction of new technology and mass-production methods was giving birth to a New Person, which was a "human machine."[110] To help it on its way required a new science of "social engineering" focused on redesigning the workers' "social psychology" through modes of body discipline and "conditioning" (*trenirovka*) as ascetic as those proposed by Chernyshevskii, and informed by the ideas of Russian Darwinists Sechenov and Pavlov.[111] In Gastev's view, this new science would be capable of affecting and transforming "even his [the worker's] intimate life," including his "aesthetic, intellectual and sexual values."[112]

The first step in this direction was for the "social engineer" to make a scientific analysis of a job starting with a "preliminary study" of various ways of doing the job, dividing it into "separate parts," choosing "the best" method for doing each element of the job, then putting these into a "series" of motions that would ensure that the work would be "economic" in terms of time taken and energy expended, and thus be "precise."[113] Within this process, photography was used as a technological and scientific adjunct to analysis. Gastev's methods were reminiscent of studies of the French laboring body undertaken variously by Paul Richer, Albert Londe, Jules Amar, and inventor of the chronocyclographic camera, Étienne-Jules Marey.[114] Initially, however, the methods were derived from the work of the Gilbreths, who had extended F. W. Taylor's ideas on the timed analysis of labor processes, to scrutinize workers' motions by the use of photography including hand-crank cinematography, and a chronocyclographic camera adapted from Marey's invention.[115] On this "scientific" basis, within TsIT's laboratories, the movements of workers were not only scrutinized with dioptic telescopes and chronocyclographic cameras, but they were also measured and analyzed for efficiency.[116]

Figure 9.8 is an example of one of Gastev's composite chronophotographic images from the early 1920s. He used a technique, pioneered by the Gilbreths of attaching little lights in order to trace the motion of a rod or hammer attached to a woman's prosthetic arm.[117] Set against the traces, on the right-hand side of the photograph, is a scale against which to measure the motion, presumably for its efficiency. Deriving from Amar's concerns with mechanizing disabled soldiers in order to make them efficient and socially

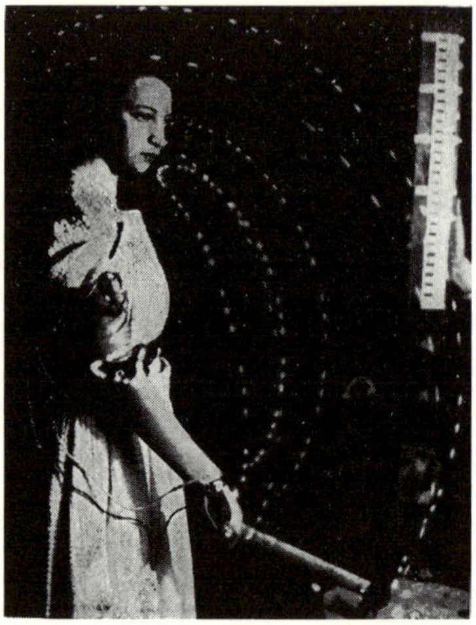

Figure 9.8 "Russian Taylorism in Gastev's Institute," composite chronophotograph, early 1920s. *Reproduced in René Fülöp-Miller,* The Mind and Face of Bolshevism *(London, 1927).*

useful "human motors," this image was not a nightmare vision of the New Person evolving into a literal cyborg.[118] Rather, it not only indicated ways of incorporating the disabled into Taylorized Soviet industry in order to increase the workforce, but also symbolized a more metaphorical symbiosis of human and machine central to the standardization of labor proselytized by Gastev's book, *Trudovye ustanovki,* published in 1923.

The body of the evolutionary, proletarian New Person had to be whole and healthy, as emphasised by TsIT's concern with monitoring health and issues of fatigue, and also by the other fields of state-supported body discipline. The proletarian New Person also was intrinsically male.

Linguistically, in Russian, *novyi chelovek* means "new person" but is a masculine form treated as gender neutral. As such, in its 1920s manifestation, the term did not exclude women, but rather offered a space for women (as honorary men) to be included with men as human beings—a concept that overturned pre-revolutionary concepts of women as not human, held particularly among the peasantry and working classes.[119] The combination of enduring misogyny and the low ratio of women in early Soviet industry, however, ensured that the proletarian ideal was commonly imaged as male, not only in general revolutionary propaganda (figure 9.9), but also in the visualizations of the evolutionary proletarian New Person offered by *Victory Over the Sun* (figures 9.1–9.3), Krinskii's poster drawings (figures 9.4 and 9.5), and the photographs by Meierkhol'd and Gastev (figures 9.6, 9.8, and 9.10).[120]

Figure 9.10 shows a staged photograph of Gastev, the "social engineer," framed by his own apparatus for scrutiny, engaged in one of the experiments he was most famous for, involving the study of metal workers hitting a chisel

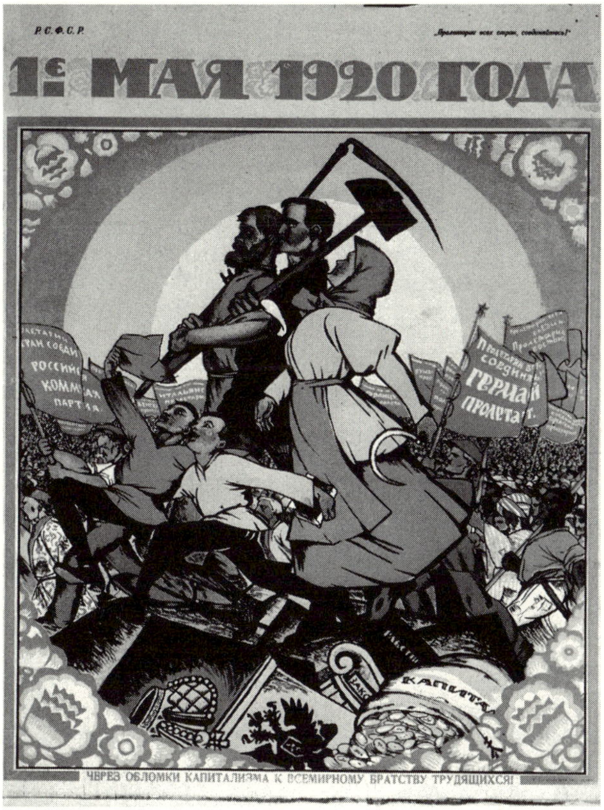

Figure 9.9 Nikolai Kochergin, 1 May 1920, poster, 1920. *RU/SU 2087: 1 May 1920, Political Poster Collection, Hoover Institution Archives, Stanford, California. © 2008. Digital image, Hoover Institution.*

with a hammer.[121] The objects of his "scientific" gaze were an aproned and bearded figure facing the camera—seemingly a composite incarnation of early revolutionary propaganda images of bearded peasants and proletarian blacksmiths (see figure 9.9)—contrasted with a more "modern" image of a clean-shaven worker in boiler-suit and cap, wielding a hammer. Although the respective roles of these two figures are ambiguous, the experiment seems to be about extracting the "best" and most efficient practice in terms of economy and precision of motion, from the skilled worker- the blacksmith—in order to train the implicitly unskilled, revolutionary proletarian and potential New Person.

In the photograph, it is possible to see apparatus for measurement, notably the giant protractor, and devices for simulating human movement—the mechanical device on a stand by the blackboard and the poseable nude model on the blackboard shelf. The arm of this figure is in the same position as those of the model, the mechanism, and the worker, and it is highly probable that the algebra on the blackboard represents a mathematical analysis of this move-

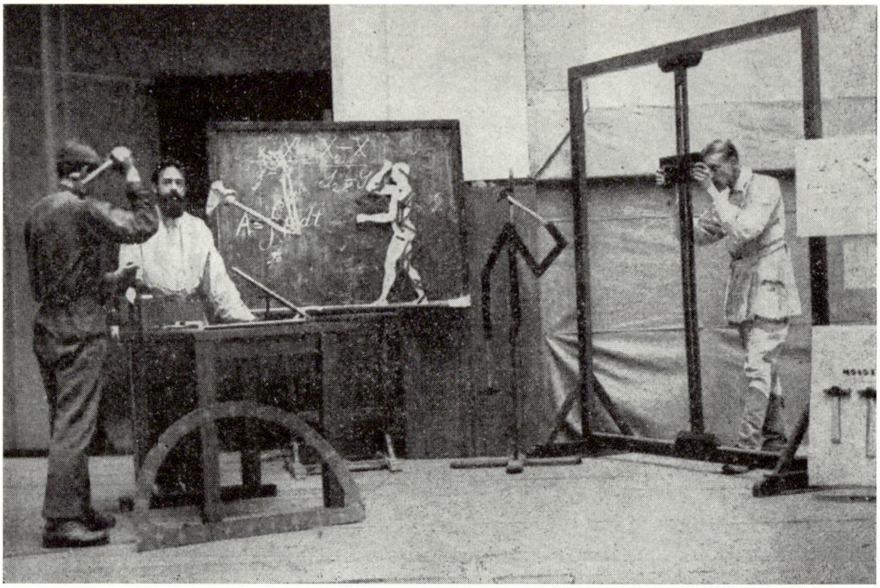

Figure 9.10 "A Demonstration at Gastev's Biomechanical Laboratory," photograph, early to mid-1920s. *Reproduced in René Fülöp-Miller,* The Mind and Face of Bolshevism *(London, 1927).*

ment. On the right-hand side of the blackboard is a ratio calculation, which may refer to inter-related movement or position change in two dimensions—traditionally in mathematics, the x-axis represents horizontal, and the y-axis vertical movement. On the left-hand side, there is an integration calculation, which is an adding-up over time, perhaps of distance covered and/or energy expended.[122] The blackboard calculations and apparatus emphasised the "scientific" nature of the study. The clothing of the workers stressed the real, practical subject of study—the proletariat—while the scientifically anatomical image of the naked male body acted as a reminder that this was the mechanical structure that needed to be improved through training and "conditioning."

Gastev's methods and ideas were criticized between 1919 and 1924 not just from within *Proletkul't*, but also from the SovNOT (Central Council of Scientific Organization of Labor) of the Commissariat of Workers and Peasants Inspection, and co-members of the Time League.[123] The main criticism was that he was dehumanizing and disempowering the workers by "transforming the living person into an unreasoning, stupid instrument."[124] This was a valid criticism.

While Gastev's chronocyclographic image did not dematerialize the worker's body—as did those of Marey and the Gilbreths—both this and the hammer experiment image did imply the control of the "social engineer" over the worker's body.[125] As Tagg and Lalvani have argued, within the laboratory process of objectifying the worker's body, the "social engineer" appropriated the knowledge of the skilled worker and re-packaged it as the property, not of the worker, but of the external "expert," diminishing the political power of the individual worker's body.[126] The photographic records made visible this disciplinary process in action, emphasizing the "scientific" necessity for the worker's body to become the mechanized and disempowered property of the state, which Foucault has described as the "docile body."[127]

This, however, does seem to be exactly what the party and state required from Gastev's project. Writing in apparently authoritative and successful defence of TsIT, Gastev cited the demand made to the Young Communists' League (*Komsomol*) in October 1923 by Nikolai Bukharin, then a leading member of the Communist Party's Central Committee: "We must direct our efforts now . . . toward creating in the shortest possible time a definite number of qualified, especially disciplined, living labor machines readily available to be put into general circulation."[128] The continuation of state funding until the late 1930s testified to an enduring state and party belief that these "living labor machines" could be, and were being, generated by TsIT. Bukharin's statement, viewed in context, moreover indicated a belief in the possibility of permanent, inheritable evolutionary change generated by this process, implying a close compatibility of Gastev's vision with Bolshevik engagement with "Darwinian" evolutionary ideas.

The shared notion of the proletarian New Person as an engineerable, indefatigable, "human machine," as I have argued, had a pedigree traceable from Darwin's ambivalence to Lamarck, through Lamarckian-style versions of "Darwinism" favored by both the Bolsheviks and the pre-revolutionary Russian Darwinists, to convergence with Engels' "revision" of the Malthusian aspect of Darwin's notion of evolutionary "struggle for existence" in relation to human society. These strands of thought variously contained emphases on organisms as physiochemical mechanisms, the evolutionary process as largely based on the inheritable effects of environment and habit, and, from Engels, the idea that social and human evolution depended on control over nature, technologization, and increased industrial productivity at the level of the individual worker. Further reinforced by the similarly "Darwinist" theories of behavioral psychologists Bekhterev and Pavlov on "conditioning" as the potential means to inheritable change, these threads were interwoven in the writings of Chernyshevskii and Bogdanov to form the basis for the Bolshevik evolutionary ideal of the mechanized, proletarian New Person propagated by *Proletkul't* after 1917.

This pedigree of "Darwinist" ideas about the evolution of the New Person, I have suggested, was held by Gastev in common not only with some of the Bolshevik leadership, but also with other members of the "leftist" avant-garde—Malevich, Ermolaeva, Lissitzskii, Krinskii, and Meierkhol'd—who were similarly inclined to become artist-engineers, putting art in the service of producing the New Person's body, no matter how wild the extrapolations. While Gastev seemingly shared with them a belief in Cubo-Futurism as the starting point for revolutionary graphic art, a major factor that distinguished Gastev's main visualizations of the evolutionary ideal from theirs, and arguably afforded his "art project" more contemporary significance, was the manner of his engagement with Taylorism.[129]

Taylorism or "scientific management," I have argued, was effectively projected by the party and state as the approved method of "conditioning" within the process of engineering the evolution of the New Person, answering to the emphasis of Engels' "revision" of Darwin, on increased productivity by appropriation of modern capitalist technologies and methods as a means to evade the Malthusian population problem. Both Krinskii and Meierkhol'd engaged with this final element of the apparently desired Bolshevik evolutionary formula. Meierkhol'd, like Gastev, produced photographic visualizations of the process that, by the commonly assumed nature of photography, appeared to offer "realistic" and thus "truthful" representations of the necessary and desired process, and indications that the process was already under way. Only Gastev's photographic visualizations, however, seem to have responded, in their entirety, to the implied practical, "Darwinist," Bolshevik ideal. They were not art-centred, as were the images and imaginings of Malevich and the Suprematists, or indeed those of Meierkhol'd, but rather, they were representations of an attempt at a seriously utilitarian creative project that was to have a broad impact on Soviet culture. What Gastev's visualizations of the New Person offered in the mid to late 1920s, was the ultimate representation, in the most practical, "scientific," empirical, and therefore ideologically acceptable form, of the evolutionary, Taylorized, conditioned, docile laboring body.

NOTES

1. G. Dokhman-Garmiza, *Chal'a Darvin v klubakh RKSM*, Politprosveta TsKRKSM (Moscow: Krasnaia nov, 1923; Moscow and Leningrad: Krasnaia nov, 1925).

2. Ludmilla J. Jordanova, *Lamarck* (Oxford: Oxford University Press, 1984), 103.

3. Ibid., 86, 104–105, 107.

4. Karl Marx, Letter to Ferdinand Lassalle in Berlin, London, 16 January 1861, in *Marx and Engels: Selected Correspondence 1844–1895*, ed. S. W. Ryazanskaya, trans. I. Lasker, (Moscow: Progress Publishers, 1975), 115; Friedrich Engels, Letter to Pyotr Lavrovich Lavrov in London, London, 12–17 November 1875, in ibid., 283; Friedrich Engels, "Ludwig Feuerbach and the End of Classical German Philosophy" (1888), in *Karl Marx and Friedrich Engels: Basic Writings on Politics and Philosophy*, ed. Louis S. Feuer (London: Fontana, 1969), 254, 268–69.

5. Jordanova, *Lamarck*, 107; Charles R. Darwin, *On the Origin of Species by Means of Natural Selection, or the Preservation of Favoured Races in the Struggle for Life* (London: John Murray, 1859), 427; Darwin, *Origin of Species* (London: John Murray, 1860), 246; Darwin, *Origin of Species* (London: John Murray, 1861), xiii, 458; Darwin, *Origin of Species* (London: John Murray, 1866), xiii, 502; Darwin, *Origin of Species* (London: John Murray, 1869), xiii, 505; Darwin, *Origin of Species* (London: John Murray, 1872), xii, 373; Darwin, "On the Tendency of Species to Form Varieties; and On the Perpetuation of Species by Natural Means of Selection," *Journal of the Proceedings of the Linnaean Society, London. Zoology* 3 (1858): 46–50; Darwin, *Journal of Researches into the Natural History and Geology of Countries Visited During the Voyage of H.M.S. Beagle Round the World* (London: John Murray, 1845, 1860), 52; Darwin, *Voyage of the Beagle* (London: John Murray, 1890), 53.

6. Michael Ruse, *Darwinism Defended: A Guide to the Evolution Controversies* (Menlo Park, Calif.: Benjamin/Cummings Publishing, 1982), 63, 143.

7. Darwin, *On the Origin of Species* (1859), 242; (1860), 242; (1861), xiv, 135, 265; (1866), xiv, 142, 289; (1869), xiv, 145, 296; (1872), xiv, 98.

8. Darwin, *On the Origin of Species* (1872), 130, 201, 443, 462–63.

9. Derek Freeman, "The Evolutionary Theories of Darwin and Herbert Spencer (and Comments and Replies)," *Current Anthropology* 15, no. 3 (September 1974): 211–37; Ernst Haeckel, "Charles Darwin as an Anthropologist," in *Darwin and Modern Science: Essays in Commemoration of the Centenary of the Birth of Charles Darwin and the Fiftieth Anniversary of the Publication of the Origin of Species*, ed. A. C. Seward (Cambridge: Cambridge University Press, 1909), 140.

10. Abba E. Gaissinovitch, "The Origins of Soviet Genetics and the Struggle with Lamarckism," trans Mark B. Adams, *Journal of the History of Biology* 13, no. 1 (1980): 1–51.

11. Theodosius Dobzhansky, "The Birth of the Genetic Theory of Evolution in the Soviet Union in the 1920s," in *The Evolutionary Synthesis: Perspectives on the Unification of Biology*, ed. Ernst Mayr and William B. Provine, 299–42 (Cambridge, Mass.: Harvard University Press, 1982).

12. Boris Gasparov, "Development or Rebuilding: Views of Academician T. D. Lysenko in the Context of the Late Avant-Garde," in *Laboratory of Dreams: The Russian Avant-Garde and Cultural Experiment*, ed. John E. Bowlt and Olga Matich, 146 (Stanford: Stanford University Press, 1996).

13. Richard W. Burkhardt, Jr., "Lamarckism in Britain and the United States," in *The Evolutionary Synthesis*, 82–89; Zhores Medvedev, *The Rise and Fall of T. D. Lysenko*, trans. I. Michael Lerner (New York: Columbia University Press, 1969); Dominique Lecourt, *Proletarian Science: The Case of Lysenko*, trans. Ben Brewster (London: New Left Books, 1977).

14. Alexander Vucinich, *Darwin in Russian Thought* (Berkeley: University of California Press, 1988), 365, 368.

15. Ibid., 152.

16. Ibid., 51.

17. Darwin, *Origin of Species* (1872), xv; Darwin, *The Descent of Man and Selection in Relation to Sex*, 2 vols. (London: John Murray, 1871), vol. 1, 205; vol. 2, 45, 49.

18. M. M. Filippov, "Darvinizm," *Nauchnoe obozrenie* 33 (1894): 1043.

19. Vucinich, *Darwin in Russian Thought*, 6, 90, 158–62.

20. Dobzhansky, "Birth of the Genetic Theory," 230.

21. Kliment A. Timiriazev, trans. and ed., Charles Darvin, *Proiskhozhdenie vidov putem esestvennogo otbora* (St. Petersburg: O.N Popov, 1896); with introduction and corrections by Nikolai I. Bukharin (Moscow and Leningrad: Sel'khogiz, 1935); edited by Nikolai I. Vavilov (Moscow and Leningrad: Sel'khogiz, 1935): edited by Vavilov and Vladimir L. Komarov (Moscow and Leningrad: Sel'khogiz, 1937); with introduction by Timiriazev (Moscow: Sel'khogiz, 1952); Timiriazev, Mikhail A. Menzbir, P. A. Petrovskii, and Aleksey P Pavlov, trans. Darvin, *Proiskhozhdenie vidov putem esestvennogo otbora* (Moscow and Leningrad: Gosudarstvennoe izdatel'stvo, 1926); introduction by Komarov (Moscow and Leningrad: Sel'khogiz, 1937); with corrections and revisions by Aleksey D. Nekrasov and Samuil L. Sobol (Moscow: Akademiia nauk, 1939), reprinted, ed. Armen L. Takhtadzhian with further revisions by A. L. Zelikman, Ia. L. Gall, A. L. Takhtadzhian, and F. I Krichevskaia (St. Petersburg: Nauka, 1991); Ivan M. Sechenov (trans. and ed.), *Proiskhozhdenie cheloveka i podbor po otnosheniiu k polu*, 2 vols. (St. Petersburg: I.M. Cherkesov, 1871–1872, 2nd rev. ed. 1873; (Moscow and Leningrad: Gosudarstvennoe izdatel'stvo, 1927); corrected and revised by Nekrasov and I. M. Poliakov with introduction and notes by Ia. Ia. Roginskii and Nekrasov (Moscow: Akademiia nauk, 1953).

22. Vucinich, *Darwin in Russian Thought*, 51–52, 71, 199, 209, 214; Walter Kofler, "I. M. Sechnov and Scientific Self-Understanding for Medical Sciences," *Journal of the History of Neurosciences* 16, nos. 1–2 (2007): 30–41.

23. Vucinich, *Darwin in Russian Thought*, 205–207, 387; Daniel P. Todes, "Darwin's Malthusian Metaphor and Russian Evolutionary Thought," *Isis* 78, no. 4 (1987): 537–51.

24. Todes, "Darwin's Malthusian Metaphor," 542–43. This volume of essays was republished seven times before Timiriazev's death in 1920: Dobzhansky, "Birth of the Genetic Theory," 229.

25. Vladimir I. Lenin, "What 'Friends of the People' Are and How they Fight the Social Democrats (A Reply to Articles in *Russkoe Bogatstvo* Opposing the Marxists)" (1894), in Lenin, *Selected Works*, 12 vols. (London: Lawrence and Wishart, 1939), vol. 11, 421–22.

26. Karl Marx, *Capital*, trans. Eden Paul and Cedar Paul, 2 vols. (London and New York: Everyman Library, 1972), vol. 1, 359; Marx, Letter to Ferdinand Lassalle in Berlin, London, 16 January 1861, in *Marx and Engels: Selected Correspondence*, 115; Friedrich Engels, Letter to Pyotr Lavrovich Lavrov in London, 12–17 November 1875, in *Marx and Engels: Selected Correspondence*, 283; Engels, "Ludwig Feuerbach and the End of Classical German Philosophy" (1888), in *Karl Marx and Friedrich Engels: Basic Writings on Politics and Philosophy*, 254, 268–69.

27. Friedrich Engels, "Preface to the English Edition of 1888," in Karl Marx and Friedrich Engels, *Manifesto of the Communist Party* (1848) (Moscow: Progress, 1969), 21; Friedrich Engels,

"Socialism: Utopian and Scientific," reprinted from *Socialism: Utopian and Scientific (An arrangement of three chapters from "Anti-Duhring")*, trans. E. Aveling, London, 1892, in *Karl Marx and Friedrich Engels: Basic Writings on Politics and Philosophy*, 126. (Moscow: Progress, 1969).

28. David R. Oldroyd, *Darwinian Impacts: An Introduction to the Darwinian Revolution* (Milton Keynes: Open University Press, 1980), 67–68.

29. Darwin, *Origin of Species* (1872), 49.

30. Ruse, *Darwinism Defended*, 26; Darwin, *Origin of Species* (1872), 50–51. In the *Descent of Man*, Darwin went further toward acceptance of Malthus's theory—perhaps providing the reason why this work was not popularly published in the USSR after the mid-1920s. Darwin, *Descent of Man*, vol. 1, 131–35.

31. Marx called it "the natural history of capitalist production," Marx, letter to Engels in Manchester, London, 7 January 1851, in *Marx and Engels: Selected Correspondence*, 47; Marx, letter to Friedrich Engels in Manchester, London, 18 June 1862, in ibid., 120; Marx, letter to Ludwig Kugelmann in Hanover, London, 27 June 1870, in ibid., 225; Engels, letter to Friedrich Albert Lange in Duisburg, ibid., 161–62; Marx, *Capital*, vol. 1, 393; vol. 2, 574.

32. Engels, letter to Lange, 161–62.

33. Friedrich Engels, *Dialectics of Nature* (Moscow: Progress Publishers, 1954), 41.

34. Daniel Todes, *Darwin without Malthus: The Struggle for Existence in Russian Evolutionary Thought* (New York: Oxford University Press, 1989), 550.

35. Marx, *Capital*, vol. 1, 359, 392.

36. Engels, letter to Lange, 161–62.

37. Ibid.

38. Edward H. Carr, introduction to *What Is to Be Done? Tales about New People*, by Nikolay G. Chernyshevsky, trans. Benjamin R. Tucker, revised and abridged by Ludmilla B. Turkevich (1864; reprint, New York: Vintage, 1961), xii.

39. Staryi Transformist (pseudonym of Nikolay G. Chernyshevshii), "Proiskhozhdenie teorii blagotvornosti bor'by za zhizn," *Russkaia mysl'* 9, no. 2 (1888): 79–114; Georgi V. Plekhanov, *Selected Philosophical Works*, 5 vols. (Moscow: Progress Publishers, 1974–1981), vol. 4, 156; Chernyshevshii, "Letter of March 17, 1876," in *Polnoe sobranie sochineniia*, 16 vols. (Moscow: Khudozhestvennaie literatura, 1939–1953), vol. 14, 643; Jordanova, *Lamarck*, 71–72; Nils Roll Hansen, "A New Perspective on Lysenko," *Annals of Science* 42 (1985): 261–78.

40. Chernyshevsky, *What Is to Be Done*; Mike O'Mahoney, *Sport in the USSR: Physical Culture—Visual Culture* (London: Reaktion Books, 2006), 22.

41. Maksim Gorkii, *Ispoved'* (Berlin: J. Ladischnikow, 1908), 196; Gorkii, "Razrushenie lichnosti," *Ocherki filosofii kollectivizma* (St. Petersburg, 1909), reprinted in *Literature and Life: A Selection from the Writings of Maxim Gorky*, trans. Edith Bone (London: Hutchinson International Authors, 1946), 112–25; Anatohi V. Lunacharskii, *Religiia i sotsializm*, 2 vols. (St. Petersburg: Shipovnik, 1908–1911); Lunacharskii, "Pered litsom roka: k filosofii tragedii," *Obrazovanie* 12 (1903): 58; Lunacharskii, "Faust and the City," in *Three Plays*, trans. Leonard A. Magnus and K. Walter (London: G. Routledge, 1923), 132, 134; Aleksandr A. Bogdanov, *Krasnaiia zvezda* (St. Petersburg: Tovarichestvo khudozhestvennyi pechati, 1908); Bogdanov, *Inzhener menni* (Moscow: Moskovskii rabochii, 1923); Bogdanov, *Vseobshchaia organizatsionnaia nauka (tektologia)* (Berlin: Grzebina, 1922).

42. Bogdanov was the revolutionary pseudonym of Aleksandr Aleksandrovich Malinovskii (1873–1928). Lecourt, *Proletarian Science*, 139.

43. Aleksandr A. Bogdanov, "predislovie" [Preface] to *Gete: bor'baza realisticheskoi mirovozzrenie*, by Vladimir O. Likhtenshtadt (St. Petersburg: np, 1920), v.

44. Vucinich, *Darwin in Russian Thought*, 159, 162.

45. Bogdanov, *Iz psikhologii obshchestva*, 2nd ed. (St. Petersburg: Pallada, 1906), 55–56; Mark B. Adams, "'Red Star': Another Look at Aleksandr Bogdanov," *Slavic Review* 48, no. 1 (Spring 1989): 1–15.

46. Todes, *Darwin without Malthus*, 118; see also *Pamiati Darvina. Sbornik statei* (Moscow: Nauchnoe slovo, 1910), a Darwin memorial anthology that included essays by Pavlov, Timiriazev, Menzbir, and Kovalevskii. Indeed, Pavlov's ideas were popularized and afforded an extra level of popular truth-value in 1926 by Pudovkin's documentary-style film, *The Mechanics of the Brain: The Behavior of Animals and Man*, Leningrad 1926.

47. Todes, *Darwin without Malthus*, 118; Marina Akimenko, "Vladimir Mikhailovich Bekhterev," *Journal of the History of Neurosciences* 16, nos. 1–2 (2007): 100–109; Michael Shterenshis and Michael Vaiman, "European Influence on Russian Neurology in the Eighteenth and Nineteenth Centuries," *Journal of the History of Neurosciences* 16, nos. 1–2 (2007): 6–18.

48. Vladimir Samoilov, "Ivan Petrovich Pavlov," *Journal of the History of Neurosciences* 16, nos. 1–2 (2007): 74–79; Anatoh I. Grigoriev and N. A. Grigorian, "I. M. Sechenov: The Patriarch of Russian Physiology," ibid.: 19–24; Ernest W. MacBride, *An Introduction to the Study of Heredity* (London: Williams and Norgate, 1924), 107–108; Ivan P. Pavlov, *Conditioned Reflexes: An Investigation of the Physiological Activity of the Cerebral Cortexes* (New York: Dover, 1960), 285; Oldroyd, *Darwinian Impacts*, 176.

49. David Joravsky, "The Stalinist Marriage of Pavlov to Marx," *Theory and Society* 4, no. 4 (Winter 1977): 457–77.

50. See, for example, Aleksandr Bogdanov, "The Proletarian and Art 1918," translation of "Proletariat i iskusstvo," *Proletarskaia kul'tura* 5 (1918): 32, and "The Paths of Proletarian Creation 1920," translation of "Puti proletarskogo tvorchestva," *Proletarskaia kul'tura* 15–16 (1920): 50–52, reprinted in *Russian Art of the Avant Garde: Theory and Criticism*, ed. John E. Bowlt, 176–82 (London: Thames and Hudson, 1988).

51. Sheila Fitzpatrick, *Education and Social Mobility in the Soviet Union 1917–1934* (Cambridge: Cambridge University Press, 2002), 9.

52. "O proletkul'takh," *Pravda* 270 (1 December 1920), cited by Christina Lodder, *Russian Constructivism* (New Haven: Yale University Press, 1983), 75, n. 9; Robert C. Williams, "Collective Immortality: The Syndicalist Origins of Proletarian Culture 1905–1910," *Slavic Review* 39, no. 3 (1980): 389–402.

53. James H. Billington, *The Icon and the Axe: An Interpretative History of Russian Culture* (New York: Vintage, 1970), 490; Igor Golomstock, *Totalitarian Art in the Soviet Union, the Third Reich, Fascist Italy and the People's Republic of China* (London: Collins Harvill, 1990), 27.

54. Vladimir M. Friche, "V poshkakh novoi krasoty," *Tvorchestvo* 1–2 (1918): 5.

55. Sergei Tretiakov, *LEF* 1 (1923): 201, cited in Golomstock, *Totalitarian Art*, 26, 28.

56. Dziga Vertov, "We—Manifesto on the Disarmament of the Theatrical Cinematography," *Kinofot* 1 (1922), trans. in *Art and Revolution*, exh. cat. (London: Hayward Gallery, 1971), 96.

57. Leon Trotsky, *Literature and Revolution* (1924), trans. Rose Strunsky (Ann Arbor: University of Michigan Press, 1968), 134, 135, 136, 145, 194–95, 199, 246.

58. Ibid., 15.

59. UNOVIS (*Utverditeli novogo iskusstva*) translates as "Affirmers of the New Art." Larissa Zhadova, *Malevich: Suprematism and Revolution in Russian Art 1910–1930*, trans. Alexander Lieven (London: Thames and Hudson, 1982), 308.

60. The Russian word *silach'* used by Malevich—usually translated as "athlete," hence the Russian title of figure 9.1—translates literally as "strong man." Vladimir Markov, *Russian Futurism: A History* (London: Macgibbon and Kee Ltd., 1969), 27, 144.

61. Ibid., 142; Stephanie Barron and Maurice Tuchman, eds., *The Avant-Garde in Russia, 1910–1930: New Perspectives* (Los Angeles: Los Angeles County Museum of Art, 1980), 146.

62. Incorporated into a portfolio offered for sale in Hanover in 1923. Lodder, *Russian Constructivism*, 250.

63. John E. Bowlt, "Body Beautiful: The Artistic Search for the Perfect Physique," in *Laboratory of Dreams: The Russian Avant-Garde and Cultural Experiment*, ed. Bowlt and Olga Matich, 37–58 (Stanford, Calif.: Stanford University Press, 1999); Isabel Wünsche, "Organic Symbiosis versus Natural Selection: How Lamarck Informed Mikhail Matiushin's Concept of Organic Culture," paper presented at the Society for Literature, Science and the Arts conference, *Evolution, Biological, Cultural and Cosmic*, New York, 9–12 November 2006. See also Charlotte Douglas, "Evolution and the Biological Metaphor in Modern Russian Art," *Art Journal* 44, no. 2 (Summer 1984): 153–61.

64. Bowlt, "Body Beautiful," 57.

65. Ibid., 49.

66. John E. Bowlt, "Pavel Filonov: His Painting and His Theory," *Russian Review* 34, no. 3 (July 1975): 290; Irene Masin-Delic, "The Transfiguration of Cannibals: Fedorov and the Avant-Garde," in *Laboratory of Dreams*, 21, 26–27.

67. Kasimir Malevich, "Suprematism: 34 Drawings," UNOVIS, 15 December 1920, reprinted in Zhadova, *Malevich*, 285.

68. Ibid., 285–286.

69. For a different interpretation, see Bowlt, "Body Beautiful," 49.

70. ASNOVA (*Assotsiatsiia novykh arkhitektorov*) was the acronym for Association of New Architects. Mikhail Matiushin, *Zakonomernost' izmeniaemosti tsvetovykh sochetanni—spravochnik po tsevtu* (Moscow and Leningrad, 1932), cited by Wünsche, "Organic Symbiosis versus Natural Selection"; Lodder, *Russian Constructivism*, 250; Zhadova, *Malevich*, 93; Mauro F. Guillen, "Scientific Management's Lost Aesthetic: Architecture, Organization and the Taylorized Beauty of the Mechanical," *Administrative Science Quarterly* (December 1977): 7.

71. GINKhUK (*Gosudarstvennyi institut khudozhestvennoi kul'tury*) was the State Institute of Artistic Culture, Petrograd. VKhUTEMAS (*Vysshie gosudarstvennye khudozhestvenno-tekhnicheskie masterskie*) was the acronym for the Higher State Artistic and Technical Workshops established in 1920. In 1928, the name was changed to VKhUTEIN (*Vysshii gosudarstvennyi khudozhestvenno-tekhnicheskii institut*), or Higher State Artistic and Technical Institute. Zhadova, *Malevich*, 94, 318, 320; Guillen, "Scientific Management's Lost Aesthetic," 693, 697–98. See also Margarethe Vohringer, "Avantgarde und Psychotechnik. Wissenschaft,

Kunst und Technik der Wahrnehmungsexperimente im postrevolutionärem Rußland" (Ph.D. thesis, Humbolt-Universität zu Berlin, Germany, February 2006).

72. Fülöp Miller's extensive caption reads: "In the top left-hand corner the old 'nichevo' Russia is symbolically struck out: below is the new Russia of mechanized activism (the "Time League" etc.). Below that is present-day Moscow: the old idyllic house with its dove-cot cheek by jowl with the skyscraper. On the right are views of the old orthodox churches transformed to meet modern needs; church towers as antennae. In the interior of a former church is an engineering shop." René Fülöp Miller, *The Mind and Face of Bolshevism* (London: G.P. Putnam's Sons, 1927), 218.

73. NOT stands for Scientific Organization of Labor (*Nauchnaia organizatsiia truda*). Vladimir I. Lenin, "Ocherednye zadachi sovetskoi vlasti" (1918), in *Sochinenia*, 4th ed., 39 vols. (Moscow: Gosudarstvennoe izdatel'stvo politicheskoi literatury, 1941–1957), vol. 29, 1948, 220–30; V. D. Banasiukevich, "V. I. Lenin I nauchnaia organizatsia truda," *Istoria SSSR* 2 (1965): 108; Kendal Bailles, "Aleksei Gastev and the Soviet Controversy over Taylorism," *Soviet Studies* 29, no. 3 (July 1977): 383.

74. Vladimir I. Lenin, "Nauchnaia' sistema vyzhimaniia pota," *Pravda* 60 (13 March 1913), reprinted in *Polnoe sobranie sochinenii*, 55 vols. (Moscow: Gosudarstvennoe izdatel'stvo politicheskoi literatury, 1958–1965), vol. 23, 1961, 18–19; Lenin, "Sistema Teilora—poraboshchenie cheloveka mashinoi," *Put' pravdy* 35 (13 March 1914), in ibid., vol. 24, 369–71; Aleksandr A. Bogdanov, *Mezhdu chelovekom i mashinoi (o sisteme Teilora)* (St. Petersburg: Priboi, 1913).

75. Daniel A. Wren and Arthur G. Bedeian, "The Taylorization of Lenin: Rhetoric or Reality?" *International Journal of Social Economics* 31, no. 3 (2004): 287–99.

76. Alec Nove, *An Economic History of the USSR, 1917–1991*, 3rd ed. (London: Penguin, 1992), 84. See also Steve Weinberg, *Armand Hammer: The Untold Story* (London: Ebury Press, 1989), 41–83.

77. Nove, *An Economic History of the USSR*, 141–46, 188–225.

78. Goeffrey Hosking, *A History of the Soviet Union, 1917–1991* (London: Fontana Press, 1992), 170.

79. O'Mahony, *Sport in the USSR*; Simpson, "Bolshevism and 'Sexual Revolution': Visualising New Soviet Woman as the Eugenic Ideal, 1917–1932," in *Art, Sex and Eugenics: Corpus Delecti*, ed. Fae Brauer and Anthea Callen, 209–38 (Aldershot: Ashgate, 2008).

80. I. N. Shpil'rein, "Nauchnaia organizatsia truda," in *Obshchestvennye nauki SSSR, 1917–1927*, ed. V. P. Volgin et al. (Moscow: Rabotnik prosveshcheniia, 1928), 62.

81. "Bor'ba za vremiia," *Pravda*, 31 July 1923, 3; Zenovia A. Sorchov, "Soviet Taylorism Revisited," *Soviet Studies* 33, no. 2 (April 1981): 246–64.

82. Guillen, "Scientific Management's Lost Aesthetic," 11; Anatole Senkevich, Jr., "The Sources and Ideals of Constructivism in Soviet Architecture," in *Art into Life: Russian Constructivism 1914–1932*, ed. Richard Andrews and Milena Kalinskova, 169–211 (New York: Rizzoili, 1990); Anatole Kopp, *Constructivist Architecture in the USSR* (New York: St. Martins, 1985), 186.

83. Sorchov, "Soviet Taylorism Revisited," 255.

84. Edward Braun, *Meierhold on Theatre* (London: Methuen and Co. Ltd., 1969), 183.

85. Vsevolod Meierhold, "The Actor of the Future and Biomechanics: A report of Meier-

hold's lecture in the Little Hall of the Moscow Conservatoire, 12 June 1922," *Ermitazh* 6 (1922): 10–11, trans. in Braun, *Meierhold on Theatre*, 199.

86. Toby Clark, "The 'New Man's' Body: A Motif in Early Soviet Culture," in *Art of the Soviets: Painting, Sculpture, and Architecture in a One-Party State, 1917-1992*, ed. Matthew Cullerne Bown and Brandon Taylor, 39 (Manchester: Manchester University Press, 1993).

87. Vsevolod Meierhold, "The Actor of the Future and Biomechanics," 200.

88. John Berger, "Understanding a Photograph" (1974), reprinted in *Classic Essays on Photography*, ed. Alan Trachtenberg, 291–94 (New Haven: Yale University Press, 1980).

89. Jules Amar, *Le moteur humaine et les bases scientifiques du travail professionnel* (Paris: H. Dunod and E. Pinat, 1914).

90. Suren Lalvani, "Photography, Epistemology and the Body," *Cultural Studies* 7, no. 3 (October 1993): 442–65.

91. Braun, *Meierhold on Theatre*, 201–202; Bowlt, "Body Beautiful," 57.

92. Kurt Johansson, *Alexej Gastev: Proletarian Bard of the Machine Age* (Stockholm: Almquist and Wiksell International, 1983), n.p., cited by John Bowlt, "Body Beautiful," 57, n. 27; Bowlt, *Russian Art of the Avant-Garde*, 230, 307.

93. Wren and Bedeian, "The Taylorization of Lenin," 290.

94. Bailles, "Aleksei Gastev and the Soviet Controversy over Taylorism," 374, 380.

95. Ibid., 383.

96. Ibid., 374, 380.

97. There were, however, further debates over the appropriateness of TsIT's methods of training in the years 1928 to 1929. Fitzpatrick, *Education and Social Mobility*, 200, f. 98.

98. Edward H. Carr, *Socialism in One Country, 1924–1926*, 3 vols. (London: Macmillan, 1958), vol. 1, 409–11.

99. Alexej K. Gastev, "Vosstanie kul'tury," originally published in *Pravda* 122 3 June 1922; no. 128, 11 June 1922; and no. 1, 3 January 1923; then as a pamphlet (Kharkov 1923); and finally reprinted in *Poeziia rabochego udara* (Moscow: Sovetskii pisatel', 1964), 236. See Charles S. Maier, "Between Taylorism and Technocracy: European Ideologies and the Vision of Industrial Productivity in the 1920s," *Journal of Contemporary History* 5, no. 2 (1970): 27–61.

100. Nikolai I. Bukharin, *Pravda* 229 (11 October 1922), cited by Alexej K. Gastev, "Shatunovshchina kak metodika," *Krasnaia nov'* (January–February 1924): 237.

101. The earliest publication about their work appeared in *American Machinist* in 1913: Fred F. Colvin, "The Latest Development in Motion Study", *American Machinist* 38 (5 June 1913): 937–39. See also Frank B. Gilbreth, *Motion Study: A Method for Increasing the Efficiency of the Workman* (New York: Van Nostrand, 1911); Frank B. Gilbreth and Lillian M. Gilbreth, *Applied Motion Study: The Efficient Method to Industrial Preparedness* (New York: Sturgis and Walton, 1917). Alexej K. Gastev, "Kak izobretat," (1924, 1927), reprinted in Gastev, *Poeziia rabochego udara*, 273.

102. Anatolii V. Lunacharskii, "Novyi russkii chelovek," in *Idealizm i materialism* (Petrograd: Puti' k znanie, 1923), 146–51.

103. Alexej K. Gastev, *Trudovye ustanovki* (Moscow: Ekonomika, 1923), 189, 206.

104. Alexej K. Gastev, "O tendentsiakh proletarskoi kul'tury," *Proletarskaia kul'tura* 9–10 (1919): 43–45.

105. Frances L. Bernstein, "Panic, Potency and the Crisis of Nervousness in the 1920s," in *Everyday Life in Early Soviet Russia: Taking the Revolution Inside*, ed. Christina Kaier and Eric Naiman 161–62 (Bloomington: Indiana University Press, 2006).

106. Nilolai K. Kol'tsov, *Omolozhenie organizma po metodu Shteinakh* (St. Petersburg: Vremia, 1922); Aleksandr A. Bogdanov, *Bor'ba za zhiznosposobnost'*, Institut perelivaniia krovi (Moscow: Novaia moskva, 1927); Pat Simpson, "The New Person's Body: Drapery and Disclosure in Stalinist Monumental Sculpture," *Sculpture Journal* 15 (Spring 2006): 1–16; Yvonne Howell, "Eugenics, Rejuvenation, and Bulgakov's Journey into the Heart of Dogness," *Slavic Review* 65, no. 3 (Fall 2006): 544–62.

107. Lecourt, *Proletarian Science*, 139.

108. Gastev, *Trudovye ustanovki*, 69; Wren and Bedeian, "The Taylorization of Lenin", 290. For a detailed account of Amar's work, see Fae Brauer, "Representing '*Le Moteur humaine*': Chronometry, Chronophotography, 'The Art of Work' and the Taylored Body," *Visual Resources* 19, no. 2 (2003): 83–105.

109. Alexej K. Gastev, "Tsentral'nyi Institut Truda," *Revoliutsiia i kul'tura* 2 (1928): 68–69; Sorchov, "Soviet Taylorism Revisited," 255, 262–63.

110. Alexej K. Gastev, "V Tsentral'nom Institute Truda," *Vestnik truda* 1 (January 1924): 73–74.

111. Alexej K. Gastev, "Kak nado rabotat," *Organizatsiia truda* 1 (1921): 18–19; Gastev, *Trudovye ustanovki*, 4, 74–79; Golomstock, *Totalitarian Art*, 26.

112. Bailles, "Aleksei Gastev and the Soviet Controversy over Taylorism," 387.

113. Alexej K. Gastev, "Chto takoe NOT?" (1927), reprinted in *A. K. Gastev, Kak nado rabotat'*, ed. N. M. Bakhrakh, 160–61 (Moscow: Ekonomika, 1972).

114. Anthea Callen, "Man or Machine: Ideals of the Laboring Male Body and the Aesthetics of Industrial Production in Early Twentieth-Century Europe," in *Art, Sex and Eugenics*, 139–61.

115. Suren Lalvani, "Photography, Epistemology and the Body," *Cultural Studies* 7, no. 3 (October 1993): 442–65; Sharon Corwin, "Picturing Efficiency: Precisionism, Scientific Management and the Effacement of Labor," *Representations* 84 (Autumn 2003): 139–65.

116. Clark, "The 'New Man's' Body," 37.

117. The method was illustrated in Colvin, "The Latest Development in Motion Study," and further elaborated in Gilbreth and Gilbreth, *Applied Motion Study*.

118. Gastev, *Trudovye* ustanovki, 69; Jules Amar, *The Physiology of Industrial Organization and the Re-Employment of the Disabled*, trans. Bernard Miall (London: George Routledge and Sons, 1920); Matt Price, "Lives and Limbs," *Stanford Electronic Humanities Review* 5, Supplement: *The Cultural and Technological Incubations of Fascism* (17 December 1996); online at http://www.stanford.edu/group.SHR/5-supp/text/price.html.

119. Valentina Zaitseva, "National, Cultural and Gender Identity in the Russian Language," in *Gender and National Identity in Twentieth-Century Russian Culture*, ed. Helena Goscilio and Andrea Lanoux, 39–47 (DeKalb: Northern Illinois University Press, 2006).

120. Victoria Bonnell, *Iconography of Power: Soviet Political Posters under Lenin and Stalin* (Berkeley: University of California Press, 1997), 23–34, 76.

121. Sorchov, "Soviet Taylorism Revisited," 251.

122. I am indebted to Dr. Chris Dillon of the Open University for the technical interpretation of the equations.

123. Aleksandr A. Bogdanov, "O tendentsiakh proletarskoi kul'ture (Otvet A. Gastevu)," *Proletarskaia kul'tura* 11–12 (1919), reprinted in *O proletarskskoi kul'ture 1904–1924* (Moscow: Kniga, 1925), 324–26. Sorchov, "Soviet Taylorism Revisited," 261, n. 3; Daniel A. Wren, "Scientific Management in the USSR with Particular Reference to the Contribution of Walter N. Polakov," *Academy of Management Review* 5, no. 1 (January 1980): 2.

124. Moscow Group of Communists Actively Interested in Scientific Management, *Pravda,* 11 January 1923, cited in Bailles, "Aleksei Gastev and the Soviet Controversy over Taylorism," 387.

125. Lalvani, "Photography, Epistemology and the Body"; and Brauer, "Representing '*Le Moteur humaine.*'"

126. John Tagg, *The Burden of Representation: Essays on Photographies and Representations* (Amherst: University of Massachusetts Press, 1988), 11, 64, 99; Lalvani, "Photography, Epistemology and the Body."

127. Michel Foucault, *Discipline and Punish: The Birth of the Prison,* trans. Alan Sheridan (New York: Vintage, 1979), 135–69, 187.

128. Nikolai I. Bukharin, *Pravda,* 11 October 1923, cited in Gastev, "Shatunovshchina kak metodika," 53–64.

129. Richard Stites, *Revolutionary Dreams: Utopian Vision and Experimental Life in the Russian Revolution* (Oxford: Oxford University Press, 1991), 154.

CHAPTER 10

Emotional Fusion with the Animal Kingdom

Notes Toward a Natural History of Surrealism

GAVIN PARKINSON

Long presented by its participants and commentators alike as an urban phenomenon with a distinguished avant-garde lineage, Surrealism seems suited to its metropolitan identity. The Surrealists, we are told, revelled in the labyrinthine complexity of the modern city, discovering mystery and intrigue behind the seemingly banal and everyday. With good reason, they have been compared to that key figure of nineteenth-century modernity, the *flâneur*, of whom Baudelaire wrote, "The crowd is his element, as the air is that of birds and water of fishes. His passion and profession are to become one flesh with the crowd."[1] Bridging the avant-garde gap between Baudelaire's solitary wanderer and their own meanderings are the poems of Apollinaire, especially his ambivalent hymn to modern Paris, *Zone* (1912) and the collection of prose writings that comprises *Le Flâneur des deux rives* (1918); the collages of the Cubists, redolent of peeling billboard posters; and the evocative, "mythic" photographs of Paris by Eugène Atget and Brassaï.

Accounts of the daily life of Parisian Surrealism given by members of the group find a place among these "documents," recording meetings held in cafés, bars, studios, and at the unofficial headquarters of Surrealism, 42 Rue Fontaine, André Breton's *atelier*. The best-known of these chronicles, Louis Aragon's *Paris Peasant* (1926) and Breton's *Nadja* (1928), continue to haunt modern literary and cultural consciousness (figure 10.1). Apparently confirming the version of Surrealism that I have sketched here, the reputation of each of these classics of "high Surrealism," and, accordingly, their conception of the movement and its activities, has been consolidated over the last thirty years by the amazing popularity achieved by the writings of Surrealism's first historian, Walter Benjamin. Focussing on Breton's *Nadja* (though he was an avid reader of Aragon, too), Benjamin's 1929 essay "Surrealism: The Last Snapshot of the European Intelligentsia," has achieved heroic status among academic writers on

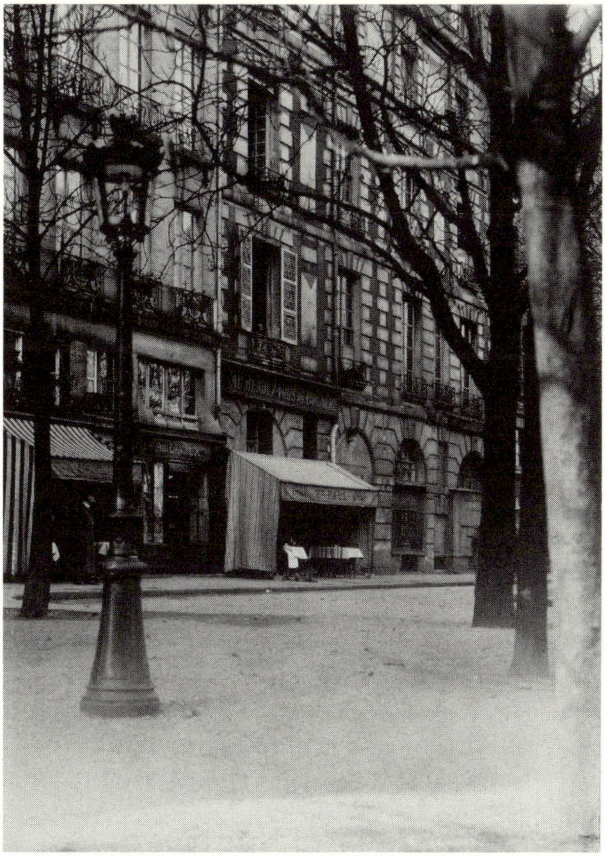

Figure 10.1 Jacques-André Boiffard, photograph from *Nadja* (1928). *Collection Lucien Treillard, Paris. Photo credit: CNAG/MNAM, Dist. RMN / © Georges Meguerditchian.*

the movement, along with its author.[2] There, Benjamin credits Breton with what he called "an extraordinary discovery": "[he] was the first to perceive the revolutionary energies that appear in the 'outmoded,'" Benjamin argued, "in the first iron constructions, the first factory buildings, the earliest photos, the objects that have begun to be extinct, grand pianos, the dresses of five years ago, fashionable restaurants when the vogue has begun to ebb from them."[3] Benjamin believed that Breton and Aragon had recognized that the revolutionary energy of the utopian dreams of the population had been siphoned off by capitalism, but that the quivering residue of that energy was still evident in and salvageable from the ephemeral, the marginal, and the discarded artifacts of capitalist consumer culture. Not surprisingly, Benjamin saw photography in Surrealism as a means of giving evidence of this. Subsequently, in pursuit of his version of Surrealism, scholars of the movement have focussed on the role it gave photography over the last quarter century, following Benjamin's Virgilean lead into the "'little universe'" of Paris, never to return.[4]

▪ ▪ ▪

Without taking issue on this occasion with the specific terms of Benjamin's argument, I want to outline three areas of *omission* that bring into question its reliability as a critical guide to Surrealism and that can help to begin the discussion of the complex roles of nature, Darwinism, and evolutionary theory within Surrealism: these can be expressed succinctly as content, date, and conflicting evidence.

At the time of writing his groundbreaking piece, Benjamin was beginning the "arcades project" (*Passagen-arbeit*), which used Paris's nineteenth-century glass arcades as the frame of reference for an ambitious Marxist analysis of the development of industrial capitalism, never to be completed. Inspired primarily by his intoxicated response to Aragon's description of the arcades in his "incomparable" book *Paris Peasant*, Benjamin characterized his 1929 reading of Surrealism as "an opaque folding screen standing before the arcades project."[5] However, Benjamin's enthusiasm for the remarkable passages of the first half of Aragon's book deflected his attention from its second half, titled ironically "Le Sentiment de la nature aux Buttes-Chaumont." There, Aragon transports his readers to the odd, artificial, nineteenth-century park of that name in the (still today) less-fashionable northeast of the city. Maintaining the book's detailed, historical commentary by observing the layout and features of the park as seen at night, Aragon's inspired descriptive powers are undiminished. Yet far from the brightly (or even dimly) lit enclosures of the ageing arcades or narrow city streets, the thematic foci of his narrative are transformed by the nocturnal silence and unpeopled, open spaces of the park. True, Breton's *Nadja* is set almost entirely in the streets of Paris, as are parts of the two other books by him open to Benjaminian readings, *Communicating Vessels* (1932) and *Mad Love* (1937). However, like *Paris Peasant*, the whole of the second half of *Mad Love* is set outside of the city, much of it taken up by Breton's rapturous response to the flora and fauna of Tenerife, host to the 1935 International Exhibition of Surrealism.[6] The distribution of city and nature in *Paris Peasant* and *Mad Love*, also gestured at in the title of the former and photographs of the latter, suggest that a *relationship* between the two spheres animated Surrealism's outlook. That relationship is not explored by those readings of Surrealism based on Benjamin's text because it was not an issue for Benjamin himself. Confirming a limited reading of the Surrealist books he admired, Benjamin's essay on Surrealism also reveals an ignorance to, or marginalization of the substantial corpus of Surrealist writings that had given a prominent role to motifs drawn from nature, since the first use of automatism ten years earlier in *The Magnetic Fields* (1920), co-authored by Breton and Philippe Soupault.[7]

If the selectivity of its contents limits its application as a guide to Surrealism, then in my view Benjamin's precocious 1929 text, celebrated as prescient by its many apologists, is further disadvantaged by its prematurity, and that is its second weakness. However debatable the exact date of Surrealism's demise, no commentator would claim that the movement had run its course by 1929. Surrealism was still young in that year, and from then on, in Breton's *Mad Love*, *Arcane 17* (1945), and *Martinique: Snake Charmer* (1948, co-authored with André Masson), as well as in his subsequent poetry, we observe an intensification of natural imagery. Furthermore, in the Surrealist-dominated journal *Minotaure* of the 1930s, natural forms proliferate, as they do in the poetry and short stories of Benjamin Péret and others. Paul Hammond has indicated a change in the direction of Surrealism—caused by the meltdown of its relationship with Communism—that postdates Benjamin's article, demonstrating that its enclosure within a Benjaminian urban paradigm is misleading:

> It was at this moment of maximum anger, frustration, fatigue, and despair over the possibility of revolution within the polarized *socius* that the Surrealists again gave primacy to the extracultural things of nature. The years 1933–1939 mark a turning point, a gradual coming to power of cognitive elements that, although present within Surrealism from the first, had remained in the background during its Freudo-Marxist high period. These tectonic shifts embraced a "theosophical" revisioning of nature, myth, and language linked to a cult of the Goddess, the displacement of historical materialism by Romantic *Naturphilosophie*, ideas of utopia prevailing over those of class struggle, anticapitalist epistemologies supplemented by precapitalist ones, a growing interest in anthropology and other peoples, the erosion of "local" interests and the attempts to internationalize the movement.[8]

While these adjustments in Surrealism's philosophy and politics, along with the expansion of its scope of influence, could not have been anticipated by Benjamin in 1929, they certainly should have been considered by those historians who have followed eagerly in his wake.

Surrealism, Psychoanalysis, Romanticism

However, while Hammond is surely right that new interests came to the fore in the mid-1930s, I would argue that "the extracultural things of nature" were never simply an afterthought within Surrealism. This is my third and main argument with Benjamin and his followers. For if Benjamin overstates the prominence of the city in Surrealism with reference to the writings of Breton and Aragon, then the visual arts within the movement, pre- and post-1929, emphatically make the case for a natural history of Surrealism.[9] Where Cubism, Expressionism, and especially Futurism offered a view of the culture of modernity and the modern city, not a single Surrealist painter consistently depicted urban spaces. This is true even of those artists—Yves Tanguy, René Magritte, Salvador Dalí, and Max Ernst—who explored the spaces inherited from Giorgio de Chirico, the one artist associated with the movement (albeit of a previous generation and never a member of the group) who extensively mapped a cityscape in his work. After early experiments with machine parts and de Chiricoesque architecture and mannequins, Ernst soon reverted to the forms of nature in his *Histoire naturelle* series of "frottages" (1925) and his forest paintings of the 1920s and 1930s; Tanguy's organicism and deep pictorial space are indebted chiefly to the landscape genre, pointing to the Brittany of his childhood; that supposed painter of the suburbs Magritte depicted domestic interiors and buildings only occasionally, preferring a universe of metamorphic bestiality that drew upon the Comte de Lautréamont's "Darwinian" epic *Les Chants de Maldoror*, presented in a partly defined natural environment well beyond the reach of any city; and the vast majority of Dalí's weird dramas are set on open plains or beaches, as recognizable from the window of his house at Port Lligat as Monet's water lilies are from the garden of Giverny.

Max Ernst is mentioned by Benjamin in his essay on Surrealism, then quickly passed over, yet his work sets a challenge to Benjamin's own assertion that "no face is surrealistic in the same degree as the true face of a city. No picture by de Chirico or Max Ernst can match the sharp elevations of the city's inner strongholds."[10] If the iconography and spaces that Ernst rendered were arrived at by way of Freud and de Chirico, then they were further modulated by the artist's taste for German Romanticism. A fascination with plant morphology handed down from Goethe informs many of his 1920–1921 works that first attracted the attention of the Surrealists, also making its impression on his *Histoire naturelle* series. The Romanticism of Caspar David Friedrich was a key source, too, for his "forest" paintings of the 1920s and 1930s, and Ernst even said "I've always had Friedrich's paintings and ideas more or less consciously in mind, almost from the day I started painting."[11] The esteem in which he held Friedrich was supplemented by his admiration for other German Old Masters inspired by the "forest tradition" of that country, such as Albrecht Altdörfer, Hans Baldung, Lucas Cranach the Elder, Albrecht Dürer, and Matthias Grünewald.[12] When Ernst *did* produce images of the city in the 1930s, as in the painting *The Entire City* (1935–1936, figure 10.2), he did not present the metropolis in a violent, apocalyptic way, or as the root of modern anxiety as did German Expressionists such as Ludwig Meidner and the Italian Futurists; rather, Ernst drew upon his knowledge of psychoanalysis (with which he had been familiar since at least 1913), and, specifically, Freud's own much-used "archaeology" metaphor, employed to illustrate the analyst's task of "unearthing" repressed memories from the unconscious. Depicting the city as a tiny proportion of the landscape, Ernst showed it resting upon layers of material in comparison to which it seems barely significant. In *The Entire City*, the city, the conscious mind, or ego, is the inhabited, man-made, "cultural" tip of a much greater whole, which is obviously the unconscious or id, here identified mainly with nature (yet not dissociable from "culture").

Freud's longest meditation on psychoanalysis as a kind of archaeology is given in his 1907 analysis of Wilhelm Jensen's book *Gradiva* (1903). In Jensen's slight tale of a young archaeologist whose encounter in Pompeii with his childhood sweetheart Zoe Bertgang releases repressed childhood desires and eases his obsession with a walking female figure seen in a relief in Rome, Freud saw mirrored the processes of psychoanalysis.[13] Both Jensen's story and Freud's exegesis were admired by the Surrealists, and they helped shape Ernst's "petrified" landscapes from 1939, created through the technique known as "decalcomania."[14] However, in the Surrealist imaginary, natural symbolism hewn from psychoanalysis was aligned with socio-political critique. Paintings such as *Europe after the Rain* (1940–1942) are monuments, then, to the revenge of the "irrational" powers of nature *and* the unruliness of unconscious desire described by Freud. Ernst and the Surrealists saw no separation between the two, expecting the first to swamp the rationally ordered spaces of the city, and the second to overwhelm the rationalizing processes of the conscious mind, as was currently happening in Europe. For similar reasons, the historical event of the destruction of the city of Pompeii by Vesuvius took on peculiar significance for Ernst and the Surrealists—as a symbolic burial of the bourgeois, Greco-Roman civilization they despised beneath the advance of nature. It manifested historically the statement in Horace's *Epistles*, which Freud had quoted and given a psychoanalytic inflection in his essay on Jensen's *Gradiva* and which was also known to Friedrich Nietzsche: "You may drive out Nature with a pitchfork, but she will always return."[15]

Elsewhere, using the same conceptual tools, Ernst extended his bank of natural imagery, linking it to notions of the "primitive" and the untamed wilderness. As readers of Freud, Ernst, and the Surrealists wished to prospect the unconscious like an unexplored continent, believing that "modern man" attained to so-called civilized behavior only through the repression of his de-

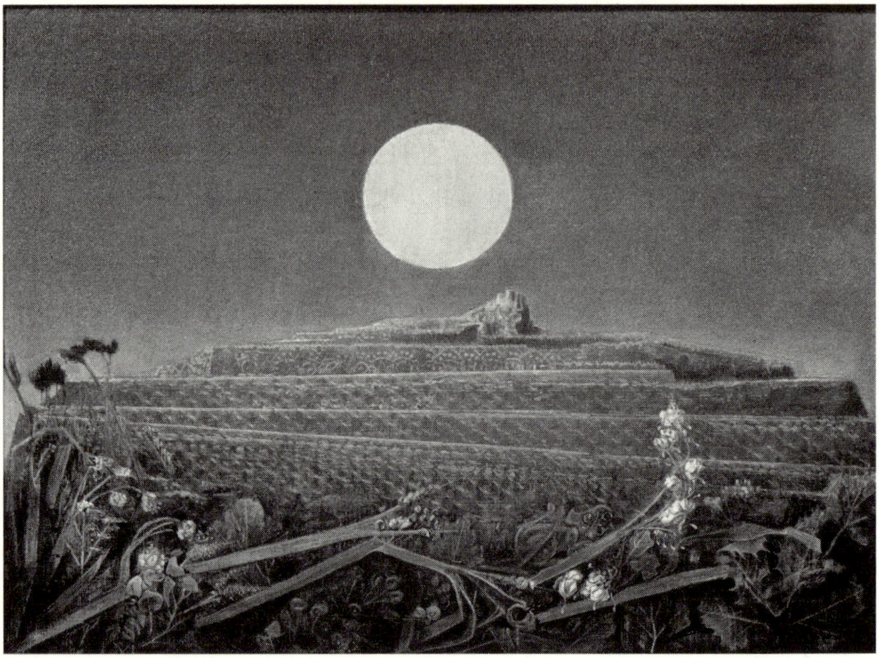

Figure 10.2 Max Ernst, *The Entire City* (1935–1936). *Kunsthaus, Zurich, Switzerland / © DACS / The Bridgeman Art Library.*

sire. With the avant-garde, the Surrealists idealized the tribal artisan, the insane person, and the child for what they saw as their refusal or inability to submit to Western-style rationalism. For the Surrealists, then, the jungle or wilderness, too, symbolized the bestial forces antithetical to the habits, customs, restrictions, and laws that characterized modern Western society. Canvases by Ernst of the 1930s like *La Joie de vivre* (1936, figure 10.3), containing semi-concealed insects and small creatures, point to the instinctual forces of desire allowed free rein outside of the organizing structures of the conscious mind. Breton himself made the same connection, confessing, uncharacteristically, to his ill-preparedness for one forest of symbols, writing of Henri Rousseau: "my investigations always pulled up sharply at the edge of Rousseau's jungle, for fear of getting lost in that inalienable adjunct of the unconscious."[16]

Darwinism, Nietzsche, Surrealism

It is fairly well known that during his early career as a research biologist, Freud subscribed totally to Darwin's ideas, and this helps to account for his

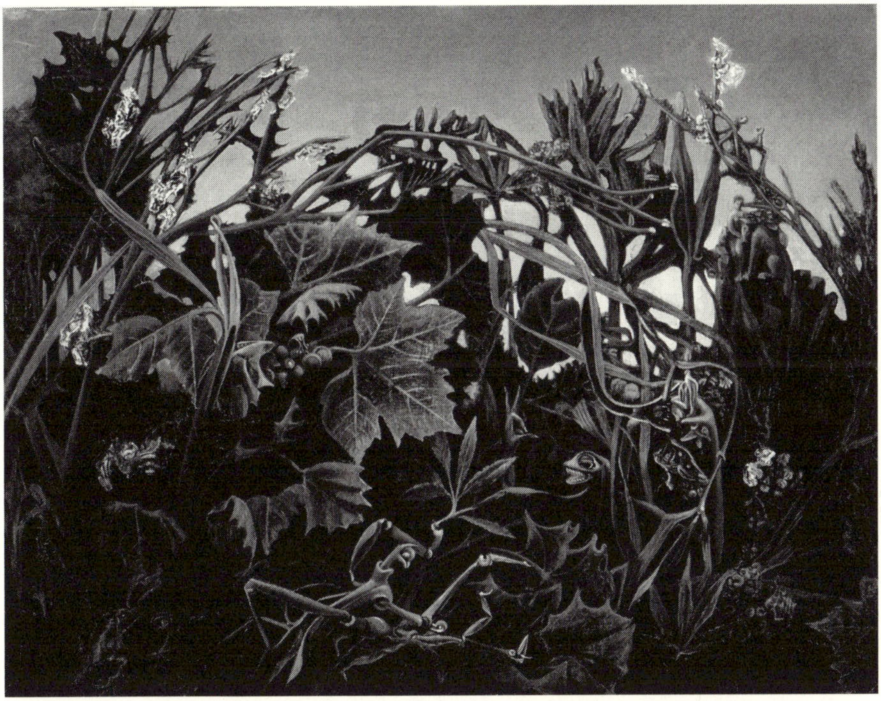

Figure 10.3 Max Ernst, *La Joie de vivre* (1936). *(oil on canvas), Scottish National Gallery of Modern Art, Edinburgh, UK / © DACS / The Bridgeman Art Library.*

use of biological analogies in his psychoanalytic writings.[17] But analogy, indispensable to psychoanalysis, has literary as well as scientific roots, as does psychoanalysis itself, allowing Frank Sulloway to argue that "the writings of the adherents of *Naturphilosophie* and Romantic medicine [anticipate] Freud's theories of dream interpretation, the unconscious, repression, the ego, the id, the superego as well as the concepts of eros and Thanatos."[18] In addition to this, it has been indicated that Goethe "played a dominant role in Freud's intellectual development," and that Goethe's work was credited by Darwin in *Origin of Species* as a forerunner of evolutionary theory.[19] Given the formative role of Darwinism, biology, and German Romanticism to Freud's thought, connections between these fields of knowledge were easily made by writers and artists steeped in psychoanalysis and associated with a 1930s Surrealism increasingly attuned to natural forces.

Forests, insects, plants, reptiles, monkeys, owls, and butterflies feature in articles and photographs carried between the covers of the Surrealist-dominated review *Minotaure* during its run of thirteen numbers from 1933 to 1939. The eclecticism of the contributions to *Minotaure* played a decisive role in the "demetropolitanization" of Surrealism, offering an important context for a discussion of Surrealism's natural history. Among these are the texts by disgruntled former Surrealist Roger Caillois on the praying mantis (subtitled "from biology to psychoanalysis") published in 1934 and the one on mimicry (in the "natural history" number of *Minotaure* that appeared under the subtitle "Le côté nocturne de la nature"), which have since gained a wide readership, partly because of their impact on the writings of Jacques Lacan.[20] Both of these articles came as further evidence of the Surrealists' tendency to anthropomorphize insects, and would be responsible for further visual imagery in that vein within the movement and on its margins.

In his essay on mimicry, Caillois meant to make observations about animal behavior that would be enlightening for theorists of human society. Dismissing the notion that insects mimic the appearance of one another in order to avoid being eaten by more powerful predators—since experiments had shown they were just as likely to be eaten as those in which the mimetic capacity had failed to evolve—Caillois argued that there was a kind of natural law that meant the organism becomes captured or "inanimated" by its environment. Undergoing a transformation, frequently in pursuit of sexual ends, in which it "abdicates that fundamentally vital difference between life and matter, between the organism and the inorganic," it is turned into a dead creature whilst still alive.[21] Caillois's rationale for the phenomenon of mimicry, then, provides a kind of analogy for the conflicting human drives toward life and procreation on the one hand, and death on the other, as theorized by Freud. Caillois footnotes the French translations of both Freud's *Interpretation of Dreams* (1899) and Darwin's *Descent of Man* (1871) in his praying mantis essay, and Alfred Russel Wallace's *Darwinism* (1889), Félix Le Dantec's *Lamarckiens et Darwiniens* (1899), and Yves Delage and Marie Goldsmith's *Théories de l'évolution* (1909) in the one on mimicry. Yet his writings on biology are symptomatic of the resistance to Darwin's theory of natural selection and the continued advocacy of the evolutionary theory of Darwin's distinguished predecessor, Jean Baptiste Lamarck, that were a feature of French science and culture at the end of the nineteenth century, had continued up to Caillois's own day, and might even be said to have carried on into ours.[22]

As a consequence of this, perhaps, it is an anti-Darwinism that characterizes Caillois's writings in those years, in the sense that both the praying mantis and mimicry essays argue for a non-utilitarian component in the behavior of insects that is *debilitating*, far from the *productive* mutability in response to external necessity that is the natural selection written of by Darwin in *Origin of Species*. Caillois continued in this vein up to and including his 1938 essay "The Function of Myth," when his approach is substantiated and complicated thanks to his discovery of Nietzsche and friendship with Georges Bataille.[23] There, Caillois extends his theory of the self-destructive instinct from the biological and social spheres to the mythic, arguing that the instinct toward a kind of self-sabotage in insects is mirrored in Nietzsche's writings by man's will toward orgiastic self-destruction, which Caillois sees projected onto the taboo-breaking hero of myth and played out by the participants in ritual. Close to Bataille at the time and active in the College of Sociology, Caillois's theory is indissociable from Bataille's notion of general economy, which describes an excessive outlay and waste without profit or return: "On the surface of the globe, for *living matter in general,* energy is always in excess."[24] Bataille's theory is itself explicitly indebted to Nietzsche's criticism of Darwin's idea of shortage and deficiency in nature when, according to Nietzsche, "in nature it is not conditions of distress that are *dominant* but overflow and squandering, even to the point of absurdity."[25] Accordingly, Caillois cites Nietzsche in opposition to Darwin when he says of the behavior of the heroes of mythology in "the Function of Myth," "this is a far cry from the all too renowned instinct of self-preservation."[26]

Darwin's remark in a letter of 1869 or 1870, "a week hardly passes without my hearing of some naturalist in Germany who supports my views," was made in the knowledge that the zoologist and Darwin acolyte Ernst Haeckel was loudly beating the drum of natural selection in Germany.[27] It is no surprise, then, to find that German-language speakers such as Freud and Nietzsche were close readers of Darwin and his followers, using his findings to their own ends.[28] Although Nietzsche counted Darwin among the "philosophical greats" and "authorities" of English intellectual life in a letter of 1877, and could write of Darwinism as "the last great scientific movement" as late as 1882 in *The Gay Science* (adding, "without Hegel there could have been no Darwin"), he was, in fact, critical of Darwin's theory, even complaining in later life that Darwin's diligence and exactitude were marks of intellectual mediocrity.[29]

Nietzsche's was not a straightforward rejection of Darwin. He drew heavily on the radical kernel of natural selection in the form of a nonconscious resource as the power and strength behind the organism's life force and behavior, but Nietzsche disagreed with Darwin over the balance between internal and external necessity, arguing "the influence of 'external conditions' is ridiculously *overestimated* by Darwin."[30] Nietzsche departs again from Darwin over Darwin's generalization of the behavior of organisms in nature, for Nietzsche did not accept that an account of species could give an accurate truth about the relations between a being and its environment, disagreeing with him in a familiar language: "Life is *not* the adaptation of internal needs to external ones," he insists, "but a will to power, which from the inside increasingly subjects and appropriates the 'external.'"[31] Nietzsche rejected what he viewed as the utilitarianism of Darwin's theory, which interpreted nature as *optimistically* holistic, balanced, and self-regulating, regarding instead this adaptation and reaction to external exigencies *pessimistically*, as promoting a levelling effect and producing mediocrity as the norm. Preservation as an outcome of natural selection did not appeal to Nietzsche so much as the self-destruction of the passionate individual through excess. Here we see the element of Nietzsche's anti-Darwinism that appealed to Caillois in "The Function of Myth," and which Caillois saw as making a neat-enough fit with his theses on the praying mantis and mimetic organisms, whose powers, he said, were not refined through their adaptation to and integration with their environment, but paralyzed by it.

A Surrealist context for Nietzsche has never been extensively plotted, because one of the curiosities about Surrealism's history, theory, and art is that for the most part they allow only a tangential relationship with the thought of Nietzsche. In spite of the congruence between Nietzsche's program of the "transvaluation of all values" and the "pure psychic automatism" espoused by the *Manifesto of Surrealism* of 1924—which identified the movement at its formation with a comparable agenda, demanding a form of expression free of aesthetic and moral concerns—Breton and those closest to him never included Nietzsche alongside the Marquis de Sade, the Comte de Lautréamont, Alfred Jarry, Arthur Rimbaud, and a handful of others in the pantheon of pre-Surrealists. Nietzsche is rarely mentioned in Breton's writings, and when he is it is usually the mad Nietzsche who makes an appearance.[32] Surrealism's interest in German thought generally—from Goethe and Hegel onward—makes Nietzsche's absence even more puzzling. Missing from the "core" theory of Surrealism, however, Nietzsche *is* made present in the art and writings of individual members of the Surrealist group and in that of others close to them. The art of André Masson offers a suitable case study.[33]

Darwinism and the Surrealist Image: André Masson

Together with the disaffected Caillois's rejection of Darwin in the pages of *Minotaure* and reception of Nietzsche in his writings of the late 1930s, Surrealism's abbreviated intellectual relationship with Nietzsche complicates any notion of a straightforward interpretation of Darwin in Surrealism, while making a Surrealist reading of Darwin through Nietzsche seem counterintuitive. It is further obscured by the "core" debates and imagery of Surrealism in the 1920s and 1930s. In its efforts to detach itself from alternative "modernisms" in the 1920s, Surrealism staked a contrary position to that of the Purism of Le Corbusier and Amedée Ozenfant that was determined in part by Darwinist trends. In the wake of the First World War, mainly between 1920 and 1925, the Purists peddled a post-Cubist, neo-Platonic philosophy that aimed to depict in painting a world beyond appearances, dwelling at excruciating length on a form-follows-function aesthetic. To their ultra-rationalist idea that modern bottles, wine glasses, plates, cars, and buildings, when compared with old ones, present an evolutionist economy of form in keeping with their function, Le Corbusier and Ozenfant attached the tag "mechanical selection."[34]

On several fronts, Surrealism opposed its "Romantic" theory to Purism's "neo-classicism," not least in its positing of the forces of the unconscious, dream, intoxication, and the irrational to Purism's adherence to reason, order, clarity, and utility; or in Nietzsche's terminology, in its promotion of Dionysian attributes in opposition to the Apollonian set of values promulgated by Purism. Surrealism also elevated nature—chaotic and unpredictable, alien and strange—in place of Purism's endorsement of the urban spaces of officialdom, administration, and organization, as can be seen in the contrast between André Masson's paintings and drawings of fishes fighting of 1926 and 1927, recalling the postwar rhetoric of social Darwinism, and Purism's cool scrutiny of desks, filing cabinets, and office materials a few years earlier in its journal *Esprit Nouveau*. This divergence is nowhere clearer than in the attack upon utility figured in the Surrealist theory of the poetic image, where the adjective so pointedly negates the object's purpose, simultaneously making it and rendering it useless, evident in Breton's at once Darwinian and unDarwinian "soluble fish," which is created and destroyed by its environment.[35] Contrast between Purism's "Darwinist" celebration of the evolution of the utilitarian object and Surrealism's negation of the object's use value is most plainly evinced in Surrealist objects of the 1930s such as Wolfgang Paalen's sponge umbrella titled *Articulated Cloud* (1938) and, more famously, Meret Oppenheim's *Fur Cup, Spoon, and Saucer* of 1936. In the metamorphosis they suggest—halfway between nature and culture—both burlesque the consumerist object, beloved of the Purists as the manifestation of capitalist "progress," which could be justified by means of a theory of Darwinian selection.

Indeed, if we view the Surrealist object as a form of hybridity—a blending, crossing, and clashing of species in the name of survival—and a subgroup of the conceptual collage that lay at the heart of Surrealism's image-making from its beginnings, then an ancestral connection between Surrealism and Darwinism is easy to make. Exemplifying the mechanism of the poetic image and extending its reach across the movement from its origins in *The Magnetic*

Fields by Breton and Soupault up to the Surrealist object in the 1930s was *Les Chants de Maldoror* (1869) by the Comte de Lautréamont (Isidore Ducasse, 1846–1870). Written in the context of the spread of Darwin's ideas throughout Europe, *Maldoror* is heavily populated by species of animals, humans, and plants furiously cross-fertilizing in a universe in which the kingdoms of man, God, and beast intermingle at war and in love. Although it bears no mention of Darwin's name or his theory, the book was conceived and written in the years following the first translation into French of *Origin of Species* (in 1862 by Clémence Royer, accompanied by a lengthy polemical preface, and republished with a new introduction in 1866) and during the subsequent scientific and philosophical debate in France. Darwin's thought did not make its way so easily into France as it had in Germany, in some quarters meeting with indifference if not outright hostility, which led Darwin to complain of "horrid unbelieving Frenchmen."[36] Born of French parents in Montevideo, the precocious Ducasse lived in Paris for most of the 1860s and, as shown by Anna Balakian, had more or less direct contact with the controversy over Darwinism from a very early age.[37]

In keeping with the universal mayhem conjured by Lautréamont, the art of Magritte aligns fable with a loose rendering of the rhetoric of "evolution" along the lines of the grotesque in paintings such as *Collective Invention* (1935). Magritte was among those Surrealist artists who illustrated a new edition of *Maldoror* in 1938, and his work can be taken as a starting point for an investigation of Surrealism's "speculative Darwinism," as can the strange paintings of "airplane swallowing gardens" by Max Ernst, odd biological concoctions of the 1930s bearing conceptual kinship with the Venus Flytrap, which, like the praying mantis was a favored organism in the Surrealist bestiary for its strange amalgamation of mythological and Freudian themes.[38]

However, the work of André Masson offers by far the best means of theorizing the reception of both Darwin and Nietzsche in Surrealism, as it demonstrates how their ideas could be loosely combined then directed along a path already cleared by Surrealism's interest in psychoanalysis and German Romanticism. More than any other artist associated with Surrealism, Masson sought to blend a diverse array of disciplines into a pictorial language founded upon motifs drawn from nature. From the time of his early pioneering experiments with automatism in 1924 that constitute his earliest contributions to Surrealism, Masson had regarded the natural world as a fund of images. Badly injured during the First World War, he had found the countryside more conducive to his health, and its roots and tendrils underpin and echo the lyrical, free-flowing line of his drawings, unifying its tangled iconography of fishes, birds, leaves, fruit, seeds, stones, and flames (figure 10.4).

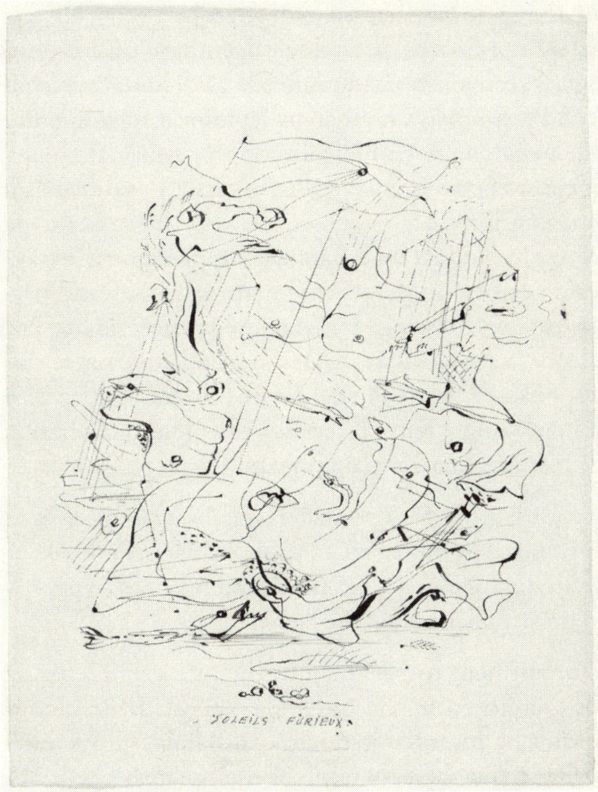

Figure 10.4 André Masson, *Furious Suns* (1925). *The Museum of Modern Art, New York. Pen and ink on paper, 16 ⁵⁄₈ × 12 ¹⁄₂ (42.2 × 3.7 cm.) Purchase. 257. 1935. © 2008. Digital image, The Museum of Modern Art, New York / Scala, Florence.*

After his break with Breton and Surrealism in the late 1920s, Masson entered into a close collaboration with Bataille, with whom he had been friendly since 1925, but his loss of day-to-day contact with the analogizing procedures of Breton and his friends led to a loss of licence in his art. The spontaneous methods that had released the freedom and lyricism of the drawings of 1923 to 1926 and his sand paintings of 1926 and 1927 fell out of favor, to be replaced by a more premeditated practice. The price was the inhibited, almost illustrative style evident in the repetitive *Massacres* drawings and paintings of the early 1930s and the imagery of the *Sacrifices* works of later in that decade, both of which were completed alongside Bataille's musings on the same themes during those years. Worse still are the bizarre insect paintings completed during his time in Spain (1934–1936) such as *Summer Divertissement* of 1934, surely linked to Caillois's *Minotaure* essays of the same period on the praying mantis and mimicry.[39] Masson escaped this ungainly literalism only after he had returned to the Surrealist fold in November 1936 following an exchange of letters with Breton from the spring of that year. Of Breton's poetry, Cauvin writes, "the very high incidence of botanical, zoological, entomological, ornithological, and ichthyological terms is striking indeed," and contact with it was vital to Masson's art.[40] Breton was an amateur lepidopterist and entomologist, and this knowledge, along with his collection of unusual stones, roots, bones, shells, feathers, and crystals, inspired Masson's art as much as it fed Breton's own poetic imagination.

His continued contact with Caillois and Bataille, supplemented by exchanges within the Surrealist milieu on poetry and nature, biology and psychoanalysis, provide a context for drawings by Masson of the mid- to late 1930s, such as his *Praying Mantis* (1940–1941). Masson blends this set of discursive currents in his response to the 1939 *enquête* in *Cahiers d'Art*, which asked, in the midst of an increasingly tense international situation, whether art could or should ignore historical and social upheavals:

> The sole justification for a work of art, for a poem, for a discovery in the field of biology or of psychoanalysis, is to contribute to the breadth of mankind's understanding, to the transmutation of social, moral, and religious hypocrisy, and consequently to the denunciation of the dominant class.[41]

Masson had touted his commitment to Marxism in the 1920s in a letter of September 1925 to Breton published in the fifth number of *La Révolution surréaliste*—an adherence that he recanted in a letter to Bataille in October 1935.[42] Having witnessed first hand the beginning of the Spanish Civil War and watched with horror as Europe lurched to the threshold of a new conflict, Masson now renewed his commitment to class war with his assessment in *Cahiers d'Art* of the revolutionary potential of diverse cultural fields. Probably embedded within this polemical statement is also an understanding of the interpretation of Darwinism by leading Marxist theorists such as Friedrich Engels and Karl Kautsky as constituting a revolutionary, emancipatory set of ideas.[43]

When Germany launched its air and ground assault on the Low Countries at dawn on 10 May 1940, Masson and his family were in Lyons-la-Forêt in Normandy where they had lived since December 1936. Like much of the population of northern France, the Massons fled south, reaching the village of Freluc in the Auvergne in June. The armistice of that month that divided the country into an occupied and a free zone left them just inside the latter. In Freluc, they stayed with Bataille who, in addition to being an old friend of Masson, was related to him through their wives, the Jewish Maklès sisters.[44] This group was soon joined by Jacques Lacan, who had known both Bataille and Masson since the early 1930s.[45]

It was during this period, when he and his family were only a step ahead of the German occupation forces, that Masson, short of painting materials, worked on many of the drawings that would be included in his book *Anatomy of My Universe* (1943).[46] He was still in Freluc when he wrote the book's prologue in October 1940. Published in English in an edition of 330 copies during the artist's subsequent wartime exile in New York, the book consists of thirty numbered, titled, and captioned drawings executed between 1936 and 1941. It has been described as Masson's *summa theologica*, a complete expression of his interests up to that time, and "an often brilliant and highly individual potpourri of ideas adopted from occultism, alchemy, astrology, Neo-Platonism, the Cabala, [and] Scholasticism."[47] More pertinently for my purposes, its pages swarm with insects, plants, and strange hybrids. Dedicated to Lacan and carrying quotations by Darwin, Herbert Spencer, Goethe, and others, it bears witness to Masson's immersion in the literatures of psychoanalysis, natural science, and *Naturphilosophie*.

In Masson's attempt to link these fields, analogy played an important part, as did the masters of analogical processes: Breton and Goethe. Masson introduces the images for *Anatomy of My Universe* with a passage from a conversation with Goethe reported by the French writer and critic Henri Blaze de Bury, where the great poet is described absent-mindedly drawing pictures of fantastic flora while simultaneously holding forth on the value of graphic expression:

> We talk too much, we should talk less and draw more. As for me, I should like to renounce the word and, like plastic nature, speak only in images. . . . In drawing, the soul recounts a part of its essential being and it is precisely the deepest secrets of creation, those which rest basically on drawing and sculpture, that the soul reveals in this way.[48]

Over the page, we encounter Masson's drawing titled *The Fraternity of the Natural Kingdoms*, comprising discrete forms relying on the intervention and operation of formal analogies to achieve its compositional coherence, which is linked by the artist to a quotation by Novalis: "The same signs occur everywhere." Novalis' ideal, identical signs "seen" in nature, parallel Goethe's professed preference for a visualized imagery over the spoken word.[49] Masson similarly conjured up and rendered analogous forms that had their source in nature and yet avoided slavish imitation. This was the feature of his art admired most by Breton, and the quotation in *Anatomy of My Universe* that attends another drawing, *Hatchings and Germinations* (figure 10.5), taken from Breton's recent text on the artist, "Prestige d'André Masson," demonstrates this: "the plastic metaphor in its pure state, I mean, untranslatable into words."[50] Although Breton used the word "metaphor," Masson's use of the

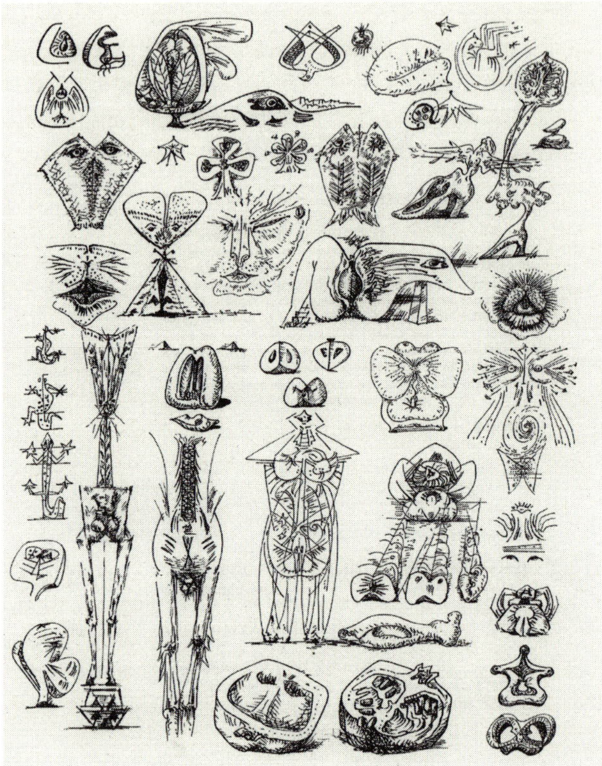

Figure 10.5 André Masson, *Hatchings and Germinations* (1938). *Present whereabouts unknown. Published in André Masson,* Anatomy of My Universe *(New York: Curt Valentin, 1943).*

word "analogy" in the title of the chapter of *Anatomy of My Universe* "The Demon of Analogy" suggests a preference for that term, because, as Dawn Ades has observed, "analogy" "could be better married to his conception of the moving flux of nature than could metaphor, a more static term."[51] If Masson's attraction to analogy and deployment of it in his work of this period was encouraged by his renewed contact with Breton, then it was certainly confirmed by Darwin, who offered a definition of "analogy" for biology in the glossary that he appended to the sixth edition of *Origin of Species* as "The resemblance of structures which depends upon similarity of function, as in the wings of insects and birds."[52]

Certain drawings in *Anatomy of My Universe,* such as *Loves of the Plants* and *Combat of Flowers,* are virtually illustrations of Goethe's anthropomorphic view of the lives, especially the sex lives, of plants. They are "Darwinian," too, in the sense of Erasmus as much as Charles, for *Loves of the Plants* is the title of the 1789 book by Charles's grandfather that gives an erotic account of plant life and behavior, as does Goethe's near-contemporary poem "The Metamorphosis of Plants," which takes the form of a botany lesson addressed to a loved one and acted as the inspiration for one of the series of Masson's Archimboldean "imaginary portraits" of Goethe of 1940, titled *Goethe and the Metamorphosis of Plants.*[53] There, as in his scientific treatise of the same name, Goethe drew analogies between the sexual lives of plants and humans, beginning and ending with allusions to the process of reproduction.[54] Accompanied by the caption "Emotional fusion with the animal kingdom," *Loves of the Plants* accordingly represents two figures, apparently male and female, formed from leaves, tendrils, seeds, fruit, and vines. Several seeds fall from the genital area of one of the figures, suggesting eroticism and procreation. But Masson's long-standing interest in Nietzschean violence is expressed in an accompanying image, *Combat of Flowers,* which, placed next to *Loves of the Plants,* represents harmony and disharmony in the plant world, where three more plant-beings fight, one of them wielding a knife. Captioned with a quotation by Heraclitus, "All things are in conflict," it gives further evidence of Masson's long-standing immersion in Nietzsche's writings, demonstrated in a contemporary letter to his dealer Daniel-Henry Kahnweiler of 4 May 1939, where he describes the "splendid pages on Heraclitus and Empedocles" in Nietzsche's discussion of the Presocratics in his *Philosophy in the Tragic Age of the Greeks,* translated into French the previous year.[55]

The most striking image of *Anatomy of My Universe* is *The Genius of the Species* (1939, figure 10.6), which bears the caption "Blason of the Darwinian epic. Totem of triumphant biology," and is a sophisticated example of Surrealism's "speculative Darwinism." A combination of the natural and the man-made in its suggestion of human, plant, insect, and ladder, *The Genius of the Species* is realized through the employment of realistic modelling and the addition of a more finished treatment than other works in the book. The spat-out seeds and human hands that threaten the fly suggest both Venus Flytrap and praying mantis. "This drawing," Masson writes in *Anatomy of My Universe,* "is the result of a deferent but still distant acquiescence in the definition of Spencer," before slightly misquoting Herbert Spencer from his 1864 *Principles of Biology,* "Life is the continual adjustment of internal to external relations."[56]

Yet this is the same Herbert Spencer who is pursued by Nietzsche throughout his writings for his scientific determinism and for his Lamarckian sponsorship of a liberal capitalist politics that insisted on the individual's freedom to adapt to economic and other circumstances. Spencer's conviction that one might adjust to one's social environment and pass on this information to one's progeny (that one might learn from experience and that economic success was available to everyone in a free market) was at one with the Lamarckian model of the inheritance of acquired characteristics—quite contrary to the

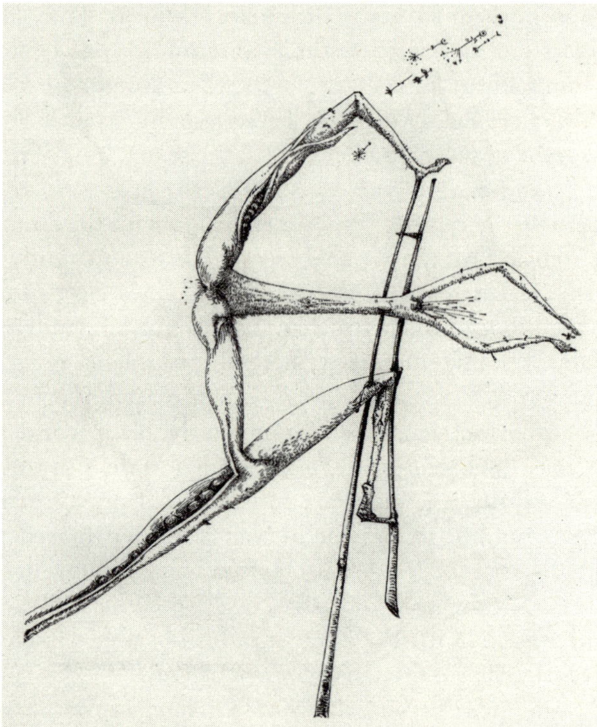

Figure 10.6 André Masson, *The Genius of the Species* (1939). *Present whereabouts unknown. Published in André Masson,* Anatomy of My Universe *(New York: Curt Valentin, 1943).*

strict Darwinist's view that an organism's unsuitability to its environment leads unwaveringly to its extinction, yet equally worthy of condemnation in Nietzsche's eyes for a morality of altruism over instinct that he believed would end in the subjugation of the strong to the weak and the annihilation of the human race.[57] Nietzsche's wholly negative attitude toward Spencer's evolutionary biology and social Lamarckism makes it sound at first as though Masson simply got his wires crossed again here by quoting Spencer in *Anatomy of My Universe* when that book is characterized by the very Nietzschean values that were formed through an antagonism toward both Spencerian and Darwinian evolutionary theory. Yet Masson certainly found this quotation from Spencer's *Principles of Biology* in the tirade against the English social philosopher that appears in Nietzsche's own 1887 *On the Genealogy of Morals,* which is only one of many diatribes aimed at him in Nietzsche's writings, but which Masson used approvingly in spite of his beloved Nietzsche's loathing of Spencerian "adjustment" or "adaptation."[58]

As we have seen, Nietzsche is present in *Anatomy of My Universe* as he is in much of Masson's work, yet we also saw Nietzsche reject the simplified

Darwinian notion of the adaptation of the organism to the environment. Equally, Masson was perfectly aware of Caillois's view on mimicry—he even referred obliquely to it years later in an interview in the 1950s—yet, as an artist essentially compiling his enthusiasms and influences, Masson was under no obligation to play the consistent theorist.[59] If *Anatomy of My Universe* is more of a compendium and assimilation of Masson's reading on biology and *Naturphilosophie* than a theory, then its inner conflicts are somehow appropriate given Surrealism's complex relationship with Darwinism as I have introduced it here (not to mention Masson's own troubled history with Surrealism), which is by no means so clear-cut as the movement's reception of the other great revolutions in thought of the modernist period, those of Marx and Freud, and should be viewed at greater length against the background of evolutionary theory in France and that country's turbulent reception of Darwin's writings and Darwinism.

Aiming to detach Masson from the Surrealists whom he saw as inveterate *citadins*, in 1958 the ex-Surrealist Georges Limbour chose the imprudent phrase "Nature et Surréalisme sont ennemis."[60] Maintaining that Surrealism was more or less Masson's Achilles heel, he went on to claim that Masson was "the non-Surrealist painter par excellence."[61] Blatantly fallacious and contradicted at every turn by Surrealism's art and poetry, Limbour's statement can only be partially explained by his own brutal expulsion from the Surrealist group by Breton thirty years before in the *Second Manifesto of Surrealism* (1929–1930) along with Masson. Another possible reason for Limbour's naïve remark is that his departure from the group in the year of Walter Benjamin's essay on Surrealism could have made him oblivious to the changes in Surrealism's relationship with the natural world in the 1930s. As he and others left in 1929, new artists and writers became attached to the group, inevitably changing its character. If the reassessment of Benjamin's interpretation of Surrealism might begin with an acknowledgment of Surrealism's debt to nature and an unpacking of its investment in Darwinism, then the extension of that discussion by means of a broader rethinking of the relationship between nature and the city in Surrealism constitutes the next, more complex task.[62]

NOTES

For their comments and guidance during the writing of this essay, I should like to thank Christopher Green, Julian Stallabrass, Sarah Wilson, Fae Brauer, and, in particular, Barbara Larson, whose suggestions and advice were invaluable.

1. Charles Baudelaire, *The Painter of Modern Life and Other Essays* (1863), trans. and ed. Jonathan Mayne (London: Phaidon, 1964), 1–41.

2. Walter Benjamin, "Surrealism: The Last Snapshot of the European Intelligentsia" (1929), in *One-Way Street and Other Writings*, trans. Edmund Jephcott and Kingsley Shorter (London: Verso, 1979), 225–39. The significance and position of Benjamin's writings generally are still difficult to judge due partly to the emotional reaction to their previous neglect and their author's deeply affecting suicide, which gave the early reception in English-language scholarship a eulogistic tone that is still present today: Hannah Arendt, "Introduction" (1968), in Walter Benjamin, *Illuminations*, trans. Harry Zorn (London: Pimlico, 1999), 7–58; Susan Sontag, "Introduction" (1979), in Benjamin, *One-Way Street*, 7–28; Terry Eagleton, *Walter Benjamin, or Towards a Revolutionary Criticism* (London: Verso, 1981). For an abbreviated history of Walterbenjamania in the context of Surrealism, see Margaret Cohen, *Profane Illumination: Walter Benjamin and the Paris of Surrealist Revolution* (Berkeley: University of California Press, 1993), 1–15. For more recent, similar refrains in the same hermeneutic groove, see Rebecca Solnit, "Paris, or Botanizing on the Asphalt," in *Wanderlust: A History of Walking* (London: Verso, 2001), 196–213; Johanna Malt, "Archaeology, Myth and the Commodity: Walter Benjamin and *Le Paysan de Paris*," *Journal of Romance Studies* 1, no. 2 (2001): 15–30; Ben Highmore, "Surrealism: The Marvellous in the Everyday," in *Everyday Life and Cultural Theory: An Introduction* (London: Routledge, 2002), 45–59. A recent publication retains while extending the familiar Benjaminian model of Surrealism as I have portrayed it here: See Michael Sheringham, *Everyday Life: Theories and Practices from Surrealism to the Present* (Oxford: Oxford University Press, 2006), 59–133. For a sceptical discussion of the Benjamin industry, see Peter Osborne, "Philosophizing Beyond Philosophy: Walter Benjamin Reviewed," *Radical Philosophy* 88 (March–April 1998): 28–37.

3. Benjamin, "Surrealism," 229.

4. Ibid., 231.

5. Ibid., 227; quoted in Cohen, *Profane Illumination*, 187.

6. "I regret," he writes, "having discovered so late these ultrasensitive parts of the earth." André Breton, *Mad Love* (1937), trans. Mary Ann Caws (Lincoln: University of Nebraska Press, 1987), 73. For an account of Darwin's passionate, failed attempts to arrange an expedition to the "scientific paradise" of Tenerife in 1831, see Janet Browne, *Charles Darwin: Voyaging* (London: Jonathan Cape, 1995), 134–36.

7. Benjamin's dialectical argument concerning the urban space, distilled in his view of the *flâneur* as one "who goes botanizing on the asphalt," is not carried into his essay on Surrealism to meet the structure of Aragon's *Paris Peasant*. Benjamin, *Charles Baudelaire: A Lyric Poet in the Era of High Capitalism*, trans. Harry Zohn (London: Verso, 1992), 36.

8. Paul Hammond, *Constellations of Miró, Breton* (San Francisco: City Lights, 2000), 92–93.

9. First published in four parts in the literary review *Literarische Welt*, Benjamin's essay was concerned chiefly with Surrealism's writings, and when he gives "the most important names at once," they are, naturally, all those of (French) writers. Benjamin, "Surrealism," 225. Some scholarship bucking the Benjaminian trend has given attention to the Surrealists' interest in natural forms, mainly in the linked contexts of collecting and the *Wunderkammer*, which relates Surrealism to postmodernist taxonomies. See, for instance, Patrick Mauriès, *Cabinets of*

Curiosities (London: Thames & Hudson, 2002), 214–24. Also see references to Surrealism and the landscape in Romy Golan, *Modernity and Nostalgia: Art and Politics in France between the Wars* (New Haven: Yale University Press, 1995).

10. Benjamin, "Surrealism," 230.

11. Quoted in Karin von Maur, "Max Ernst and Romanticism: Between the Lyrical Celebration of Nature and the Aesthetics of Horror," in *Max Ernst: A Retrospective* (London: Tate Gallery, 1991), 341–50.

12. Ernst included all of these artists except Dürer in a double-page, "typographical collage" titled "Max Ernst's Favourite Poets/Painters of the Past," *View* 2, no. 1 (April 1942): 14–15. To my knowledge, the published scholarship on Ernst has never fully discussed his forest paintings in this context.

13. Sigmund Freud, "Dreams and Delusions in Jensen's *Gradiva*" (1907), reprinted in *Art and Literature*, Penguin Freud Library, vol. 14 (Harmondsworth: Penguin, 1990), 27–118.

14. Invented in 1936 by Oscar Domínguez, in decalcomania, gouache or oil paint is placed on a sheet of paper or on canvas, then another sheet of paper or piece of glass is pressed on top of this, slowly peeled away, reapplied, and peeled away until the paint is almost dry. The outcome is a furry, textured surface, often of enticing forms that can be worked into more recognizable motifs by the artist.

15. "Naturam expelles furca, tamen usque recurret," quoted in Freud, "Dreams and Delusions in Jensen's *Gradiva*," 60. Noted in the context of remarks about the stubborn recurrence of ancestral "plebeianism" by Nietzsche, *Beyond Good and Evil* (1886), trans. Helen Zimmern (Buffalo, N.Y.: Prometheus Books, 1989), 240. See Horace, *Epistles*, Book I (Cambridge: Cambridge University Press, 1994), 69.

16. André Breton, "Henri Rousseau A Sculptor?" (1961), reprinted in *Surrealism and Painting*, trans. Simon Watson Taylor (New York: Icon Editions, 1972), 369. I am referring to Breton's well-known Baudelairean statement, "Interpretive delirium begins only when man, ill-prepared, is taken by a sudden fear in the forest of symbols." Breton, *Mad Love*, 15.

17. Lucille B. Ritvo, *Darwin's Influence on Freud: A Tale of Two Sciences* (New Haven: Yale University Press, 1990), 42–43.

18. Frank. J. Sulloway, *Freud, Biologist of the Mind: Beyond the Psychoanalytic Legend* (London: Burnett Books, 1979), 146.

19. Harald Leupold-Lowenthal, "Analysis Finite and Infinite," in *On Freud's 'Analysis Terminable and Interminable,'* ed. Joseph Sandler, 70 (New Haven: Yale University Press, 1991). According to Freud, it was "hearing Goethe's beautiful essay on Nature" that made him decide to become a medical student. Quoted in Ritvo, *Darwin's Influence on Freud*, 24. Ritvo adds that the poem "Fragment uber die Natur" (1780) was, in fact, the work of Goethe's friend of the time, the Swiss theologist Georg Christoph Tobler.

20. Roger Caillois, "La mante religeuse: de la Biologie à la Psychanalyse," *Minotaure* 5 (1934): 23–26; "Mimetisme et psychasthenie légendaire," *Minotaure* 7 (1935): 5–10. Although Lacan did not mention the texts by name, Caillois's writings inform some of his key theoretical statements. See Jacques Lacan, "The Mirror-Phase as Formative of the Function of the I as Revealed in Psychoanalytic Experience," in *Écrits: A Selection*, trans. Alan Sheridan (London: Tavistock, 1977), 1–7; "The Line and Light," in *The Four Fundamental Concepts of Psychoanalysis*, trans.

Alan Sheridan, (Harmondsworth: Penguin, 1994), 91–104. See also Denis Hollier, "Mimesis and Castration, 1937," *October* 31 (Winter 1984): 3–15.

21. Hollier, "Mimesis and Castration, 1937," 11.

22. "French biology has continued largely isolated from the evolutionary theories developed elsewhere. . . . Even today, it is said that the majority of French biologists refuse to take the modern synthesis of genetics and the selection theory seriously." Peter J. Bowler, *The Eclipse of Darwinism: Anti-Darwinian Evolution Theories in the Decades around 1900* (Baltimore: John Hopkins University Press, 1983), 117. The materialist philosopher Le Dantec was one of France's leading writers on evolution in the late nineteenth century, and he continued in a Lamarckian vein up to 1910—a bias demonstrated in the section of his book that was one of Caillois's main sources, "Mimétisme darwinien et mimétisme lamarckien," in *Lamarckiens et Darwiniens* (Paris: Félix Alcan, 1899), 100–53. The 1908 statue of Lamarck by Léon Fagel that stands at the entrance of the Jardin des Plantes carries the inscription "Fondateur de la doctrine de l'évolution" (and would have been seen toward the end of his life by Henri Rousseau, whose jungle paintings, so admired by Breton and Ernst, were inspired by his visits to that establishment). For more on debates around Darwin, Darwinism, evolution, natural selection, and Lamarck in France from the publication of the *Origin of Species* to the beginning of the twentieth century, see Thomas Henry Huxley, "On the Reception of the *Origin of Species*," in Charles Darwin, *The Life and Letters of Charles Darwin*, vol. 2, ed. Francis Darwin, 179–204 (London: John Murray, 1887): Robert E. Stebbins, "France," in *The Comparative Reception of Darwinism*, ed. Thomas F. Glick, 117–63 (Chicago: The University of Chicago Press, 1988); Barbara Larson, *The Dark Side of Nature: Science, Society, and the Fantastic in the Work of Odilon Redon* (University Park: Pennsylvania State University Press, 2005), 17, 51–56; Bowler, *Eclipse of Darwinism*, 58–106, 107–17. For a retrospective account contemporary with Caillois, see Jean Rostand, *L'Evolution des espèces: Histoire des idées tranformistes* (Paris: Hachette, 1932).

23. Roger Caillois, "The Function of Myth," in *The Edge of Surrealism: A Roger Caillois Reader*, ed. Claudine Frank, 113–23 (Durham: Duke University Press).

24. Georges Bataille, *The Accursed Share: An Essay on General Economy*, vol. 1, *Consumption* (1949; reprint, New York: Zone, 1991), 23. This book is Bataille's most comprehensive account of general economy. For more detail than I can allow in this essay, see his key statement of 1933, "The Notion of Expenditure," in *Visions of Excess: Selected Writings, 1927–1939*, trans and ed. Alan Stoekl (Minneapolis: University of Minnesota Press, 1985), 116–29; Jacques Derrida, "From Restricted to General Economy: A Hegelianism without Reserve" (1967), in *Writing and Difference*, trans. Alan Bass (Chicago: University of Chicago Press, 1978), 251–77; Michele H. Richman, *Reading Georges Bataille: Beyond the Gift* (Baltimore: John Hopkins University Press, 1982); Jean Piel, "Bataille and the World: From 'The Notion of Expenditure' to *The Accursed Share*," in *On Bataille: Critical Essays*, ed. Leslie Anne Boldt-Irons, 95–106 (New York: SUNY, 1995).

25. Friedrich Nietzsche, *The Gay Science* (1882), trans. Walter Kaufmann (New York: Vintage Books, 1974), 292. Nietzsche restated this position a few years later in *Twilight of the Idols* (1889) under the heading "Anti-Darwin": "the general aspect of life is *not* hunger and distress, but rather wealth, luxury, even absurd prodigality." Nietzsche, *Twilight of the Idols, The Anti-Christ*, trans. R. J. Hollingdale (Harmondsworth: Penguin, 1968), 75.

26. Caillois, "Function of Myth," 117.

27. Darwin, *Life and Letters*, vol. 3, 118. For more on the reception of Darwin in Germany, see William M. Montgomery, "Germany," in *The Comparative Reception of Darwinism*, 81–116.

28. For Freud's own, brief remarks on his intellectual "relationship" with Nietzsche, see Peter Gay, *Freud: A Life for Our Time* (London: Macmillan, 1989), 45–46.

29. Margot Norris, *Beasts of the Modern Imagination: Darwin, Nietzsche, Kafka, Ernst, and Lawrence* (Baltimore: The John Hopkins University Press, 1985), 76; Nietzsche, *Gay Science*, 305. "Behind Darwin lurks Hegel," writes Allan Stoekl in his discussion of Georges Bataille's 1930s Nietzschean-Freudian theory of the evolution of modern man and society. Space restrictions preclude consideration here of the location of Bataille in the larger Surrealist reception of Darwinism. Bataille, *Visions of Excess*, xii. My thanks to Arkady Plotnitsky.

30. Quoted in Norris, *Beasts of the Modern Imagination*, 76.

31. Quoted in ibid.

32. See lines 216–18 of Breton, "Fata Morgana" (1940), in *Poems of André Breton*, trans. and ed. Jean-Pierre Cauvin and Mary Ann Caws, 131–55, 149 (Austin: University of Texas Press, 1982); and Breton, "Friedrich Nietzsche 1844-1900," in *Anthology of Black Humor* (1939), trans. Mark Polizzotti et al., 129–31 (San Francisco: City Lights, 1997). There is a further rare and apparently favorable reference to Nietzsche in the form of a quotation in Breton, *Communicating Vessels* (1932), trans. Mary Ann Caws and Geoffrey T. Harris (Lincoln: University of Nebraska Press, 1990), 23.

33. Described by Breton as the artist closest to Surrealism at the time of the *Manifesto*, Masson was already a great admirer of Nietzsche, and it was probably on his suggestion that Nietzsche was mentioned alongside Kant, Hegel, Schelling, Marx, and Max Stirner in the Surrealists' 1925 broadside expressing for the first time their sympathy toward Communism and the Russian Revolution: "La Révolution d'abord et toujours," *La Révolution surréaliste* 5 (15 October 1925): 31–32.

34. For a full and clear account, see Briony Fer, David Batchelor, and Paul Wood, "'This Liberty and this Order': Art in France after the First World War," in *Realism, Rationalism, Surrealism: Art between the Wars* (New Haven: Yale University Press, 1993), 19–30.

35. See André Breton, "Soluble Fish" (1924), in *Manifestoes of Surrealism*, trans. Richard Seaver and Helen R. Lane (Ann Arbor: University of Michigan Press, 1972), 49–109.

36. Stebbins, "France," 122. In the letter quoted above to the French naturalist Jean Louis Armand de Quatrefages de Bréau, in which Darwin wrote of the growing acceptance in Germany of his views, he also contrasts the German and French responses to his theory: "It is curious how nationality influences opinion; a week hardly passes without my hearing of some naturalist in Germany who supports my views, and often puts an exaggerated value on my works; whilst in France I have not heard of a single zoologist, except M. [Jean Albert] Gaudry (and he only partially), who supports my views." Darwin, *Life and Letters*, vol. 3, 118. In a letter of 1868 to the English-German physiologist William Thierry Preyer, Darwin wrote, "The support which I receive from Germany is my chief ground for hoping that our views will ultimately prevail," whereas a letter to Gaudry of the same year expresses disappointment at the rejection of the mutability of species in "the country which gave birth to Buffon, the elder Geoffroy, and especially to Lamarck." Ibid., vol. 3, pp. 88, 87.

37. Anna Balakian, *Surrealism: The Road to the Absolute* (1959; reprint, London: Unwin

Books, 1972), 53–66. The 1959 date of the first edition of Balakian's book suggests her speculations might well have been prompted by the centenary of *Origin of Species.*

38. "The Surrealist bestiary gives pride of place, above all other species, to animals that are sui generis and have an aberrant or decadent appearance such as the platypus, the praying mantis, or the anteater." André Breton, "Caught in the Act" (1949), reprinted in *Free Rein,* trans. Michel Parmentier and Jacqueline d'Amboise (Lincoln: University of Nebraska Press, 1995), 129.

39. Masson himself conceded of the work he completed in Spain: "Je ne crois pas que ce soit le meilleur de mon œuvre." Georges Charbonnier, *Entretiens avec André Masson* (Paris: René Julliard, 1958), 176. According to the list of books he borrowed from the Bibliothèque Nationale, Bataille read extensively on the subject of insect instincts and societies in April 1933 and on evolution toward the close of 1934. Bataille, *Oeuvres complètes,* vol. 12 (Paris: Gallimard, 1988), 590, 598.

40. Jean-Pierre Cauvin, "Introduction: The Poethics of André Breton," in *Poems of André Breton,* xvii–xxxviii, xxxvii.

41. Masson, *Cahiers d'Art* 14 (1939): 72–73.

42. In the first he writes, "le seul bouleversement social valable en ce temps, est le Dictature du Prolétariat telle que l'ont conçue et rendue virtuelle Karl Marx et Lénine." *La Révolution surréaliste* 5 (15 October 1925): 30; and in the second, "on est oblige de *détester d'abord le Marxisme.*" André Masson, *Les années surréalistes: Correspondance 1916–1942,* ed. Françoise Levaillant (Paris: La Manufacture, 1990), 90, 281.

43. See Lewis Call, "Anti-Darwin, Anti-Spencer: Friedrich Nietzsche's Critique of Darwin and 'Darwinism,'" *History of Science* 6, pt. 1, no. 111 (March 1998): 1–22.

44. Freluc is near Bataille's birthplace, Billom, which itself is only twenty miles south of Vichy, a city that was about to find its place in history.

45. Martica Sawin, *Surrealism in Exile and the Beginning of the New York School* (Cambridge, Mass.: MIT Press, 1995), 114.

46. André Masson, *Anatomy of My Universe* (New York: Curt Valentin, 1943).

47. William Rubin and Carolyn Lanchner, *André Masson* (New York: Museum of Modern Art, 1976), 155.

48. Masson, Anatomy of My Universe, n.p.

49. "I would like to stop talking altogether. I should like to speak as Nature does: merely in signs." Goethe quoted in Willy Hartner, "Goethe and the Natural Sciences," in *Goethe: A Collection of Critical Essays,* ed. Victor Lange, 151 (Englewood Cliffs, N. J.: Prentice-Hall, 1968).

50. Published in *Minotaure* 12/13 (1939): 151–54.

51. Dawn Ades, "Movement and Metamorphosis," in *André Masson: Line Unleashed* (London: Hayward Gallery, 1987), 33.

52. Darwin, *On the Origin of Species by Means of Natural Selection, or the Preservation of Favoured Races in the Struggle for Life* (New York: Penguin, 1985), 464.

53. In the midst of the threat posed by Germany, Masson's "imaginary portraits" of Goethe, Nietzsche, Hölderlin, Kleist, and Richter constituted a provocative gesture on a par with that of the Surrealists after the previous war where "[t]heir support for the revolutionary tradition of German thought had political implications." Franklin Rosemont, *André Breton and the First*

Principles of Surrealism (London: Pluto, 1978), 33. Masson completed a series of portraits of Breton around the same time apparently comparing him with Goethe, as Michel Foucault did when interviewed shortly after Breton's death: "Breton bringing knowledge into expression (with psychoanalysis, ethnology, art history, and so on) is, in a sense, our Goethe." Foucault, "A Swimmer Between Two Words" (1966), in *Aesthetics, Method, and Epistemology*, ed. James Faubion, trans. Robert Hurley et al., 172 (London: Penguin, 2000).

54. For a discussion, see Matthew Bell, *Goethe's Naturalistic Anthropology: Man and Other Plants* (Oxford: Clarendon Press, 1994), 221.

55. Masson, *Correspondance*, 415. Malcolm Bowie points out that Lacan would have found a fund of imagery in keeping with his concept of the "fragmented body" of the "Mirror Stage" in the writings of Empedocles, whose fanciful theory of evolution is recorded in his *On Nature*. Bowie, *Lacan* (London: Fontana, 1991), 28–29. In "Analysis Terminable and Interminable" (1937, French translation 1939), Freud alluded to his recent discovery that his theory of the conflict between Eros and the death instinct had a distinguished precedent in Empedocles, and given Masson's recent reading of Nietzsche and the presence of both Lacan and Bataille, this passage probably was discussed at Freluc in the summer of 1939, and may very well have been known to Surrealists such as Breton and Ernst. Freud, "Analysis Terminable and Interminable," in *The Standard Edition of the Complete Psychological Works of Sigmund Freud*, vol. 23, trans. James Strachey (London: The Hogarth Press, 1964), 216–53.

56. "The broadest and most complete definition of Life will be—*The continuous adjustment of internal relations to external relations*." Herbert Spencer, *The Principles of Biology*, vol. 1 (London: Williams and Norgate, 1864), 80.

57. See Call, "Anti-Darwin, Anti-Spencer," 4, 15–16. As well as drawing together most of Nietzsche's references to Darwin and Spencer, Call's text brings out the complexity of the relations within them, which is beyond the scope of an essay of this length.

58. "The concept of 'adaptation'—a second-order activity, a mere reactivity—has been pushed to the forefront, and even life itself has been defined as an ever-more expedient inner adaptation to external circumstances (Herbert Spencer)." Friedrich Nietzsche, *On the Genealogy of Morals: A Polemic*, trans. Douglas Smith (Oxford: Oxford University Press, 1998), 59.

59. In a discussion of figurative art in the context of Lacan and psychoanalysis, Masson clearly has both Caillois's mimetism and Lacan's Mirror Stage in mind. Charbonnier, *Entretiens avec André Masson*, 145–56.

60. Ibid., 22.

61. "Il est le peintre non-surréaliste par excellence," quoted in ibid.

62. Further complications are introduced by Benjamin's own interest in Romanticism and Goethe, which might be brought into productive dialogue with his reading of Surrealism, though this is not attempted among the essays recently collected by Beatrice Hanssen and Andrew Benjamin, ed., *Walter Benjamin and Romanticism* (New York: Continuum, 2002).

CHAPTER 11

Darwin on the Threshold of the Visible

Contemporary Art and Evolution

SARA BARNES AND ANDREW PATRIZIO

Into Visibility

Art does not reproduce the visible; rather, it makes visible.
—Paul Klee, "Creative Credo," 1920

Every effort to understand destroys the object studied in favour of another object of a different nature; this second subject requires from us a new effort which destroys it in favour of the third, and so on and so forth until we reach our lasting presence. . . . the point from which we began.
—Claude Lévi-Strauss, *Tristes Tropiques*, 1955

The shaping presence of Charles Darwin on visual art has not been felt only before the contemporary period. Rather, it has moved through the last century and on into the present one. Art of today, the main focus of this essay, has engaged with spatial and temporal formations of evolutionary thought, to a greater or lesser extent in relation to Darwin's writings. However, in order to make some sense of what is an extraordinary legacy of pertinent work, we focus chiefly on a few exemplary artists, framed within metaphors of imaginary projection, the geological, inter-speciality, the genetic, and the search beyond the visible. Darwin may have been the archetype of his age's predilection for gazing intently and deeply on forms and behavior in the natural world. Some contemporary artists, primarily prompted by invited commissions, have drawn directly on Darwin's life and work, such as Jamie Shovlin's *Aggregate* (2002), which represented various editions of *Origin of Species*; Shirley Chubb's *Thinking Path* (2004), inspired by Darwin's "Sand-walk" around Down House, Kent; and *Stage* (2008) by Dorothy Cross, responding both to Darwin's own collections and to the artist's visit, with actor Fiona Shaw, to the Galápagos Islands.[1] The Darwin double centenary celebration in 2009 is itself producing new artifacts, such as those created for the competition by the Natural History Museum, London, to produce a permanent work honoring Darwin, won by Tania Kovats.[2] However, in this chapter we employ the rather different approach of examining artists that respond to post-Darwinian natural history from oblique angles rather than head on. We have found, appropriately enough perhaps, that many of the most inventive artists engaged in scientific ideas often find their own route around the panoramic set of inspirations we call "the natural world" via detours, meanders, asides, digressions, excursions, erasures, and ruptures. These are not flippant or irresponsible strategies as against the direct gaze of science, but a way of creating spaces for interaction, re-imagination, and deeper understanding through the tangential. As Gillian Beer puts it in her essay collection *Open Fields*, "Forms of knowledge do not readily merge; they may lie askance or cross-grained. But that does not imply failure. Dis-analogy can prove to be a powerful heuristic tool."[3] The methods of both the artists we examine here and of Darwin, we propose, represent projections into the natural world and therefore can be aligned for our purposes.

A recurrent mode within the Darwin scientific model involves imagining the invisible and the barely discernable. The long narrative of geological time and the unfolding nature of species variation, for example, are not directly observable in the lifetime of a single human being, yet scientific enquiry, such as Darwin's, involves imagining questions the answers to which may be unobservable and the evidence for which may require imaginative projection. Nineteenth-century natural science increasingly relied on models that promoted the impossibility of stability. Species stasis became a term assaulted simultaneously in the natural world by the combined effects of natural selection and mutation.[4] Darwin's concepts have formidable forward momentum—"What explains the vitality of Darwinism is the . . . power of the concepts that Darwin left to his followers: variation, competition, inheritance, chances of survival and reproduction, descent and genealogical arrangement."[5] This attention to ideas that demonstrate force, pressures, vectors, momentum, and the like have attracted attention within culture production as a whole, including the visual arts.

Geology

Jim said to me, a volcano buries itself. It perpetually erases its own history.
—Ilana Halperin, *Towards Heilprin Land*

. . . a grain of sand turns the balance.
—Charles Darwin, notebooks

In her essay "The Representation of Time in Painting: A Study of William Dyce's *Pegwell Bay: A Recollection of October 5th, 1858*" (1978), Marcia Pointon states that it is a painting "about time explored through an image of a particular moment in time," capturing a glimpse of Donati's comet on the specific day it passed over the south coast of Britain.[6] Pointon considers Dyce's 1860 painting to be a "portrayal of the concept of geological time in opposition to human, daily time," placing the painting within the Victorian milieu of scientific thinking according to James Hutton, Abraham Gottlob Werner, and Charles Lyell (figure 11.1).[7] Dyce draws attention to the figures on the shoreline, backs turned to the ancient cliff face and the unfolding, barely visible trajectory of the comet beyond. Pointon argues that it was not Dyce's intention to produce an accurate and literal depiction of Pegwell Bay, nor to illustrate contemporaneous scientific debates, but to offer an intellectual response to the environment that engaged with a "discourse in pictorial terms on the nature of the universe."[8] The year 1858 is, of course, significant in the context of evolutionary thinking—Darwin's and Alfred Russel Wallace's theories were presented to the Linnean Society in July of that year and it may very well be the case that Dyce was working on his painting in 1859, the year the first edition of *Origin of Species* was published.[9]

As is well known, Darwin was (primarily) a geologist during and in the years immediately following his voyage on the *Beagle*, and Lyell's *Principles of Geology* was highly influential on his early scientific career.[10] Darwin's scientific interpretations and field observations frequently were disseminated, however, by an aesthetic narrative that is comparable to a Romantic discourse bordering on the sublime. In James Paradis's tracing of these dual theoretical and aesthetic impulses in Darwin's published works, he suggests that the Romantic tradition as expressed in Wordsworth and Coleridge was a continuing influence on Darwin's development of scientific theory.[11] For our purposes, the significance of this lies in Paradis's assertion regarding the conflicting theories of perception to be found in the Romantics and the natural scientists. What this amounts to is an understanding of experience of time through one's own aging or experiences within a nature that changes cyclically or abruptly through natural events, and knowledge of time based on the naturalist's or evolutionist's measuring of it in the study of nature that has developed over millions of years.[12] Just as Dyce's human figures are composed against the backdrop of the geological layers and geomorphology of the cliffs at Pegwell Bay, oblivious to the singular event of Donati's comet, time "in the naturalist's nature was beyond the possibilities of human sensation, the geological and evolutionary record dwarfing the human moment.."[13]

This pitting of man against or within the monumentality of nature (mountainous ranges, deep river valleys) and singular natural events (the erupting volcano, the earthquake) was the backbone of the pictorial as well as the liter-

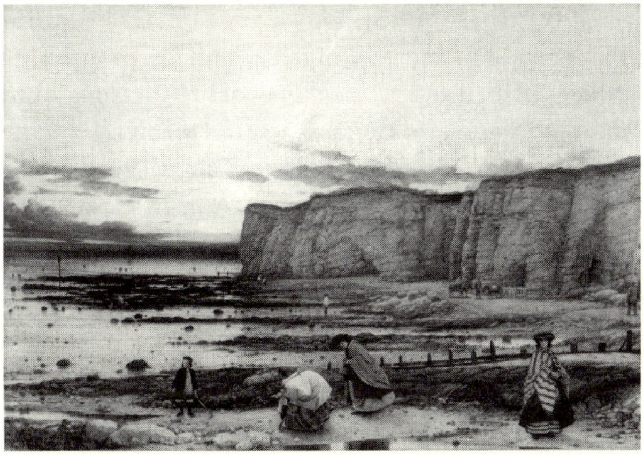

Figure 11.1 William Dyce, *Pegwell Bay: A Recollection of October 5th, 1858*, 1858–1860, oil on canvas, 37 ½ × 42 inches. © *Tate, London 2008.*

ary Romantic sublime, their significance measured in human terms. For Darwin and his predecessors such as Humboldt and Herschel, however, it was the relations between such events and observable, recordable facts that were indexical of the measurement of geological time and the development of both geological and biological evolution. The human element, the human scale of time, could not be accommodated in such a system. The human element, placing the individual as central to the experience of geological and evolutionary time, encapsulates the position of artists still intent on engaging with some sense of that which is impossible to capture.

As in Darwin and Dyces' lifetime, geological processes such as uplift, erosion, and sedimentation over millions of years are compounded by the continual presence of an entropic rupturing of the Earth's crust and core on a daily basis—Darwin himself experienced both an active volcano and an earthquake on his *Beagle* travels.[14] The observable traces of these geological processes in the structures, properties, and surfaces of rocks and landforms and the immediate human experience of witnessing (perhaps virtually) tremendous, earth-shattering events, provides a rich record of geological and evolutionary evidence for creative exploration. But how is the aesthetic impulse made manifest in an era of scientific geological exploration that now involves the seismic measuring of volcanic activity and the ability to predict a tsunami, the development of accelerator mass spectrometers capable of measuring cosmogenic isotopes (that is, isotopes created by the interaction of cosmic radiation with target nuclei of particular elements on Earth), or the sending of remote devices to evaluate life and evolution on Mars? Perhaps surprisingly, for many artists it remains just as Pointon stated, an intellectual response to the environment that engaged with a "discourse in pictorial terms on the nature of the universe." Today, however, artists are as likely to utilize those scientific measuring instruments and raw materials and communicate in the language of evolutionary geology and biology in order to produce work that incorporates sound and tactility in addition to pictorial elements.[15]

The availability of technological hardware and software and the collaborative relationships between artists and scientists—frequently in the field—highlight how artists are wooing the markers of the unseen: the Earth's barely detectable, but constant shifts only made observable by scientific data or the concrete results of evolutionary time itself. Physical traces (fossils, fulgurites, rocks, fissures, temporary islands, ancient lava flows) are the bedrock of a creative practice made manifest in what artist Robert Smithson referred to as "abstract geology"—the artistic union of the perceptual and the conceptual.[16] For Darwin, the fossil record of mineralized replicas and vacated molds, for example, represented the only direct source of information on the history of life and are indexical of the necessity for reflection, guesswork, and imaginative projection that he and his contemporaries were engaged in. Diverting from the traditional descriptive and chronological classification of empirical geological research, the influence of Lyell in terms of speculating and theorizing was likened by Darwin to "the pleasure of gambling."[17]

Whether art references or directly incorporates the material objects of geological time and events, they function as metaphors for what Rhea Anastas has called "an operative proposition for how an art object might not merely comment on but also carry an expanded range of significance."[18] As metaphors for a whole range of human and social experience, artists such as Allan McCollum and Ilana Halperin reinstate the human element denied by the nineteenth-century naturalists, fusing the abstract, temporal, and physical terrain of evolution with a meditation on "where and how we stand in relation to here and now and not here and now."[19]

McCollum has been making works that replicate naturally occurring objects since the early 1990s, building upon his long-term interests in copying, reproduction, and the political and symbolic relationships that underpin and are integral to the production of art—issues commensurate with the collection and exchange value of natural objects.[20] McCollum's *Natural Copies from the Coal Mines of Central Utah* (series begun 1995) consists of manufactured serial copies of dinosaur footprints taken from the original natural casts of dinosaur tracks discovered in the roofs of coal mines in Central Utah and displayed in the Eastern Utah Prehistoric Museum (figure 11.2). McCollum's copies establish the stamp of human activity: the commercial strategies of coalmining and excavation; the community's collecting of the fossils for their own pleasure; the historical scientific interest for the local museums; and the

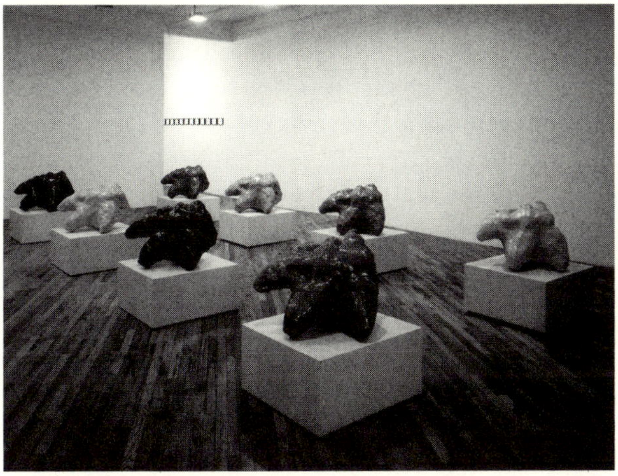

Figure 11.2 Allan McCollum, *Natural Copies from the Coal Mines of Central Utah* (series begun 1995). Enamel paint on cast polymer-enhanced hydrocal, 22 × 26 × 20 inches each. *Courtesy of Friedrich Petzel Gallery, New York.*

necessity of generating income. Darwin may have been one of the first to recognize the importance of fossils in the theory of evolution, but if we accept that both Darwinism and evolution are acknowledged today as cultural and political, as well as biological constructs, the physical phenomena of evolutionary evidence are redolent with imprint of the recent past regardless of whether one considers evolution, natural selection, and modification as given fact or remaining in the realm of dangerous theory. Darwin's interest in the fossil in terms of gradual evolution makes way for the rapid production methods of local economy and artistic output.

Fossils, rocks, and natural casts have accrued meaning and value as something other than merely the natural, but also scientific, cultural, and political artifacts removed from their status as objects transfixed in specific time. McCollum, in producing his art object copies of natural objects, highlights this accumulation of meaning and value when he states that meaning, "might adhere to an artwork in the way meaning becomes attached to any other common object, perhaps in the way a pearl forms around a grain of sand, or perhaps in the way a concretion might accrete around a seed, or a pebble, in the sands of an ancient sea."[21]

For Halperin, the accumulation of meaning registers as other forms of human engagement with geological time, and the significance of events is manifest less in the formal properties of geological landforms and objects than as the poetic communication of human experience. Such experiences hover between the tragic, the adventuresome, the awe-inspiring, and the sense of being on a quest, always on the verge of discovery. Halperin's drawings, photographs, literary texts, and performance lectures rehabilitate the

Romantic sublime as it has been related to the aesthetics of Edmund Burke and Immanuel Kant, placing the artist resolutely within the natural environment of cataclysmic events or their aftermath and focussing upon a subjective projection onto nature rather than the properties of the object as physical evidence.[22]

Halperin's numerous first-hand contacts with the effects of singular events, coupled with her museological and scientific research, reflect Pointon's remark regarding Dyce's *Pegwell Bay*—"time explored through an image of a particular moment in time"—but Halperin's human figures are not oblivious to the momentous events that contribute to our understanding of nature and evolution, they have been at the centre of it, physically, emotionally, scientifically.[23] Often, that human figure is Halperin herself and her travelling companions, marking human time in a geological landscape and reflecting Darwin's own delight in discovery: "the first day's partridge shooting or first day's hunting," he wrote in a letter to his sister Catherine, "cannot be compared to finding a fine group of fossil bones, which tell their story of former times with almost a living tongue."[24] This storytelling with its foundation in the distilled geological past and former human experiences is encapsulated in an acute personal investment by the artist. When Halperin was celebrating her own thirtieth year, she undertook an expedition with companions to Heimaey (an island off the south coast of Iceland) that had a volcano that had erupted in 1973, the year of Halperin's birth.[25] Approaching the summit of the volcano, the travellers met with the ruins of homes along the remains of the lava flow, partially swallowed and fractured structures such as staircases pungent with daily domesticity. They collected pieces of lava to present to all Halperin's friends turning thirty that year. Touching upon the vast natural physicality of Earth's disrupted landforms, the artist stands on the threshold of activity that is imperceptible and set apart from its traces in the visible world (figure 11.3).

Halperin attempts to make human and aesthetic sense of the immensity and monumentality of the geological processes that have made a theory of evolution possible: from the initial research to the trekking and documentation to the presentation of facts, retold experiences, and imaginative projections. When Gillian Beer states that, "evolutionary history is first a form of imaginative history. It cannot be experimentally demonstrated sufficiently in any present moment," we are aware that Darwin's theory of evolution was based on an accumulation of observations through contact with nature and projection.[26] Halperin likewise plays into a phenomenological strain of creative practice by drawing on the body and empiricism, even if her quest is immaterial rather than evidential.

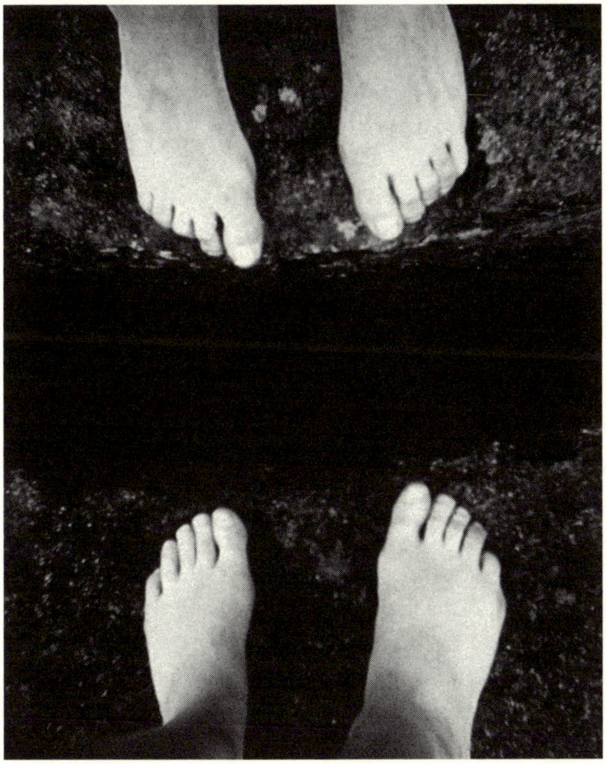

Figure 11.3 Ilana Halperin, *Meeting on the Transatlantic Ridge,* 1999. C-print on mdf, 24 × 20 inches. *Courtesy of the artist and doggerfisher, Edinburgh.*

The Animal

. . . community of descent is the hidden bond . . .
—Charles Darwin, *Origin of Species,* 1859

The phenomenological imperative is also apparent in the work of artists obliquely addressing the Darwinian evolutionary driving forces of difference, variation, and mutation of species through a physical embodiment and heightened use of the senses, but it is invariably matched by immaterial processes rather than concrete outcomes and an emphasis on the invisible domains of human and animal consciousness. Underlying the tantalizing possibilities brought about by the realizations that animals and humans are both like us and not like us are evolutionary conclusions made by those in the Darwin circle such as T. H. Huxley that humans have a close taxonomic affinity with apes.[27] Reiterating this, Darwin's *The Descent of Man* (1871) firmly placed humans within the animal species and demonstrated at the same time the human threads in the processes of evolution that endow *Homo sapiens* with a distinctiveness based partially in higher intellectual faculties. This distinctiveness has led to human dominance within the animal species and is noted by Darwin as "powers of observation, memory, curiosity, imagination, and reason."[28] Yet Darwin was aware that even here connections with the animal world were continuous.

The Expression of the Emotions in Man and Animals (1872) sets out the similarities of reactive behavior and expressions in animals and humans by the three principles of association of useful habits (involuntary association, habit, and inheritance); antithesis (involuntary expressive movements that may be the opposite of the state of mind, but may be highly expressive nonetheless), and direct action of the nervous system (expressions independent of the will and formed perhaps by habit such as trembling, perspiration, expressions of rage or terror).[29] These are made manifest in expressive behavior that also function as a communication tool to others—humans and animals respond to the expressions of other humans and animals with their own expressive actions.

Darwin's theory of natural selection may be considered the scientific progenitor of our increasing acceptance of artificial distinctions between humans and animals, an acceptance fuelled by biological research revealing, for example, that humans share 98 percent of genetic makeup with bonobo apes. But our consent in acknowledging these dissolving boundaries on a scientific basis is paralleled by corresponding philosophical, technological, and cultural shifts relating to our changing perceptions of what it means to be animal and/or what it means to be human and the further disintegration of these constructed boundaries.[30] This is succinctly captured by Cary Wolfe in arguing that we need to "disarticulate the problem of a properly post-modern pluralism from the concept of the human with which progressive political and ethical agendas have traditionally been associated—and to do so, moreover, *precisely by taking seriously* pluralism's call for attention to embodiment, to the specific materiality and multiplicity of the subject . . . the "human," we now know, is not now, and never was, itself."[31]

If we accept both the human and the animal as constructs, we are provided with an opportunity for the maneuvring required to break down the barriers between human and nonhuman on more than the biological level, by augmenting the expressive modes common to animals and humans as stated by Darwin. The possibility then emerges of exploring models of perception and experience external to those we know through being human. Although there exists a long and richly varied catalogue of artists working with animals in a wide variety of media and conceptual approaches, the current plethora of artists interested in going beyond merely using animals as subject matter owe much to the seminal work of Joseph Beuys. As with many of his contemporaries, Beuys can be said to have been keying in to a post-war dissatisfaction with the industrialized subject made manifest in certain types of performance art and earthworks (see Smithson above). It was a discourse being played out, for instance, by the Arte Povera group, including Germano Celante who wrote, "Animals, plants and minerals take part in the world of art. The artist feels attracted by their physical, chemical and biological possibilities . . . [and] discovers also himself, his body, his memory, his gestures—all that which directly lives."[32] Beuys was a self-described shaman whose performances endeavored to heal the fractured relationship between humans and nature. He lived with a coyote in a New York Gallery for three days in the performance *I Like America and America Likes Me* (1974) and cradled and talked to a dead rabbit in *How to Explain Pictures to a Dead Hare* (1965). In numerous ways—socially, politically, aesthetically—Beuys was highlighting alienation, but as he explained with respect to *How to Explain Pictures to a Dead Hare*: "This was a complex tableau about the problem of language and about the problems of thought, of human consciousness and of the consciousness of animals, and of course the ability of animals. This is placed in an extreme position because this is not just an animal but a dead animal . . . Even a dead animal preserves more powers of intuition than some human beings with their stubborn rationality."[33]

Beuys' nod to the consciousness of humans and animals mobilizes an aesthetic desire of humans to experience becoming-animal, an imperceptible becoming that transcends the phenomenology of gestural communication, language, or imitation. Going beyond the scientific experimental ventures of artists working with artificial breeding techniques and genetics (see below), becoming-animal addresses the question of interspecies blending that belies both biological essentialism and biological hybridization and denies the taxonomical pre-Darwinian hierarchy of species, each of which was believed to have specific individual characteristics. Instead, Darwin's proposal that hidden bonds bind all of nature through a common ancestry—a proposal that debunked both the autonomy of species and the hierarchy that positioned humans as the pinnacle of species—permits artists to consider how, "Animals offer us the possibility to think through another kind of subjectivity and to contemplate a point of view that has perhaps a more multiplicitous relationship to time/space."[34]

Marcus Coates interrogates the idea of a common consciousness in his work as an integration of the ethological and the ethnological arenas of animal behavior and human social coding. In a series of self portraits—*Red Fox* (1998); *Goshawk* (1999), in which he perches in a tree (figure 11.4); *Stoat* (1999);

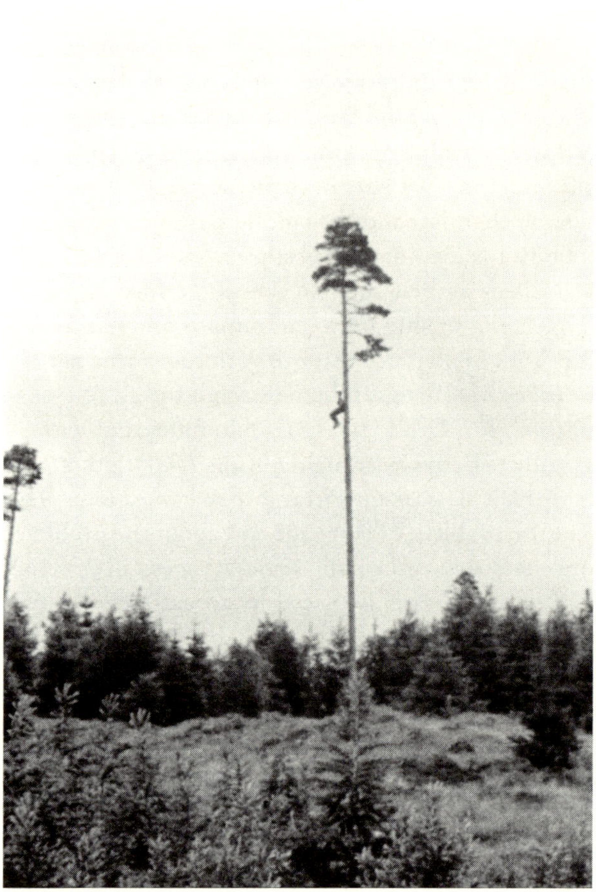

Figure 11.4 Marcus Coates, *Self Portrait as a Goshawk,* 1999. *Courtesy of the artist. Photo: Jet.*

Sparrowhawk Bait (1999); and *Deers* (2001)—Coates embraces the philosophy that to understand animals we must learn to think like them. Drawing upon his own early life experiences with nature in a suburban environment when he believed there was a "direct line to animals and nature, an unspoken language and an innate understanding," he "developed a long lasting romantic and primitivist outlook, where everything could be related to or understood on the same level. If God was in everything then I was in everything, why then wouldn't an otter understand me?"[35] In order to achieve this, a degree of relinquishing adult knowledge and rational thinking and a willingness to submit to a "mysterious and unknowable connection with the world" is required. The "confusion, contradiction and uncertainty" this creates for the artist, provides "a dynamic and energetic state that helps you stand outside of society. For me this is an exciting position, it requires you to lose control or lose yourself."[36] This uncertainty and dynamism in the aesthetic conceptual and experiential unfolding of species integration (that is, an integration that does not imply transgenic or xenotransplantation techniques, but relies upon a speculative outlook regarding intersubjectivity) involves a unified performativity by Coates that blurs the boundaries between the physicality and consciousness of human and nonhuman activity. *Goshawk* required the assistance of local foresters in hoisting and fixing the artist to the upper branches of a Scots pine tree so that he could see the immediate world around him as though through the eyes of a hawk scanning for prey. In such instances, it is direct observational and experiential knowledge rather than theoretical projection that feeds into the transformative desires of the artist.

While Coates acknowledges that we cannot escape our humanness, echoing Thomas Nagel's dictum that we cannot know what it's like to be a bat from the bat's perspective, and that we project our humanness onto other animals, nevertheless the artist strives for an affinity with nonhumans.[37] For Jacques Derrida, such an affinity of intersubjectivity cannot occur until we yield to the gaze of the animal, that is to say, instead of perpetuating the animals as objects of our gaze, we become the object of the animal's own looking at us.[38] It is only then that we can go on to imagine the experience of being an animal by posing the ultimate empathetic question, "do animals suffer?"[39] For Derrida, the intersubjectivity of interspecies conceptualization rests upon this ethical position.

Derrida's contribution to the extensive literature on the gaze, looking, and objectification highlights the pre-eminence of experience in the aesthetic disclosure of becoming-animal. Whether Coates looks like, sounds like, or acts like an animal is moot, the imperative is the process of becoming, yet the observable and audible elements of his work are undeniable as he takes on the vocal and physical attributes of birds and mammals, albeit as initially observed from the human perspective. This inevitably raises the question of imitation and an emphasis on corporeality, on form and language that is at odds with the cultural concept of becoming-animal as derived from the writing of Gilles Deleuze and Félix Guattari.[40] This highly influential work asserts that there are no absolute distinctions within the living world between animal, vegetable, and mineral, including humans, because underpinning the living world and continually coursing through it are multiple and imperceptibly interconnected forces or intensities indifferent to fixed characteristics of identity and subjectivity. This sets up the problem of form—and thus representation—for the artist in becoming-animal, an aesthetical paradox discussed by Steve Baker in *The Postmodern Animal* (2000).[41] Baker draws attention to Deleuze and Guattari's emphasis upon the experience of movement and speed as events, so that the individual subject is transformed into an event. As such, in compliance with their insistence that becoming-animal "produces nothing other than itself"—no subject, no resemblance, no imitation—artists such as Marcus Coates who ultimately cannot escape their humanness, can create work that, in its "movements, becomings and affects are 'below and above the threshold of perception.'"[42]

It is important that Deleuze and Guattari's concept of becoming is not understood as a progressive or regressive trajectory from one form or state to another, but rather as heterogeneous flux, based on alliances and affinities rather than kinship. This is clarified in their statement that becoming is "not evolution, at least not an evolution by descent, and filiation" and that "if evolution includes any veritable becomings, it is in the domain of *symbioses* that bring into play beings of totally different scales and kingdoms, with no possible filiation."[43] Instead, they put forward the term "involution" to express a creative faculty that runs between and beneath the processes of becoming and propose that the social theory of neo-evolutionism has some value in becoming-animal because it allows for defining the animal by populations and movement by transversal communication, rather than generic types and purely filiative production.[44]

As we have seen, for Coates the imperceptibility and reality of becoming-animal lies in consenting to affinity both physically and through consciousness; it is not possible for us to know our evolution corporeally. "Can we have a sense of our inherited humanness, from ancient cultures or when we inhabited very different bodies or even further back when we were unrecognisable as mammals?" he asks. "In our present condition we have no signs of our genetic heritage beyond our generational ancestry, but perhaps our being holds an awareness or corporeal memory of the first taste of consciousness. By corporeal I mean an innate sense of physical connectivity."[45]

However, in the work of artists such as Patricia Piccinini (figure 11.5), imperceptibility and reality are to be discovered in the manipulations of genetic material resulting in corporeal manifestations of becoming-animal that, from the human perspective of normative morphology, appear as monstrous, as excess. The vast literature excavating the biological, sociological, technological, anthropological, and cultural variations of "otherness" engendered by the term "monstrous" cannot be examined here, but is raised in order to make explicit the emphasis on difference by Darwin and by Deleuze and Guattari, an emphasis that is indexical of a natural propensity for the creation of monstrosity and as such both a material and philosophical marker of evolutionary diversity.

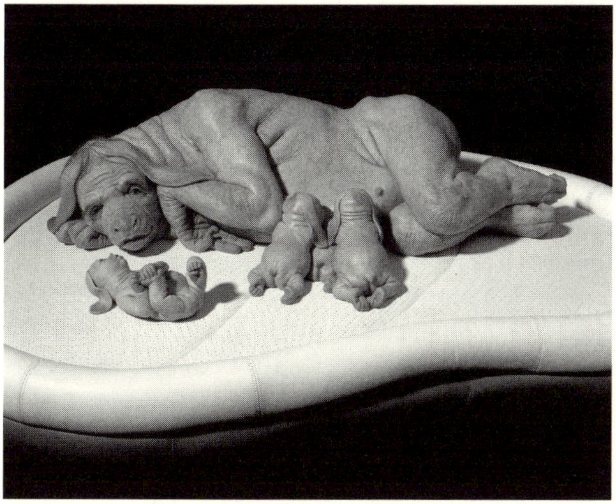

Figure 11.5 Patricia Piccinini, *The Young Family*, 2002. Silicone, polyurethane, leather, human hair, plywood. 85 cm high × 150 cm long × 120 cm wide approximately (33½ × 59 × 47 inches). *Courtey of the Artist. Photo: Graham Baring.*

Beyond the Visible

One must go beyond logic in order to experience what is large in what is small.
—Gaston Bachelard, *The Poetics of Space*, 1958

Transversal communications between different lines scramble the genealogical trees.
—Gilles Deleuze and Félix Guattari, *A Thousand Plateaus*

Darwin projected from the large landscapes of geological formation but also from minute observations of smaller natural specimens, looking at difference and similarity locked within detail. Darwin's method, particularly following from the publication of *Origin of Species*, found visual expression in Ernst Haeckel's graphic vision of what David Brody vividly calls the "microbial baroque."[46] Haeckel's influence, from the Darwin-inspired *General Morphology* (1866) up to the visual feast of *Kunstformen der Natur* (Art Forms in Nature) (1899–1904), which continues in print today, was substantial in art of his generation. In the spirit of Robert Hooke's *Micrographia* (1665), Haeckel's value for art also lies within the invisible conjured into visibility, where there was a discernable rupture between the observed and the intangible but graphically rendered—a rupture that continues to feed contemporary visualizations. "Miniscule and Small-Scale Art 1964–1996" was the subtitle of an important exhibition curated by Ralph Rugoff, "At the Threshold of the Visible." Projects on this theme by current artists included that of Hagop Sandaldjian (1931–1990), some of whose tiny carved objects were to conjure up the invisible world of a single blood cell. Rugoff writes: "Sandaldjian's microminiatures steadily lead us toward the recognition that 'reality' embraces an endless succession of orders of magnitude, levels of perception, and degrees of perspective, and so lies ultimately beyond the grasp of any single viewpoint."[47]

The arboreal/corporeal reality of the tree of life, however resilient, has required re-imagining in the wake of the modelling of genetics and DNA. Systems of biological classification have long been based on easily visible structural characteristics (numbers of legs, wing structure, and the like). This empirical form of comparative taxonomic enquiry with its heyday in the nineteenth century has inspired contemporary artists, the most significant of which include Mark Dion and Suzanne Anker.[48] In the early twentieth century, it was possible to picture the Tree of Life with four major branches or kingdoms: animals, plants, fungi, and prokaryotes (the latter a catch-all term for huge rafts of micro-organisms.) Since the 1960s with the application of precise DNA information, visible morphologies became only one taxonomic tool. The new "wheel" of life branches into three major living domains: the eukarytos (all cellular, nonbacterial life), the bacteria, and the archaea (fundamentally different DNA structures that might make up to 10 percent of the world's biomass). This map consists largely of invisible life, with animals, plants, and fungi compressed into one tiny part of the eukarytos. This model, continually being redrawn by geneticists since the 1990s, is based entirely on DNA differences across species and organisms large and small.[49] This new, genetically based tree puts humans, a tiny percentage of the Earth's biomass, in a marginal domain. This could be seen as a late reverberation of the "Darwinian trauma" as first described by Freud and reiterated by Derrida, yet more evidence of our relative invisibility in the universal scheme of things. This background is important when we look at artists whose work responds to this marginality or conversely expresses a kind of utopian humanism purposefully "blind" to such a perspective.

Art responsive to evolutionary and Darwinian principles could and has appeared in many recent artistic forms, including an empathetic parallel between evolution and the digital. Says Artificial-Life researcher Thomas Ray, of his virtual world of Tierra:

> Life on Earth is the product of evolution by natural selection operating in the medium of carbon chemistry. However, in theory, the process of evolution is neither limited to occurring on the Earth, nor in carbon chemistry. Just as it may occur on other planets, it may also operate in other media, such as the medium of digital communication. And just as evolution on other planets is not a model of life on Earth, nor is natural evolution in the digital medium.[50]

Given the current diversity of acceptable artistic techniques and media, artists such as those involved in Biota and Knowbotics Research can work within materials that *are* evolutionary, rather than those that only depict the evolutionary. Peter Weibel's 1993 event Ars Electronica was concerned with artificial life, biological origins, and, relevant to our focus on the micro- and macrocosmic, the extreme range of genetic research from the molecular to whole population systems. Available technology is key to this new cultural front. Art practice and scientific work can employ identical software and hardware, as recognized some time ago by Barbara Stafford: "Advanced information technologies of interpretation have given raw data a malleability previously unconceived."[51] Karl Sims' "artificial evolutionary" work *Galápagos* using computer-derived fractal geometries altered by audience interaction is one among many similar recent projects.[52]

It is a commonplace that Darwin examined the interventionist procedures of animal and plant breeding to make projections about the kind of mutations and effects that would occur over much longer periods of time under natural selection. This began as early as 1839 with *Questions about the Breeding of Animals*, through to *Origin of Species*, and then with *The Variation of Animals and Plants under Domestication* (1868). Contemporary artist George Gessert is perhaps the most explicitly indebted to this aspect of Darwin's work. He is interested in plant domestication and ways that human aesthetic preferences affect evolution. He has proposed in papers such as "Notes on Genetic Art" and "A Brief History of Art Involving DNA" that plant and animal breeders represent the pre-history of genetic art, employing both functional and aesthetically based rules of selection to create new forms. Gessert's own art project centers on the breeding of hybridized flowers, in particular irises, in a series started in 1994, *Natural Selection*, for example *Hybrid 488* (figure 11.6). Directly in relation to Darwin's contribution to art, Gessert asserts that "Challenge to . . . dualism came not from philosophy but from biology and animal breeding . . . From pigeons kept for aesthetic pleasure, Darwin confirmed evolutionary processes that affect all life . . . Domesticated and wild creatures are parts of a single whole that is dynamic, orderly, and intricately connected . . . [Darwin] described nature as if it were an authorless and boundaryless artwork symbolizing nothing . . . Joy and suffering, beauty and terror flow in and out of one another. His vision of evolution is classically sublime."[53]

Hybrid plants and animals, too, populate the remarkable paintings of Alexis Rockman, such as *Hot House* (2004) with its moist floral explosions, and the geological fantasy of *Neozoic Era* (1999), with its dinosaur/animal hybrids traversing a desert landscape under which already lies the detritus of

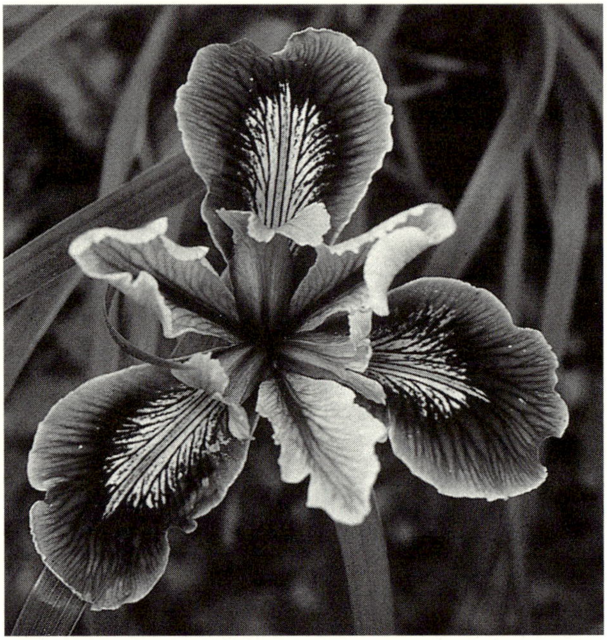

Figure 11.6 George Gessert, *Hybrid 488*, from *Natural Selection* (detail), series begun 1994. Dye sublimation prints with text. Selected leaves, 7 ¾ × 5 ¼ inches each leaf. *Courtesy of the artist, copyright Smithsonian Institution.*

contemporary urbanism (figure 11.7). Plant-like space rockets move to attack in a seeming return to the catastrophic paradigms so dominant in Darwin's day, as in our own (Neozoic being our own geological era). In his youth, Rockman was inspired by early encounters with animal displays through his archaeologist mother, acting as Margaret Meade's assistant at the American Museum of Natural History in New York. On one level, Rockman follows the concerns of Darwin with the eruption of the hybrid into the environment of the species. For example, as the latter noted in his *Beagle* diary of 1831–1836: "The mule always strikes me as a most surprising animal: that a hybrid should possess far more reason, memory, obstinacy, powers of digestion and muscular endurance, than either of its parents.—One fancys art has here out-mastered Nature."[54] Since Darwin's time, Surrealism and the ambitions of genetics have intervened, reflected in Rockman's self-styled "psychedelic eco-tourism." Perhaps art's out-mastery of nature can be read as a metonym for humankind's assault on nature as a whole. Rockman is one among many artists who re-imagine the world and so encourage us to consider it afresh. For paleontologist Stephen Jay Gould (incidentally also inspired early by the American Museum of Natural History), Rockman's role is concerned with "showing us the prejudices of our categorizations by creatively expanding the range of natured forms, and by fracturing boundaries in an overt manner

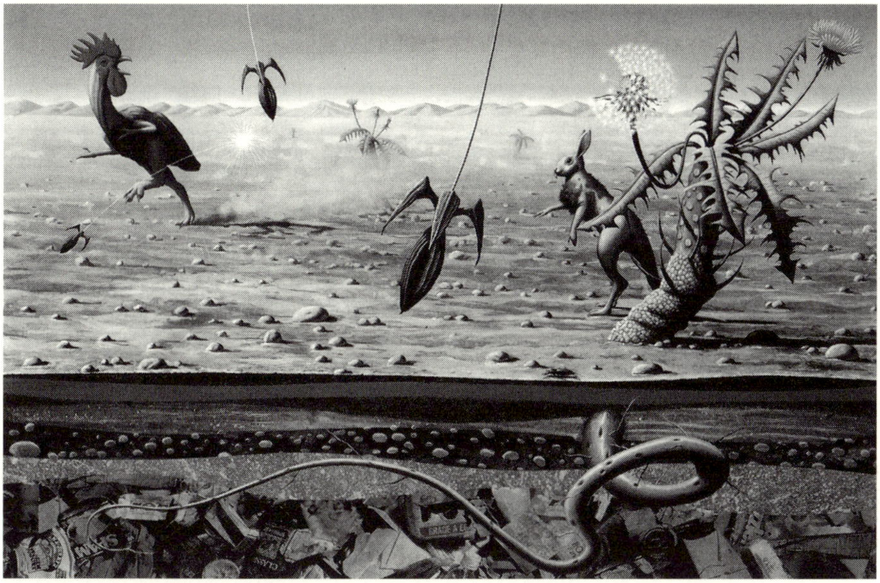

Figure 11.7 Alexis Rockman, *Neozoic Era*, 1999. Oil, acrylic and collage on wood panel, 40 × 60 inches. *Courtesy of the artist and Leo Koenig Inc.*

while nature's own breakages, as subtle in concept or invisible to plain sight, are much harder to grasp, but surely understandable by analogy to artistic versions."[55]

There has been substantial interest in "post-evolution" and the "post-human" in recent decades, responding to the technical possibilities of adding artificial stages to Darwinian human evolution. Unsurprisingly, cultural commentators have struggled to reach firm conclusions. For example, Jeffrey Deitsch ponders in the 1992 exhibition catalogue *Post-Human*: "It is quite unclear whether the post-human future will be better, or worse, or whether it will even be post-human at all."[56]

With some access to genetic technology, a growing group of artists, singular and collective, such as SymbioticA (who use "wet biology practices"), and Bioteknica (Shawn Bailey and Jennifer Willet), have been molding life rather than creating images.[57] Virilio has called it "an art of beings, an art of the bio-techno, and no longer an art of fixed, pictorial forms.[58] Bioteknica, carefully traversing the boundary between corporate genotechnology, public awareness of science, and art installation, is concerned with decoding the fundamental principles of life and placing the power of genetic supremacy in the hands of humanity itself.

Genetic or transgenic art in which the genes of one organism are transplanted into another, has faced a number of challenges in its aspiration to be taken seriously. How might lasting work be created that has commercial value within the economies of art? On the conceptual level, how do genetic artists respond to the attack on the claims of genetics to be the driver of identity—the genetic essentialism critiqued by Dorothy Nelkin (see note 48)? Are artists powerless in the face of multinational corporate efforts aimed at translating this coded landscape into marketable commodities? Genetic technology is, for Donna Haraway, "the translation of the world into a problem of coding . . . in which . . . all heterogeneity can be submitted to disassembly, reassembly, investment, and exchange . . . The organism has been translated into problems of genetic coding and read-out . . . In a sense, organisms have ceased to exist as objects of knowledge."[59]

If high art aspires to escape some of its technical limits (true for printmaking just as much as transgenic art), this poses problems for genetic-based art whose medium is very much the message. The "tactical" collective Critical Art Ensemble (CAE), founded in 1987, offer some escape from this impasse by explicitly politicizing genotechnology, within the associated developments in brain and DNA mapping, organ production, and reproductive processes that they term "a third frontier of vision."[60] Through open-source publications and live projects, they warn us that "the body is on the verge of being placed under new management, and like all exterior cultural phenomenon, it will be made to function instrumentally so that it may better fulfill the imperatives of pancapitalism (production, consumption, and order)."[61] CAE challenges the positivist inflections prevalent in genetic science and its commercialization, countering the rhetoric around "mastery of life" narratives, and the fundamental manipulation, shaping, and radicalizing evolution in the active choreography of life. Stephen Wilson's proselytization that, "Today, artists and engineers are beginning to work together with evolution. In the future, it may be possible for artists to work in collaboration with evolution to produce works of art whose beauty and complexity approach that of organic life," seems far from Darwin's fascination with the gentle regimes of domestic breeding and naïvely unaware of genetic discrimination, surveillance, and commercial intervention, or as Virilio calls it: "industrializing the species itself."[62]

Art using genetic processes imports an aesthetic paradigm around "free-expression" that in turn may pay greater or lesser attention to ethical boundaries patrolled within medical research. "But where," Virilio asks, "does the liberty of expression stop in the realm of the sciences? If it doesn't stop, Mengele will be a prophet."[63] Some of these issues, though intractable, are second order, internal to the ethically loaded, hybrid processes of artistic intervention within biotechnology. What is of first-order importance is that the very fabric of organic life is implicated directly, so that bio-art confuses entirely the relationship between the maker and the made. Again, Virilio has captured this fear around aesthetic production: "to say that the transgenic art is an art like the others—it's not, because it exterminates the source of the other arts. The living organism is irreplaceable. The living organism is not of the same nature as what produces it."[64]

Despite these concerns, it is still possible to produce successful artworks using genetic material referencing nineteenth-century cultural aspirations that Darwin might have recognized. For example, Marc Quinn's *A Genomic Portrait: John Sulston* (2001) was made from colonies of bacteria grown from Sulston's own DNA (figure 11.8). Once the culture, grown in agar jelly, reached the point of visibility, the process was stopped and the artwork was complete. This ironic cultural re-presentation of one of the pioneers in genomic mapping, commissioned by the National Portrait Gallery, London, plays with the Victorian notion of portraiture as a direct source of moral inspiration.

Genetic technological innovation is still unfolding rapidly over the early part of the twenty-first century, so its future shape and management is still uncertain. Equally uncertain, given the inadequacy of some of the resulting artwork, is whether, in representational or direct form, art concerned with genetics is up to re-imagining some of the forceful conundrums that the post-Darwinian world is fabricating.

Novel Results

Recent arts practice as discussed here embodies the possibilities of a more radical re-reading of how the paradigm-shifting work of a natural scientist and associated ideas affects cultural production. Direct linear connections and influences are only one way of re-imagining *Origin of Species*. Darwin is a starting point, and sometimes only a tangential one at that, for artwork that goes beyond that very starting point. As Merleau-Ponty writes, "a philosophy, like a work of art, is an object that can arouse more thoughts than those that are 'contained' in it (can one enumerate them? Can one count up a language?), retains a meaning outside of its historical context, even has meaning only outside of that context."[65]

Furthermore, contemporary artists involved in the natural sciences are only working within a Darwinian context in a somewhat limited sense. We have already cited less-arboreal models of evolution. A new emphasis on co-operation, around Lynn Margolis's concept of endosymbiosis, for example, shows current and future evolutionary biology attending to a possibility that

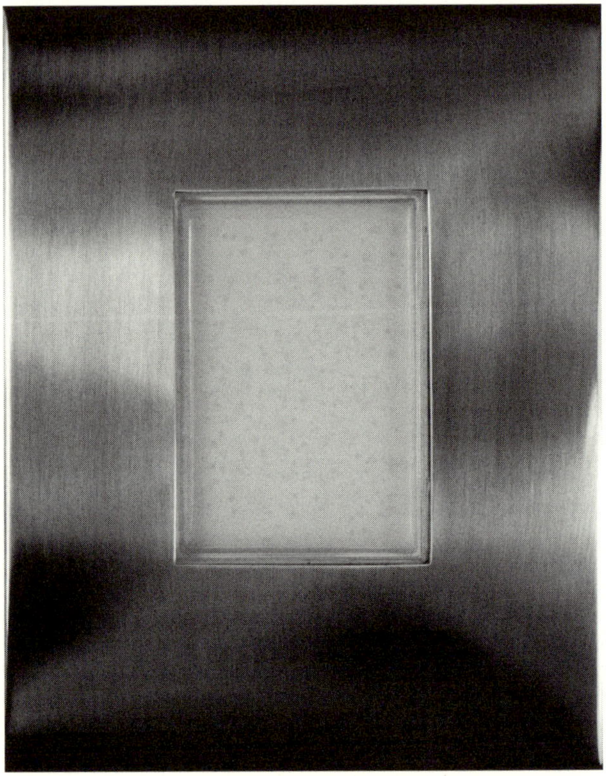

Figure 11.8 Marc Quinn, *A Genomic Portrait: John Sulston*, 2001. Sample of sitter's DNA in agar jelly mounted in stainless steel, 5 × 3⅜ inches. *Courtesy of White Cube, London, © National Portrait Gallery, London.*

major fusion events might occur between evolutionarily remote groups, threatening the ever-extending tree model further. On the occasions in which artists share an "asymmetrical enthusiasm" with natural scientists, precisely these kinds of ruptures and tension can be explored imaginatively. Two convergent factors seem likely to further enhance the imaginative possibilities in Darwin's work for contemporary artists. One is the existing clarity embodied in his texts, as described by Antony Flew: "Overwhelming though it is, *The Origin of Species*—quite unlike *Principia*—can be understood immediately by the intelligent layperson. The combined effect was, and remains, to make it imperative of anyone with any pretensions towards a rational and comprehensive world outlook to try to come to terms with Darwinism."[66] Second is the immediate availability of Darwin's published and manuscript works, including his journals and their accompanying images represented by the Darwin Online project run by John van Wyhe at the University of Cambridge.[67] This work has set aside an open field for artistic inspiration, as well as scholarly record.

Imaginative projection is the most fruitful link between the methods of Darwin and of today's creative artists. Projection is the art of transference, gap-vaulting, and bringing aspects of the world together in surprising new combinations. And imagination? Darwin himself offers us a characteristically simple yet effective formulation in *The Descent of Man*: "The Imagination is one of the highest prerogatives of man [sic]. By this faculty he unites, independently of the will, former images and ideas, and thus creates brilliant and novel results."[68]

NOTES

1. Pat Fisher, et al., eds. *Jamie Shovlin: Aggregate*, exh. cat. (New Forest, U.K.: ArtSway, 2006); Shirley Chubb, *Thinking Path*, exh. cat. (Shrewsbury, U.K.: Shrewsbury Museums Service, 2004); Dorothy Cross, *Stage*, commissioned by Shrewsbury Museums Service; Galápagos Islands residency funded by Calouste Gulbenkian Foundation.

2. Kovats' *Darwin Canopy* is to be a cross-section of a 200-year-old oak, cut lengthwise and inserted into the ceiling of the museum. It symbolizes Darwin's original "tree of life" image, common origins, and the interconnectedness of all living things.

3. Gillian Beer, *Open Fields: Science in Cultural Encounter* (Oxford: Oxford University Press, 1996), 115.

4. Brian Charlesworth and Deborah Charlesworth, *Evolution: A Very Short Introduction* (Oxford: Oxford University Press, 2003), 9.

5. Jean Gayon, "From Darwin to Today in Evolutionary Biology," in *The Cambridge Companion to Darwin*, ed. Jon Hodge and Greg Radick, 260 (Cambridge: Cambridge University Press, 2003).

6. Marcia Pointon, "The Representation of Time in Painting: A Study of William Dyce's *Pegwell Bay: A Recollection of October 5th, 1858*,'" *Art History* 1, no. 1 (March 1978): 99–103.

7. Ibid., 103.

8. Ibid.

9. Wallace had written to Darwin from Indonesia regarding a theory of natural selection that was akin to Darwin's own theories. The meeting at the Linnean Society was on 1 July 1858, although neither author was able to attend.

10. In the 1840s, Darwin published "The Structure and Distribution of Coral Reefs" (1842); "Geological Observations on the Volcanic Islands Visited during the Voyage of H.M.S. *Beagle*" (1844); and "Geological Observations on South America" (1846). Darwin read the three volumes that made up Lyell's *Principles of Geology* (1830–1833) during the *Beagle* voyage.

11. James Paradis, "Darwin and Landscape," in *Victorian Science and Victorian Values:*

Literary Perspectives, ed. James Paradis and Thomas Postelwait, 550 (New York: New York Academy of Sciences, 1981).

12. Ibid., 99.

13. Ibid.

14. Charles Darwin, *Voyage of the Beagle* (1839; reprint, London: Penguin, 1989), chapter 16.

15. Two recent examples include Stephen Hurrel's *Beneath and Beyond* (2008), an installation based on a specially developed computer program monitoring one hundred seismic stations around the world, and Katie Paterson's *Vatnajökull (the sound of)* (2007) inviting gallery visitors to make a telephone call connected to an Icelandic glacier to hear the sounds of ice melting.

16. Robert Smithson, "A Sedimentation of the Mind: Earth Projects," *Artforum* 7, no. 1 (September 1968).

17. Charles Darwin, letter to W. D. Fox from Botofogo Bay, near Rio de Janeiro, May 1832, in *The Life and Letters of Charles Darwin, including an Autobiographical Chapter*, ed. Francis Darwin, vol. 1, 251 (London: John Murray, 1887).

18. Rhea Anastas, "Allan McCollum: The Kansas and Missouri Topographical Model Project" (Kansas City, Mo.: Grand Arts, 2003); online at http://home.att.net/~allanmcnyc.

19. Mungo Campbell, "Journey through the Surface of the Earth," in *Ilana Halperin* (London: Camden Arts Centre, 2005).

20. These include fossilized dinosaur bones (*Lost Objects*, series begun 1991), dinosaur footprints preserved as sandstone (*Natural Copies from the Coal Mines of Central Utah*, series begun 1995), fulgurites (*The Event: Petrified Lightning from Central Florida (With Supplemental Didactics*, series begun 1997), topographical maps (*The State Topographical Models Project*, series begun 2003), sand spikes (*Signs of the Imperial Valley: The Sand Spikes of Mount Signal*, 1998–2001), and the natural mold of a dog "smothered" in the A.D. 79 eruption of Vesuvius (*Dog from Pompeii*, series begun 1990)

21. Allan McCollum, "Where Does the Meaning Come From?" Statement from the artist's website in reference to the *Signs of the Imperial Valley: The Sand Spikes of Mount Signal*, 1998–2001, online at http://home.att.net/~amcimages/introduction.html.

22. Edmund Burke, *A Philosophical Enquiry into the Origin of Our Ideas of the Sublime and Beautiful* (1757); Immanuel Kant, Critique of Judgment (1790). It was a lack of observable, physical evidence of the processes of incremental change that propelled Darwin into imagining the lapse of time inferred from form. This leads to the theory of space-time substitution in geomorphology, that is, inferring change of form over time from change of form in space. The ideal example is the coral reef model. Thanks to Prof. Mike Summerfield, Institute of Geography, University of Edinburgh, for discussion on this.

23. Including Heimaey, Iceland, the subsequent new landmass of volcanic ash, Eldfell, and the Krafla volcano fissure; the temporary appearance of Ferdinandea in the Mediterranean; a voyage around the disintegrating glaciers of Greenland.

24. Charles Darwin, letter to his sister Catherine from the Falkland Islands, 6 April 1834, in *Charles Darwin's Diary of the Voyage of H.M.S. Beagle*, ed. Nora Barlow, 9 (Cambridge: Cambridge University Press, 1933).

25. See Halperin's artwork, *The Eldfell Birthday Event*, 2003 (www.ilanahalperin.com).

26. Gillian Beer, Darwin's Plots: Evolutionary Narrative in Darwin, George Eliot and Nineteenth-Century Fiction (London: Routledge & Kegan Paul, 1983), 8.

27. Thomas H. Huxley, *Evidence as to Man's Place in Nature* (London: Williams & Norgate, 1863).

28. Charles Darwin, *The Descent of Man and Selection in Relation to Sex*, vol. 1, (London: John Murray, 1871), 137.

29. Charles Darwin, *The Expression of the Emotions in Man and Animals* (London: John Murray, 1872)

30. See, for example, the influential work of René Girard's *Violence and the Sacred* (1977), Jacques Derrida's *The Animal That Therefore I Am* (1977; new full edition, ed. Marie-Louise Mallet, N.Y.: Fordham University Press, 2008), Julia Kristiva's *Powers of Horror* (1980), and Slavoj Zizek's *Looking Awry* (1991).

31. Cary Wolfe, "Introduction," in *Zoontologies: The Question of the Animal* (Minneapolis: University of Minnesota Press, 2003), emphasis in the original, xiii.

32. Germano Celant, "Arte Povera" (1969), in *Art in Theory 1900–1990*, ed. Charles Harrison and Paul Wood, 886–89 (Oxford: Blackwell, 1992).

33. Tate Modern website, "Joseph Beuys Films," at http://www.tate.org.uk/modern/eventseducation/film/josephbeuysfilms2819.htm.

34. Diana Thater, *Knots and Surfaces* (New York: Dia Centre for the Arts, 2002), 16.

35. Marcus Coates, interviewed by Alec Finlay in an email correspondence and reproduced at http://www.alecfinlay.com/autumn.html, and in part in Marcus Coates and Alec Finlay, eds. *Journey to the Lower World* (London: platform projects, morning star, 2005).

36. Coates and Finlay, *Journey to the Lower World*, unpaginated.

37. Thomas Nagel, "What Is It Like to Be a Bat?" *The Philosophical Review*, 83, no. 4 (October 1974): 435–50.

38. Jacques Derrida, "The Animal That Therefore I Am (More to Follow)," trans. David Wills, *Critical Inquiry* 28,, no. 2 (2002): 369–418.

39. Derrida is referencing the eighteenth-century philosopher Jeremy Bentham. See also Peter Singer, *Animal Liberation: A New Ethics for Our Treatment of Animals* (New York: New York Review/Random House, 1975).

40. Gilles Deleuze and Félix Guattari, *A Thousand Plateaus: Capitalism and Schizophrenia*, trans. Brian Massumi (Minneapolis: University of Minnesota Press and Continuum International Publishing Group, 1987); see chapter 10, "1730: Becoming-Intense, Becoming-Animal, Becoming-Imperceptible."

41. Steve Baker, *The Postmodern Animal* (London: Reaktion, 2000), chapter 6.

42. Ibid., 138.

43. Deleuze and Guattari, *A Thousand Plateaus*, 238. See also J. B. S. Haldane, "On Being the Right Size" (1928), reprinted in *Cabinet* 28 (Winter 2007/2008), outlining the evolutionary purpose that for "every type of animal there is an optimum size." Deleuze and Guattari's symbiosis would overturn this evolutionary principle.

44. Deleuze and Guattari grant Darwinism with two fundamental contributions to what they refer to as a science of multiplicities: 'the substitution of populations for types, and the substitution of rates or differential relations for degrees." Deleuze and Guattari, *A Thousand Plateaus*, 48.

45. Coates and Finlay, *Journey to the Lower World*, n.p.

46. David Brody, "Ernst Haeckel and the Microbial Baroque," *Cabinet* 7 (Summer 2002).

47. Ralph Rugoff, *At the Threshold of the Visible: Miniscule and Small-Scale Art 1963–1996*, exh cat. (New York: Independent Curators Incorporated, 1996), 67.

48. See, for example, Lisa Corrin, Miwon Kwon, and Norman Bryson, *Mark Dion* (London: Phaidon, 1997); and Susanne Anker, and Dorothy Nelkin, *The Molecular Gaze: Art in the Genetic Age* (New York: CSHL Press, 2004).

49. Margaret Wertheim, "Figuring Life," *Cabinet* 27 (Autumn 2007): 54–59.

50. Thomas Ray, "What Is Tierra?" in *Information Arts: Intersections of Art, Science, and Technology*, ed. Stephen Wilson, 352 (Cambridge, Mass: MIT Press, 2002).

51. Barbara Maria Stafford, *Body Criticism: Imaging the Unseen in Enlightenment Art and Medicine* (Cambridge, Mass: MIT Press, 1991), 84.

52. Wilson, *Information Arts*, 258–61.

53. George Gessert, "A Brief History of Art Involving DNA," *Art Papers* 20 (October 1996): 22. See also Dmitry Bulatov, *BioMediale: Contemporary Society and Genomic Culture* (Kaliningrad: The National Centre for Contemporary Art and The National Publishing House "Yantarny Skaz," 2004).

54. Charles R. Darwin, (15 September 1834), in *Charles Darwin's Beagle Diary*, ed. Richard D. Keynes, 293 (Cambridge: Cambridge University Press, 2001).

55. Stephen J. Gould, *Second Nature*, quoted in *Information Arts*, 143.

56. Jeffrey Deitsch, *Post-Human*, exh cat. (New York: DAP, 1992), 15.

57. "Symbiotica A: Centre of Excellence in Biological Arts," University of Western Australia website at http://www.symbiotica.uwa.edu.au/; and see, for example, http://www.subtletechnologies.com/2007.

58. Paul Virilio, *Crepuscular Dawn* (New York: Semiotext(e), 2002), 118.

59. Donna Haraway, "A Cyborg Manifesto: Science, Technology and Socialist Feminism in the Late Twentieth Century," in *Simians, Cyborgs, and Women: The Reinvention of Nature* (London: Free Association Books, 1991), 164.

60. Quoted from Critical Art Ensemble essay "On Biology," in Wilson, *Information Arts*, 84.

61. Critical Art Ensemble, *Flesh Machine: Cyborgs, Designer Babies, Eugenic Consciousness* (Brooklyn: Autonomedia, 1998) 5. Online at http://www.critical-art.net/books/flesh/index.html.

62. Wilson, "Evolution as Art," in *Information Arts*, 353; Virilio, *Crepuscular Dawn*, 103.

63. Virilio, *Crepuscular Dawn*, 124.

64. Ibid., 126.

65. Maurice Merleau-Ponty, *The Visible and the Invisible* (Evanston, Ill.: Northwestern University Press, 1968), 199.

66. Anthony Flew, *Darwinian Evolution* (London: Paladin, 1984), 14–15.

67. "The Complete Work of Charles Darwin Online," http://darwin-online.org.uk/.

68. Darwin, The Descent of Man, 46.

About the Contributors

Sara Barnes is Research Associate at the Edinburgh College of Art, specializing in art and science intersections. Her most recent projects are the exhibition and award-winning catalogue *Anatomy Acts: How We Come to Know Ourselves* (2006) and *Species of Origin*, on the life and work of Charles Darwin and recent art practice.

Robert Michael Brain is Associate Professor of History at the University of British Columbia, where he specializes in the cultural history of science, including evolution and the mind, brain, and behavior. He is author of the forthcoming *The Pulse of Modernism: Experimental Physiology and the Artistic Avant-Gardes: 1840–1930*.

Fae Brauer is Research Professor for Visual Theories at the University of East London School of Architecture and the Visual Arts and Senior Lecturer in Art History and Theory at the University of New South Wales College of Fine Arts. Her books include *Corpus Delecti: Art, Sex and Eugenics* (2008) and *Modern Art's Centre: The Paris Salons and the French "Civilizing Mission"* (2009). While her essays are published in a wide range of books and journals, she is Chief Investigator of the project *Art and Genetics: The Cultures of Eugenics and Biogenetics in America, Australia, Britain and Europe* and the Australian Research Council–funded project *Regenerating the Body: Modern Art, Neo-Darwinism and the Fitness Imperative*.

Janet Browne is Aramont Professor in the History of Science at Harvard University, where she specializes in the work of Charles Darwin. Dr. Browne is author of the two-part biography of Darwin, *Charles Darwin: Voyaging* (1995) and *Charles Darwin: The Power of Place* (2002).

James Krasner is Associate Professor of English at the University of New Hampshire. He is author of *The Entangled Eye: Visual Perception and the Representations of Nature in Post-Darwinian Narrative* (1992).

Barbara Larson is Associate Professor of Art History at the University of West Florida. She is author of *The Dark Side of Nature: Science, Society and* *the Fantastic in the Work of Odilon Redon* (2005), and has written many art and science essays that have appeared in exhibition catalogues and in journals such as *Science in Context, The Art Bulletin, Revue d'art canadienne,* and *Artibus et Historiae.*

Marsha Morton is Professor of Art History at Pratt Institute, where she specializes in art and science at the end of the nineteenth century. She has written a number of articles on German art and Darwin and is author of the forthcoming *Between Darwin and Freud: The Graphic Vision of Max Klinger.*

Gavin Parkinson is Lecturer in European Modernism at The Courtauld Institute of Art, University of London. He is author of *Surrealism, Art and Modern Science: Relativity, Quantum Mechanics, Epistemology* (2008) and *The Duchamp Book* (2008).

Andrew Patrizio is Director of Research Development and Professor at Edinburgh College of Art. He has held curatorial posts at Glasgow Museums and the Hayward Gallery, London, and has published numerous books and exhibition catalogues. He was the 2007–2008 recipient of an Arts and Humanities Research Council grant on Charles Darwin and contemporary art.

Phillip Prodger is Curator of Photography at the Peabody Essex Museum. A specialist in science and photography, he is author of the annotated *Catalogue of Illustrations of Human and Animal Expression from the Collection of Charles Darwin* (1998), "Illustration as Strategy in Charles Darwin's *Expression of Emotions in Man and Animals,*" in *Inscribing Science: Scientific Texts and the Materiality of Communication,* ed. Timothy Lenoir (1998), and the forthcoming *Darwin's Camera: Art and Photography in the Theory of Evolution.*

Pat Simpson is Reader in Social History of Art at the University of Hertfordshire. She has published extensively on Soviet art and culture in journals such as *Art History, Oxford Art Journal, Sculpture Journal,* and *Russian Review,* and has contributed chapters on Soviet representations of women to *Gendering Landscape Art* (2000), *Work and the Image* (2000), and *Corpus Delecti: Art, Sex, and Eugenics* (2008).

Index